PREACHING THROUGH LUKE

James C Goodloe IV

Preaching through Luke

The Gospel as Catechism

James C. Goodloe IV

WIPF & STOCK · Eugene, Oregon

PREACHING THROUGH LUKE
The Gospel as Catechism

Wipf & Stock
An Imprint of Wipf and Stock Publishers
199 W. 8th Ave., Suite 3
Eugene, OR 97401

www.wipfandstock.com

ISBN 13: 978-1-62564-239-4

Manufactured in the U.S.A.

Dedicated to
Deborah Campbell Goodloe,
my most faithful hearer,
my most discerning critic,
the love of my life

"It seemed good to me also, having followed all things closely for some time past, to write an orderly account for you, most excellent Theophilus, that you may have certainty concerning the things you have been taught [i.e., catechesis]."

—Luke 1:3–4 (ESV)

Contents

Contents

Contents

Preface

IT WAS HUGHES OLIPHANT Old, in his *Worship That Is Reformed According to Scripture*,[1] who first opened my eyes to the history and importance of *lectio continua* preaching, which is reading and preaching through the Bible, book by book, chapter by chapter, and verse by verse, in order, without omitting sections. He also gave me courage to pursue such preaching yet today.

Old's book has been reissued in a revised and expanded edition as *Worship Reformed According to Scripture*. Here is some of what he has written about our goodly heritage of *lectio continua* preaching:

> Origen (ca. 185–ca. 254) . . . preached through the books of the Old Testament one by one. Today we have some twenty of his sermons on Genesis, about fifteen on Exodus, and a similar number on the other historical books. . . . The ministry of Origen was to preach through the whole of the Bible, book by book, chapter by chapter.

> John Chrysostom (ca. 347–407) . . . preached through most of the books of the New Testament. We have eighty-nine sermons on the Gospel of Matthew. When we look at these sermons, we discover that he proceeds through the whole of the Gospel explaining the text verse by verse.

> Ambrose of Milan (ca. 339–97) . . . preached in Milan, the capital of the Western empire, at the same time John Chrysostom filled the pulpit in Antioch. Ambrose fascinated his congregation with his expositions of the Old Testament.

> Augustine of Hippo (354–430) . . . preached a *lectio continua*.

> Ulrich Zwingli (1481–1531) . . . started out by taking the Gospel of Matthew and preaching through it verse by verse, day after day for a whole year. To use the technical term, he preached a *lectio continua* of the Gospel of Matthew. . . . Zwingli began his reform with a return to the classical practice of systematic expository preaching. . . . Like a Swiss John Chrysostom he preached through the Bible, verse by verse, one book at a time.

1. Old, *Worship That Is Reformed*, "Ministry of the Word," 57–85.

John Oecolampadius (1482–1531) . . . became preacher at St. Mark's Church, where he set to work preaching, just as John Chrysostom had done, through one book of the Bible after another.

Matthew Zell (1477–1548) . . . began his ministry by preaching through the four Gospels.

Wolfgang Capito (1478–1541) . . . preached through Isaiah, Jeremiah, and Ezekiel.

Martin Bucer (1491–1551) . . . did a long series of sermons on the Gospel of Matthew, the Gospel of John, the first epistle of Peter and the book of Psalms. . . . If the Gospels were preached though in course on Sunday morning, then the New Testament Epistles were preached through either later on Sunday, at vespers perhaps, or else at the daily preaching services. It was the same with the Old Testament books.

John Calvin (1509–64) introduced [this approach] to Geneva and . . . those who were exiled during the reign of Queen Mary (1553–58) took [it] with them when they returned to England and Scotland. *The exposition of Scripture in course became one of the biggest planks in their platform of Christian revival. To them it was an essential component of Christian worship that was according to Scripture and after the example of the early church.* . . . Sunday morning Calvin normally preached through the Gospels or the Acts of the Apostles. At Sunday vespers he would preach through the Psalms or perhaps a New Testament epistle. On weekday mornings he preached through Old Testament books. . . . Calvin preached through most of the books of the Bible, and he preached his way slowly through each book. Normally, he took three to six verses at a time. This system produced, for example, 123 sermons on Genesis, 200 sermons on Deuteronomy, 159 sermons on Job, 176 sermons on 1 and 2 Corinthians, and 43 sermons on Galatians. . . . His life's work was to preach through the whole Bible.

John Knox (1513–72) . . . became preacher at St. Giles Cathedral in Edinburgh. There he exercised as dramatic and powerful a preaching ministry as any preacher in the history of Christendom. . . . He did this in the course of expository preaching, never departing from the text of Scripture.[2]

How could I do any other? So it was that at Gilwood Presbyterian Church, in Concord, North Carolina, I began preaching through the books of the Bible, particularly the New Testament. I spent more than five years going through Matthew (1991–1992), Mark (1992–1993), Luke (1993–1995), and John (1995–1996). I can honestly say that it was the most important thing I have ever done in regard to preaching. After

---

2. Old, *Worship Reformed*, 63–78, emphasis added. For a fuller treatment, see Old, *The Reading and Preaching of the Scriptures*, seven volumes.

that, I preached through some of the shorter letters. I am very grateful to Gilwood for the opportunity and privilege of doing this.

Subsequently I was called to be the pastor of Grace Covenant Presbyterian Church, in Richmond, Virginia. In addition to preaching through Matthew (1999–2001), Mark (2002–2003), Luke (2004–2006), and John (2006–2007) again, I also preached through the Acts of the Apostles (2001–2002), Romans (2003–2004), Philippians (1999), 1 and 2 Timothy (2006), Titus (2006), Philemon (2006), 1, 2, and 3 John (1999), and Jude (2006), as well as substantial portions of other letters. Again, I am very grateful to Grace Covenant for the opportunity and privilege of doing this.

Most recently, it has been my privilege to supply the pulpits of Mattoax and Pine Grove Presbyterian Churches of Amelia County, Virginia. My wife, Deborah Campbell Goodloe, who is a deacon and a Christian educator, grew up in the Pine Grove Church. Her father, William Wallace Campbell, who was an elder, is buried there. It has been good for us to reconnect with these churches, and the sermons in this volume were preached there. I am grateful to Mattoax and Pine Grove for the opportunity and privilege of revisiting 1, 2, and 3 John, Jude, and Philemon, and now also Luke, preaching from all of them yet again.

The following collection of sermons could be titled "Questions for Theophilus." Luke notes in 1:4 that the volume had been written "that you may have certainty concerning the things you have been taught [i.e., catechesis]." The rest of the gospel contains a barrage of questions, almost catechetical in nature. Many of those are reflected in the titles of these sermons. The questions usually point to what is important in the passage, both for Theophilus and for us.

For instance, the very first question in the gospel and, not insignificantly, in response to gospel, comes from Zechariah: "How shall I know this?" (1:18). This is a question of knowledge, particularly of the basis of saving faith. It would be a good first question for Theophilus and for us. The answer given by the angel Gabriel is that we shall know by the word of God (1:19). Even with Gabriel no longer present, that continued to be the case for Theophilus and continues to be so for us.

The second question comes from Mary: "How will this be?" (1:34). This is a question not so much of biology as of theology. The issue is not so much virgin birth as incarnation. The question is how the Son of God can become human. That would be a good second question for Theophilus and for us. The answer, again from Gabriel, is that it will be by the power of God (1:35). Again, this continues to be valid for us.

The third question comes from Elizabeth: "Why me?" (1:43). Why should the gospel of Jesus Christ come to her, or to Theophilus, or, even more strangely, to us yet today? Why? As Mary answers in her song, it all has to do with God's choice, election, mercy, and salvation (1:47–55). It has nothing to do with us, our deservingness, or even the lack thereof. It is sheer grace.

The fourth question comes from the neighbors of Elizabeth and Zechariah, through all the hill country of Judea, in regard to the birth of their child of the Lord's great mercy, strangely named John: "What then will this child be?" (1:66). This time Zechariah, who once again can speak, gives the answer that he will be a prophet of God (1:76–79). John is not the Christ, but he will go before the Christ. No one else, prophet or apostle, priest or preacher, is the Christ. Jesus alone is Christ.

Thus begins the catechism according to Luke, a series of questions for Theophilus and so for us, in order that both he and we may have certainty concerning the things we have been taught. The catechism continues to the end of the gospel, with the risen Lord Jesus Christ himself asking the last questions. See Appendix A below for additional consideration of the questions in Luke.

Note that these first four questions in Luke have to do with epistemology, agency, election, and identity. These lay the groundwork for everything else. Moreover, the answer to the first question ("How shall I know?") is the word of God; how very interesting that the first chapter of the Westminster Confession of Faith is on the Bible. The answer to the second question ("How Will This Be?") is the power of God; the second chapter of Westminster is on God. And the answer to the third question ("Why Me?") is divine election; the third chapter of Westminster is on God's eternal decrees. I am not suggesting that Westminster consciously followed the order of Luke. I am saying that this is a good order in which to treat these questions.

Through most of the years of my preaching, I have used the Revised Standard Version of the Bible. After years of anticipation, I used the New Revised Standard Version briefly. In fact, I was reading Mark 8 the day I put it down. Verse 34 reads, according to the NRSV, "If any want to become my followers, let them deny themselves and take up their cross and follow me." Besides being perfectly barbarous English (how many people would be on that cross?), using plurals to avoid male pronouns, those very evasions made it also seem to me to fall under the condemnation of the subsequent verse 38: "Those who are ashamed of me and of my words in this adulterous and sinful generation, of them the Son of Man will also be ashamed when he comes in the glory of his Father with the holy angels" (NRSV, again with the unwarranted plurals). By the time I preached the following sermons, I had begun to use the English Standard Version (ESV), which I have found to be a most faithful and felicitous translation.

I should note that in my studies of the Bible I have learned much from the commentaries of John Calvin. I should also note that in my study of theology I have learned much from John Calvin and from John H. Leith. The latter also did much to encourage my preaching.

As I have continued forward in *lectio continua* preaching, I have been much encouraged by the preaching ministries of my colleagues David Wood and Steve Bryant, who joined me along the way in this adventure. I have recently learned of others who also preach *lectio continua*: Ron Scates, Jeffrey Wilson, Louis Williams, and Bob Fuller. I am also grateful for help and encouragement not only from Hughes Oliphant Old but also from Stan Hall (now deceased) and Richard A. Ray. In fact, following the publication of a few articles about this in *Presbyterian Outlook*, I identified more than fifty ministers who preach in this way. I would appreciate hearing from others who do so.

My daughter, Campbell Goodloe Hackett, was a student at Princeton Theological Seminary. One of her New Testament professors, the late Dr. Donald Juel, once introduced a text from Mark to the class and suggested that almost no one had ever heard a sermon on it. My daughter put up her hand. He was dubious, but Campbell said that she had grown up in a church where the minister preached straight through the books of the Bible, including Mark. Juel was shocked that anyone did that. My question is, why is such preaching unusual? It could and should be the norm.

I am more keenly aware of the shortcomings of the following sermons than are any who heard them or any who will read them. I offer them here less for any illusions I have about the value of their content and more for the importance of the substantive and historic pattern of preaching the Bible *lectio continua*, submitting ourselves to the authority of the Word. That can still be done today! Here is the proof. It is my prayer that others will be made bold to follow in this way and to do better than I have done.

Dr. James C. Goodloe IV
Executive Director
Foundation for Reformed Theology
4103 Monument Avenue
Richmond, VA 23230
www.foundationrt.org
August 2, 2013

1

How Shall I Know?

LUKE 1:1–25; DANIEL 9:1–15, 20–23

"INASMUCH AS MANY HAVE undertaken to compile a narrative of the things that have been accomplished among us, just as those who from the beginning were eyewitnesses and ministers of the word have delivered them to us, it seemed good to me also, having followed all things closely for some time past, to write an orderly account for you, most excellent Theophilus, that you may have certainty concerning the things you have been taught."

Here in the first sentence of the Gospel according to Luke we have a statement of the purpose of the book: it was written in order that "you"—which at the time referred to Theophilus but which now includes all of us who read the gospel—"may have certainty concerning the things you have been taught." This whole book is here today for us to know the gospel of Jesus Christ, for us to know the content of the Christian faith, for us to know the good news of God, and for us to believe it and to obey it. Thanks be to God!

Given this purpose of the Gospel according to Luke, it is no accident that the first question asked in this book, by the first person we meet in this book, is simply, "How shall I know this?" "How shall I know?" Zechariah asks this in regard to what Gabriel has told him, but it also has a broader meaning and application. Luke records it because it is a good and important question for Theophilus. More than that, Luke records it because it is a good and important question for us. The purpose of the book is for us to have certainty, and the first question is, "How?" How shall we know? How shall we know the gospel of Jesus Christ? How shall we know the good news of God? How shall we know the content of the Christian faith? How shall we know? This is still our question. We need an answer, here at the beginning of the gospel, before we go any farther. How shall we know? We need an answer, on this day in our lives, so that we may move forward in the faith. How shall we know?

The answer is swift. "The angel answered him, 'I am Gabriel, who stands in the presence of God, and I was sent to speak to you and to bring you this good news.'" It is as if Gabriel was astonished at the question. His answer, in effect, is, "I just told you! That is how you will know." And yet, there is much more going on here. And even if Gabriel was astonished at Zechariah's question, we are not, because his question is our question, and we want to know the answer. So what is this answer?

The word "angel" means "messenger." A messenger is someone who carries and delivers a message for someone else. A messenger does not invent the message. A messenger does not write the message. A messenger is not to interpret the message. A messenger is not to tamper with the message. A messenger carries and delivers a message for someone else. This is what the word "angel" means.

In this case, Gabriel is an angel of the Lord. That is different. Gabriel stands in the presence of God. Gabriel is sent from God to speak to Zechariah, just as he had been sent to speak to Daniel. That is who Gabriel is. That is what Gabriel does. He is an angel of the Lord who carries a message from the Lord to the people of God. On the one hand this sounds fantastic. Very few people have contact with angels. And yet on the other hand, this very device, this very method of delivering the message, plays down the importance of the messenger and plays up the content of the message itself. That is, the angel is not the point of the story. The message that the angel brings, the word from God to the people of God, *that* is the point of the story. And we have the message. It would not matter if we never had access to an angel again. What the angel brought is the word of God, and that, my friends, we still have today. That is what we have in this very gospel. That is the answer to our question. That is how we shall know. We shall know by the word of God. Thanks be to God!

It has been observed that angels appear in connection with the birth of Jesus Christ and in connection with the resurrection of Jesus Christ, before his resurrections appearances. In the time between his birth and resurrection, and in the time of his resurrection appearances, it is Jesus himself who speaks for, and on behalf of, God. Thus we have not only the word of angels who as messengers bring the word of God, but we have also and even more the word of Jesus Christ himself. Again, none of us has ever met him in the flesh. It appears that Theophilus had not done so. And yet, we still have the teachings of Jesus Christ. We have his words. We have what he said. We have his gospel. That is what is written down in this book through which we are about to read, hear, preach, and listen. It is not the "Gospel *of* Luke." Instead, it is the "Gospel *according to* Luke." That is because it is the gospel *of* Jesus Christ! This is the word we have. This is how we shall know.

Short of meeting Jesus Christ in the flesh, short of receiving a visit from Gabriel, how are we to know that the word of Scripture is the word of God? This is an extraordinarily important question and one that has engaged the church for centuries.

Several possible answers have been considered and then set aside as inadequate. For instance (1), we do not regard the Bible as the word of God simply because it is ancient. Other writings are as old or older. And there was a day, of course, when the Bible was brand new. So, its antiquity does not establish that it is the word of God. Again (2), we do not regard the Bible as the word of God simply because the church says so. That would be to get things backwards. It was the word of God, communicated through the Bible, which called the church into existence. The church acknowledges the Bible as the word of God, but the acknowledgment does not make it so. And the church's authority is not sufficient to make it so. Moreover (3), we do not regard the Bible as the word of God because of its internal coherence, though it does demonstrate a remarkable coherence for a document written by many human hands over several centuries in at least three different languages. Finally (4), we do not regard the Bible as the word of God because it measures up to any outer standard, for that would in and of itself acknowledge something else as a higher standard than the word of God, which would be a contradiction.

Instead, we do acknowledge the Bible as the word of God because, and only because, it produces within us the inner conviction that it is the word of God. Yes, that is circular. But it is also personal. The word of God is self-authenticating. Either it convinces us, or it does not. If it does, nothing can take that away from us. If it does not, nothing else can give that to us. In that division of humanity, between those who acknowledge the Bible as the word of God and those who do not, lays a great mystery. The division does not have to do with intelligence. It does not have to do with prior faith. Faith comes from the word of God, not the other way around. It does not have to do with our deserving, for then none of us would receive the word. The mystery seems, instead, to have to do with the election of God, with the free and not outwardly determined choice on the part of God alone as to whom he wishes to hear and to believe.

That is to say, the word of God is independent. It is outside and beyond our control. It cannot be tamed. It cannot be domesticated. It can, perhaps, be used and abused, but not for long. It will not tolerate such foolishness. The word of God is a great and consuming fire, and it is also a spring of living water. It is an absolute standard which humbles us, and it is a word of grace which lifts us up and makes us alive. If you know it, you know what I am talking about.

As for the personal aspect of the word, consider these parallels: If your wife tells you that she loves you, either she convinces you of that or she does not. No one else can convince you of it. If your husband tells you that he loves you, either he convinces you of that or he does not. There are outward patterns of behavior that tend to confirm that or not, that are consistent or not, that are supportive or not, that are appropriate or not. Those are extraordinarily important. And some of us men are not too bright! And yet, a profession of love either awakens a corresponding awareness of love or it does not. Thus, a profession of love is personal. It is not academic. It is not scientific.

It is not political. It is personal. And it is either convincing or not. The word of God is at least somewhat like that. Either you hear the word of God as the word of God, or you do not. Either you hear the voice of our creator, or you do not. Either you hear the grace of our redeemer, or you do not. If so, you know it is the word God, more surely than you know anything else. If not, there is nothing else I can do to convince you. I can only encourage you to keep listening. God is good. God is gracious. Many millions before you have listened and heard. Many millions before you have heard and believed. Many millions before you have believed and obeyed. Keep listening.

"How shall we know?" How shall we know the gospel of Jesus Christ? How shall we know the good news of God? How shall we know the content of the Christian faith? There is only one way. We shall know by the word of God alone. That does not mean that we have to see an angel. That does not mean that we have to meet Jesus Christ in the flesh. And it does not mean that we can put it into a test tube and measure it. It is not that kind of knowing. But it does mean that we will be encountered by God as God has chosen to make himself known in and through the word of God as revealed to the prophets, as embodied in Jesus Christ, as entrusted to the apostles, as written and recorded in the Bible. Thanks be to God!

The Gospel according to Luke was written in order "that you may have certainty concerning the things you have been taught." This whole book is here today for us to know the gospel of Jesus Christ, for us to know the content of the Christian faith, for us to know the good news of God, and for us to believe it and to obey it. If that is of interest to you, you are in the right place. If you want to know all of these things, the first question is, "How shall we know?" And the answer to that question, given in the text itself, is, "We shall know by the word of God alone." That is where we start. There are many more questions and answers. Luke has them all lined up for us, like a catechism. We will face them one by one. I invite you and urge you to immerse yourself in hearing this word, in being engaged by this word, and so in making it your very own.

"Inasmuch as many have undertaken to compile a narrative of the things that have been accomplished among us, just as those who from the beginning were eyewitnesses and ministers of the word have delivered them to us, it seemed good to me also, having followed all things closely for some time past, to write an orderly account for you, most excellent Theophilus, that you may have certainty concerning the things you have been taught."

To God be the glory forever and ever! Amen.

2

How Will This Be?

THE ANGEL GABRIEL SAID to Mary, "Behold, you will conceive in your womb and bear a son, and you shall call his name Jesus. He will be great and will be called the Son of the Most High. And the Lord God will give to him the throne of his father David, and he will reign over the house of Jacob forever, and of his kingdom there will be no end." And Mary said to the angel, "How will this be?" That is a very good question! "How will this be?" At one level, the question is, "How will a virgin conceive?" And yet, at another level, the question is, "How will the Son of God become human?" That is far more difficult and far more interesting. Thus does Mary pose to the angel a profound question, "How will this be?"

Before we get to the answer, consider with me the nature and purpose of the question. It is significant that in the first sentence of the Gospel according to Luke we have a statement of the purpose of the book: it was written in order that "you"—which at the time referred to Theophilus, for whom the book was first written, but which now includes all of us who read the gospel—"may have certainty concerning the things you have been taught." This whole book is still here today in order for us to know the gospel of Jesus Christ, for us to know the content of the Christian faith, for us to know the good news of God, and for us to believe it and to obey it. That is why it was written, that is why we have it, and that is why we read and preach it today. So let us seek this certainty which it intends.

Given this purpose of the Gospel according to Luke, how does it go about carrying out that purpose? How does it fulfill that purpose? The rest of the gospel, from the first sentence to the end of the book, contains a barrage of questions and answers. It is my contention not only that the questions point to what is important in each

5

part of the gospel story, but also that the questions were of continuing significance to Theophilus, and even that the questions are still of continuing significance to us. That is to say, the book we have before us is not only a gospel story but is also a gospel catechism, a question-and-answer teaching device intended to communicate the Christian faith, intended to be learned and even memorized, intended to engage the learner in the great questions of the faith, an early catechism in the form of a story, indeed a catechism embedded in the gospel.

We have here, in logical order, a series of questions of faith and doubt, life and death, good and evil, truth and falsehood, reality and unreality. We have here the questions that we ask, or that we should ask, about who we are, whose we are, and what we are about. We have here a gift from God, who knows us better than we know ourselves. If we follow these questions, appropriate them as our own, and receive the answers into our hearts and minds, we can have certainty of the truth of the gospel we have been taught. Would you like that?

Given this purpose of the Gospel according to Luke, it is no accident that the first question asked in this catechism, before today's reading, is simply, "How shall I know this?" How shall I know? Zechariah asked this in regard to what Gabriel told him, but it has a broader meaning and application. This is a question of knowledge, particularly knowledge of the basis of saving faith. Luke recorded it because it is a good and important first question for Theophilus and also for us. The purpose of the book is for us to have certainty, and the first question is, "How shall we know?" The answer for Zechariah, for Theophilus, and for us is that we shall know by the word of God, and by the word of God alone. Even with Gabriel no longer present, that continued to be the case for Theophilus and continues to be so for us. Thus begins the catechism according to Luke, a series of questions and answers for Theophilus and for us, in order that he and we may have certainty concerning the things we have been taught. It continues to the end of the gospel, with the risen Christ himself asking the last questions.

In today's reading, the second question asked in this catechism, by the second person we meet in this book, following Gabriel's announcement that Mary will bear the Son of the Most High, is simply, "How will this be?" That is, "How will a son of Mary also be the Son of God?" "How will the Christ enter the world?" Mary asks this in regard to what Gabriel has told her, but it also has a broader meaning and application. Luke records it because it is a good and important second question for Theophilus and also for us.

"How will this be?" This is a question not so much of biology as of theology. The issue is not so much virgin birth as incarnation. The real question is how the Son of God can become human. The whole rest of the gospel depends upon this premise. If the Son of God becomes human, his parables make sense, his healings make sense, his crucifixion makes sense, his resurrection makes sense, his forgiveness of sins makes sense, and his promise of the resurrection makes sense. Apart from his becoming human, none of these would make sense at all. So, "How will this be?"

The answer comes swift on the wings of an angel. "The Holy Spirit will come upon you, and the power of the Most High will overshadow you; therefore the child to be born will be called holy—the Son of God. . . . For nothing will be impossible with God." Remember that the word "angel" means messenger. The angels in the Scripture are messengers from God. The significance of this is that the words of the angel are the words of God. "The Holy Spirit will come upon you, and the power of the Most High will overshadow you; therefore the child to be born will be called holy—the Son of God. . . . For nothing will be impossible with God." "How will this be?" How will a son of Mary also be the Son of God? How will the Christ enter the world? How will the Son of God become human? The answer for Mary, for Theophilus, and also for us is that it will be by the power of God, and by the power of God alone. It will be because God says so. What more explanation could we need?

Job wanted answers about the terrible suffering in his life. For thirty-five chapters Job questioned God. Then in chapter 38, God broke the silence of the heavens:

> Where were you when I laid the foundation of the earth?
> Tell me, if you have understanding.
> Who determined its measurements—surely you know!
> Or who stretched the line upon it?
> On what were its bases sunk,
> or who laid its cornerstone,
> when the morning stars sang together
> and all the sons of God shouted for joy? (38:4–7)

This continues through chapters 39–41. God's answer is, in effect, "I am God, and you are not God."

Job got it. Job realized that God had the power and that he did not. More than that, Job realized that God is good. Even though Job was a good and righteous man, his seeing and realizing the goodness of God was so overwhelming that Job despised his own petty goodness. He repented. That is to say, the power of God is not simply raw power, or sheer power, but is the power of goodness. It is the power that expressed itself in the creation of the world and all that is in it. It is the power that expresses itself in providing for the needs of the world and all its creatures. It is the power that expresses itself in redeeming the world from sin and in saving the world. It is the power by which the Son of God can even become human.

So it was that the angel Gabriel said to Mary, "Behold, you will conceive in your womb and bear a son, and you shall call his name Jesus. He will be great and will be called the Son of the Most High. And the Lord God will give to him the throne of his father David, and he will reign over the house of Jacob forever, and of his kingdom there will be no end." What will the power of God at work here accomplish in all of this? At the center of this angelic announcement of the birth of Jesus Christ stand the words of ancient prophecy, "He will reign . . . forever." This announcement offers to us a new and different citizenship and a new and different life. We are invited to acknowledge the eternal reign of Jesus and so to enter his kingdom. We are invited to realize that our home is not here, where the world is fading away, but there, with him, where our life is forever and ever. Are you fearful of the transience of life? Do you want to escape the terror that stalks at night? Do you want to come in out of the cold? Do you want to turn away from decay and from the relentless march toward death, before it is too late to turn away? Do you want to turn toward life and eternity? Are you ready to acknowledge the eternal lordship of Jesus Christ? Or, having already acknowledged him, are you ready to continue to grow in the Christian faith and life?

This is what the angel Gabriel announces to us: Jesus will be the son of Mary, as any mother's child. And yet, Jesus will be also the Son of God, the mediator apart from whom we have no useful knowledge of, or access to, God, but together with whom we have everything. Just as God created the heavens and the earth by the power of his word, so now does God provide for the incarnation of his eternal Son into this new human life by the power of his word, without the agency of an earthly father. This conception is a new beginning for all the world. In this birth is the rebirth of all of humanity. In this life alone the window is open for us to see God and the door is open for us to return to God. And in his death and resurrection are the forgiveness of our sin and the promise of our eternal life with him.

So it is that Jesus Christ, born of Mary, Son of God, reigns forever and stands over against all the pretenders to lordship. It may appear that violence and terrorism have taken over the lordship of this world, but they shall not reign forever. Military powers can put on impressive shows of force, but they shall not last forever. We may act as if we believe the dollar is almighty, but there shall be an end to this and all other economies. The intellectual and psychological framework of the modern world is largely hostile to the Christian faith, and that of the postmodern world may be even more so, but the announcement that Jesus is Lord and will reign forever gives us the courage to go on.

The Gospel according to Luke was written in order "that you may have certainty concerning the things you have been taught." This whole book is here today for us to know the gospel of Jesus Christ, for us to know the content of the Christian faith, for us to know the good news of God, and for us to believe it and to obey it. If that is of interest to you, you are in the right place. The first question is, "How shall we know?" The answer to that question is, "We shall know by the word of God alone." The second question is, "How will this be?" The answer to that question is, "This will be by the power of God." There are many more questions and answers. Luke has them all lined up for us, like a catechism. We will face them one by one. I invite you and urge you to immerse yourself in hearing this word, in being engaged by this word, and so in making it your very own.

"How will this be?" Gabriel said to Mary, "The Holy Spirit will come upon you, and the power of the Most High will overshadow you; therefore the child to be born will be called holy—the Son of God. . . . For nothing will be impossible with God." Whereupon Mary said, "Behold, I am the servant of the Lord; let it be to me according to your word." May God grant us the grace to be so faithful and obedient before the power of the goodness of God.

To God be the glory forever and ever! Amen.

3

Why Me?

LUKE 1:39–56; JEREMIAH 31:7–14

ELIZABETH WAS FILLED WITH the Holy Spirit, and she exclaimed with a loud cry, "Why is this granted to me that the mother of my Lord should come to me?" "Why is this granted to me that . . . my Lord should come to me?" "Why is this granted to me?" "Why . . . me?" You see, at one level this is a question occasioned by geography: Why was Mary, who was newly pregnant and from Nazareth, in Galilee, visiting her relative, Elizabeth, also pregnant, in the hill country of Judah? Luke does not say. But there is more to this than geography, of course. At another level this is a question of recognition: How did Elizabeth recognize Mary as the mother of her Lord? And how did the unborn John the Baptist know to leap for joy at the approach of the unborn Jesus Christ? That seems peculiar, at best. It is suggested that Elizabeth acted at the prompting of the Holy Spirit, and we can assume that the same was true of young John. So now they have told us who is who. But having said that, what else is to be said?

The point is that at yet another level the real question here is, "Why me?" The main question for Elizabeth was, "Why has the Lord come to me?" Indeed, the overwhelming question for Mary was, "Why has the Lord come to me?" And so the pressing question for Theophilus, for whom the Gospel according to Luke was written, continued to be, "Why has the Lord come to me?" And yes, the real question for each of us yet today, in all awe and amazement, is still, "Why has the Lord come to me?" "Why has the Lord come to me?" "Why me?"

Before we get to the answer, it is important to understand the significance of the question. The first sentence of the Gospel according to Luke contains a statement of the purpose of the book: it was written in order that "you"—which at the time referred to Theophilus, for whom the book was written, but which now includes all of us who read the gospel—"may have certainty concerning the things you have been taught." This Gospel according to Luke is still here today in order for us to know the gospel of Jesus Christ, for us to know the content of the Christian faith, for us to know the good news of God, and for us to believe it and to obey it. That is why it was written, that is why we have it, and that is why we read and preach it today.

Moreover, it is my contention that the Gospel according to Luke carries out its purpose of establishing certainty by posing a series of questions—good questions, serious questions, important questions, questions of life and death, questions for which the gospel is the answer. It does this in such a way that the questions are not only in the story but are also the questions of the story, and are the very questions of human life and existence, so that they engaged Theophilus in the matters of the faith and so that they continue to engage us in the same matters of the faith. That is to say, the book we have before us is not only a story but also a catechism, a question-and-answer teaching device intended to communicate the Christian faith, intended to be learned and even memorized, intended to engage the learner—even each of us yet today—in the great questions of the faith; an early catechism in the form of a story, indeed a catechism embedded in the gospel.

We have here, in logical order, a series of questions of faith and doubt, life and death, good and evil, truth and falsehood, reality and unreality. We have here the questions that we ask, or that we should ask, about who we are, whose we are, and what we are about. Indeed, we have here a gift from God, who knows us better than we know ourselves. If we follow these questions, appropriate them as our own, and receive the answers into our hearts and minds, we too can have certainty of the truth of the gospel we have been taught.

Only two questions in this catechism come before today's question. Zechariah the priest asked Gabriel the angel the first question in the book, "How shall I know?" This is a question of knowledge, particularly of the basis of saving faith. It is a good first question for Theophilus and also for us. The answer for Zechariah and for all the rest of us is that we shall know by the word of God and by the word of God alone. Gabriel soon left, of course, but Theophilus still had the written word of God, and so do we. So do we. And it is by this word that we shall know.

It was the virgin Mary who asked Gabriel the second question in the book, "How will this be?" That is, "How will a son of Mary also be the Son of God?" "How will the Christ enter the world?" This is a question of agency. It is a good second question for Theophilus and also for us. It is a question not so much of biology as of theology. The issue is not so much virgin birth as incarnation. The question is how the Son of God can become human. The whole rest of the gospel depends upon this premise. How will this be? The answer for Mary, for Theophilus, and also for us, is that it will be by the power of God, and by the power of God alone. It will be because God says so. What more explanation could we need?

Thus begins the catechism according to Luke, a series of questions and answers for Theophilus and so for us, in order that he and we may have certainty concerning the things we have been taught. It continues to the end of the gospel, with the risen Christ himself asking the last questions. And so it is that today we come to Elizabeth, wife of Zechariah, mother-to-be of John the Baptist, relative of the virgin Mary, the mother of her Lord, who asks for us the third question, "Why is this granted to me that . . . my Lord should come to me?" "Why me?" This is not a question of geography. This is not simply a question of recognition. This is a question of divine election. This is a question of divine choice. This is a question of why the grace of God comes to us even though we do not deserve it one tiny bit.[1] This is a question of amazement, joy, wonder, and gratitude. "Why has the Lord come to me?" "Why me?"

This time, Mary gives the answer. In a beautiful song, known as the "Magnificat" because of the first word in the Latin translation, a song reminiscent of Hannah's song in the Old Testament when she gave her son, Samuel, to the Lord, Mary tells of the grace of God, the always-prior grace of God, and thus of divine initiative, choice, and election.

> My soul magnifies the Lord,
> > and my spirit rejoices in God my Savior,
> for he has looked on the humble estate of his servant.
> > For behold, from now on all generations will call me blessed;
> for he who is mighty has done great things for me,
> > and holy is his name.
> And his mercy is for those who fear him
> > from generation to generation.
> He has shown strength with his arm;
> > he has scattered the proud in the thoughts of their hearts;
> he has brought down the mighty from their thrones
> > and exalted those of humble estate;
> he has filled the hungry with good things,
> > and the rich he has sent empty away.
> He has helped his servant Israel,
> > in remembrance of his mercy,
> as he spoke to our fathers,
> > to Abraham and to his offspring forever.

That is to say, the answer to question "Why me?" for Elizabeth, for Theophilus, and so for us is that the Lord comes to us by the sheer choice of God alone. It is not up to

---

1. It is striking that these first three questions and answers follow the same order as the first three chapters of the Westminster Confession of Faith: "Of the Holy Scripture," "Of God, and of the Holy Trinity," and "Of God's Eternal Decrees." This is not to say that the Westminster divines were consciously following the order of the questions in Luke. It does, however, suggest that both have come upon a good and reasonable order for presenting the faith. *Book of Confessions*, "Westminster Confession of Faith," 121–26.

us. It is not up to anyone else. It is not up to anything else. It is by the sheer choice of God alone.

God chose Mary not only for her sake but also for the sake of her people, Israel. For God had chosen Israel too for a special part in his salvation of world. Israel was not a mighty nation or empire. Israel was not wealthy or prominent. Israel was not important by the standards of the world. By the time of Mary, Israel was a conquered nation, without citizenship, an occupied nation on the fringe of the empire. And yet, God had chosen Israel from all the countries of the world to bring the Christ into the world, for the sake of the world, for the sake of humanity, for your sake and mine. God has a plan and purpose for humanity, and it is being worked out in history, politics, and economics, down through the centuries. We have come this far. God will not abandon us now.

That is to say, God does not tolerate evil forever. He does not put up with it indefinitely. God has brought down the power of evil. He has put it away. He has destroyed it. In Mary's son, the powers of sin, death, and evil met their match and more; they met their conqueror, they met their end, they met the one who undid them forever. So, the powers-that-be in this world shall not rule for long. They have had their day. They have had their chance. They have had their opportunity to do good, and for the most part have failed. They have run their course. Their day is over. The kingdom of God will come.

So, the Lord comes even to us by the sheer choice of God alone. Thanks be to God! To be sure that we realize what this means, consider that God does not come to us because of our deservingness or because of anything else outside of God. If you think that God comes to you because you are good, where are you going to be on that hard day when you realize that you are not nearly so good as you had imagined? If you think that God comes to you because you are rich or because you are poor, you are in for a rude awakening. Those have nothing to do with it. If you think that God comes to you because you are white or black, Asian or Indian, nothing could be farther from the truth. In that God takes the initiative to choose us and come to us, the grace of God rules out any basis in us of our deserving his love and grace. Instead, he loves us despite ourselves.

The other thing that the grace of God rules out is any other determinant outside of God. God does not answer to anyone else. If he did, he would not be God. God does not depend upon anything else. If he did, he would not be God. So God does not have to make his choices based on any standards external to himself, such as other notions of goodness, fairness, justice, or deservingness. If he had to answer to higher standards, they would be above him, and he would not be God. That is to say, again, that God's choice to come to us is based on the inscrutable will of God and on the inscrutable will of God alone. The basis of that decision is not available to us. The reason for that decision is not ours to know. The mind and will of God are not ours to know. But what we do know of God is Jesus Christ. What we do know of God is the extent of his love and grace. What we do know of God is that Christ was willing to die for us. What we do know of God is that he raised Christ for us. And this gives us faith and confidence.

So, for all of our freedoms, we are not free to decide whether God will come to us in Jesus Christ. That is already done. We are not free to decide whether God will love us. God already loves us, more than we can comprehend. We are not free to decide whether God will call us to be his own and to carry out his mission. The call has already been issued. The matters which we are free to decide are these: Shall we believe in God? Shall we be grateful to God? Shall we praise God? Shall we rejoice in and obey God?

Mary, the mother of Jesus, tells us what God has done for us in Jesus Christ, and in her faithful response to the grace of God she provides a model for any who would be Christian today. Just as Mary believed in the word and the promises of God, so are we called upon to believe in the word of God. We are called upon to trust God. We are invited to be confident in the promises of God. We are encouraged to be loyal to the purposes of God set forth in Christ and in the Scripture. God has come to redeem us and to make us whole. The one who died on the cross is now the living Lord of the universe. The one who would not save himself is now the Savior of all! Let us believe in God and in his Christ, with all our heart and soul.

Elizabeth was filled with the Holy Spirit, and she exclaimed with a loud cry, "Why is this granted to me that . . . my Lord should come to me?" "Why . . . me?" And yes, the real question for each of us, in all awe and amazement, is still, "Why has the Lord come to me?" "Why me?" Shall we join Mary, Mother of Jesus, in singing to God:

> My soul magnifies the Lord,
>> and my spirit rejoices in God my Savior,
> for he has looked on the humble estate of his servant. . . .
> He who is mighty has done great things for me,
>> and holy is his name.
> And his mercy is for those who fear him
>> from generation to generation.
> He has shown strength with his arm;
>> he has scattered the proud in the thoughts of their hearts;
> he has brought down the mighty from their thrones
>> and exalted those of humble estate;
> he has filled the hungry with good things,
>> and the rich he has sent empty away.
> He has helped his servant Israel,
>> in remembrance of his mercy,
> as he spoke to our fathers,
>> to Abraham and to his offspring forever.

To God be the glory forever and ever! Amen.

4

What Then?

Luke 1:57–80; Jeremiah 1:1–10

"All these things were talked about through all the hill country of Judea, and all who heard them laid them up in their hearts, saying, 'What then will this child be?' For the hand of the Lord was with him." The newborn baby was the son of a priest, Zechariah, but he was named John. He was not given his father's name. He was not given his father's father's name. He was not given his mother's father's name. In fact, he was not given a name from any of his relatives. This was very strange. Heads were shaking. Tongues were wagging. "All these things were talked about through all the hill country of Judea."

Moreover, the newborn baby, John, was the son of a previously barren woman, Elizabeth. The whole thing set off centuries-distant echoes of Sarah, who was given her firstborn Isaac in her old age; of Rachel, who was given Joseph after long barrenness; and of Hannah, who after years of prayers was given Samuel. Each of those births had been an extraordinary gift of the grace of God, leading to unlikely patriarchs and prophets. Thus was the question raised of John, "What then will this child be?" "What then will this child be?"

Something was afoot. Something was stirring. Something new and different was happening. God was at work in the world again! No wonder that it was said of John, "the hand of the Lord was with him." But to what end? For what purpose? What might God be doing now? "What then will this child be?" Who was John going to be? And, of course, what does it have to do with us yet today? How will this ancient reality affect or change us? What then will we be? That was the question for Zechariah and Elizabeth. That was the question for all their relatives and neighbors through all the hill country of Judea. That was the question for Theophilus, for whom the Gospel according to Luke was written. And yes, that is still the question for us: "What then will this child be?" And therefore, what then will we be?

Before we get to the answer, let me take a moment to consider the setting of this question and thus to establish its significance. This is the last of four questions here in the first chapter of the Gospel according to Luke, and the questions not only occur in the story but also carry the point of the story all the way down to us. The first sentence of the gospel contains a statement of the purpose of the book: it was written in order that "you"—which then referred to Theophilus, but now includes all of us who read the gospel—"may have certainty concerning the things you have been taught." This whole Gospel according to Luke is still here today in order for us to know the gospel of Jesus Christ, for us to know the content of the Christian faith, for us to know the good news of God, and for us to believe it and to obey it. That is why it was written, that is why we have it, and that is why we still read and preach it today.

Three of the four questions are asked before today's question. First (1), Zechariah the priest asked Gabriel the angel, "How shall I know?" This is a question of knowledge, particularly of the basis of saving faith. It is a good first question for Theophilus and also for us. The answer for Zechariah and for all the rest of us is that we shall know by the word of God and by the word of God alone. Gabriel soon left, of course, but the point is that Theophilus still had the written word of God, and so do we. It is by that word that we shall know.

Second (2), the virgin Mary asked Gabriel, "How will this be?" That is, "How will a son of Mary also be the Son of God?" "How will the Christ enter the world?" This is a question of agency. It is a good second question for Theophilus and also for us. The issue is the incarnation. How can the Son of God become human? The whole rest of the gospel depends upon this premise. The answer for Mary, for Theophilus, and also for us is that the incarnation will be by the power of God, and by the power of God alone. It will be because God says so.

Third (3), Elizabeth, wife of Zechariah, mother-to-be of John the Baptist, relative of the virgin Mary, asked, "Why is this granted to me that . . . my Lord should come to me?" This is a question of divine election. This is a question of divine choice. This is a question of why the grace of God comes to us even though we do not deserve it. "Why has the Lord come to me?" Mary gave the answer in a beautiful song known as the Magnificat. She told of the always-prior grace of God, and thus of divine initiative, choice, and election. That is to say, the answer to question "Why me?" for Elizabeth, for Theophilus, and so for us is that the Lord comes to us by the sheer choice of God alone.

These three questions and answers and all the ones that follow have convinced me that the book we have before us is not only a story but is also a catechism, a question-and-answer teaching device intended to communicate the Christian faith, intended to engage the learner, even each of us yet today, in the great questions of the faith. That is to say, the questions are not only in the story but are the story, and are the very questions of human life and existence, so that they engaged Theophilus in the matters of the faith and so that they continue to engage us in the same matters of the faith. We have here the questions that we ask, or that we should ask, about who we are, whose we are, and what we are about. If we follow these questions all the way to the end and appropriate the answers into our hearts and minds, we too can have certainty of the truth of the gospel we have been taught.

Thus begins the catechism according to Luke, a series of questions and answers for Theophilus and so for us. First (1), "How shall I know?" This is a question of knowledge. We shall know by the word of God. Second (2), "How will this be?" This is a question of agency. It will be by the power of God. And third (3), "Why me?" This is a question of divine election. The Lord comes to us by the sheer choice of God alone.

Now we come to the fourth question (4) asked in this book, asked by the neighbors of Elizabeth and Zechariah, new parents by the mercy of God: "What then will this child be?" This is a question of identity. Who will John be? What will God do in and through him? By extension, it raises the same questions for us. What then shall we be? What will God do in and through us?

This time Zechariah, who asked the first question in the book and who had not spoken during the nine or so months since, gave the answer in a wonderful poem or song: "Blessed be the Lord God of Israel, for he has visited and redeemed his people." Most of the song is about Jesus Christ, as well it should be. And the rest of the gospel is about Jesus Christ. But Zechariah concludes the song with words directed at his son, later to be known as John the Baptist, and these words answer the fourth question of the gospel:

> You, child, will be called the prophet of the Most High;
>   for you will go before the Lord to prepare his ways,
> to give knowledge of salvation to his people
>   in the forgiveness of their sins,
> because of the tender mercy of our God,
>   whereby the sunrise shall visit us from on high
> to give light to those who sit in darkness and in the shadow of death,
>   to guide our feet into the way of peace.

The strangely named child, by human reckoning untimely born, was to be a prophet of God Almighty! That was his identity. That was what he would be. John would be a prophet. Indeed, he was to go before the Lord Jesus Christ and prepare his ways. So, John's identity was defined by his relationship to Jesus Christ. Hear that again: John's identity was defined by his relationship to Jesus Christ. So is ours.

What Zechariah had to say about his son is important both for what it says and also for what it does not say, or what it rules out. The first thing (1) it says is that the Lord is coming. The long-prophesied, long-awaited, long-expected Savior of Israel was about to come into the world. This is the deep and underlying good news of this reading. This is the good news of this whole book. This is the gospel that has come down even to us, that Christ has come to save the world. Thanks be to God!

The second thing (2) Zechariah's song says is that John would be the Lord's prophet. The Lord was coming, and John would prepare his way. More specifically, he would "give knowledge of salvation to his people in the forgiveness of their sins." So it was that John, son of Zechariah, came to be known as John the Baptist. That is who he was and what he did. "He went into all the region around the Jordan, proclaiming a baptism of repentance for the forgiveness of sins" (3:3). We will hear more about that later.

The third thing (3) Zechariah says, by virtue of the second, is that John would not be the Christ. John would be the prophet of the Lord, but he would not be the Lord himself. It is important not to get those confused! It was important for John. It was important for those whom John baptized. It is still important for us. If John had misunderstood this, he would have detracted from the ministry of Christ and failed in his own ministry. Everything John did was to point beyond himself to Christ. If those whom John baptized had misunderstood this, they would have missed the point, blindly following him instead of the Lord. If we misunderstand this, we will be falsely honoring the messenger while simultaneously disregarding his message. This prophet pointed ahead to Christ. We are grateful for his work, and we honor him by going where he directs us.

So this is more than a history lesson. The question for Theophilus is also a question for us. The answer that Zechariah gave still informs our lives. What then shall we be? Our identity is defined by our relationship to Jesus Christ. Our identity may not be—indeed cannot be—the same as John the Baptist's. But his identity and ours are both defined by our relationship to Jesus Christ.

Consider this: Mary was told that she would be the mother of Jesus Christ. No one else can do that. But, in her obedience to her calling, she became a model for all subsequent Christian discipleship. So it is with John the Baptist. It was said that he would be a prophet of God, preparing the way of the Lord. That has been done. The Lord has come. No one else can prepare for him to come. But, in his obedience to his calling, John became a model for all subsequent Christian discipleship. That is to say, just as he was called to be a prophet of God then and to prepare the way of the Lord, so are we called to be disciples of the Lord Jesus Christ now and to follow in his way. Let me say that again: Just as John was called to be a prophet of God then and to prepare the way of the Lord, so are we called to be disciples of the Lord Jesus Christ now and to follow in his way. This is our identity. This is who we are. This is what we are about. Thanks be to God!

Just as with John, this is important for us both for what is says and also for what it does not say, or what it rules out. First of all (1), it says that the Lord has come. The Lord for whom John was to prepare *then* is the Lord whom we are to follow *now*.

Second (2), we are to be the Lord's disciples. What a glorious calling this is! We are not accidents of the cosmos. We are not children of the devil. We are not cogs in the giant wheels of the economy. We are not slaves of alien masters. We are disciples of Jesus Christ! Let me say that again: We are disciples of Jesus Christ! And no one can ever take that away from us.

Third (3), in that we are disciples of the Lord Jesus Christ, we are not the Lord. It is so important not to be confused about this! God is God, and we are not. Jesus is Lord, and we are not. Jesus is Savior, and we are the saved, not the mighty savior ourselves. We are to be grateful for what God has done for us, not to assume that we have done it ourselves. This is true of us individually, and it is true of the church as a whole. The church does not exist for its own sake. The church exists to point beyond itself to our Lord and Savior, Jesus Christ.

"All these things were talked about through all the hill country of Judea, and all who heard them laid them up in their hearts, saying, 'What then will this child be?' For the hand of the Lord was with him." Heads were shaking. Tongues were wagging. But Zechariah the priest, who had been struck dumb, was filled with the Holy Spirit and prophesied, answering the question by saying:

> You, child, will be called the prophet of the Most High;
> for you will go before the Lord to prepare his ways,
> to give knowledge of salvation to his people
> in the forgiveness of their sins,
> because of the tender mercy of our God,
> whereby the sunrise shall visit us from on high
> to give light to those who sit in darkness and in the shadow of death,
> to guide our feet into the way of peace.

To God be the glory forever and ever! Amen.

5

What Good News?

Luke 2:1–21; Micah 5:1–5a

"Behold, I bring you good news of a great joy that will be for all the people." What good news is this? What good news could there be for shepherds in the field? What good news could there be for all the people? What good news could there be that might reach all the way even to us? Yes, the angel said, "Behold, I bring you good news of a great joy that will be for all the people." But that raises the question: What good news? What good news could there be for us?

We live in what seem to us to be strange times. I am not sure how different they are from other hard times, but they seem strange to us. We are at war with a largely non-geographic enemy, or at least a non-national enemy. We are under attack for our faith, or at least for not having another faith. All that we hold dear is at stake: gospel, freedom, democracy. Terror stalks the night. The nation hovers in the aftermath of an election, not sure which way to go. Young men and women prepare for war. Some whom we know are already there. Then, in the midst of it all, there steals upon the ear the distant song of angels: "Behold, I bring you good news of a great joy that will be for all the people." But still that raises the question: What good news? What good news could there be for us?

Presumably the good news is not financial. Presumably it is not political. Surely it is not military. At the same time, it cannot be philosophical or ideological. Nor can it be merely social. These all represent broad areas of human concern, but they do not get at the root of the problem. They do not address our most serious concerns. They do not touch our deepest wound. But what does? What good news is there for us?

The answer is short but comprehensive: "For unto you is born this day in the city of David a Savior, who is Christ the Lord." Here is the "good news of a great joy that will be for all the people." "For unto you is born this day in the city of David a Savior, who is Christ the Lord." The weight of the world is carried in these three words: (1) Savior, (2) Christ, and (3) Lord. What good news do they carry for us?

First (1), in the birth, in the person, and in the life, death, and resurrection of Jesus we have our Savior. He is not merely a teacher. He is not simply a moral guide. He is not an example. He is not a counselor. He is not an assistant. Jesus is our Savior! He does for us what we cannot do for ourselves. If we could save ourselves, we would not need saving, or at least we would not need a savior. But Jesus is our Savior! He saves us. He rescues us. He delivers us. He redeems us. According to the angel—and we remember that the word "angel" means messenger, in this case a messenger from God, speaking the word of God and bringing good news from God—the Savior of humanity, the Savior of the world, your Savior and mine, was born in Bethlehem, was born on earth, was born into humanity. This is good news.

Second (2), Jesus our Savior is also Christ. The Savior of the world is also the long-expected, long-awaited Christ. The word is familiar to us, but it must have been shocking in this first announcement. "Christ" is the Greek word used in the New Testament for the Hebrew word "Messiah," used in the Old Testament. They both mean "the Anointed One." It has connotations of royalty. Just as we inaugurate presidents, just as some countries crown kings, so did ancient Israel anoint their kings. The Anointed One was king of Israel. But when this announcement was made to the shepherds, Israel did not have a king of their own. They had not had a king for centuries. In fact, they suffered much under alien kings who served under the Roman emperor. The shepherds probably looked over their shoulders to make sure no Roman soldiers were near to hear such treasonous news.

And yet, there had been an ancient promise. God had told King David that his dynasty would rule forever. And Bethlehem was the city of David! The prophets, such as Micah, had spoken the word of the Lord that his Anointed One would come. Could it be? Could it possibly be? A thousand years after King David, when hope had worn thin and expectation had vanished, could it be that the Anointed One was to come? And now more than that, the Christ who was to come would be not only King of Israel but also Savior of the world. This is good news. Thanks be to God!

Third (3), Jesus our Savior who is Christ is also the Lord. This is the most astounding of all. For the Savior to come was wonderful beyond comprehension. For the Savior to be the Christ was a blessing beyond all deserving. But for the Savior and Christ also to be the Lord, also to be God Almighty, was absolutely unanticipated, unheard of, unimaginable, unexpected, never dreamed of, and incomprehensible. God is God, and we are not God.

And yet, by the choice, initiative, love, and wisdom of God, God came to us as one of us, and nothing has been the same ever since. Jesus our Savior is not just any savior. Our Savior is not a military general or a political liberator. And Jesus our Savior is not only the Christ of ancient hope, the Anointed One sent from God. Instead, Jesus our Savior and Christ is also the Lord God Almighty, Creator of heaven and earth and of all that is in them. Now that is good news! That is hope beyond hope! That is reason to rejoice. Though all the world be against us, the creator of the world is with us, and the Lord of the universe is for us. Nothing can count against that. Not the emperor. Not the cold of night. Not the threat of terror. Nothing.

"Behold, I bring you good news of a great joy that will be for all the people. For unto you is born this day in the city of David a Savior, who is Christ the Lord." An implication of this good news is, of course, the reality that we need good news. Outward appearances to the contrary, we are poor beggars in the night. Apart from this announcement that we have a Savior, we might not even have realized that we needed to be saved. But now that we have been told, it would be foolish and fatal to deny our neediness. Now that the Christ has come, it would be insane to turn away from Bethlehem. Now that the Lord is with us, it would be the height of ingratitude, that sin of sins, to try to go our own way.

What is the bad news to which the good news of Christ is the answer? We who were created to be God-centered have fallen instead into being self-centered. And once having started down that road, there is nothing we can do, our*selves*, by our own efforts, to become un-self-centered. It is simply impossible. And so we wither and die.

And yet, God has come to us in Christ our Savior to recenter us upon the Lord God Almighty. God does this at Bethlehem, coming down from heaven to earth to be with us. "This will be a sign for you: you will find a baby wrapped in swaddling cloths and lying in a manger." God does this on the cross at Golgotha too, lifting us out of our self-centeredness to see the extent of his sacrifice for us. And God does this again at the empty tomb creating new life out of death. In all of these, God does for us what we cannot do for ourselves. Christ is our salvation. Thus do we thrive and live. Only thus do we thrive and live. The gone-wrongness of our existence is undone by the One who is greater than us. Thanks be to God!

It took the church centuries of reflection to articulate this good news of Savior, Christ, and Lord in what we know as the Nicene Creed:

> We believe in . . . one Lord Jesus Christ,
> the only-begotten Son of God,
> begotten of the Father before all worlds,
> God of God,
> Light of Light,
> Very God of Very God,
> begotten, not made,
> being of one substance with the Father;
> by whom all things were made;
> who for us men, and for our salvation,
> came down from heaven,
> and was incarnate by the Holy Spirit of the Virgin Mary,
> and was made man.

Here is the heart of the Christian faith, without which there is no Christian faith: Jesus, the son of Mary, *is* the Lord God Almighty in the flesh. God himself is with us. This good news stands over against anything else that can be said about us or to us. God himself is with us in Jesus Christ. This is not a general truth. This is a particular reality. Jesus Christ was born in Bethlehem, about two thousand years ago, a real human being. God himself is with us in Jesus Christ alone. There are no other saviors. There are many pretenders, but there are no other saviors. Do not be deceived.

"Behold, I bring you good news of a great joy that will be for all the people. For unto you is born this day in the city of David a Savior, who is Christ the Lord. And this will be a sign for you: you will find a baby wrapped in swaddling cloths and lying in a manger." What does this now ancient good news have to do with us? We have already said that we have a Savior. And we have already said that we have been saved from ourselves, from our self-centeredness. By extension, we can understand that we have been saved from sin, death, and evil.

But what we have not said yet is that we have been saved to and for God. This is extraordinarily important. We are saved to and for God. We are not saved to ourselves! We are saved from ourselves. If we were saved to ourselves, that would be more of the same. We are saved to and for God. We are not saved for ourselves! We are saved from ourselves. If we were saved for ourselves, that would be more of the same. We are saved to and for God. The point of salvation is God, not us. A lot of people miss that point, and when they miss that point, they miss the main point. The point of salvation is God, not us. That is to say, we are not saved to or for ourselves. We are saved to and for God. That is good news.

Why are we saved to and for God? To what end? For what purpose? For what reason? For the glory of God, of course! For the glory of God! That is the greatest goal of all. That is the reason we live. That is the reason we breathe. That is the reason we worship. That is the reason we are saved. Do you remember the parting words of the angels? "Glory to God in the highest! Glory to God in the highest! Glory to God in the highest, and on earth peace among those with whom he is pleased!" And that is good news.

If it had been for the glory of humanity, it would have been announced to Caesar Augustus in Rome. As it turns out, by his decree for a census, Augustus unwittingly served God's larger purposes. If it had been for the glory of humanity, it could have happened in Jerusalem. But it happened in tiny Bethlehem. And it was announced to shepherds, of all people. At least they were unpretentious enough to get the message. After visiting the manger, after seeing their Lord and our Lord, "the shepherds returned, glorifying and praising God for all they had heard and seen, as it had been told them." They got it. And so does this good news call us too back to our proper lives of praise and thanksgiving.

"Behold, I bring you good news of a great joy that will be for all the people." What good news? "For unto you is born this day in the city of David a Savior, who is Christ the Lord." This is good news! So let us sing with the angels:

> *Glory to God in the highest, and on earth peace*
> *among those with whom he is pleased! Amen.*

6

How Long?

LUKE 2:22–40; ISAIAH 49:1–6

"THERE WAS A MAN in Jerusalem, whose name was Simeon, and this man was righteous and devout, waiting for the consolation of Israel,"—waiting for the consolation of Israel, waiting for the consolation of Israel—"and the Holy Spirit was upon him. And it had been revealed to him by the Holy Spirit that he would not see death before he had seen the Lord's Christ." How long would that take? "It had been revealed to him by the Holy Spirit that he would not see death before he had seen the Lord's Christ." How long would he have to wait for the consolation of Israel? How long have you and I waited for salvation? How long are we willing to wait for redemption? How long are we to wait? How long?

We live in strange times. We live in a land of untold wealth, but we exist in an age of increasing insecurity. We are largely free to do as we please, but we are often not pleased with what we freely do. We are fiercely proud of our freedom of religion, but for many that means merely freedom from religion, freedom not to worship God at all, freedom not to be grateful or gracious, freedom not to be respectful, freedom in fact to be dismissive of God. We know the name of Jesus Christ, but do we honor that as one name above all others, or do we dishonor that as only one name among many? The times in which we live seem strange even to us, and yet, even that strangeness unites us with the rest of humanity across all time and places in our waiting—waiting for better times, waiting for the right time, waiting for consolation, waiting for salvation, waiting for redemption, waiting for God and for his Christ, either by name or not. How long are we to wait? How long?

Simeon "came in the Spirit into the temple, and when the parents brought in the child Jesus, to do for him according to the custom of the Law, he took him up in his arms and blessed God and said,

> Lord, now you are letting your servant depart in peace,
>> according to your word;
> for my eyes have seen your salvation
>> that you have prepared in the presence of all peoples,
> a light for revelation to the Gentiles,
>> and for glory to your people Israel.

Here is good news! When Simeon saw the infant Jesus, the Holy Spirit worked within him so that he realized that his wait was over, that the long night of Israel had ended, that the day of salvation had dawned, that the light had risen, that God has sent his Christ, and that the consolation of Israel had begun. Thanks be to God! No wonder he blessed God with a hymn. And what a hymn it was! Simeon sang, in effect, that he could die happy having seen Jesus Christ.

All his life he had waited for the Christ. Now that the Christ had come he could depart in peace. His life was fulfilled in seeing and announcing the Christ—yes, seeing and announcing the Christ. That is to say, his was not a private experience. It was not just Simeon and Jesus. This was, instead, a highly public encounter. It was in the temple. It was at a time of worship. Simeon lifted up the child and lifted up his voice to proclaim salvation in Christ, quoting Isaiah 49 about the servant of the Lord. It could not have been lost on his hearers that his acknowledgment of salvation in Christ stood in direct opposition to the teachings of the Roman Empire that Caesar Augustus was savior. There was not room for two saviors. Simeon was making a radical, exclusive, dramatic profession of faith—expensive faith, dangerous faith, challenging faith, all-or-nothing faith.

To say that Jesus is Savior is to say that no one else is Savior. To say that Jesus is Lord is to say that no one else is Lord. To say that Jesus is the light of the world is to say that no one else is the light of the world. Jesus is not one among many or one among several. Jesus is the one and only. With him, it is all or nothing. And so, Simeon's wait was over. And because his wait was over, our wait is over. How long are we to wait? How long? No longer! No longer! The Christ has come, and his name is Jesus. Thanks be to God!

John Calvin, a pastor and theologian in Geneva in the 1500s, has made an interesting observation of this passage. If the sight of Christ as an infant was sufficient for Simeon to approach death cheerfully and confidently, he asks, how much more reason is there for us to live confidently and peacefully today, since we have seen not only the birth but also the life, death, and resurrection of Jesus Christ?[1] We have seen all

---

1. Calvin, *Harmony of the Gospels*, 1:92.

parts of our salvation complete in Christ. That gives us a tremendous advantage over Simeon and therefore an increased responsibility.

Simeon's faithful waiting for the consolation of Israel raises for us the implied question, "How long are we to wait?" How long are we to wait for salvation? For Simeon, the waiting was for a lifetime. And yet, before he died he saw the Christ. And so he died in peace with the blessing of God. And the implied question points us directly to the gospel answer that the salvation that Simeon saw was not just for himself but was also for the world, for Israel and for the Gentiles, and, yes, for you and for me. Because his wait is over, our wait is over. We do not need to wait any longer. We do not need to look to the future for any other salvation. Salvation has come. Redemption has come. Consolation has come. Christ has come. Nothing needs to be added or can be added to what he has done. It is complete. God has been glorified. The wait is over.

This was true for Simeon. This was true for Joseph and Mary. This was true for Luke. This was true for Theophilus, to whom Luke dedicated this gospel. And, yes, this is true for you and me. However long we have waited, however dark and cold the night has been, however lonely the watchfulness has been, however deep the depths we have plumbed, however far we have fallen, however strenuously we have run away, however grievous the sin we have committed, however blind and ungrateful we have been, however deadly our self-inflicted wounds, all of that has come to an end. Christ has come. Our waiting is over. Now we are living in the fullness of time. Thanks be to God!

No sooner had Simeon made his public announcement of Christ than he pulled Mary aside for a more private revelation, which we get to overhear: "Behold, this child is appointed for the fall and rising of many in Israel, and for a sign that is opposed (and a sword will pierce through your own soul also), so that thoughts from many hearts may be revealed." That is to say, salvation is not cheap. The glory of God is not without cost. All that is not well with life cannot be made well by the simple say so of God. Instead, Christ paid the price of being opposed, hated, resented, accused, blamed, convicted, and crucified in order to bear away our sin and to reconcile us to God. No wonder some would rise and some would fall! That is to say, some would believe and some would reject. Some would receive the reconciliation that was extended and some would persist in their brokenness. We should not be surprised even today by opposition to the gospel. The only question for us is, which will it be for us? Shall we rise by Christ, or shall we fall by Christ? In Jesus, do we see God's Christ, or just another teacher? As we see Jesus, are we turned and drawn toward God, or are we turned away?[2] This is our defining moment. Nothing else in our lives is more important than this.

In case there is any hesitation, in case there is any more undue waiting, in case someone needs a little more convincing, Luke shares with us another witness also. "Anna . . . did not depart from the temple, worshiping with fasting and prayer night and day. And coming up at that very hour she began to give thanks to God and to

---

2. Craddock, *Luke*, 39.

speak of him to all who were waiting for the redemption of Jerusalem." At that very hour! At that very moment! At the very instant of their presentation of Jesus to the Lord, according to the Law of the Lord, this prophetess, Anna, gives her thanks to God and gives her testimony to all who would listen that Jesus was the Christ bringing the redemption of Israel and so of the world. Luke has preserved this for us, so that it is as if we were there. This pious woman tells us yet today that Jesus Christ and Jesus Christ alone is our redeemer. This is her testimony to us. Shall we receive it or not?

From time to time, people stand before these congregations to join the church by professing their faith in Jesus Christ as Lord and Savior or by reaffirming their faith in Jesus Christ as Lord and Savior. When they do this, it is because they have heard the good news. They have believed in Christ. They have responded in faith. They want to be part of these congregations of the people of God. And in their professions and reaffirmations of faith they give to all of us the gift of the opportunity to reaffirm our own faith. Will we do that?

From time to time, people come to this sanctuary to present their children to the Lord, not according to the law of the Old Testament but according to the commandment of Christ in the New Testament, for the sacrament of baptism. When they do this, it is because they have heard the good news. They have believed in Christ. They have responded in faith. They want their children to be part of these congregations of the people of God. And in their presentations they give to all of us the gift of the opportunity to reaffirm our own faith. And when they do this, will old men sing and bless the Lord? Will prophetesses prophesy? They already have! Can we sing that with them?

"There was a man in Jerusalem, whose name was Simeon, and this man was righteous and devout, waiting for the consolation of Israel, and the Holy Spirit was upon him. And it had been revealed to him by the Holy Spirit that he would not see death before he had seen the Lord's Christ." How long are we to wait? No longer! Our wait is over. For Simeon "came in the Spirit into the temple, and when the parents brought in the child Jesus, to do for him according to the custom of the Law, he took him up in his arms and blessed God." May God grant us the grace and faith to join him yet today in singing:

> Lord, now you are letting your servant depart in peace,
>   according to your word;
> for my eyes have seen your salvation
>   that you have prepared in the presence of all peoples,
> a light for revelation to the Gentiles,
>   and for glory to your people Israel.

To God be the glory forever and ever! Amen.

7

Did You Not Know?

LUKE 2:41–52; ISAIAH 45:18–25

"WHY WERE YOU LOOKING for me? Did you not know that I must be in my Father's house?" These are the first recorded words of Jesus Christ. This is the only story we have from his childhood. And already the great affirmations of the gospel are imbedded in the words of this early question: "Did you not know that I must be in my Father's house?" Listen together with me as we hear yet again what Jesus still has to say to us yet today.

First (I), "Why were you looking for me? Did you not know that I must be in my Father's house?" I take it that the second question is simply a restatement of, and an expansion upon, the first. The most striking part of this second sentence is at the end, perhaps for the greatest emphasis, where Jesus calls the temple in Jerusalem "my Father's house." So let us start here at the end and then work back to the beginning. Jesus calls the temple in Jerusalem "my Father's house." Perhaps this has become commonplace among us. We sometimes refer to a church building as God's house. We acknowledge Jesus as the Son of God. But this was the first time it was ever said! This was explosive! Jesus, as a twelve-year-old boy, sitting in the temple at Jerusalem, called it "my Father's house." Even his earthly parents, who twelve years earlier at the time of his birth had learned from the shepherds what the angels from heaven had said about him—"To you is born this day a Savior who is Christ the Lord"—at this time they "did not understand the saying that he spoke to them." They took him back home to Nazareth. But years later, after Christ's crucifixion and resurrection, Luke understood what this saying about God meant. And so Luke has preserved it even for us.

"Did you not know that I must be in my Father's house?" Young Jesus, son of Mary, fully human, spoke plainly and straightforwardly of God Almighty as "my

Father." The angel Gabriel had prophesied this to Mary. The virgin Mary had given birth to Jesus. Then the years went by, years of growth and nurture, years of worship and, apparently, of Bible study. And now, for the first time of which we know, Jesus himself said it out loud: "My Father." "My Father!" But what does this mean? How could this be? What are its implications?

"Did you not know that I must be in my Father's house?" Here, for the first time, Jesus teaches his earthly parents and so teaches us that the God of Israel is his Father. It would not be the last time that he teaches this. We especially remember him addressing God as "Father" when he prayed on the Mount of Olives that his Father's will be done, and again when he prayed from the cross that his Father forgive those who crucified him. Those who would dismiss such Father language as the later invention of the church stubbornly deny the plain language of the text and stupidly fail to understand who Jesus is. For Jesus to call God "my Father" is for him to teach us that he is the Son of God. And for Jesus to be the Son of God is not for him to be some strange creature but instead means that none other than God himself is with us in Jesus Christ.

This, in turn, has several gospel implications. The first (1), of course, is that God exists. To those who would deny this, who would say that this world, this visible, material, physical world, is all that there is, we would say, "How do you know?" "Where can you stand to say that there is nothing beyond what you know?" The first thing that Jesus affirms and teaches us here is that there is a God, that God does exist, and that Jesus knows him as Father. That is to say, the very Creator and Judge of the world is none other than the Father of Jesus Christ.

The second implication (2) of God being with us in Jesus is that if we were to divide the world—by which I mean the universe, all that is—between that which is God and that which is not God, Jesus would be on the side with God. Jesus is divine. That is what it means for him to be the Son of God. "Son of God" does *not* mean anything less than or other than God. Not at all! Instead, "Son of God" means precisely that Jesus is God. Jesus is God among us, God with us, and God for us. In Jesus the God of Israel, the Creator and Judge of the world, of whom the prophets spoke, has come to be with us and to save us. This is what it means. No wonder no one at the time understood. This was absolutely new and different.

"Did you not know that I must be in my Father's house?" Now, once we hear that Jesus has said that God is his Father, so that Jesus is the Son of God, God himself with us and for us, we are faced with several possibilities. Others have pointed these out before. One possibility (1) is that Jesus was a fool. That is, one possibility is that he did not know what he was saying, that he did not know what he was talking about, that he was self-deceived and out of his mind. But with all of his great teachings, with all of his followers, with all of his influence, I do not know of anyone who thinks he was a fool. A second possibility (2) is that Jesus was a liar. That is, maybe he knew better but just made up all of this. But with all of his love and compassion, with his refusal to defend himself, I do not know of anyone who thinks he was a liar. The third and only remaining possibility (3) is that Jesus is who and what he said he is: the Son of God, God with us and for us. If he is not to be dismissed as a fool, and if he is not to be condemned as a liar, then he is who he says he is: the Son of God. And, as we have already said, this means nothing less than that God has come to be with us and for us in Jesus Christ. And that, my friends, is pure gospel, good news. As Paul has written, "If God is *for* us, who can be against us?" (Romans 8:31b).

This is what it means that Jesus calls the great temple in Jerusalem "my Father's house." This is his very first teaching recorded for us, when he was twelve years of age. Those today who would claim to be admirers of Jesus but not his followers, those who acknowledge him as teacher but deny that he is anything more than a teacher, have failed to hear this, his very first teaching. His very first teaching is that he is the Son of God. For so-called admirers to set aside this teaching would mean either that (1) Jesus was not a very good teacher, so that we might as well set aside the rest of his teachings too, or that (2) those who want to set aside this teaching are not even very good admirers, let alone followers. Since even they have already said that he is a good teacher, we must conclude that they are very poor students. If they were good students, they would have to acknowledge this first teaching of Jesus, that he is the Son of God, God with us and for us. And so this teaching raises the question for us: Do we acknowledge that Jesus is the Son of God? Do we?

We need to make one more connection here. The prophet Isaiah received a word from the Lord that God is the only Savior:

> I am the LORD, and there is no other. . . .
> I the LORD speak the truth;
> > I declare what is right. . . .
>
> > . . . And there is no other god besides me,
> a righteous God and a Savior;
> > there is none besides me.
>
> Turn to me and be saved,
> > all the ends of the earth!
> > For I am God, and there is no other. . . .
> "To me every knee shall bow,
> > every tongue shall swear allegiance."
>
> Only in the LORD, it shall be said of me,
> > are righteousness and strength. . . .
> In the LORD all the offspring of Israel
> > shall be justified and shall glory. (Isaiah 45:18–25)

So, given (1) that Jesus is God and (2) that God is Savior and the only Savior, it follows (3) that Jesus is Savior and the only Savior. It is Jesus who saves us, which is good news, and it is Jesus alone who saves us, so that there is no other who can save us, which means we are to look no farther. In Jesus, God himself has come to be with us and for us. Thanks be to God!

There is more to the question, a second part (II). "Why were you looking for me? Did you not know that I must be in my Father's house?" Given that the most striking part of this sentence is at the end, where Jesus calls the temple "my Father's house," the second element of his teaching for us here is in the middle of the sentence—that Jesus must be in his Father's house. It is a matter of divine necessity that Jesus must be in the temple, must be in his Father's house, must be where his Father is, must be about his Father's business. This is who he is. This is what he is about. This is what he does. Jesus is in the temple. Jesus must be in the temple.

And more than simply being there, he was engaging the teachers in conversation. "After three days they found him in the temple, sitting among the teachers, listening to them and asking them questions. And all who heard him were amazed at his understanding and his answers." Let me say that again: "All who heard him were amazed at his understanding and his answers." The twelve-year-old Jesus was there in the midst of all the teachers of the temple—perhaps comparable to today's seminary professors, teachers of other teachers of the faith. Jesus was there impressing them with his knowledge of the Word of God. This is who Jesus is. This is what Jesus does. He knows the Word of God, and he communicates it to us. He knows the will of God, and he communicates it to us. He did it then. He does it now. We would do well to listen to him and to learn from him. We would do well to appropriate his gospel teachings and to absorb them into our very being.

There is one more part to the question, a third part (III). "Why were you looking for me? Did you not know that I must be in my Father's house?" "Did you not know?" Given that the most striking part of this sentence is the end, where Jesus calls the temple "my Father's house," and that the second element of his teaching is in the middle, that Jesus must be in his Father's house teaching the Word of God, the third part is at the beginning, and that is that God intends for all of this to be known. The question begins, "Did you not know?" The implication of this question, the meaning of the way it is asked, and therefore the very expectation of this question, is that the hearer should know about Jesus and his Father. That is to say, God intends for all of this to be known. Jesus says that we should know all of this. It may seem strange that Mary and Joseph did not know at that time. No one but Jesus knew then. But does this mean that his question was pointless? No, not at all! It means that his question was aimed beyond them. In due time, Luke came to know. Then Luke wrote this down so that Theophilus would know. And God has providentially preserved this question precisely so that even you and I might know today.

That is to say, the question in today's reading is aimed right at us. You and I are to know that Jesus is the Son of God. You and I are to know that he teaches the word of God and the will of God. And since Jesus must be in his Father's house teaching it, in that this is who he is, then it follows that we who would follow him and bear his name must also be in his church hearing the word of God—hearing, learning, and so knowing the word and will of God. This, my friends, is who we are! Did you not know? Did you not know? What could be more important?! What in all the world could be more important? What in all of life could be more important? Why would be we anywhere else other than here?

Dr. John H. Leith has written this about coming to know God:

> We also come to know God by participating in the fellowship of those who affirm the reality of God and who worship his name. It is doubtful if any faith conviction can be maintained apart from a supporting community, and this is especially true in the instance of faith in God. Christian life as well as theology is based on the conviction that we come to know God by the power of the Holy Spirit, especially as the Holy Spirit speaks through the words of scripture in the fellowship of the church. Persons come to know God in a great variety of ways. God's spirit is free. It is possible that the Spirit of God will deeply move one who is playing golf on Sunday morning, but it is more likely that the Spirit of God will deeply move our hearts and renew our minds in the conviction that God is and, more than that, that God knows us and that God loves us through participation in the worshiping, believing community of Christian people.[1]

That is, again, we are expected to know what Jesus teaches, and this—the gathered and worshiping community, where the Word of God is read, preached, and heard—is where we come to know. How could we do any other than come to church? How can we not bring our friends and neighbors with us, so that they may know?

As a part of the ongoing life of these two congregations, we are in the midst of an annual transition of elders on the session, or governing body, of these churches. Some are completing their service. Others have been elected and are being trained for their office. Upon successful completion of an examination by the current session, to be conducted tomorrow night, the new elders are to be ordained and installed, after which the new session will be convened and will begin to function. As a part of that ordination and installation service, the newly elected elders will be asked the following four questions, among several others, and expected to answer them affirmatively:

a. Do you trust in Jesus Christ your Savior, acknowledge him Lord of all and Head of the Church, and through him believe in one God, Father, Son, and Holy Spirit?

b. Do you accept the Scriptures of the Old and New Testaments to be, by the Holy Spirit, the unique and authoritative witness to Jesus Christ in the Church universal, and God's Word to you?

---

1. Leith, *Basic Christian Doctrine*, 65.

c. Do you sincerely receive and adopt the essential tenets of the Reformed faith as expressed in the confessions of our church as authentic and reliable expositions of what Scripture leads us to believe and do, and will you be instructed and led by those confessions as you lead the people of God?

d. Will you fulfill your office in obedience to Jesus Christ, under the authority of Scripture, and be continually guided by our confessions?[2]

You can hear in these ordination and installation questions that it is built into the very structure of the Presbyterian Church that all of our officers—ministers, elders, and deacons alike—are expected to learn and to affirm exactly what all of us have heard today in this reading from the gospel: (1) that Jesus is God, with us and for us, as Savior; (2) that Jesus teaches us the Word of God; and (3) that he expects us to know it.

"Why were you looking for me? Did you not know that I must be in my Father's house?" These are the first recorded words of Jesus Christ. This is the only story we have from his childhood. The great affirmations of the gospel are imbedded here in the words of this very question, addressed not only to Mary and Joseph but also to us yet today: "Did you not know that I must be in my Father's house?" "His mother treasured up all these things in her heart." How could we do any less? So I urge us all to be faithful in our worship of God and diligent in our study of the Bible.

To God be the glory forever and ever! Amen.

---

2. Presbyterian Church, *Book of Order*, 122.

8

What Shall We Do?

LUKE 3:1–20; ISAIAH 40:1–11

"WHAT THEN SHALL WE do?" Thus the crowds asked John the son of Zechariah. "Teacher, what shall we do?" Thus the tax collectors, also, as crooked as they were, said to John, for a second time, in case we missed it from the crowds. "And we, what shall we do?" Thus even the soldiers, also—Roman soldiers!—asked John, for a third time, in case we missed it from the tax collectors and from the crowds. This is one of only two passages in this entire gospel where a single question is asked three times. What is the significance of that? This question is asked three times for us, for you and me, and for our benefit. It points us as strongly as possible toward what is important in today's reading from the gospel.

"What shall we do?" The question points both forward and backward. Obviously, it points forward to some kind of action. But before that, it points backward to some kind of cause. That is, what shall we do *about what*? We will want to tend to both of these directions, backward and forward, cause and action. The question demands it. And it is appropriate that we deal with first things first. So, what is the cause that leads to this question?

I.

The question asked first by the crowd, second by the tax collectors, and third by the soldiers, all three recorded for our benefit, was asked in response to what John had said. And how are we to understand what he said? Near the beginning of today's reading, it is written that John "went into all the region around the Jordan, proclaiming a baptism of repentance for the forgiveness of sins." And near the end of today's reading, it is also written that "with many other exhortations he preached good news to the people." So this is what he was doing, proclaiming the forgiveness of sins and preaching good news. And the first thing for us to do, of course, is to hear this good news of forgiveness. All else depends upon that.

John "went into all the region around the Jordan, proclaiming a baptism of repentance for the forgiveness of sins." Can you imagine how this must have sounded? The people of Israel were a people of the law. The Roman Empire was known for law and order. The law means that people paid for what they did and got what they had coming to them. That is justice. And yet, the gospel says our sin is forgiven. The gospel says the price has been paid for us. The gospel says that we do not get what we deserve. That is mercy. That is pure, divine mercy. And that is the gospel.

No wonder the people wanted to know what to do! John built upon this good news of forgiveness to issue a call to repent, to turn around, to quit promoting our own interests and to be focused and centered upon God. In the face of the announcement of forgiveness, there is no place to stand on self-righteousness. There is no way to pretend to be innocent. It is not enough, for instance, to say that we are children of Father Abraham. It is not enough even today to say that we are members of the church. The good news of the forgiveness of our sin rightly leads to a profound dissatisfaction with who we are, with what we are about, with what we have done, and with where we are headed. The good news of the grace of God calls upon us to repent, to turn around, to quit relying on our own failing strength, and to cast ourselves upon the mercy of God. He is our only hope. No wonder the people wanted to know what to do!

Now think with me about the context within which this announcement of forgiveness occurred, and what that continues to mean for us in the world within which we live. "In the fifteenth year of the reign of Tiberius Caesar, Pontius Pilate being governor of Judea, and Herod being tetrarch of Galilee, and his brother Philip tetrarch of the region of Ituraea and Trachonitis, and Lysanias tetrarch of Abilene, during the high priesthood of Annas and Caiaphas, the word of God came to John the son of Zechariah in the wilderness." On the one hand, this dates the story. It means that this happened around the year of our Lord 28 or 29.

Yet, on the other hand, and far more importantly, it also means that the word of God did not come to Tiberius Caesar in the supposedly eternal city of Rome. It came to John. To expand upon that, the word of God did not come to Pontius Pilate governing in Judea. It came to John. The word of God did not come to Herod ruling in Galilee, or to Philip ruling in Ituraea and Trachonitis, or to Lysanias ruling in Abilene. It came to John. Moreover, the word of God did not come even to Annas or Caiaphas, high priests in Jerusalem. No, instead the word of God came to John son of Zechariah, in the wilderness. John's name seems almost laughable at the end of this list of dignitaries. While the high and mighty were exercising their inherited powers, John was the first and only child of an elderly and obscure couple, Zechariah and Elizabeth.

While the rulers were in their palaces and temples, John was in the wilderness. And yet, the word of God came there to John, not to them.

This long list of names helps to indicate not only a point in time but also the division of all history into those times before the gospel was preached and those times during which it is preached, the move from the Old Covenant into the New, the beginning of the end for all the old kingdoms of the world and the coming of God's Christ and of his new kingdom of peace and justice. The times were changing, and a host of people who thought they were important would no longer be so important anymore. Today, we know longer count our years by the reign of Tiberius. But we do count our years from the birth of the Christ, about whom John the Baptist preached.

How the word of God came to John we do not know, other than to say that it happened within the grace, power, providence, wisdom, goodness, and initiative of God. Now, what significance did the word of God have to John? What impact did it make on him, and what difference did it make for him? That we *do* know. As a result of the word of God, the one great truth of John's life was that Jesus Christ was about to come. More important than name, rank, or circumstance was this single, overriding reality: that the Son of God, the Anointed One, the Savior of the world, the Lord of the universe, was about to come. This put the Roman Empire, with its power, wealth, and glory and with its armies, oppression, and atrocities, into perspective. It too would pass away. This put the whole history of the people of Israel into perspective, for the ancient prophecies were being fulfilled and the priestly sacrifices on the altar in the temple would find their climax and conclusion on the cross.

We share with John this significance of the word of God, for the word of God has come to us too. The word of God has come to us through John's preaching of the gospel. The word of God has come to us in the word made flesh in Jesus Christ. The word of God has come to us in the written record of and witness to Jesus Christ in the Bible. And the word of God has come to us in the reading, preaching, and hearing of the gospel today.

The one great truth of John's life was that Jesus Christ was about to come, and we share this with John. The one great truth of our lives is that Jesus Christ has come and is coming again. Still more important than name, rank, or circumstance, standing over against all that counts against us at work, school, or home, and standing over against all that beats us down, is this single, overriding reality: that the Son of God, the Anointed One, the Savior of the world, the Lord of the universe, has come and is coming again. John lived before the first coming of Christ, while we live after the first coming and before the second coming, or the return, of Christ. And yet, we share with John the reality that this is the one great, defining truth of who we are.

We share with John the passing from the old to the new. For him, that meant the transition from prophecy to fulfillment, which in written form came to be the distinction between the Old and the New Testament. Eventually it meant the fall of the Roman Empire, which was thought to be eternal and whose rulers were regarded as divine. They were neither divine nor eternal, and yet the gospel of Jesus Christ is both, and it lives on. What new world do we enter yet today?

The old power of death no longer reigns supreme over us. We all still must die, unless Christ first returns, yet the power of death is broken. Christ died and lives again that we might live. The resurrection of Jesus Christ is the promise of our own.

The old power of sin no longer reigns supreme over us. We still sin, not only in our worst actions but even in our best, yet the power of sin is broken. Our sin is forgiven, our sickness is healed, our lives are reoriented and made new.

The old power of loneliness no longer reigns supreme over us. No matter what our circumstance in this world, we are not alone, because God has come to us in Jesus Christ. We are reconciled to God and therefore to each other.

The old power of meaninglessness no longer reigns supreme over us. Our lives have been given meaning, purpose, and direction in the service of our Lord. Nothing can take that away from us. This is the gospel of our Lord.

II.

"What then shall we do?" Having heard the good news of the forgiveness of our sin, "What shall we do?" The good news of Jesus Christ demands a response. So, "What shall we do?" If we are not moved to respond, we have not heard the good news. And if we have heard the good news, if our hearts are aching as we yearn to respond appropriately, it is fitting that we seek some guidance on exactly what we are to do.

The first response, of course, is to believe the gospel. The very question itself implies such belief, for otherwise the question would not be asked. Faith itself is a gift that comes in the proclamation of forgiveness. The baptism of repentance is the outer sign of the same. And yet, to be sure that it is not missed, let us say clearly that the first response is faith. And with faith comes gratitude. And with gratitude comes praise. And with praise comes worship. And with worship comes hope. And with hope comes the love of God. Other than saying that faith comes first, I do not mean to imply any order of events with all of these other gifts. It is simply to say that with the gift of faith come all these other treasures: gratitude, praise, worship, hope, and love. Thanks be to God!

There are also clear and profound implications for how we relate to each other. That is to say, having been reconciled to God, we are to be reconciled to each other. Having been loved by God, and having loved God, we are also to love one another. This is the working out of the baptism of repentance. Repentance is not the earning of our salvation. It is the living out of our salvation. So it is that John told his hearers that they were to share what they had, not to cheat each other, and not to extort money from each other. These continue to apply to us.

To expand upon that, whoever has two coats is to share with anyone who has none. Whoever has food is to share with anyone who has none. Whoever has a kind word is to share it with those who need it. If this world were final, if this life were all there were to life, there might be some reason to hang onto these things, to keep them to ourselves and for our own. Since, however, we are only passing through here, on our way home, we can certainly help some others along the way. So it is that the reality of the coming of Jesus Christ has a great leveling effect in the world. The high and mighty are brought low, the weak and lowly are lifted up. The highway is made smooth, "and the rough places a plain."

Moreover, it became important for John to say that he was *not* the Messiah or the Christ, but that he was only a prophet or a messenger pointing people to Christ. Again, this becomes an important model for who we are and what we are about as the church. We point people to Jesus Christ. There are a lot of other things we do, but we must never lose sight of this: we point people to Jesus Christ. When we call attention to ourselves, we have become confused and lost our way. We cannot save anyone. We can, however, preach the word of God which has come to us. We can tell the story of Jesus Christ. We can share the good news of forgiveness. We point people to Jesus Christ.

While John prepared the way of the Lord for the first coming of Christ, we in the church are to continue to prepare the way of the Lord for the second coming of Christ. We do not talk about this very often in the Presbyterian Church. However, it is a good and important way of understanding who we are and what we are about as the church of Jesus Christ.

In these ways and more, we are stepping from the old world into the new. We continue to live in a time of transition, the time in between the first and second comings of Jesus Christ. And it is precisely in this time that we affirm that the greatest and most important truth and reality about our lives is our Lord, Jesus Christ. "In the fifteenth year of the reign of Tiberius Caesar, Pontius Pilate being governor of Judea, and Herod being tetrarch of Galilee, and his brother Philip tetrarch of the region of Ituraea and Trachonitis, and Lysanias tetrarch of Abilene, during the high priesthood of Annas and Caiaphas, the word of God came to John the son of Zechariah in the wilderness." Today, the word of God has come to us. What then shall we do?

To God be the glory forever and ever! Amen.

9

Whose Son?

LUKE 3:21–38; ISAIAH 42:1–9

"Now when all the people were baptized, and when Jesus also had been baptized and was praying, the heavens were opened, and the Holy Spirit descended on him in bodily form, like a dove; and a voice came from heaven, 'You are my beloved Son; with you I am well pleased.'" Therein lies the question: Whose son? Whose son is Jesus? This is more than a biology question. This is more than a history question. This is more than a question of ethnicity. This is more than a social or political question. Whose son is Jesus? This is a personal question, in terms of its impact on you and me. This is a religious question. This is a question of life and death, good and evil, meaninglessness and purposefulness, lostness and salvation. Everything depends upon this question and its answer.

First (I), whose son is Jesus? Is he the son of Mary? Yes, undoubtedly. Is he the son of Joseph? So it appeared. Or, as the scripture reads, "as was supposed." Certainly he was legally accepted as Joseph's son. In the second chapter of Luke, it is reported that Joseph did his fatherly duty, presenting Jesus to the Lord, taking him to the temple, and so forth. And yet, even then, the boy Jesus began referring to another as his Father. And even more importantly by today's reading, it becomes apparent that to think of Jesus as the son of Joseph would be to miss his true identity and his true importance. So we are back to our original question: Whose son is Jesus?

"A voice came from heaven, 'You are my beloved Son; with you I am well pleased.'" This happened after Jesus was baptized and while he was praying, and the use of the second-person pronoun suggests not only that it was addressed to Jesus but also that Jesus alone heard it. Of course, it was recorded for our benefit, so now we too have heard it. Obviously, the voice from heaven is meant to be understood as coming from

God Almighty, the King of heaven, the Lord of the universe. The voice of God is saying to Jesus, and so through Luke even to us yet today, that Jesus is the Son of God.

Then, in case we missed the point of the voice from heaven, Luke tells us exactly whose son Jesus is, tracing his genealogy back through his adoptive father, strangely enough, seventy-seven generations, all the way back to the beginning, all the way back to the source, so that Jesus is not only the son (as was supposed) of Joseph, not only the son of King David, not only the son of Father Abraham, and not only the son even of Adam, but also and especially and even more so the Son of God. Whose son is Jesus? He is the Son of God, the Lord, the Almighty, the Creator, Judge, and Redeemer of the universe.

The next question (II) is, of course, what does that mean? Beyond the bold words of the affirmation, what does it mean that Jesus is the Son of God? Again, this is more than a biology question. This is more than a history question. This is more than a political question. What does it mean that Jesus is the Son of God? This is a personal question, in terms of its impact on you and me. This is a religious question. This is a question of life and death, good and evil, meaninglessness and purposefulness, lostness and salvation. Everything depends upon this question and its answer.

That Jesus is the Son of God means, of course, that Jesus is more than human. Jesus is more than the son of Mary. Jesus is more than a good teacher. Jesus is more than a moral example. Jesus is more than a prophet. Jesus is more than a friend. Jesus is more than a leader. Yes, Jesus is all of those things, but he is also more than all of these things. He is not only quantitatively more than even the sum of these, but he is also qualitatively different from these.

That Jesus is the Son of God means precisely that Jesus is of God, that Jesus is God himself, and that Jesus is God with us and for us. This relationship of Father and Son is one of identity, not of subordination. That Jesus is the Son of God means precisely that the one who thought of us before we were, the one who created us, the one who holds us and sustains us in existence from one moment to the next, the one who judges us, the one who saves us, and the one who will welcome us home, is present with us and for us in Jesus. We have not been abandoned. We have not been left alone. We have not been forsaken. We have not been forgotten. We have not been neglected. We are not being tricked, fooled, frowned upon, or laughed at. God has come to us in Jesus. This is what it means that Jesus is the Son of God. This is why Luke tells us so.

So again, first, whose son is Jesus? Jesus is the Son of God. And second, what does that mean? Jesus is God with us and for us. Then, of course, the third question (III) is: What difference does that make for us? Again, this is more than a history question. This is more than a political question. What difference does it make for us that Jesus is the Son of God? This is a personal question, in terms of its impact on you and me. This is a religious question. This is a question of life and death, good and evil, meaninglessness and purposefulness, lostness and salvation. Everything depends upon this question and its answer.

First of all (1), it means that we are not coincidences of the cosmos but are instead creatures of the Creator. This is a huge difference. We are not chance gatherings of atoms and molecules but are the purposeful creations of the kind, benevolent, and powerful Creator. We are not animals, and we are not automatons, but instead we are beings created to be in relationship with God and with each other. And now God has come to be with us in the person of Jesus. This is remarkable, exciting, and good cause for great gratitude.

Second (2), it means that we are not a law unto ourselves but that we answer to a higher authority. This is a huge difference. Standards have been set for human life. We are not free to amend them or to tamper with them. The notion that we could somehow break the Ten Commandments is, in some sense, an illusion. It would be more true to say that we find ourselves broken upon them. The presence of God in Jesus emphasizes that these ancient commandments are not alien or arbitrary but are the express will of God for our lives.

Third (3), it means that the brokenness of our lives does not have the final word about who we are. God has not left us to our own devices but has provided for our care, redemption, and well-being. This is a huge difference. Thanks be to God! God has come to us in Jesus to save us from ourselves, to save us from our sin, and to save us to and for God. We are only at the beginning of our reading of the gospel now, but this is where the story is heading. Jesus, the Son of God, offers himself for us, pays the price for our sin, settles our debt, takes our gone-wrongness and uncleanness upon himself, turns our lives around, and reorients us toward God.

Fourth (4), we do not have to seek the one we are to worship. Instead, God has come to us and found us. This is a huge difference. We do not address our prayers, "To Whom It May Concern." We do not worship an unknown God. We do not worship a nameless God. We do not worship the spirit in the sky. We do not have to imagine whom we worship. We worship the God and Father of our Lord and Savior Jesus Christ. This is who we are. This is what we do. The whole point of our lives is "to glorify God and enjoy him forever." Jesus has made this both possible and imperative.

Fifth (5), the alienations of our lives do not have the final control over who we are and what we do. Instead, God has provided for us to be reunited with each other. This is a huge difference. Having separated ourselves from God, we have separated ourselves from each other by gender, race, economics, class, politics, nation, war, and violence. That is not the way life is meant to be. And we cannot overcome this on our own. But look around the church. The ancient feuds of humanity are being overcome. We still have a long way to go. Look around the church. See what God has started. Jesus has gathered us from the far corners of the earth, male and female, young and old, rich and poor, of many races, from many nations, and even many languages. Thanks be to God!

Sixth (6), we are not to be turned inward upon ourselves but to be turned outward toward others, witnessing, helping, caring, serving, and loving. This is a huge difference. If Jesus were anyone else, we might have good reason to continue to be self-serving. But since he is the Son of God, and since he has come to serve us, so are we set free from self to serve others, and so are we commanded to serve others. All those who are in need are also those for whom the Son of God came to earth. We can do no other than to serve them gladly.

Seventh (7), it is not the case that our lives simply run their course down to the end so that this life is all there is. Not at all! The lives we live here are a part of our eternal lives. This is a huge difference. In Jesus, the Son of God, God is with us now in order that we may be with God forever. That is the goal. That is the purpose. That is the end effect of it all. Our lives are put into proper perspective. Distant horizons open before us. We are not simply part of the passing earth. We are children of eternity.

This list could go on and on. The implications for us are endless. The difference it makes for our lives is incalculable. All of this grows out of who Jesus is and whose son he is. Whose son is Jesus? He is not only the son of Mary. He is not only the son (as was supposed) of Joseph, not only the son of King David, not only the son of Father Abraham, and not only the son even of Adam. No, something far greater than that is going on here. "When all the people were baptized, and when Jesus also had been baptized and was praying, the heavens were opened, and the Holy Spirit descended on him in bodily form, like a dove; and a voice came from heaven, 'You are my beloved Son; with you I am well pleased.'"

To God be the glory forever and ever! Amen.

10

Whom Shall You Serve?

LUKE 4:1–13; DEUTERONOMY 6:1–15

WHOM SHALL YOU SERVE? God or the devil? That is the question that came to Jesus Christ, and now it comes to us. Whom shall you serve? God or yourself? Whom shall you serve? God or your country? God or your race? God or your favorite cause? God or anyone or anything else? Whom shall you serve? We realize, of course, that not serving is not an option. To live is to serve someone or something. To breathe is to have a master. The question, then, is not whether you shall serve. The question is, whom shall you serve? Shall you serve God or not? In particular, shall you have the faith and courage to serve the God and Father of our Lord Jesus Christ, or shall you settle for something less? Therein lies the question for you and for me.

This is the question that the devil asked Jesus in the second temptation, which is the central temptation and, I believe, the main temptation in the wilderness. "The devil took him up and showed him all the kingdoms of the world in a moment of time, and said to him, 'To you I will give all this authority and their glory, for it has been delivered to me, and I give it to whom I will. If you, then, will worship me, it will all be yours.'" "If you . . . will worship me, it will all be yours." "If you . . . will worship me." That is all he asked. Of course, that is everything.

By the way, we have to remember that the devil is a liar! We have to remember not to believe anything he says. I do not believe for a moment that all the authority and the glory of the kingdoms of the world had been delivered to the devil. It may appear sometimes that the nations of the world have been given over to him, but I do not believe it. Their authority and glory had not been given to the devil, and they were not his to give to whomever he willed, so he could not have given to Jesus what he did not have.

Nevertheless, this is the offer of glory with which the devil tempted Jesus: "To you I will give all this authority and their glory, for it has been delivered to me, and I give it to whom I will. If you, then, will worship me, it will all be yours." Jesus, of course, understood the underlying question. Jesus knew what was at stake. Jesus realized the consequences of his response as he looked beyond the wilderness and toward the cross. The underlying question both in the wilderness and on the cross was, "Whom shall you serve?" The temptation was for Jesus not to serve his God and Father, not to fulfill his calling, not to be who he was, but instead to flee from the wilderness, to come down from the cross, and so to turn his back on all humanity. That would have been the easy thing to do. That would have been the self-serving thing to do. That would have saved his life. "Whom shall you serve?" Does it seem to you a simple matter? The future of the universe hung in the balance. Jesus knew.

And he answered with a quotation from the scriptures, from the word of God, decisively exposing, rejecting, repudiating, and eliminating what the devil was offering. "Jesus answered him, 'It is written, "You shall worship the Lord your God, and him only shall you serve."'" Here it is, in all its beauty and simplicity: "You shall worship the Lord your God, and him only shall you serve." Jesus answered with a quotation from the scriptures, a verse that he studied and learned and remembered and with which alone he dismissed the greatest lies and temptation of the devil. "You shall worship the Lord your God, and him only shall you serve." Jesus did not answer from philosophy! Jesus did not answer from history. Jesus did not answer from personal experience. Jesus did not answer from psychology. Jesus did not answer from politics. Jesus did not answer from feelings. Whom shall you serve? "You shall worship the Lord your God, and him only shall you serve." Period. End of discussion. Next question.

I am not saying this was easy! By this answer, given before he ever preached his first sermon, Jesus set his face toward the cross. He had to know that. This answer set him along the path to his death. And yet, without hesitation, he gave this answer for himself and so for us. He served God alone both for the glory of God and also in order to save us. Thanks be to God!

In that sense, in regard to the decisive battle between good and evil, the victory was won. God in Jesus did for us what we could not do for ourselves. We cannot save ourselves, nor do we need to save ourselves, because he has already done it for us. And yet, the question and his answer continue to have an ongoing application for our answers to temptation and thus for our lives. What Jesus did for us not only saved us but also provides an example for us, and therefore a teaching for us. When the devil still asks us, as he does every day, "Whom shall you serve?," let us remember and be guided by the brave and faithful answer Jesus gave: "You shall worship the Lord your God, and him only shall you serve." Yes, he did this for us once for all in the wilderness and on the cross. He also did it so that we might follow him in this way every day of our lives.

Perhaps at this point we could strengthen our understanding of what he accomplished by looking at the other two temptations also, and how he responded to them. First of all, after forty days of fasting—obviously humanly impossible, and clearly a sign of God's sustaining mercy—Christ was tempted, not to extravagance, but to the apparently simple satisfaction of human hunger by the transformation of a single stone into a single loaf of bread. What harm could have been done by this? The most obvious harm is that Jesus would have misused his power to help himself instead of to help others. Again, "Whom shall you serve?" The underlying temptation was for Jesus to quit relying on the hidden grace of God, to quit believing in the sustaining mercy of God, to abandon faith in God his Father, to take matters into his own hands, to take care of himself, and to provide for his own food. This was the temptation not simply to eat, but to give up on God, to serve himself, and so to eat. In response to this, Jesus quoted Moses to the effect that our lives are based not only on food but also, and even more, on the will and mind and word and purpose of God. Christians have realized that even when we do have access to food, it is of no benefit without God's mercy. Therefore we pray yet today, "Bless this food to the nourishment of our bodies . . ."

The third temptation became more severe, for the devil himself began to quote Scripture. "Throw yourself off the temple, because it is written that God's angels will take care of you." What was going on there? Jesus was no longer in the wilderness, but back at Jerusalem, at the temple, where he had been taken as a baby, where he had visited the teachers as a boy, and where with disciples he would soon be again. Was the temptation to make a spectacle of himself? Was the temptation to try to manipulate mass conversions? Or was the temptation to try to take control, to try to force God's hand? That is, shall you serve God, or shall you try to make him serve you? Jesus—Jesus the Son of God!—realized that he was the one being tested, not the one who was to be conducting the tests, especially not to be conducting tests on God! And again, he responded with a word from the Scriptures. So the devil departed for a while. We will not hear the devil's voice again in Luke until this last temptation is echoed in the words of the rulers and the soldiers at the crucifixion, urging Jesus to come down from the cross and so to save himself.

Again, Jesus resisted and so defeated temptation for us, once for all, both in the wilderness and again on the cross. He also did it so that we might follow him in this way every day of our lives. So, Christ's responses to his temptations provide us with models for the living of our lives and for resisting the temptations we face. As the church, we are yet today engaged in a struggle for the hearts, souls, minds, and strength of all the people of the world. And we are not the only player on the field. There are powerful forces of evil at work, tempting people to go other directions. So God's grace does not give us reason to be lazy or anything less than diligent, even for a moment. Instead, God's grace provides the only possible foundation and reason for the effort of discipleship and the life of obedience.

Think with me about the history of humanity and of our individual lives. There are four steps here: as we are created, as we have fallen, as we are redeemed, and as we are yet to be glorified. First (1), we human beings were created able to sin. We did not have to sin, but, given the ability and freedom of will to do so, we sinned. Second (2), once we sinned, we were not able not to sin. Everything we do has become infected by our sin. Having turned away from God, we are not capable of turning back to God. Having become self-centered, even an effort to end this is self-centered and doomed to fail. This is why Jesus Christ had to come and to die in order to defeat sin and evil and to reclaim us as his own. Third (3), when God does forgive and convert someone, that person becomes able not to sin, at least on a good day, in small and broken ways, and for brief moments. Every once in a while, I am capable of an unselfish action. Of course, as soon as I realize it, I become so proud of myself that my self-centeredness reaches levels higher than ever before, so my ability not to sin does not last for long! But the ability of the redeemed not to sin is real, even if severely limited. The fourth part (4) of this history is that human beings will not be able to sin. What a wonderful freedom that will be, when sin is no longer an option! This we understand will happen only in heaven.

Today, we are interested in the third stage of human history, the state of being redeemed, of being made able not to sin, at least in small ways. Jesus resisted temptation not only to win the victory for us, but also to work out the victory in us. The gospel brings about not only forgiveness but also renewal. The point is for us not only to be saved but for us also to be sanctified, for us to be made holy, for us to follow our Lord, Jesus Christ, in resisting temptation and serving God.

So, Christ's responses to his temptations do provide us with models for the living of our lives and for resisting the lesser temptations we face. On every occasion Jesus was able to respond appropriately and successfully with the word of God. This encourages us in diligence as students of the word. On every occasion Jesus chose to trust God rather than to take matters into his own hands. This encourages us in faith, confidence, and patience. In particular, while we are not tempted to turn stone into bread—partly because we have plenty of food and even more so because that is not within our power—nevertheless we do have to ask, what false ways for providing for ourselves are within our power? Cheating, fraud, and dishonesty come to mind. So, Christ's successful resistance of temptation calls us to work hard and honestly at the tasks to which God has called us.

Are we tempted by the glory and authority of the kingdoms of the world? That has not been offered to me! Again, we are led to ask, for what lesser glories have we been willing to sell our souls? Or, what besides God have we been willing to worship? Whom shall you serve? The pressures for success are very real in our society and even in church. Jesus, our Lord, our model, was an apparent failure. His disciples deserted him. He was arrested, convicted, and executed. But he kept the faith. Do we risk losing the faith when we pursue worldly standards of success at any cost? The lust after wealth is very real. Jesus died a poor man. Why is money so all-consuming to our world? Whom shall you serve?

Are we tempted to put God to the test? I have not been carried to the pinnacle of the temple. However, are we not in grave danger of the same temptation when we complain about God's apparent failure to take better care of us? Are we not in danger when we ask God, "Why did you let me get sick? Why did you let this happen to me?" These questions may not be sinful in and of themselves, but we need to be aware that with them we are skating on thin ice, way too close to the edge.

Despite all the problems of the world and all the problems of our lives, God has the means to overcome sin, death, and evil, and he has provided both for our salvation and also for the renewal of our lives by Christ's victory over temptation. Whom shall you serve? God or the devil? That is the question that came to Jesus Christ in the wilderness, and now it comes to us in the wilderness of our lives. Whom shall you serve? God or yourself? Whom shall you serve? God or your country? God or your race? God or your favorite cause? God or anyone or anything else? Whom shall you serve? Jesus said, "You shall worship the Lord your God, and him only shall you serve." Period. End of discussion. Next question. Let us hear this, receive this, remember this, rely on this, and so live our lives accordingly.

To God be the glory forever and ever! Amen.

11

Is Not This . . . ?

LUKE 4:14–30; ISAIAH 61:1–11

"THE SPIRIT OF THE Lord is upon me, because he has anointed me to proclaim good news to the poor. He has sent me to proclaim liberty to the captives and recovering of sight to the blind, to set at liberty those who are oppressed, to proclaim the year of the Lord's favor." Didn't Jesus read nicely? "All spoke well of him and marveled at the gracious words that were coming from his mouth." "The Spirit of the Lord is upon me, because he has anointed me to proclaim good news to the poor." And, what is more, "Today this Scripture has been fulfilled in your hearing." Then it began to sink in. And that was when they said, "Is not this Joseph's son?" Who does he think he is?

Jesus said, "The Spirit of the Lord is upon me." And they said, "Isn't this Joe's boy? He can't talk to us like that. Get him!" "When they heard these things, all in the synagogue were filled with wrath. And they rose up and drove him out of the town and brought him to the brow of the hill on which their town was built, so that they could throw him down the cliff." So much for the young man's homecoming. It did not seem an auspicious beginning for his ministry. Indeed, the shadow of the cross fell across his path from day one.

Who is this strange Jesus? There could hardly be any question in your life more important. One cannot imagine a more significant issue. This is not a history question. This is a question about who you are and how you are going to live. Who is this strange Jesus? The people of Nazareth had their opportunity to answer, and they failed the test. Years later, Luke realized that the question continued to be a live one, so he preserved it for his reader, Theophilus, and gave him the right answer. And still today, as we look back to the birth and life of Jesus, and as we live in an increasingly hostile, volatile, and violent world, the question of his identity and therefore of our identity is posed ever more sharply. That is to say, the gospel hinges on the answer to this question: "Who is this man Jesus?" Is he merely a man? Or, being a man, is he also something more than human? And what does he have to do with us?

So it is that today's reading about the beginning of his adult ministry brings us directly into the realities and affirmations of his sonship. "Is not this Joseph's son?" That is one way of looking at Jesus. It has a certain plausibility about it. It involves little or no commitment on our part. It is safe—or so it seems. It does have certain problems related to it, and we will get to those. But it is an understandable position. "Is not this Joseph's son?" Or, "The Spirit of the Lord is upon me." That is quite another way of looking at Jesus. It raises the stakes. It demands a response. If it is true about Jesus, it has certain implications and consequences for us. To acknowledge the lordship of another would be to humble ourselves. To reject the lordship of another would be to assume an adversarial position against a possibly powerful opponent. Even not to answer is, of course, to answer. So, there is no in between. No wonder the people of Nazareth got agitated.

But we are not here today to put down the people of Nazareth. There would be no point in that. We are not here today to second-guess Theophilus. His answer is between him and his Creator. We are here today to answer for ourselves. We are here today to answer for our time and to bear witness to our world. We are here today to take our stand so that our children and our children's children can see, hear, and know who we are. "Is not this Joseph's son?" Or, "The Spirit of the Lord is upon me." Which shall it be for us? How do we perceive Jesus? How do we understand him? How shall we know him? How shall we believe in him? How shall we acknowledge him? How shall we follow him? How shall we obey him? How shall we serve him? How shall we live for him? "Isn't this Joe's boy?" Or, "Is this the one upon whom is the Spirit of the Lord, for whom alone we shall live, for whom we shall die, and by whom we shall live again?" Therein lies the question. Therein lies the question of the centuries. Therein lies the great question of humanity. Now it is our turn and our question. We cannot avoid answering it.

I submit to you that the question raised by Jesus and about Jesus through his reading and preaching of the word of God is far more interesting, provocative, faithful, and fruitful than the question raised by the onlookers. "The Spirit of the Lord is upon me" and "Today this Scripture has been fulfilled in your hearing." Could it be, can it be, that the Spirit of the Lord is upon this person in a unique and special way? Could it be, can it be, that this one is not simply the son of Joseph but is actually the Son of God? Could it be, can it be, that in this one person God has come down from heaven and is present here with us and for us? Could it be, can it be, that in this one the Creator has visited his creatures, the Redeemer has come to the ones he would redeem, the silence of the heavens has been broken, the light has shined in the darkness, healing has poured forth upon the world, and grace has claimed its victory?

This is at least part of what it would mean for the Spirit of the Lord to be upon this one in this time and in this place. For the Spirit of the Lord to be upon this one would mean none other than that the Lord is present in this one. This is new. This is different. This is unique. This is previously unheard of. This sets this one, Jesus, apart from every other one. And therein lies the offense, yet today.

The world is comfortable with many lords, which is to say, with no lords. For if many are lords, then none is lord, and none has to be obeyed. And yet, if none is lord, then many are lords, and many must be obeyed. In the world's attempt to free itself from its rightful service to its one Lord, it has fallen into a terrible subservience to many lords, many evil and terrible lords. Surely this latter duty is harder than the first.

This is what happens when Jesus is regarded as none other than Joseph's son. The son of Joseph only would be, finally, not different from the son of John, or the son of William, or the son of Charles, or the son of anyone else. The son of Joseph only would be only one of us. Such a one could not help us anymore than we can help ourselves, which is not at all. Therein lies the problem if Jesus were merely human.

If Jesus were the best teacher in the world but not more than the best teacher in the world, he could not teach us anything that we do not already know. We need far more than that. If Jesus were the best example in the world but not more than the best example in the world, he could not show us anything beyond our inherent possibilities, and that is not enough. We need far more than that. If Jesus were the greatest leader in the world but not more than the greatest leader in the world, he could not lead us to where we need to go, for we are not that good of followers. We need far more than that. If Jesus showed the greatest love in the world but not more than the greatest love in the world, he could not heal us of our universal disease of self-love. We need far more than that. We need teaching from the word of God. We need a divine example. We need the Good Shepherd. We need self-giving love that can heal us, turn us around, reclaim us, remake us, and redeem us. In short, we need a savior, not only one more son of Joseph.

With this in mind, hear again what Jesus has to say to us: "The Spirit of the Lord is upon me, because he has anointed me to proclaim good news to the poor. He has sent me to proclaim liberty to the captives and recovering of sight to the blind, to set at liberty those who are oppressed, to proclaim the year of the Lord's favor." And, "Today this Scripture has been fulfilled in your hearing." This is who he is and what he is about. To be the one upon whom the Spirit of the Lord is has certain definite implications. First of all, he is the Anointed One. The Greek word for that is "Christ." Moreover, he is the Anointed One specifically in order to proclaim good news to the poor. The poor are not generally the recipients of good news—not then, not now, not ever. This is no merely human endeavor. This is the act of God in and through the Son of God to care for those whom the world despises. This turns everything upside down. This sets the rich and powerful on notice. The Empire of Rome never quite knew what hit it in the birth and ministry of Jesus Christ. But finally, the arrogance of the Empire and the humility of the Christ could not coexist. So, the Empire is no longer with us. That raises the question as to who might be next.

Jesus went on, in this first recorded sermon in Luke, to define his ministry even more specifically. It would have to do with liberty for the captives, and it has continued to do so. Millions have been set free from sin, free from guilt, free from damnation, free from addiction, free from perversion, free from loneliness, free from despair, free from slavery, free from hatred, free from contempt, free from self-loathing, free from war, free from prison, free from the past, free from all that bound them. If we would follow him, surely we are to be both the recipients of this ministry of freedom and also the agents of its continuation throughout the world.

His ministry would also have to do with giving sight to the blind. What a wonder, what a miracle, what a gift this has been! At his touch, those who had not seen could see and have seen. At his touch, ancient prejudices have dissolved. At his touch, unforeseen possibilities have arisen and come into sight. In his name, countless hospitals have been built around the world and those who were blind now see. Indeed, how many millions have sung of his amazing grace, "I once . . . was blind, but now I see"?

The ministry of Jesus Christ is also "to set at liberty those who are oppressed, to proclaim the year of the Lord's favor." This is why he was sent. This is why he came. This is what he has done and what he is doing. In him alone is true freedom from all that oppresses humanity. In him alone does the saving grace of God pour out upon all humanity. In him, ancient prophecy came true and was fulfilled. In him, even we have received grace upon grace. In him, even we, unworthy servants though we are, are called upon to continue to share his good news with all those about us. Can we do that?

I pray that you will join me in realizing that the question "Is not this Joseph's son?" inevitably diminishes and distorts the reality of who Jesus is and leads us in the wrong direction. Setting that aside, do we dare to take up instead that far more interesting question, that far more faithful question, that far more provocative and complicated question, that far more involved and involving question, that far more challenging and fruitful question, that far more grace-filled, eternity-glimpsing, and heaven-bound question: "Is not this the one upon whom the Spirit of the Lord is?"

To God be the glory forever and ever! Amen.

12

What Is This Word?

LUKE 4:31–44; DEUTERONOMY 18:9–18

JESUS "WAS TEACHING THEM on the Sabbath, and they were astonished at his teaching, for his word possessed authority." That was new. That was different from the word of their usual teacher. That got their attention. You know what I mean. That woke them up. That opened their eyes. "His word possessed authority." In fact, as the service went on, with great signs and wonders, "They were all amazed and said to one another, 'What is this word? For with authority and power he commands the unclean spirits, and they come out!'" Something really happened at church that day. "What is this word?" Therein lies an extraordinarily important question for them, for Luke, for Theophilus, to whom Luke wrote his gospel, and, yes, even for us, even for you and me yet today. "What is this word?" Whence comes its power? What is the basis of its authority? Most importantly, who is the one who speaks it? What is it saying to us? What is he saying to us? "What is this word?"

According to this scripture, Jesus Christ is the one who speaks the very word of God. At the very least, Jesus is the new prophet like Moses, who led the people of God out of the land of Egypt, out of the house of slavery. Of course, that ancient prophecy was fulfilled more immediately in the person of Joshua, who succeeded Moses and led the people of God into the Promised Land. But that immediate fulfillment does not mean that the prophecy has not been fulfilled even more completely in the person and work of Jesus Christ, who still leads the people of God out of sin and guilt and into eternal life.

In fact, it may be significant that the English name Jesus comes from the New Testament Greek *Iesous*, from the Aramaic *Yeshua*, and from the Old Testament Hebrew *Yoshua*, which, of course, comes directly into English as Joshua. That is, it is the same name. And it means, "He will save his people." If Joshua was the immediate successor to Moses, Jesus is the eventual successor to Moses, the new prophet like Moses, indeed the new Moses, the one whom God has raised up—another interesting word, having to do also with the resurrection of Jesus Christ—the one whom God has raised up to speak the word of God to the people of God, even to us yet today.

According to this scripture, Jesus Christ is the one who speaks the very word of God. This means, of course, that Jesus is even more than the new Moses. Jesus not only speaks the word of God, not only teaches the word of God, not only preaches the word of God, but also lives the word of God, embodies the word of God, *is* the word of God. "What is this word?" What is this word of authority and power? This word is none other than the very word of God, and the one who speaks it, the one who speaks it with authority and power, the one who teaches like no other, the one who rebukes demons and whom they obey, the one who heals with a word or a touch, the one who preaches like no other, the one who was sent for the very purpose of preaching good news, this one is in fact none other than God himself with us. And that, of course, is what the gospel is all about. The good news is that God himself is with us in the person and life of Jesus Christ—with us in order to be for us, for us in order that we might be with him—all of which he began to make known in this scripture about the teaching, healing, and preaching of Jesus.

"What is this word?" With this, the people asked a very good question. There is no evidence in today's reading that they learned the answer then. Maybe they did later on, and it was not recorded. Luke knew the answer, of course, which is why he preserved the question. But the fact that the people in the story did not know the answer at that time raises now the additional question of whether we, the people reading and hearing the story today, know the answer. We shall return to that in a moment.

For now, consider who did know the answer at that time. The demon whom Jesus rebuked in the synagogue cried out, "I know who you are—the Holy One of God." And demons who came out of many in the house of Simon also cried out, "You are the Son of God!" This is extraordinary. Somehow these spiritual forces, even though they were unclean and evil forces, knew the identity of Jesus and recognized the presence of God in him. They had met the one who could control them with a word. It must have been strange for them, liars that they were, to speak the truth. And it must have been a greater truth than the people were ready to bear, before the cross and the resurrection, for each time the demons cried out, Jesus silenced them, not because they were wrong but "because they knew that he was the Christ." And knowing was not enough. It was not salvific for the demons. In fact, it seems to have been agonizing for them. Salvation comes by faith, not by bare knowledge. Still, Luke has preserved these once silenced truths for us both to know and also to believe: "I know who you are—the Holy One of God" and "You are the Son of God!"

Consider also the significance of the exorcisms and healings that Jesus performed. Those seem to us quite extraordinary and fascinating in and of themselves.

But in the Scriptures, they are not ends in and of themselves. They are, instead, the results of his teaching, the outcome of his teaching, evidence of his teaching, indicators of his authority, and signs of his power. They point beyond themselves to him, to who he is and what he is about. This should warn us against misunderstanding Jesus. He is not only an exorcist, as wonderful as that is for those relieved of demons. He is not only a healer, as grateful as we are for the healing of sicknesses and diseases. We could even want more of each of these. But these are not who Jesus is. These are pointers to something much greater.

"What is this word?" With this, the people asked a very good question. There is no evidence that they learned the answer then. But their not knowing the answer at that time raises the additional question of whether we, the people reading and hearing the story, know the answer yet today. Do we know what this word is? Do we know who it is that speaks this word? Do we know who we are in relation to him? This reading is not, after all, a history lesson. This sermon is an encounter with the living God. The godliness of Jesus Christ was communicated through his word, which we still have even though Jesus is not here in the flesh, and which we are still grappling today, right now.

"What is this word?" Thus Luke queries Theophilus in this catechism. And thus Luke queries us. "What is this word?" As in all catechisms, the answer is supplied. This authoritative, exorcizing, astonishment- and amazement-producing, powerful word of teaching is none other than the word of God. This fever-healing, service-inspiring word is none other than the word of God. This sickness- and disease-healing, demon-rebuking word is none other than the word of God. This good-news, kingdom-of-God, purposeful-preaching word is none other than the word of God. And therefore, the one who speaks this word is "the Holy One of God," "the Son of God," "the Christ," and truly is God. That is the answer. That is *the* answer. It is in the text. So now the tables are turned, and the question is asked of us: Is *the* answer our answer? Can we make it our answer? Do we dare to make it our answer?

If we do, there are at least four ways for us to respond to this word of God. The first way (1) for us to respond is to listen. If the people then were astonished and amazed, we can at least listen. We can at least take the Scriptures seriously. We can at least read and study them, pray with and through them, come to classes about them, and gather to hear them read and preached. We can listen to the word of God and to the one who speaks the word of God.

In addition to listening, the second way (2) for us to respond is to believe. Even the dirty demons knew that Jesus is "the Holy One of God," "the Son of God," "the Christ," but knowing is not enough. We need to believe. Surely we who have the benefit of the Gospel according to Luke, and of two thousand years of Christian preaching and teaching, can believe. Surely we can listen and believe that Jesus speaks the very word of God, and that Jesus is God himself with us.

In addition to listening and believing, the third way (3) for us to respond is to obey. To acknowledge Jesus as God is to admit that we are not God. To acknowledge Jesus as God is to recognize him as Lord. To acknowledge Jesus as God is to realize that he—and not we ourselves—is in charge of our lives. When Jesus teaches us to love the Lord our God with all our heart, soul, mind, and strength, surely we can obey. When Jesus teaches us to love our neighbor as ourselves, surely we can obey. How could we do any less than to listen, believe, and obey?

In addition to listening, believing, and obeying, the fourth way (4) for us to respond is to serve. The people of the synagogue were only astonished and amazed. The demons were rebuked and silenced. Of the people who were healed, it does not say what they did. It does say that the next day, "people sought him and came to him, and would have kept him from leaving them." That, in and of itself, was a refreshing change from the people of his hometown church, who wanted to throw him down a cliff. But Jesus could not stay there, for he was sent for the purpose of preaching the good news of the kingdom of God to the other towns as well. Perhaps this means that we are not to try to keep Jesus to ourselves but are instead to share him and his good news with all the world. But none of these responses gives us a model of service.

But did you hear what Simon's mother-in-law did? She was ill with a high fever. They appealed to Jesus on her behalf. He stood over her and rebuked the fever, just as he had rebuked the demons, and the fever left her. "And immediately she rose"— again, the same word as the resurrection—"and began to serve them." Now, that probably means that she cooked dinner for them! It has always appalled me that this poor woman got up from her sick bed and cooked dinner for Simon and Jesus! I am sure she was glad to be able to get up. But there is something more than cooking going on here. The word for serve is *diekonei*, the Greek verb from which we get the English noun "deacon." Here is the first deacon, and this deacon is female, Simon's mother-in-law. Moreover, her service is more than cooking, as wonderful as that is. Her service is the glad and faithful service of a Christian disciple. Her service is a model for us. Surely, we too can (1) listen, (2) believe, (3) obey, and (4) serve.

"What is this word?" Whence comes its power? What is the basis of its authority? Who is the one who speaks it? What is it saying to us? What is he saying to us? These are the questions this scripture poses to us. What is our answer? And therefore, how shall we respond?

To God be the glory forever and ever! Amen.

13

Let Down Your Nets!

LUKE 5:1–11; ISAIAH 9:1–7

"OF THE INCREASE OF his government . . . there will be no end." "Put out into the deep and let down your nets." "Of the increase of his government . . . there will be no end." "Do not be afraid; from now on you will be catching men." "Of the increase of his government . . . there will be no end." "They left everything and followed him." On the one hand we have an ancient prophecy of the birth of Jesus Christ and of the growth and eternity of his kingdom. On the other hand we have its fulfillment in the life of Jesus Christ, with his ministry (1) symbolized in the catching of fish, (2) specified in the catching of men, and (3) actualized in the conversion of Simon Peter. "Of the increase of his government . . . there will be no end." Simon was the first person included in that endlessly increasing government. James and John were the second and third. Now it has grown for two thousand years. Has it included you yet?

Who is this strange and powerful governor whose birth and life we celebrate? Who is this Christ whom we adore and serve? What is the nature of his kingdom? What are the means of his government? What is the peace that he has accomplished? The prophet Isaiah told us who Jesus would be seven hundred years before he was born, in words that we still rejoice to hear: "For to us a child is born, to us a son is given; and the government shall be upon his shoulder, and his name shall be called Wonderful Counselor, Mighty God, Everlasting Father, Prince of Peace" (Isaiah 9:6). In this person, given as a child to the people of Israel and through them given to all the people of the world, God himself is present with and for us. That is to say, Jesus is the Lord of the universe. And the reason for his birth, the purpose of his life, the goal and accomplishment of his ministry, is to gather us all under his gracious government and thus into the kingdom of God.

This is the wonder and the joy of the birth and life of Jesus Christ. God has not deserted us. God has not left us without hope. God has not left us here alone. Instead, God has come to be with us, as one of us, and yet as more than one of us. He came to us as a child who became a man, and yet, that child and man was, even as he still is, the Lord of the universe. As Lord of the universe, he shall rule over every alien power. He shall rule over the power of sin. He shall rule over the power of disease. He shall rule over the powers of war and strife. He shall rule over the power of evil. He shall rule over the power of death. He shall rule over them all.

And at the same time, he shall rule over us. He shall gather us to himself, no matter how lost and scattered we are, no matter how far away we have wandered, no matter how hard we have run. He shall gather us to himself, call us his very own, and so make us his own. He shall incorporate us into his kingdom, which is to say, into the kingdom of God. And he shall adopt us as his own and receive us as good citizens, reprobates though we are, in his ever-increasing reign. For this is what it means for there to be no end of the increase of his government and therefore of peace. It means that he shall rule and not any other. It means that he shall be Lord and not any other. It means that he shall quell every enemy, displace every foe, and win every victory, not only for us, but even against us and our rebellion. And that is good news. That is gospel. That is what the Christian faith is all about.

So think with me now about this child given to us, this son given to us, upon whose shoulder the government is, whose name is called "Wonderful Counselor, Mighty God, Everlasting Father, Prince of Peace." In his ministry, in his life, in his work, what Jesus had to share with the crowds pressing in upon him was not magic, was not a good show, and was not esoteric philosophy, but was instead the word of God. He did not have good advice, as such. He did not offer financial assistance. He did not have a political platform. He did not offer news and commentary. He did not give book reviews. But what Jesus did have was the word of God, the word of God alone, the word of God pure and undiluted. Thanks be to God that he had that!

Jesus had the word of God because he is the Son of God. He taught the word of God to us because it is by the word of God that we are able to live. And it is by that word of God that Jesus shares the grace of God, the forgiveness of our sin, and the promise of eternal life. It is by that word of God that the increase of his government knows no end. It is by that word of God that he draws us into his reign, into his grace, and into his sustaining mercy. No wonder the crowds pressed in upon him. May God grant us the grace to be so eager today to hear the word of God!

Of all those people who crowded around Jesus, one person became the focus of Christ's attention. He borrowed Simon's boat as a platform from which to teach the crowds. He also borrowed Simon's boat as an occasion to engage Simon at some greater depth. You have heard the story. "Put out into the deep and let down your nets for a catch." At first Simon was hesitant, but soon he consented. After a night of catching nothing, fish filled the nets to the breaking point, then filled two boats to the sinking point. But this catching of the fish was only a symbol of his ministry, which was being actualized in much greater ways. A much larger catch than the fish was taking place inside the boats, inside the hearts and minds of the fishermen. A much more important event was occurring in the kingdom of God and the governance of Jesus Christ. A new disciple was being born. Jesus was claiming Simon as his very own.

At the heart of today's reading is a subtle but important transition. At one point Simon answered Jesus, "Master, we toiled all night and took nothing! But at your word I will let down the nets." Moments later he said to him, "Depart from me, for I am a sinful man, O Lord." The first was respectful, perhaps. It was at least obedient. But the latter was worshipful. The latter was fall-down-on-your-face worshipful. The latter was "Woe is me for I am lost!" worshipful. The latter was "My Lord and my God" worshipful. The latter acknowledged the lordship of Jesus. "Depart from me, for I am a sinful man, O Lord." And in that moment, with that acknowledgment of Jesus as Lord, with that transition from respect to worship, with that conversion, Jesus drew Simon Peter into his service, into his kingdom, into his endlessly increasing government. Jesus claimed Simon Peter as his very own, and so he was. And thus it all began.

James and John were close behind. All three "left everything and followed him." Simon Peter, James, and John left family and friends, work and livelihood, community and tradition, and means of employment. They left everything and followed Jesus! Here is the miracle in today's reading. You thought the miracle was the fish? Those were an important indicator of the identity of Jesus. But the miracle is that Simon Peter, James, and John were converted to a living faith in Jesus Christ as Lord and Savior. And the incontrovertible, outward sign of that miracle was that they left everything and followed Jesus, answering his words with their lives. Can the miracle of faith, obedience, and discipleship happen again, right here, today? Can those who have followed him for years follow ever more obediently? Can those who have never followed him at all start on that journey today?

The original impact of this first affirmation of Jesus as Lord may be difficult for us to realize. The Jews believed in one God in heaven, and could not comprehend that God had also come to earth as a human. The Greeks believed in many gods who went back and forth from heaven to earth all the time and they thought it foolish that Jesus was the one Lord. And so this single confession of faith spelled the end of both those worlds of faith, even as it does for any of our alternatives today. For us to say that Jesus is Lord is to realize that God is God and that we are not God, and that God is in control of our lives, not we ourselves. To say that Jesus is Lord is to rule out all the pretenders. The president is not Lord. The dollar is not Lord. The nuclear bomb is not Lord. Life itself is not Lord. Youth is certainly not Lord. Sin and evil are not Lord. The devil, prince of lies, is not Lord. Even death, our old and powerful enemy, is not Lord over us. Death's most powerful weapon is to make us fear that death is Lord. But from this false and oppressive lie faith in Jesus as Lord sets us free.

Immediately Jesus put Peter to work. Immediately the attention turned from Peter being caught by Jesus to Peter catching men for Jesus. "Put out into the deep and let down your nets." There is the symbolic imperative. "Do not be afraid; from now on you will be catching men." There is the specification of his ministry. The fisherman who had become a disciple would soon become an apostle and an evangelist. That is the trajectory of the Christian faith and life. Christ came to increase the kingdom of God. So it is that we have been included. So it is that we are put to work.

It is a direct implication of this reading that Jesus is calling on us yet today, at Mattoax and Pine Grove Presbyterian Churches, to let down our nets for a catch, not to be afraid, and to be catching men, women, and children with his gospel, for his kingdom, and into his church, into these churches. This is why Jesus came. This is what the Christian faith and life are all about. This is its direct implication for us. Are we doing this? Are we fulfilling our duty? Are we being Christians?

At least two questions emerge. First (1), are we preaching the gospel of Jesus Christ? Sometimes the gospel turns some people away. I know that. But the normal result is that people hear, believe, rejoice, and obey. The normal result is that people are attracted to the forgiveness of sin and the promise of eternal life and so the church grows. If people are turning away from church, we need to preach the gospel more faithfully, more powerfully, and more winsomely than ever before. How do we do that? The word of God, pure and undiluted, full of grace and truth, is the only word we have. Let us speak no other.

Second (2), are our members believing the gospel of Jesus Christ? It is not enough for gospel to be preached rightly; it must also be heard rightly. And for the gospel to be heard rightly is for the word of God to be believed, obeyed, and shared. Are we living, vital witnesses to our Lord Jesus Christ? Are we naming his name for others to hear and know? Do people see our lives and want to know what it is that we have? Do they see our example and come pressing to hear word of God?

So, what will it be? Shall we put out to the deep water and let down the nets for a catch? Or, shall we sit idly on the shore and watch the Lord use some other churches to build up the kingdom? God shall build up his kingdom. There will be no end to the increase of the government of Jesus Christ. The only question is: Shall we be a part of the kingdom? Shall we be a part of the increase? Shall we be a part of that service? Shall we be a part of Christ's church? Or shall we be left aside?

In today's reading, everyone who saw the large catch of fish was astonished. But astonishment is not enough. Only three of those who saw the catch—Simon Peter, James, and John—left everything and followed Jesus. Only three responded correctly. That is, only three believed. Only three were converted. Only three became disciples. "When they had brought their boats to land, they left everything and followed him." Simon Peter, James, and John left family and friends, work and livelihood, community and tradition, and means of employment. They left everything and followed Jesus!

Here is the miracle in today's reading: they were converted. Here is the proof of the miracle: they followed Jesus. God is inviting us to the same response even today.

"Of the increase of his government . . . there will be no end." "Put out into the deep and let down your nets." "Of the increase of his government . . . there will be no end." "Do not be afraid; from now on you will be catching men." "Of the increase of his government . . . there will be no end." "They left everything and followed him." On the one hand we have an ancient prophecy of the birth of Jesus Christ and of the growth and eternity of his kingdom. On the other hand we have its fulfillment in the life of Jesus Christ, with his ministry (1) symbolized in the catching of fish, (2) specified in the catching of men, and (3) actualized in the conversion of Simon Peter. "Of the increase of his government . . . there will be no end." Simon was the first person included in that government. James and John were the second and third. Now it has reached all the way to us. Shall we acknowledge Jesus as Lord? Shall we honor his government and kingdom? Shall we let down our nets for a large catch of men, women, and children? Shall we follow him?

To God be the glory forever and ever! Amen.

14

Who Can Forgive?

LUKE 5:12–26; ISAIAH 11:1–9

"WHO CAN FORGIVE?" "THERE shall come forth a shoot from the stump of Jesse." "Who can forgive sins?" "There shall come forth a shoot from the stump of Jesse, and a branch from his roots shall bear fruit." "Who can forgive sins but God alone?" "There shall come forth a shoot from the stump of Jesse, and a branch from his roots shall bear fruit. And the Spirit of the LORD shall rest upon him, the Spirit of wisdom and of understanding, the Spirit of counsel and might, the Spirit of knowledge and the fear of the LORD. And his delight shall be in the fear of the LORD." "Who can forgive sins but God alone?" Jesus answered them, "Which is easier, to say, 'Your sins are forgiven you,' or to say, 'Rise and walk'? But that you may know that the Son of Man has authority on earth to forgive sins . . . I say to you, rise, pick up your bed and go home." And the man did it! No wonder "amazement seized them all, and they glorified God and were filled with awe, saying, 'We have seen extraordinary things today.'"

You see, the teachers of the law of God were right. No one but God can forgive sins. Of course that is right! Sin is against God, so no one but God can forgive sin. And yet, the teachers of the law of God were also wrong. Jesus was not speaking blasphemies. If anyone else had presumed to forgive sins, that one would have been speaking blasphemies. But Jesus was not speaking blasphemies when he forgave sin. There was one possibility that the teachers of the law of God had not even considered. Suppose, for a moment, that God was in Christ, that Jesus was God with us and for us, that he spoke on behalf of God, and that as God he forgave sin. Then it would not be blasphemy. Then it would be truth and grace. And that, of course, is precisely what did happen. That was the unthinkable possibility that the teachers of the law of God had missed. But that is the good news. God was in Christ, Jesus is God with us and for us, he speaks to us on behalf of God, and as God he forgives sin, even our sin, yet today. This is truth and grace. This is gospel. The ancient prophecies of the Messiah came true. Thanks be to God!

There is more. The scripture we have read today goes to the very heart of the gospel. A simple action tells the whole story. Jesus touched the man who had leprosy. He touched him. And that is the story of the gospel. Why? It was against the law to touch anyone who had leprosy. Leprosy was understood to be unclean, and uncleanness was understood to be catching. So to touch an unclean person was, by law, to become unclean. When Jesus touched the man with leprosy, Jesus became, by law, unclean. He legally took the man's uncleanness upon himself. He became, in effect, a man with leprosy himself. No wonder he left the cities and went into the desolate places. It was against the law for him to enter the cities. Those with leprosy had to stay outside. Of course, Jesus also healed the man of leprosy. And the uncleanness he contracted from him turned out to be no match for the cleansing power of holiness that burned within him.

But think for a moment about that first touch. Jesus could have healed him with a word. Jesus could have healed him from a long distance. There are examples of him doing both of those in Scripture. But instead, Jesus chose to touch him. Instead, he chose to come and be with him as well as for him. Instead, he chose to share the man's pain and suffering. Instead, he chose to address not only the man's physical ailment but also the aching of his heart, his profound and deep loneliness, his alienation from God and humanity. Jesus touched the man. And is not this what Jesus does for us all? Is not this what his very birth into humanity means? Is it not the case that in Jesus of Nazareth, born of Mary, Christ the Son of God has drawn near to us all, and touched us in all our filth and misery, and become one of us? He was born as one of us! He became human! He took on our frailty! He took on our weakness! He took on our brokenness! Thanks be to God! He touched us.

Yes, Jesus is more than human. If he were not more than human, there would be no point to the gospel. But what an entrance! What a starting point! What a way to begin! We will get to Easter soon enough. We will come to the grand conclusion of the gospel, the victory won through death and resurrection. But now, we celebrate and rejoice in this grand, humble beginning: Jesus touched us and became one of us. He took our humanness upon himself and so became human—truly human, fully human. He knows us inside out. He knows us through and through. He knows us from beginning to end. He knows us better than we know ourselves. That is why this one can help us. This one alone can help us. He can forgive our sin. He can make us clean. He can restore us to God. He can, and he does.

This is the one before whom the man with leprosy fell on his face and begged, "Lord, if you will, you can make me clean." How odd that we usually think that worship should be face up, as if we want to rejoice in how good we are and to tell God what we have done for him. How very often in the Bible, instead, when people realize they are in the presence of God, they fall down on their face and do not presume to look up. They know they are not worthy to look upon God. And in this instance, the man with leprosy addressed Jesus as "Lord." In the verses immediately prior to these, it took a tremendous miracle for Simon Peter to move from addressing Jesus as "Master" to addressing him as "Lord." That transition was his conversion. Today's reading does not describe this man's conversion. It does not tell us how he was led to believe in Jesus. It does not tell us when or where he overheard what the angels had told the shepherds: "Fear not, for behold, I bring you good news of a great joy that will be for all the people. For unto you is born this day in the city of David a Savior, who is Christ the Lord." But here was a man who both recognized the Lord and also realized his own neediness. Here was a man who both appreciated who Jesus was and also realized how much he needed him. Here was a man with a broken heart who also knew that Jesus could help him. Would this be of interest to you? Would this be of interest to anyone you know and love? Is not Jesus someone of whom the world is still in need yet today? Do we not still have good reason to celebrate this wonderful news in our own lives?

It is no accident that the man with leprosy asked to be made clean. It was a wasting disease, outwardly. It was a devastating disease, inwardly. The common assumption was that leprosy was a punishment from God. Such a severe punishment indicated profound displeasure which must have been judgment upon great evil. So the person with such a disease bore a double burden. Whether the man who asked to be made clean meant it this way or not, the request certainly has connotations of inner as well as outer cleaning. "Take away my sickness and forgive my sin. Take away my uncleanness and restore me to God. Take away my filthiness and renew a right spirit within me." That is why Jesus touched him. Indeed, that is why Jesus came.

It is not insignificant that after this healing, this cleansing, this mighty act of God, Jesus withdrew to pray. The very Son of God, God himself with us and for us, withdrew for prayer. This always amazes me. And it always raises questions for me. If it was important for Jesus to pray, how much more important must it be for me? If he sought the mind of God, if he sought the guiding of the Spirit, if he poured out his heart in thanksgiving, how much more should I do so? If not only his ministry of teaching and healing but also his very life on earth was undergirded by frequent, prolonged, in-depth prayer, how much more should my ministry and life be based upon, and sustained by, the same? Even by this quiet example, Jesus teaches us what makes for peace and cleanness.

All that is symbolized in the cleansing of the man with leprosy is made explicit in the healing of the man who was paralyzed. Even as Jesus went beyond the call of duty by touching the man with leprosy, so also did he look beyond the obvious paralysis when he said to this second man, "Your sins are forgiven you." That was not why his friends had brought him there. That was not the presenting issue. And that was not the underlying cause of the paralysis. If it had been, the paralysis would not have required a second act by Jesus to be healed. But the man's sinfulness was a more serious issue, a much greater problem, and a more severe neediness than his paralysis. So Jesus dealt with first things first.

The men carrying the man who was paralyzed got more than they had bargained for! They brought a friend to be healed of paralysis; what he got was forgiveness of his sins! They had hoped for the restoration of his limbs; what he got was the salvation of his soul! They had hoped that he could work again and be a productive member of human society; what he got was adoption as a child of God, enlistment into the kingdom of God!

And as I have lived long enough to see beneath the surface of life, how much more have I appreciated the profundity of these words of Jesus: "Your sins are forgiven you." How much more have I realized how much I need to hear and long to hear myself these words of Jesus: "Your sins are forgiven you." Surely this is why we celebrate the birth and life of this one, the one and only one who can and does say this to us and who makes it so: "Your sins are forgiven you."

If only on the day of judgment my sins will be forgiven, if only I will be admitted into heaven as the least of the least, if only I can sit on the back row in the far corner or even stand in the narthex just inside the door, for that I will give thanks forever. So it is that this ancient miracle of forgiveness still has much to tell us about the Christian life. Our best thoughts, words, and actions are tainted by self-interest. None of our actions are ever as good as we think. None of the actions of our enemies are ever as bad as we think. We are always standing in the need of forgiveness, usually more than we realize. We are also always standing in the need of forgiving others, usually more than we want to forgive. We live, finally, not by our own strength or goodness, not by our own wits or wisdom, but by the forgiving grace of God alone.

Part of what the gospel is all about, and part of what today's reading is all about, is that this miracle has already occurred. These gracious words have already been spoken. We do not have to wait until the end of time to hear the gospel: "Your sins are forgiven you." We hear it now. We hear it today. I just read it. I am preaching it now. This gospel reading from long ago is speaking God's word to us today. Just as the men carried their friend who was paralyzed into the presence of Christ, so does this story carry us into the very presence of Jesus Christ right now. He is here. We are here. And the good news is that God has already provided for the forgiveness of our sin in the birth and life of Jesus Christ, as well as in his death and resurrection, so his forgiveness is extended to us here and now, even in this life. Thanks be to God!

I still want to hear those words again at the end of time. I still long for my forgiveness to be confirmed then. I would delight to hear it from his own lips, if possible. But the more important thing is that I already know even now that it is true, and in this I rejoice. "Your sins are forgiven you." And these words are for you too, here and now, at this very moment.

This gospel of forgiveness is the starting point for any ministry we have here, for any life we have together, for any good news we carry into this city. Into the midst of the brokenness of our lives, into the gaping wounds we have suffered as well as the ones we have caused, we are to pour this healing balm. This miracle of forgiveness stands at the heart of the gospel. Without this, there would be no gospel. But with this, we have grace upon grace. Insist upon my telling you this over and over. You will never tire of hearing it.

Perhaps the men who carried their friend to Jesus give us a model for Christian discipleship and for the evangelistic ministry of the church. What better work could we do in the world than to carry people to Jesus, to carry people to the public preaching of his gospel, to carry people to his church? Surely this is the foundation of our parenting, that we bring our children to hear the word of God, to hear the preaching of the gospel, to learn both the need and the reality of forgiveness. There is nothing more important for us to do. This is not just one more extracurricular activity. Surely this is the basis of our witness, that we bring our friends and neighbors here to Mattoax and Pine Grove Presbyterian Churches, bring them to hear the word of God, bring them to hear the preaching of the gospel, bring them to learn both the need for and the reality of forgiveness. There is no greater gift we can give our friends and neighbors than to bring them here to Jesus. This is important to us as an act of obedience. This is also important for the life, health, and well-being of these two congregations. Surely this is the basis of peace in this city and peace in the whole world, that we bring the world to hear the word of God, to hear the preaching of the gospel, to learn both the need for and the reality of forgiveness. This is our world mission. Surely this is what the gospel itself is all about. "Glory to God in the highest, and on earth peace among those with whom he is pleased!" Christ has come to us that we might bring people to him.

The dark side of this story is that there is no evidence that even the healing of the man's paralysis brought the teachers of the law to the point of conversion. There is no record that they were brought to saving faith. Their charge of blasphemy was repeated later in the trial before the crucifixion of Jesus. But at least man who had been paralyzed realized what was going on. Not only did he walk out of there, but also he glorified God. He got it. There was no confusion in his mind about Jesus being a magician, trickster, or blasphemer. He knew the one to whom gratitude was due: the God and Father of Jesus Christ. So he answered the question on which the teachers of the law were stuck.

"Who can forgive?" "There shall come forth a shoot from the stump of Jesse." "Who can forgive sins?" "There shall come forth a shoot from the stump of Jesse, and a branch from his roots shall bear fruit." "Who can forgive sins but God alone?" "There shall come forth a shoot from the stump of Jesse, and a branch from his roots shall bear fruit. And the Spirit of the LORD shall rest upon him, the Spirit of wisdom and of understanding, the Spirit of counsel and might, the Spirit of knowledge and the fear of the LORD. And his delight shall be in the fear of the LORD." "Who can forgive sins but God alone?" Jesus answered them, "Which is easier, to say, 'Your sins are forgiven you,' or to say, 'Rise and walk'? But that you may know that the Son of Man has authority on earth to forgive sins . . . I say to you, rise, pick up your bed and go home." And the man did it! Does this not seize you with amazement? Can we all glorify God and be filled with awe, saying, "We have seen extraordinary things today"?

To God be the glory forever and ever! Amen.

15

Why with Sinners?

LUKE 5:27–39; ZECHARIAH 7:4–10

"WHY DO YOU EAT and drink with tax collectors and sinners?" Of all the things to complain about! Levi threw a feast for Jesus, and this was the best his opponents could come up with. The Pharisees and their scribes grumbled at his disciples, saying, "Why do you eat and drink with tax collectors and sinners?" "Why with sinners?" Why not with nice, respectable people like us? That is what they were asking. Why not with us?

Their question has to do, of course, with more than eating and drinking. It has to do with life. It has to with people. It has to do with family and society, race and ethnicity, church and nation, poverty and wealth, male and female, likes and dislikes, every distinction we make between "us" and "them." "Why with sinners?" Why with those other people? Why with those not like us? Or, why not with us? Of course, the more pressing question is: Why did Jesus come at all to be with any of us by being born as one of us? What strange news is Christ's coming to us! They did not deal with that.

"Why with sinners?" The complaint was made to his disciples, but Jesus answered them directly. "Those who are well have no need of a physician, but those who are sick. I have not come to call the righteous but sinners to repentance." Why with sinners? Because they are the ones who need help! That makes sense. The doctor does not come for people who are well. The doctor comes for those who are sick, for those who need help. And that raises another question: How are you doing today? Do you want to see the Good Doctor?

What is this help that Jesus extends to sinners? "I have not come to call the righteous but sinners to repentance." The good news here is that Jesus calls people out of one way of life and into another, out of darkness into light, out of despair into joy, out of gone-wrongness into made rightness, out of rebellion into service, out of sin into repentance, out of death into life, out of damnation into salvation, out of lostness into foundness, out of alienation into reconciliation, out of the cold into the house, out of loneliness into love. Is that a kind of change you would like to make? Is that a kind of transition that would be good for you? Is that a turn in life that you would like to take? Does that speak to the aching and yearning of your heart?

The good news here is also that when Jesus calls, people listen. When Jesus calls, people come. When Jesus calls, lives are changed. He makes it happen. Look at what he did to Levi. Jesus "went out and saw a tax collector named Levi, sitting at the tax booth. And he said to him, 'Follow me.' And leaving everything, he [Levi] rose and followed him." Just like that. There was no looking back. There was no thinking about it. There was no getting a second opinion. There was no taking of polls. "Leaving everything, he rose and followed him." Just like that. There is the miracle in today's reading.

What is more, "Levi made him a great feast in his house." John Calvin pointed out from this that while Levi resigned from his tax office, he used his house and means for the ministry of Christ. He put aside all hindrances but not all household interests.[1] The feast was not the point of the calling, and that was not the reason that Jesus called him, but the feast did become the occasion for "a large company of tax collectors and others"—others meaning, of course, other sinners—to be "reclining at table with them." The calling of one sinner just brought in more! Of course, if you are looking for sinners, that is good. If you came for sinners, that is good. If your purpose in life is to help sinners, that is good. At our best, the church still works that way today. We bring in one sinner, and that sinner brings in many more. Thanks be to God! For now, remember where it started: "Leaving everything, he [Levi] rose and followed him [Jesus]." Just like that.

Our ancestors in the faith have named this "Effectual Calling," meaning that by his calling God accomplishes what he says. As it is written in the Westminster Confession of Faith:

1. All those whom God hath predestinated unto life, and those only, he is pleased, in his appointed and accepted time, effectually to call, by his Word and Spirit, out of that state of sin and death in which they are by nature, to grace and salvation by Jesus Christ: enlightening their minds, spiritually and savingly, to understand the things of God, taking away their heart of stone, and giving unto them an heart of flesh; renewing their wills, and by his almighty power determining them to that which is good; and effectually drawing them to Jesus Christ; yet so as they come most freely, being made willing by his grace.

2. This effectual call is of God's free and special grace alone, not from anything at all foreseen in man, who is altogether passive therein, until, being

1. Calvin, *Harmony of the Gospels*, 1:262.

quickened and renewed by the Holy Spirit, he is thereby enabled to answer this call, and to embrace the grace offered and conveyed in it.[2]

That means that when God calls a person, God's very calling brings about what it intends. The call is effectual or, as we might say today, effective. It effects what is included in the call. The call itself makes the intended results happen. Again, Jesus called Levi to follow him, and so he did. That is to say, Levi is not the hero of the story. The point of the story is not what a wonderful man Levi was. He was a tax collector! He was collecting money for Rome, the foreign, occupying military force, from his own poor and oppressed people. He was working for the enemy. He was probably as corrupt as the day was long. If anything, that is what this reading is all about. Levi was *not* such a wonderful man. Jesus called him anyway. Maybe there is hope for us.

The point of the story is that Jesus made Levi a disciple. Jesus called him to follow, and so he did. Jesus called him to be a disciple, and so he was. Jesus named him one of his own, and that naming made it so. I am not saying that Levi's response was unimportant. But I am saying that the call of Jesus made Levi's response possible and, more than that, actually brought it about. So the good news for us is not about Levi. The good news for us is about Jesus Christ coming to us about the healing, calling ministry of Jesus Christ, and about the powerful, saving, transforming gospel of Jesus Christ. And he continues to call us today. "Follow me." Do we hear him?

The Pharisees and their scribes grumbled at his disciples, saying, "Why do you eat and drink with tax collectors and sinners?" "Why with sinners?" This is a dangerous question. This is a dangerous question because it assumes that the sinners are over there instead of right here. It is pointing the finger at others instead of examining oneself. And, in so doing, it is running the risk of attempting to set oneself beyond the pale of the stated intent of Christ's ministry, calling sinners to repentance. Therein lies the danger. Far be it from us that we think so highly of ourselves as to assume that we do not need the help that Christ so graciously extends to us. So this dangerous question—"Why with sinners?"—is recorded in Scripture and remembered through the centuries not merely as a history lesson but even more so as a current warning to us of a clear and present danger.

Do we not run the risk of thinking of sinners as everyone else out there except us? Do we not run the risk of thinking of ourselves as basically okay or maybe even pretty good, decent, respectable, and upstanding? And is not the real risk not simply that we might be haughty and arrogant toward all those other people, as bad as that is, but even more that we might try to exclude ourselves from the grace of the Lord Jesus Christ, to cut ourselves off from the love of God, and so to eliminate ourselves from the communion of the Holy Spirit? Do we really regard ourselves as so well that we need no help from the Great Physician? Never underestimate the power of self-delusion.

2. Presbyterian Church, *Book of Confessions*, 134.

Let me offer an alternative. Instead of worrying about all those sinners out there, let us do three things. First (1), let us identify with the sinners. That is to say, let us confess our sin. Let us realize and admit that we are the ones whom Jesus came to help. As John Calvin, again, has said of this passage, "The grace of Christ is only of benefit to us when we are conscious of our own sins, and come to him in humility, groaning under their weight."[3] So, confession and repentance are not something we can do once and be through with it. This is a part of our continuing and deepening conversion throughout our lives.

Second (2), let us profess our faith in Jesus Chris as Lord and Savior and so give thanks to God that it is for us that Jesus came. God's faithfulness to us calls forth faith from us. God's grace elicits our gratitude. We are not called to be one of the first disciples or one of the apostles. But we are called to be believers, to be followers, to be Christians, and so to be members of his church.

Third (3), let us rise and follow Jesus. Leaving everything, let us rise and follow him. Leaving all our self-importance, leaving all our self-righteousness, let us rise and follow him. Those old things need to make way for the new. Leaving the surety of our self-estimates, whether good or bad, let us take his calling of us as the true measure of our lives. Let us rise from the graves of our sinfulness, let us rise from the tombs of our selfishness, and follow him. Let us follow him into church, let us follow him into the world, let us follow him into mercy and compassion, into witness and mission, into worship and gratitude, into justice and righteousness, into peace, into all things good. Let us follow him into life, and let us follow him into heaven.

In just a moment, a young couple is going to stand before us, profess their faith, and so present their infant daughter for baptism. It is no accident that the affirmations we will ask them to make follow exactly the pattern I have just set forth: (1) confession of sin, (2) profession of faith, and (3) promise of faithfulness. Let us all use this occasion as a time for our own reaffirmation of faith and rededication of service. In fact, our whole order of worship follows this pattern: (1) praise and confession at the beginning, (2) proclamation of the gospel and affirmation of faith in the middle, then (3) commitment and thanksgiving at the end. That is a pattern for worship, a pattern for discipleship, and a pattern for life.

As we gather once again to hear the word of God, to hear the gospel of Jesus Christ, and today to hear the call of Christ to follow, let me ask you these questions. Has this week been all that you had hoped? Has this past year been everything you had hoped? Has your life been what you had once hoped and imagined? Is everything going absolutely great for you? Or could you use some help? Could you use some medicine from the Good Doctor? Could you use some turning around? Could you use some repentance? If so, we have good news. That is why Jesus came. The Pharisees and their scribes grumbled at his disciples, saying, "Why do you eat and drink with tax collectors and sinners?" "Why with sinners?" Jesus answered them, "Those who

---

3. Calvin, *Harmony of the Gospels*, 1:265.

are well have no need of a physician, but those who are sick. I have not come to call the righteous but sinners to repentance."

To God be the glory forever and ever! Amen.

16

Good or Harm?

LUKE 6:1–11; 1 SAMUEL 21:1–6

"IS IT LAWFUL ON the Sabbath to do good or to do harm, to save life or to destroy it?" Therein lies the question. "The Son of Man is lord of the Sabbath." Therein lies the good news. When Jesus Christ is Lord, every day is a good day for doing good. Thanks be to God!

Consider the healing in today's reading. It was not an emergency. The man in church was not bleeding to death. He was not having a heart attack. He was not in respiratory failure. The man had a withered hand. It could have waited another day. Jesus healed him anyway. He told the man to stand up right in front of the whole congregation, and he healed his hand. Jesus did not have to wait for an emergency to act. Any day was a good day for healing someone. Any day was a good day for doing good. Any day was a good day for saving life. And by this healing, Jesus took another step closer to the cross. His Sabbath healing inspired the undying fury of those who eventually killed him.

Part of the good news is that God was in Jesus Christ breaking through the world's restrictions to heal, to do good, and to save life. That is the great joy in this reading. It was against the law to harvest on the Sabbath, as the onlookers were quick to point out. But Jesus is Lord over the Sabbath. It was against the law to practice medicine on the Sabbath, as the onlookers were waiting to see. But Jesus says it is always legal to do good and to save life. Those particular laws are foreign to us. And yet, there are other restrictions that bind and constrict our lives as much today. There are other boundaries set up for us not to cross. Jesus steps across them to reach us and to heal us. God breaks through all the barriers to make us well and whole and to reclaim us as his own. Is that of interest to you? God in Jesus Christ has paid the price for healing the gone-wrongness of our lives. And that healing is not cheap. As Christ bore away the sin of the world, it cost him his own life. He has already paid the price for healing the gone-wrongness of our lives. What a shame it would be for us to reject the healing, or to neglect it and so let it slip away, when Jesus has already paid that terrible price.

By way of contrast, there is also a deep sadness in this reading. Jesus did not heal the hardened hearts of the Pharisees. He did not soften, warm, touch, or convert their poor, shriveled up hearts. Instead, the Pharisees remained suspicious, accusing, and angry to the end. It is very sobering to ponder their unwillingness to rejoice in his doing good. It is frightening to consider their fury at his saving life. Their refusal to accept Christ is incomprehensible. Their hearts must have been harder to heal than the man's withered hand! More to the point, in not admitting their sickness, they did not want Christ to heal them. The question for us is: What are we doing? How are we responding to the ministry of Jesus Christ? What direction shall we go? Pray that God will spare us the kind of hardness of heart that is incurable. Pray that God will unfailingly turn our hearts to himself and hold us safe for all eternity.

One of the hard realities of life today, made all the more obvious by this reading, is that Jesus does not heal all of our sicknesses. Despite the miracle in today's reading, he does not take away all the diseases of our loved ones. God does not alleviate all the suffering of the world, let alone prevent it, as we have learned again this week with the earthquake and the tsunami. We do not know why God allows such horrible things. So, what can we say about this? How can we read this gospel about healing so that it is not simply a cruel reminder of something that is beyond our reach? Let me offer four considerations about this.

First (1), we must say there are healings still today for which there is no other explanation than the mercy of God. There have been times when healing has come after the doctors and nurses have said there was nothing else they could do. In fact, a proper understanding would be that God is the source of all healing. Sometimes God works through medical care; sometimes God works beyond it. So, to admit that God does not heal all of our sicknesses is not to say that God does not heal at all. We continue to pray for healing with good hope, and with confidence in God's mercy and power.

Second (2), we do not know how much suffering God has prevented. Nor do we know how our prayers have been involved in that. The suffering we have seen in the world has been massive, even incomprehensible. But who is to say that it could not have been worse? And we will not know until the end of time how our prayers have availed. So, until then we will pray without ceasing.

Third (3), by following the example of our Lord in doing good and saving life, we can help to alleviate much suffering. That is the purpose of, for instance, our Five-Cents-per-Meal offering, which goes to combat hunger here and around the world. John Calvin had a good insight from this reading about the importance of doing good and saving life. "He who takes a man's life is guilty of doing evil, but those who do not trouble to help the needy are little different from murderers."[1] That is strong language. To withhold from the needy what they need is little different from killing them. And as Fred Craddock has written in our own day:

> Jesus poses the issue so as to make inactivity before human need no real option at all. One will be *doing* something: to act is to do good (save life); to refuse to act is to do evil (destroy life). The choice is not whether to do or whether not to do but *what* will I do? Jesus answers his question by his act of doing good: he heals the man. The message is clear: it is never the wrong day to help another, to minister to human need.[2]

Fourth (4), the word of God in this reading applies not only to physical healings but also to spiritual healings. There are millions of times as many people who suffer from withered souls as from withered hands. Are you one of them? Is your soul withered and wasted away and almost useless? Is your heart hard and cold? Is your life reduced to nothingness? Are your relationships strained and broken? God can work in Jesus Christ to break through everything that is crushing your heart and soul and life and relationships. God can restore them to what he means for them to be. Jesus Christ came to earth and went to his death on the cross to heal you and me and to make us whole again. Is that of interest to you? Is that something you might want for yourself, for your loved ones, for your neighbors, for your world? If it is, you are in the right place. Here we speak again the good word of God's love, Christ's forgiveness, and the life and power of the Holy Spirit.

"Is it lawful on the Sabbath to do good or to do harm, to save life or to destroy it?" Therein lies the question. "The Son of Man is lord of the Sabbath." Therein lies the good news. When Jesus Christ is Lord, every day is a good day for doing good. So, what are some of the ways that this ancient reading applies to our lives today? What do we hear the living God saying through this? In some important ways, our situation into which it speaks today is very different from the one into which it was first spoken. The burden of our age is not that people are too scrupulous about obeying the law, whether religious, civil, or criminal. If anything, the burden of our society is its rampant lawlessness. There is an utter disregard for the value of human life and property. So, oddly enough, the true application of the reading today might run exactly opposite the reading itself.

In Christ's day, some people intended to obey the law even if it meant that others went hungry and suffered. In our day, people break the law just because it is there. They would as soon shoot you as look at you. It is a different world. Jesus broke the law to do good and save life. Today, as his followers we need to uphold the law in order to do good and save life. Our society is impersonal, brutal, crushing, and despairing. We need to teach our children, and all the children, the value of life and law.

1. Calvin, *Harmony of the Gospels*, 2:32.
2. Craddock, *Luke*, 82.

Thus, we remind ourselves that human life is valuable because God values each of us as a child of God. If we base our value on our economic worth, that can be taken away. If we base our value on our work, that can end. If we base our value on our social standing, that can change. If we base our value on our race or our party or our nationality, those of different races and parties and nationalities will challenge it. But when we realize that our lives are valuable because God values us, nobody can take that away from us. God's valuing of us provides the only viable basis for human family, society, civilization, and well-being.

Another application has to do with remembering this reading not only as history but also as a warning to the church. The church is always in danger of ossifying and fossilizing. Have you ever seen fossilized dinosaur bones? They stood still too long. They died and they turned to stone. We do not want that to happen to the church. The Pharisees maintained the letter of the law even at the price of the hunger and suffering of other people. The church runs the risk of focusing on itself while disregarding the suffering of others. As we try to be faithful today and tomorrow, we will extend the healing ministry and gospel of Jesus Christ to other people. We need to be on the move. We need to be on the lookout. We need to reach people whom we have never reached before. We need to bring here as many people as we can for Jesus to heal.

Another application has to do with the spiritual healing we have received from God through the ministry of Jesus Christ, the restoration of our withered souls. Our sin has been forgiven. Our life has been renewed. We who were lost have been found. We who were dead have been made alive. We have been made whole again. This is the same healing that we are now to extend in Christ's name to all those about us. Christ set the example of doing good and saving life so we might follow his example and extend his ministry. Ben Campbell Johnson, former Professor of Evangelism at Columbia Seminary, has written, "Evangelism is that peculiar task of the church to communicate the good news of God's love to persons so that they may understand the message, place their trust in Christ, become loyal members of his church, and fulfill his will as obedient disciples."[3]

It is the joyful task of the whole of these two congregations to share the good news of Jesus Christ—his healing, doing good, and saving life—with all those about us. Everyone needs this healing. Everyone needs to hear the gospel of Jesus Christ. Not all will respond positively. Nevertheless, we all need it. We have all sinned and fallen short of the glory of God. Jesus has already paid the price for the healing of us all. Far be it from us not to tell others. Far be it from us not to share with others. Far be it from us to us to restrict, restrain, and distort the ministry and gospel of Jesus Christ. We do not want to behave as if our hearts were still cold and hard and shriveled! And remembering that the healing of the withered hand took place within worship encourages us to bring people with withered souls into the worship of the church of Jesus Christ. Here we can expose them to his gospel, love, and healing.

3. Johnson, *Evangelism*, 12.

The Word of God read and preached today calls for a decision. Do we rejoice in the radical freedom of doing of good? Do we accept Christ's costly healing, and go about gladly doing good and saving life by sharing his healing with others? Or, do we keep our familiar but shriveled old hearts and souls?

"Is it lawful on the Sabbath to do good or to do harm, to save life or to destroy it?" Therein lies the question. "The Son of Man is lord of the Sabbath." Therein lies the good news.

To God be the glory forever and ever! Amen.

17

Blessing or Woe?

Luke 6:12–26; Jeremiah 17:5–8

"Blessed are you who are poor, for yours is the kingdom of God." "But woe to you who are rich, for you have received your consolation." "Blessed are you who are hungry now, for you shall be satisfied." "Woe to you who are full now, for you shall be hungry." "Blessed are you who weep now, for you shall laugh." "Woe to you who laugh now, for you shall mourn and weep." "Blessed are you when people hate you and when they exclude you and revile you and spurn your name as evil." "Woe to you, when all people speak well of you, for so their fathers did to the false prophets." Blessing or woe? Woe or blessing? Which shall it be for us? Which is it for us?

This Sermon on the Plain seems strange to us. Jesus assembled a great crowd of his disciples, and a great multitude of other people was there, not only from the city of Jerusalem and the surrounding countryside of Judea but also from the faraway and foreign place of the seacoast of Tyre and Sidon. The people came to hear. They came to be healed. They wanted to touch him. Jesus had them in the palm of his hand. Did not the pronouncement of woes as well as blessings, let alone the strange blessings themselves, run the risk of emptying the house, of alienating the seekers, and perhaps of dividing the flock? So it would seem. And those things are not to be taken lightly. But he said what he said.

The word of Jesus Christ does not simply draw people together. It separates, and then it draws people together. The word of Jesus Christ does not simply comfort. It pierces, and then it comforts. The word of Jesus Christ is not all sweetness and light. It is a consuming fire, and then it is light by which to see. The gospel of Jesus Christ both attracts and repels. That is the nature of the gospel. If it does not attract, it is not gospel. That should be obvious. But if it does not repel, it is not gospel. That may not be so obvious. That is the strange part. And that is the dangerous part. It is dangerous for preachers today because we preachers do all sorts of other things on our own that drive people away and we want to believe their departure is because of the gospel. Preachers must be held accountable for that. And it is far more dangerous for all of us who are hearers of the gospel, including preachers, because we may find in our pride that we do not want to be forgiven, that we do not want to be helped, that we do not want to be loved, that we do not want to be transformed. That would be a curse indeed.

The pattern from which Jesus started, particularly as we find it in Jeremiah, seems easy enough to understand. "Cursed is the man who trusts in man." "Blessed is the man who trusts in the LORD." "Cursed is the man who . . . makes flesh his strength." "Blessed is the man . . . whose trust is the LORD." "The man who trusts in man . . . is like a shrub in the desert." "The man who trusts in the LORD . . . is like a tree planted by water." All of that makes sense. We may not see it every day. Sometimes the evil appear to prosper. Sometimes the holy suffer. But we understand the distinction. We understand the blessing and the curse. They make sense. In the long run, those who rely on the flesh will fail. Those who rely on the Lord will flourish.

What Jesus does with this is not out of line with what Jeremiah says. It is not discontinuous with it. But Jesus intensifies it and absolutizes it almost to the breaking point. "Woe to you who are rich." That is trusting in man. "Blessed are you who are poor." That is trusting in God. When you cannot depend upon your own financial resources, all that is left is trusting in God. "Woe to you who are full now." That is trusting in the flesh. "Blessed are you who are hungry now." That is trusting in the God. It may seem to us simple necessity. Jesus elevates it to faith. "Woe to you who laugh now." That is a sign of self-confidence. "Blessed are you who weep now." That is evidence of self-awareness and of awareness of one's need for God. "Woe to you, when all people speak well of you." What could be wrong with that? "Blessed are you when people hate you." For those of us who are not hungry, this may seem harder than going hungry. For those of us who want to be liked, this makes the least sense of all. For those of us gathered in the crowd to hear Jesus, this one makes us wonder. What is going on here? What does he mean? What does this have to do with me? These questions are as fresh now as they were then.

Of all the four blessings and four woes, short and cryptic, this last blessing is expanded. This one is elaborated upon. This one has additional instructions and explanations attached. Maybe it can give us a clue to the rest. "Blessed are you when people hate you and when they exclude you and revile you and spurn your name as evil, on account of the Son of Man! Rejoice in that day, and leap for joy, for behold, your reward is great in heaven; for so their fathers did to the prophets."

For starters, note the qualifier to the blessing. Being hated, excluded, reviled, and spurned is no blessing in itself. I suspect many people can testify to that. Instead, being hated, excluded, reviled, and spurned has to do with blessing only when it takes place "on account of the Son of Man," on account of Jesus Christ. I give people plenty of other reasons to hate, exclude, revile, and spurn me. Those reasons do not count. The question is: Is there anything in my faith, life, and witness visibly connected to the faith, life, and gospel of Jesus Christ? If anyone were to look at me, could they see anything of him at all? And if so, could they see enough of him in me to form the basis of any objection? That is where the blessing comes in. If there is enough of Jesus Christ in my life that people hate, exclude, revile, and spurn me on account of him, then I am on the right track.

This is tricky. It can be hard to sort out. I may want to believe that people are objecting to all the Jesus they see in me, when really it is only me that they see in me. I can give plenty of reason for offense on my own without any help from him. So, it can be hard to sort out. But given that, and once it is sorted out, to whatever extent that people object not only to me but to all of us for his sake, to that extent we are blessed. We are blessed not because being hated, excluded, reviled, and spurned are good in and of themselves. Not at all. They are not good. We know that. We are blessed because, in the great scheme of things, we have been drawn to the right side of life and history, to the side of the Creator, to the heart of the Redeemer. Thanks be to God!

Moreover, consider the instructions and reasons attached to this expanded blessing: "Blessed are you when people hate you and when they exclude you and revile you and spurn your name as evil, on account of the Son of Man! Rejoice in that day, and leap for joy, for behold, your reward is great in heaven; for so their fathers did to the prophets." Not only are these rejections considered blessed, but also they are the occasion for rejoicing. They are the occasion for rejoicing because they are evidence of the reality of Jesus Christ in our lives. Why are we to rejoice? Because our "reward is great in heaven." Not here, mind you, but in heaven. Why is our reward great in heaven? Because "so their fathers did to the prophets."

To be hated, excluded, reviled, and spurned on account of Jesus Christ is to be in community with, and in continuity with, the very prophets of the word of the Lord in the Old Testament. In fact, to be hated, excluded, reviled, and spurned on account of Jesus Christ is to be in community with, and in continuity with, the twelve apostles of the gospel of the Jesus Christ in the New Testament. Indeed, to be hated, excluded, reviled, and spurned on account of Jesus Christ is to be in community with, and in continuity with, Jesus Christ himself. That is the point of this all. He was hated. He was excluded. He was reviled. He was spurned. He was falsely accused. He was wrongly convicted. He was executed. Jesus Christ suffered under Pontius Pilate. He was crucified, died, and was buried. He descended into hell for your sake and for mine. That, and that alone, makes sense of these blessings and woes that he pronounces upon us.

That first congregation from Judea and beyond could not yet have known all of this about Jesus Christ. But Luke knew this and wrote it down, so that now we know it, too. We know where Jesus' life was headed. We know what he went through. And we know where he ended up. The cross was not the end. Even the empty tomb was not the end. "The third day he rose again from the dead; he ascended into heaven, and sitteth on the right hand of God the Father Almighty." That is why there is blessing in him. Suffering is not good in itself. No one is saying that. We know better than that. But through the cross, Jesus won the crown. Through the cross, Jesus won the victory. Through the cross, Jesus calls us to himself, names us his very own, and pours out his blessings upon us. Is that of interest to you? Or do you still want to try to make it through life on your own? You cannot have it both ways. Which way do you prefer?

"Blessed are you who are poor, for yours is the kingdom of God." "But woe to you who are rich, for you have received your consolation." "Blessed are you who are hungry now, for you shall be satisfied." "Woe to you who are full now, for you shall be hungry." "Blessed are you who weep now, for you shall laugh." "Woe to you who laugh now, for you shall mourn and weep." "Blessed are you when people hate you and when they exclude you and revile you and spurn your name as evil." "Woe to you, when all people speak well of you, for so their fathers did to the false prophets." Blessing or woe? Woe or blessing? Which shall it be for us? Which is it for us?

To God be the glory forever and ever! Amen.

18

What Benefit?

LUKE 6:27–36; 1 SAMUEL 26:6–12

"IF YOU LOVE THOSE who love you, what benefit is that to you?" "And if you do good to those who do good to you, what benefit is that to you?" "And if you lend to those from whom you expect to receive, what credit is that to you?" These three questions constitute an attack upon our ordinary goodness, and they challenge us to extraordinary goodness. These three questions—"What benefit is that to you?," "What benefit is that to you?," and "What credit is that to you?"—undercut the working presuppositions of polite society. Indeed, these three questions peel away the veneer of respectability and self-righteousness and so open the door to the gospel of God and the righteousness of Jesus Christ.

"If you love those who love you, what benefit is that to you?" "And if you do good to those who do good to you, what benefit is that to you?" "And if you lend to those from whom you expect to receive, what credit is that to you?" In order best to understand the truth to which these three questions point us, I want first to explore the assumptions behind them, second to consider the comments added to them, and third to return to the questions themselves. Consider first (1) the three assumptions behind these three questions: "If you love those who love you," "If you do good to those who do good to you," and "If you lend to those from whom you expect to receive." That is what we do. We love the people who love us. We do good to those who do good to us. We lend to those from whom we expect to receive. That is what good people do. In fact, surely it would be bad not to love those who love us, not to do good to those who do good to us, and not to lend to those from whom we expect to receive. What kind of world would that be? So surely the point is not for us to quit doing good, to quit loving, or to quit lending.

What, then, is the point? Consider, second (2), the three comments after these three questions. "If you love those who love you, what benefit is that to you? For even sinners love those who love them. And if you do good to those who do good to you, what benefit is that to you? For even sinners do the same. And if you lend to those from whom you expect to receive, what credit is that to you? Even sinners lend to sinners, to get back the same amount." The presumed ordinary goodness that we share with the rest of humanity is nothing more than, and nothing other than, the self-interested and self-serving strategy of sinners trying to make it on their own. "Even sinners love those who love them." "Even sinners" do good to those who do good to them. "Even sinners lend to sinners, to get back the same amount." Even sinners meet these minimum standards of human interaction. So these can hardly be considered virtues.

Now, having looked at the assumptions and the comments, let us return third (3) to the three questions themselves. "If you love those who love you, what benefit is that to you?" "And if you do good to those who do good to you, what benefit is that to you?" "And if you lend to those from whom you expect to receive, what credit is that to you?" Given that even sinners do all of those things, the answer is that none of these things is of any benefit to us and none of these things brings any credit to us. That is not to say that we are to stop loving, stop doing good, or stop lending. In fact, we are to do them even more. We shall get to that in a moment. The point here is that, given that even sinners do all of these things, none of these things is of any benefit to us and none of these things brings any credit to us. They may form a minimum standard of human interaction, but they count for nothing before God. They get us nowhere with God. They are of no benefit to us with God. They gain us no credit with God. So, we are still penniless, beggarly sinners.

These negative answers to the three questions seem to imply that we should do something more, something above and beyond the minimum, in order to be of benefit to us with God, in order to build up some credit with God. If even sinners love those who love them, should we not love those who do not love us? Would not that be of benefit to us? If even sinners do good to those who do good to them, should we not do good to those who do not do good to us? Would not that be of benefit to us? If even sinners lend to sinners from whom they expect to receive, should we not lend to sinners from whom we do not expect to receive? Would not that be of credit to us? Well, yes and no. Yes, we should do all this and more. We shall get to that in a moment. But no, even these increased activities will not earn us any benefit or credit with God. That is not the way it works. The truth that our minimal standards are not of benefit to us seems to imply that if we do more we will earn more. But that is not the way it works.

Instead, here is where the gospel of Jesus Christ provides a correction to our natural way of thinking. Listen not only to the implied behavior but even more to the gospel reason behind it: "Love your enemies, and do good, and lend, expecting nothing in return, and your reward will be great, and you will be sons of the Most High, for he is kind to the ungrateful and the evil." "He is kind to the ungrateful and the evil." "He is kind to the ungrateful and the evil." Thanks be to God! There is the gospel. "He is kind to the ungrateful and the evil." We do not have to earn our way into heaven. Heaven is not a benefit we receive for our good works. Heaven is not purchased by building up credit. The God and Father of Jesus Christ "is kind to the ungrateful and the evil." And that, my friends, reaches far enough to include even us. We do not earn God's kindness. God is kind even to those of us—all of us—who do not deserve it.

Here is the gospel key to it all. It still has implications for our behavior. We shall get to those in a moment. But stop and consider the great gospel behind all the questions, behind the all assumptions and the implications, and behind all the critiques and the challenges. The God and Father of Jesus Christ "is kind to the ungrateful and the evil." That is not a reason for us to strive to be ungrateful and evil. But we do not have to strive to be ungrateful and evil. We already are. That is where we are. That is who we are. That is reality. So God has come to us where we are. He loves us where we are. He also loves us into another place where we are not yet. But he starts with us as we are. We do not have to earn his attention and care. Forgiveness is not a benefit of behavior so good as not to need forgiveness. Neither is eternal life purchased on credit.

In case we missed this gospel, Jesus gives it to us again in a slightly different form: "Be merciful, even as your Father is merciful." Again, we shall get to "be merciful" in just a moment. For now, consider the foundation: "Your Father is merciful." That is it. "Your Father is merciful." That is the good news. Jesus does not say, "If you are good enough, God will look kindly upon you." How terrifying that would be! Jesus says, "Your Father is merciful." Jesus does not say, "If you try hard enough, God will credit your effort toward your account." How terrifying that would be! Jesus says, "Your Father is merciful." The foundation, the good news, the underlying reality of all that is said here is the grace and mercy of God Almighty.

Now, finally, it is time to look at the implications for our behavior. Now that we have the underlying truth, now that we have the gospel, now we are ready to ask what it means for our lives. This is very different from what we first thought the implications were. Instead of seeking to earn God's favor, now we are in a position of seeking to respond to God's prior favor. Jesus does not say, "Be merciful, *so that* your Father *will be* merciful to you." That is not the gospel. That would be terrifying. Instead, Jesus does say, "Be merciful, even as your Father is merciful." That is the gospel. That is grace. That is full of life and hope. Either way, the implication could be worded, "Be merciful." Either way, some of the outer actions would look the same. But the foundation is different, so the motivation is different, and so the resulting Christian life is different.

Jesus says, "Be merciful, even as your Father is merciful." We could put that in chronological order to say, "Because your Father is merciful, therefore be merciful." That is the gospel. Because God has already shown mercy to us, let us show mercy to each other. Because God has already forgiven us, we do not have to live in the anxiety of wondering whether or not we have been forgiven. Instead, we are set free from that worry and set free to be forgiving of those around us. Because God has already promised us eternal life, we do not have to live this life in fear and worry about the next life. Instead, we are set free from that worry and set free to be of help to those around us in this life. Do you see the difference? Instead of seeking to earn God's good favor, we are told that he has already poured it out upon us. Instead of seeking to establish our own benefit and credit, we are set free to live in joy and gratitude, responding to the benefit and credit already given us.

In terms of these three questions, what, then, if anything, is the additional benefit to us of good behavior? What beyond salvation is the credit we receive? Not that we earn some future favor, but that even now we shall be drawn closer and closer to God. "Your reward will be great, and you will be sons of the Most High." What a wonderful benefit that will be! The reward is not extrinsic or arbitrary. The reward of godliness is being children of God. The reward of gratitude is being grateful. The reward of graciousness is being gracious. The reward of mercy is being merciful. The reward of goodness is being good. The reward of generosity is being generous. The reward of kindness is being kind. There can be no higher reward. That is the benefit. That is the credit, if you will. "Your reward will be great, and you will be sons of the Most High." Is this of interest to you? Is this something you would like to do? Does this appeal to you?

And now we are ready to hear about how we are to go about living out this wonderful grace of God in our day-to-day lives. "I say to you who hear, Love your enemies, do good to those who hate you, bless those who curse you, pray for those who abuse you." Do you see how expanded this is? Not only are we to love those who love us—Jesus never says for us to stop loving them—but also we are to love even our enemies, those who do not love us, even those who hate us and seek our harm. We are to love them and seek their well-being. That love would reflect the love of God. Not only are we to do good to those who do good to us—Jesus never says for us to stop doing good to them—but also we are to do good to those who hate us, even to those who do not do good to us, even to those who wish us harm, even to those who work for our demise. That goodness would reflect the goodness of God.

Not only are we to bless those who bless us—Jesus never says for us to stop blessing them—but also we are to bless those who curse us, even those who do not bless us, even those who are not neutral toward us, even those who despise us and spit upon us. We are to bless them despite what they do to us. That blessing would reflect the blessing of God. Not only are we to pray for those who pray with and for us—Jesus never says for us to stop praying with and for them—but also we are to pray for those who abuse us, even for those who do not pray for us, even for those who actively work against us, even for those who injure and humiliate us. We are to pray for them. It is easy to pray for family and friends. It is easy to pray for fellow Christians. It is easy to pray for the weak and needy. But to pray for the strong and mighty? To pray for those who lord it over us and wrong us? Such prayer would reflect the very heart of God.

"I say to you who hear . . . To one who strikes you on the cheek, offer the other also, and from one who takes away your cloak do not withhold your tunic either." Now Jesus has gone from prayer and blessing to actually suffering injury, wrong, and loss. To strike back when injured would be to fall to the level of the offender, to take matters into our own hands, and to deny the love and mercy of God. To stand and take the injury is to bear witness to the suffering love of God, particularly as made manifest in the suffering of Jesus Christ on the cross. This does not say that we are not to protect others. But it does say that we are to suffer personal injury without striking back or seeking retaliation. And this extends even to property loss. If someone takes your overcoat, do not withhold your jacket either. This is not the way to get ahead in the world. And it is not meant to encourage thievery. But it would reflect the extravagant mercy of God.

"I say to you who hear . . . Give to everyone who begs from you, and from one who takes away your goods do not demand them back." Is this for real? Does Jesus mean this literally? I see no indication that he does not. I see no way out of this. He says what he means and means what he says. People come to these churches every day seeking help. People throughout this county and commonwealth need help. People in Japan need help today. People in Korea need help today. People in around the world are crying out for help. Do we hear them? Can we help them? "I say to you who hear . . . As you wish that others would do to you, do so to them." We recognize this as the Golden Rule: "Do unto others as you would have them do unto you." It may or may not work as a strategy. The others may still do something else unto us. But we cannot control them. We are, however, responsible for our own actions.

Again, "Love your enemies, and do good, and lend, expecting nothing in return, and your reward will be great." "Expecting nothing in return." Ostensibly, that refers to the persons to whom the good is done. We are not to seek anything back from them. And yet, it may have a larger reference too. We are not to do good deeds to others in expectation of a return from God. That is not the way it works. We are not to do this to seek benefit. We are not to do this to seek credit. We are not to do this to curry favor. We have already received good from God. We have already been forgiven. We have already been promised eternal life. Any little good we do is in response to that prior grace. Any little good we do is an act of thanksgiving, an act of praise, and act of joy and of gratitude. Let us so live our lives as to celebrate the goodness of God.

"If you love those who love you, what benefit is that to you? For even sinners love those who love them. And if you do good to those who do good to you, what benefit is that to you? For even sinners do the same. And if you lend to those from whom you expect to receive, what credit is that to you? Even sinners lend to sinners, to get back the same amount. But love your enemies, and do good, and lend, expecting nothing in return, and your reward will be great, and you will be sons of the Most High, for he is kind to the ungrateful and the evil. Be merciful, even as your Father is merciful."

To the God of mercy be the glory forever and ever! Amen.

19

Why Do You Call Me "Lord"?

LUKE 6:37–49; ISAIAH 55:1–3, 6–13

"Why do you call me?" "Why do you call me 'Lord'?" "Why do you call me 'Lord, Lord,' and not do what I tell you?" This question that Jesus asks drives a wedge between our stated faith and our contradictory action. To acknowledge someone as Lord is to become that person's servant. That is what Lord means. But to disobey that same one is to disavow him as Lord. That is what disobedience means. And where there is a discrepancy between our faith and our action, our actions speak louder than our words. This is not to say that Jesus seeks silence. He does not. This is not to say that Jesus does not want a profession of faith. He does. But this is to say that Jesus seeks our obedience along with our faith and that he seeks congruence between our faith in his lordship and a Christian life of obedience to his lordship.

The good news behind today's reading, the gospel underlying this reading, is that Jesus is Lord. No one else is our Lord. Jesus is ruler of the universe. Jesus is the embodiment of God Almighty. Jesus is the presence of God with us and for us. Apart from this truth and reality, this reading would make no sense at all. But with this truth and reality, this reading is pure gospel, good news, life-changing proclamation.

One consequence of Jesus being Lord is that at least some people are able to acknowledge him as Lord. At least some people are able to believe in him. At least some people are able to call him Lord. This is as it should be. Christian faith is a real possibility within human life and one to which we should aspire. It is appropriate that we call him Lord. Again, Jesus never says that he is not Lord. He never says that people should not call him Lord. He simply points out that those who do call him Lord should also obey him. That, after all, is what being Lord means.

This, of course, leads to a second consequence of Jesus being Lord. His questioning why people disobey indicates that obedience is at least possible. If obedience were not possible, the question would be nonsensical. But Jesus is not capricious. He does not ask of us that which is not possible. So his questioning of our disobedience and the concomitant possibility of obedience indicate that not only Christian faith but also the Christian life are both real possibilities in human life and ones to which we can and should aspire. It is appropriate that we seek not only to call him Lord but also to obey him in our lives.

What, then, are we to do? How are we to seek both Christian faith and Christian life?

> Everyone who [1] comes to me and [2] hears my words and [3] does them, I will show you what he is like: he is like a man building a house, who dug deep and laid the foundation on the rock. And when a flood arose, the stream broke against that house and could not shake it, because it had been well built. But the one who hears and does not do them is like a man who built a house on the ground without a foundation. When the stream broke against it, immediately it fell, and the ruin of that house was great.

We are familiar with the contrast between the house built on the rock and the house built without a foundation. But consider what the man who built the house on the rock is meant to illustrate: "Everyone who [1] comes to me and [2] hears my words and [3] does them." Here is the model. Here is the threefold pattern. Here is the single invitation to Christian faith and Christian life. "Everyone who [1] comes to me and [2] hears my words and [3] does them" is like the man who built the house on the rock. Do you want to be like that man? "Everyone who comes to me and hears my words and does them" is a person of both Christian faith and Christian life. Is that of interest to you?

There are three steps to this invitation. First (1), "Everyone who comes to me." Come to Jesus. Come to God. Come to God's church. Come to the preaching of the gospel of Jesus Christ. Come here to where God has promised to meet us, promised to comfort us, and promised to make himself known to us. It is as Isaiah said, so many years ago:

> Come, everyone who thirsts,
> > come to the waters;
> and he who has no money,
> > come, buy and eat!
> Come, buy wine and milk
> > without money and without price.
> Why do you spend your money for that which is not bread,
> > and your labor for that which does not satisfy?
> Listen diligently to me, and eat what is good,
> > and delight yourselves in rich food.

> Incline your ear, and come to me;
>> hear, that your soul may live;
> and I will make with you an everlasting covenant,
>> my steadfast, sure love for David. . . .
>
> Seek the LORD while he may be found;
>> call upon him while he is near;
> let the wicked forsake his way,
>> and the unrighteous man his thoughts;
> let him return to the LORD, that he may have compassion on him,
>> and to our God, for he will abundantly pardon. (Isaiah 55:1–7)

Now, that is an invitation! That is God's invitation. He has opened the door. He has cleared the way. Jesus invites us to come to him and so to come to God. Let us not linger too long. Let us not keep him waiting. It would be rude, and it would be a shame for us to squander and lose such an invitation as this.

Second (2), "Everyone who comes to me and hears my words." It is not enough to come to God. It is also necessary to hear the word of God. Or rather, without such hearing, there would be no true coming to God. But with and by such hearing, we have arrived in the very presence of God. Hearing the word of God read and preached is the way we come to God. It is the way that God himself has given to us. It is the way that he has provided for us. It is the reason we are here. Again, as Isaiah said:

> For my thoughts are not your thoughts,
>> neither are your ways my ways, declares the LORD.
> For as the heavens are higher than the earth,
>> so are my ways higher than your ways
>> and my thoughts than your thoughts.
>
> For as the rain and the snow come down from heaven
>> and do not return there but water the earth,
> making it bring forth and sprout,
>> giving seed to the sower and bread to the eater,
> so shall my word be that goes out from my mouth;
>> it shall not return to me empty,
> but it shall accomplish that which I purpose,
>> and shall succeed in the thing for which I sent it. (Isaiah 55:8–11)

It is through the word of God as recorded in the Scriptures and as proclaimed from the pulpit that God speaks to us. It is through the word of God that God communicates with us. It is through the word of God that God comforts us and challenges us. It is through the word of God that God gives his gospel to us. It is through the word of God that God pours out his grace upon us and gives us faith. Let us hear the word of God.

Third (3), "Everyone who comes to me and hears my words and does them." Again, it is not enough for us simply to come to God. It is not even enough for us to hear the word of God, if that hearing does not take root deep in our hearts, souls, and minds, and lead to real change in our lives. This is the main point of today's reading. It is also necessary, in addition to our coming to God, and in addition to our hearing the word of God, for us to do the word of God, to obey what Jesus says. Without such obedience, there has been no coming or hearing. But with such obedience, there has been and is true and genuine coming and hearing.

> For no good tree bears bad fruit, nor again does a bad tree bear good fruit, for each tree is known by its own fruit. For figs are not gathered from thornbushes, nor are grapes picked from a bramble bush. The good person out of the good treasure of his heart produces good, and the evil person out of his evil treasure produces evil, for out of the abundance of the heart his mouth speaks.

So let us seek the good treasure from God and ask that he plant it deep within us so that we might produce good.

This life of Christian obedience involves a departure from slavery in and to sin and a departure from the exile of alienation from God and from each other. This obedience constitutes a new exodus, a rescue into a new life, a salvation into a great joy. Again, as Isaiah said so long ago:

> For you shall go out in joy
>   and be led forth in peace;
> the mountains and the hills before you
>   shall break forth into singing,
>   and all the trees of the field shall clap their hands.
> Instead of the thorn shall come up the cypress;
>   instead of the brier shall come up the myrtle;
> and it shall make a name for the LORD,
>   an everlasting sign that shall not be cut off. (Isaiah 55:12–13)

How could we not do this?

What then will this new, Christian life look like?

> Judge not, and you will not be judged; condemn not, and you will not be condemned; forgive, and you will be forgiven; give, and it will be given to you. Good measure, pressed down, shaken together, running over, will be put into your lap. For with the measure you use it will be measured back to you.

Do you see how strange and wonderful this is? This world teaches us to live by taking. Christ teaches us to live by giving and forgiving. The two could not be any more different. This is how to live the Christian life. And this new, Christian life is no easy, human accomplishment. It is a gift from God himself.

This, then, is the pattern for Christian faith and life, for becoming Christian and being Christian: (1) Come to Jesus, (2) hear his words, and (3) do them. It is no accident that this threefold pattern of Christian faith and life is reflected in our threefold pattern of worship. You can see it in the three boldface headings in our bulletin. First (1), we gather to glorify God. That is why we come here—to be in the presence of God, to be with God, to sing his praises, to worship him, and to glorify his holy name.

Second (2), we hear the word of God. We hear the word of God both read and preached. This is what we do in worship. It is not that we just sit. We hear. We listen. We absorb. We receive. We believe. And therefore, we obey. Hearing the word of God is the center of our service. Without hearing the word of God, there would no glorifying God and there would be no giving thanks to God. But with the hearing of the word of God, and on the basis of our hearing the word of God, we do in fact affirm our faith in God.

Third (3), we give thanks to God. The grace of God elicits and calls forth both our gratitude to God and our graciousness to each other. We express our gratitude in thanksgiving begun here and carried throughout our lives. We live out our graciousness in obedience begun here and carried throughout our lives. Thus, the very pattern of our worship intends to proclaim the gospel, to communicate the Christian faith, and to inculcate the Christian life, in direct and explicit fulfillment of what Jesus teaches us in today's reading.

"Why do you call me?" "Why do you call me 'Lord'?" "Why do you call me 'Lord, Lord,' and not do what I tell you?" This question that Jesus asks drives a wedge between our stated faith and our contradictory action. To acknowledge someone as Lord is to become that person's servant. That is what "Lord" means. But to disobey that same one is to disavow him as Lord. That is what disobedience means. And where there is a discrepancy between faith and action, actions speak louder than words. This is not to say that Jesus seeks silence. He does not. But it is to say that Jesus seeks our obedience along with our faith, and that he seeks congruence between our faith in his lordship and our life of obedience to his lordship.

So let us be "like a man building a house, who dug deep and laid the foundation on the rock. And when a flood arose, the stream broke against that house and could not shake it, because it had been well built."

To God be the glory forever and ever! Amen.

20

Say the Word!

LUKE 7:1–17; 1 KINGS 17:17–24

"SAY THE WORD!" "SAY the word!" "Say the word, and let my servant be healed." The centurion of Capernaum understood that the very power of God Almighty, Creator and Lord of the universe, resided in the word of Jesus Christ. The centurion's plea points to what is important in this reading. The power of God to create, the power of God to heal, indeed the power of God to raise the dead resides in the word of Jesus Christ. It was true then. It continues to be true now. The centurion understood this. And Jesus recognized this understanding as nothing less than saving faith.

There are three accounts of the power of the word of Jesus Christ in today's reading. One (1) has to do with the centurion's servant. Jesus healed him from a distance, without seeing him, without touching him, with only a word. Another (2) has to do with the dead son of the widow of Nain. Jesus raised him from the dead—and not the freshly dead, but on-the-way-to-the-cemetery dead—with only a word. The third account (3) has to do with the centurion himself, who "heard about Jesus," and hearing he believed, for only in believing did he ask for help. And this third account of the power of the word, this conversion of a centurion to saving faith, is perhaps the greatest miracle of the three.

Do you see the significance for us yet today of this healing, this raising from the dead, and this conversion, all by the power of the word? Jesus (1) did not see or touch the centurion's servant. Jesus (2) performed no ritual over the dead son of the widow. And Jesus (3) never met the centurion of Capernaum. Instead, he dealt only with the elders and friends whom the centurion sent to him. The one thing Jesus gave all three of these people was his word. He spoke, and they were healed, raised, and converted. So it is with us. We cannot see or be seen by Jesus in the flesh. We cannot touch or be touched by Jesus in the flesh. But we can and do hear the word of Jesus. We can and do hear the gospel of Jesus. We can and do hear that gospel word yet today. And the power of God Almighty still resides in the word of Jesus Christ.

When Jesus talks, even the dead listen! Of course, we all know that is not possible. The dead cannot hear. But in this reading, the dead man hears and obeys. So it is possible! In the providence of God, even the impossible is possible. And in that impossible possibility we find the very gospel of Jesus Christ.

For instance (1), it is not possible that I, as a sinner, could or would turn to God. The very nature of sin rules that out. And yet, when God calls me by name, his calling turns me around to himself. Thus, it is part of the gospel of Jesus Christ that God's word speaks to my human impossibility and creates not only a possibility but even a new reality.

Again (2), it is not possible that I, lost in a sea of self-concern and self-centeredness, could or would become centered upon God and concerned about others. Self-centeredness is a quicksand from which the self cannot escape by the self's own actions. And yet, when God's Son, Jesus Christ, our Lord and Savior, willingly and obediently suffers and dies on the cross, without deserving it, God draws my attention away from myself and refocuses it upon the majesty of God. So, it is part of the gospel of Jesus Christ that the terrible price paid by Christ in the crucifixion overwhelms my human impossibility and creates a new reality.

Furthermore (3), it is not possible that I, having caused so much pain to God and others and myself, could or would ever be forgiven, restored, and reconciled into the joy and fellowship of the people of God. The wounds are too deep. And yet, when God calls me his own, so I am. Thus, it is part of the gospel of Jesus Christ that the power of God Almighty, which created the universe by God's word, continues to work today, taking our human impossibilities and making from them a new reality, even a divine fellowship.

Humanly speaking, none of this is possible. And yet, by the grace and power of God, all of this is not only possible but also even real. Jesus Christ has said the word. And his word is gospel and life for us yet today.

Consider this: In today's reading, life and death were on a collision course. Jesus and his disciples and a large crowd that went with him were approaching the gateway of the town of Nain. Just at that moment, a funeral procession was coming out through the gate. The dead man, his mother's only son, was being carried at the front, and she was already a widow. There was a large crowd with her coming out from the town.

Custom and courtesy dictate that those meeting a funeral possession stop and get off the road. We still do that today. But Jesus stood his ground. He did not get out of the way. Instead, he made the funeral procession stop for him. In fact, he turned the procession around. Jesus knew that with the loss of both her husband and now her only son, the widow was alone and had no means of support. He knew that when bad things happened, people regarded them as punishments from God, so this woman would be ostracized, pushed aside, and left to fend for herself. And Jesus had compassion on her.

That is when Jesus stopped the funeral procession in its tracks. The crowds must have gasped when he touched the stretcher with the dead body on it. Dead bodies were considered ritually unclean. His touching it suggests a wonderful exchange, by which he absorbed the very uncleanness of death itself into himself and gave to the young man the gift of his life in return. Our minds run ahead all the way to the cross, of course, where Jesus exchanged his sinless obedience for all the sin of the world, for your sin and for my sin, and after which he died and was buried so that we might rise and live forever. That is what this reading is all about.

When the pallbearers stood still, Jesus told the dead man to get up! And the dead man heard the word, sat up, and began to speak! Jesus spoke, and the man lived. Jesus restored him to life, to conversation, and so to community. Then Jesus gave him to his mother. What a wonderful gift! The funeral procession was stopped dead cold. It fact, it was reversed. Instead of a burial, they turned around and had a celebration of life. They all worshiped and glorified God, as the two crowds become one, disciples celebrating and, perhaps, former mourners becoming disciples themselves. While the prophet Elijah had to cry out to God three times to restore a widow's son to life, Jesus gave life to this widow's son without prayer and instead simply with his own command. Thus the people cried out not only, "A great prophet has arisen among us!"—that is not the half of it—but also, "God has visited his people!" God himself has visited his people, in the person and work of Jesus Christ. Their confession of faith is an invitation for us to confess our faith today.

Now, what does it mean to us that when Jesus talks, even the dead listen? First (1), it means that God wills life and not death. Christ's raising of the dead man to life points ahead to God's raising of Jesus Christ on the first Easter to a new and different kind of life. Moreover, Christ's resurrection is the promise of our own. God has plans for us that even death cannot destroy. God's power to create life out of nothingness can also restore life even from the darkness of death. These are words of assurance and eternal hope for us.

Second (2), the reality that even the dead listen to Jesus means that all the self-righteous schemes by which we presume to contribute something—anything—to our own salvation are shown to be false. We can no more save ourselves than the dead man could hear or rise on his own. His rising to life was completely the work of Jesus Christ, and so is our salvation. Four hundred fifty years ago, John Calvin wrote of this passage, "Here we have a shining example of [Christ's] free mercy, in reviving us from the dead."[1] By "free mercy" Calvin means that God in Jesus Christ acted to restore the dead man to life, not because the man deserved it, but simply out of God's sheer goodness.

---

1. Calvin, *Harmony of the Gospels*, 1:252.

In the twentieth century, William Temple elaborated upon this as follows:

> *All is of God; the only thing of my own which I can contribute to my own redemption is the sin from which I need to be redeemed.* My capacity for fellowship with God is God's gift in creation; my partial deliverance from self-centeredness, my response to truth, beauty and goodness is God's gift through the natural world which he sustains in being and the history of man which he controls. One thing is my own—the self-centeredness which leads me to find my apparent good in what is other and less than the true good. This true good is the divine love and what flows from it appreciated as its expression. In response to that good, man finds his only true freedom, for only then does the self act as what it truly is and thus achieves true self-expression.
>
> . . . As the experience of grace becomes deeper, the conviction of its all sufficiency becomes more inevitable and more wholesome, until at last a man knows, and is finally "saved" by knowing, that all good is of God alone. *We are clay in the hands of the potter and our welfare is to know it.*[2]

Third (3), the reality that even the dead listen to Jesus Christ means that the very power and the goodness of God are present in the word of God, in the reading and preaching of the gospel of Jesus Christ, even today when Jesus is no longer physically present among us. Consider especially the account of the healing of the centurion's servant. The centurion was not a member of the people of Israel. He was a Gentile, an outsider, just as we are. He felt unworthy to have Jesus come into his home, and yet he was confident that Jesus could heal his servant by the power of his word, even at a distance. Jesus marveled at the centurion's confidence in the authority of his word as an instance of faith, better than any faith he had found in Israel. This reading is for all of us who have lived long after the time of Christ's earthly life, who have never seen Jesus in the flesh, and who have never heard his voice, but who have—thank God!—heard and believed his word, and who have been healed, forgiven, and raised to new life by his gospel. The power and goodness of God are present in the word of God, in the reading and preaching of the gospel of Jesus Christ, even when Jesus is no longer physically present among us. This is the one thing the church has to offer to the world: the word of God, the gospel of Jesus Christ, which we read and preach from this pulpit every single Sunday.

So, what does the word of Jesus Christ in this reading from the gospel do for us yet today? First (1), it gives us the courage to die. The power that death holds over us is the fear of death, the fear of its finality, the fear of nothingness. The gospel tells us that the God and Father of Jesus Christ is stronger than death. This reading portrays God's power in terms of restoration to this life, which we understand, in order to tell us of resurrection to another life, which we can scarcely imagine. This gives us

---

2. Temple, *Nature, Man and God*, 401–2. Cited in Leith, *Basic Christian Doctrine*, 228.

no encouragement to hasten death. But it allows us to face and approach death with dignity and poise, confident in the greater power of God.

Therefore, and second (2), this word from the gospel also gives us the courage to live. Since the fear of death robs us of the joy of life, the destruction of the fear of death gives us, in turn, the courage to live our lives in joy. We are here today by the will of God Almighty, whom we love, serve, and obey. Given the knowledge of the will of God for life, we are set free from despair, free to live life fully and faithfully. We are invited and commanded to arise from death, to arise from fear, to arise from complacency and lethargy, to arise from sin, to arise from self-centeredness and satisfaction. Christ calls us out of death into the impossible possibility of genuine, authentic, faithful, loving, joyful human life.

Third (3), this word from the gospel gives us the courage to share the word of God, the gospel of Jesus Christ, with others. God intends for the good news of his Son, Jesus Christ, to reach all the people of the world. We, the people of his church, are his instrument for sharing that good news with everyone around us. Do you have members of your family who seem deaf to the good news, or dead to the gospel? Do you have neighbors who might benefit from a kind word about the love of God in Jesus Christ? Do you know people who are poor, despised, ill, suffering, and lost, who need to learn from us the ministry of the healing compassion of Jesus Christ? Is there anyone in our entire greed-driven, drug-numbed, and crime-infested society who does not need to hear the good news about the power of God that is greater than the bondage and fear of death, about the love of God, who loves us when we least deserve it, and about the fellowship of forgiven sinners formed into the community of the people of God? We cannot keep this good news to ourselves. Share the word about Jesus Christ, and bring people here to church to hear his gospel read and preached Sunday after Sunday. After all, when Jesus talks, even the dead listen! So, "Say the word!" "Say the word!" "Say the word" of Jesus Christ that this needy world might be healed.

To God be the glory forever and ever! Amen.

21

Who Is to Come?

LUKE 7:18–35; DEUTERONOMY 18:15–22

"ARE YOU THE ONE who is to come, or shall we look for another?" Thus John the Baptist sent his disciples to ask Jesus. And Luke has made sure that we get to hear the question again when they do ask him, "Are you the one who is to come, or shall we look for another?" The question assumes the ancient prophecy of Moses that God would send a prophet like Moses, the one for whom they were looking, the one to speak the word of God to the people of God. And throughout Luke, the questions have pointed the way to what is good and true and important in each passage. So for this question to be repeated is a way for Luke not only to proclaim, but to proclaim boldly, gladly, and emphatically, the good news that Jesus is the one who is to come, so that we do not need to look for another. Thanks be to God!

It is no accident that John's question continues to be our question. It is the great question of human life. So we continue to ask Jesus yet today, "Are you the one who is to come, or shall we look for another?" That is, are you the one in whom we are to believe, or shall we look for another? Are you the one we are to trust, or shall we look for another? Are you the one we are to obey and to follow, or shall we look for another? Are you the one on whom we are to stake our lives, all that we are and all that we have, or shall we look for another? Are you the one? So it is that Luke continues to proclaim boldly, gladly, and emphatically the good news for us yet today that Jesus is the one who is to come, so we need not look for another.

Consider the answer that Jesus gives to John's disciples: "Go and tell John what you have seen and heard: the blind receive their sight, the lame walk, lepers are cleansed, and the deaf hear, the dead are raised up, the poor have good news preached to them. And blessed is the one who is not offended by me." He points us to what he has been teaching and doing, to what can be seen and what can be heard. He supplies the information we need, and he also insists that we answer our own question. More than enough information is given here to establish that Jesus is the Christ. That is true whether we know it or not, whether we believe it or not, whether we like it or not, whether we obey him or not. But we have to answer our question for ourselves. This has to do with our faith, our belief, our decision, our commitment with all our heart and all our soul and all our mind and all our strength. "Are you the one who is to come?" "Go and tell . . . what you have seen and heard."

Note what Jesus does: "the blind receive their sight, the lame walk, lepers are cleansed, and the deaf hear, the dead are raised up, the poor have good news preached to them." Why these? Why these particular deeds? These deeds fulfill the Old Testament prophecies of what would happen when God himself came to rescue his people and to establish his kingdom. And it was all coming true in the person and work of Jesus Christ. The kingdom of God, for which the people had yearned for centuries, was coming into being before their very eyes. The sick were healed. The outcasts were made clean and brought into the community. Those who had never heard anything could hear Jesus teaching. The dead were raised. And most remarkable of all, more than the healings and even the raising of the dead, the poor had good news preached to them. The poor, whom everyone was sure that God despised, were told the good news of God's love, forgiveness, and salvation. The poor of this world are welcomed with open arms into the kingdom of God. The poor, who seem too count for nothing, count dearly in the eyes of Jesus. They are the recipients of his good news. That is to say, Jesus is not only the prophet like Moses, the one who was to come to speak the word of God to the people of God. In that the kingdom of God is coming, Jesus is also the Anointed One sent from God, the Christ, the very Son of God.

Now we too have seen and heard what Jesus has said and done. We have listened to his teachings and learned his parables. We have known the mystery of prayer answered, of people healed. We have known the joy of forgiveness, and we have seen people reconciled to each other by the grace of God. We do not get to see the ministry of Jesus firsthand, but we have seen and heard enough of the teaching and healing of the resurrected and living Jesus Christ to make up our minds. The only question for us is: Do we believe in Jesus as the Christ or not?

There is always the terrible possibility that we shall fail to believe. John raises that question: "Shall we look for another?" But if we despaired of God in Christ, for whom would we look? Would we turn to the stars and to fate if we tired of the will of God? Would we trust our own wits or our own goodness instead of the grace of Jesus Christ? Would we put our confidence in money and success instead of the Savior who joins us in our suffering? Upon whom do we depend? In whom do we trust? Upon what do we base meaning, purpose, value, and direction in our lives? Who are we, and whose are we? To whom do we belong?

It would help us to avoid the temptation to look for someone else if we would realize the deeper question about salvation and the deeper answer about salvation in this passage. We need to remember and to realize that John the Baptist was not only in prison but also soon to be executed. For all the good news to the sick and the dead and the poor, there is not a single word here about release to the captives. There is a lot about that elsewhere in the Scriptures, but none at all here. The silence is deafening. The point is that John never got out of prison alive. Instead, he got his head cut off. So what good news did Jesus have for John? John's being on the way to being executed did not invalidate Christ's identity or undo who Jesus is. In fact, John's being on the way to being executed did not put him beyond the reach of God's gospel. But that was not at all obvious then, nor is it obvious now. So we need to look deeper.

I submit to you that John was called to that high and difficult faith of believing in Jesus as his Savior even when Jesus did not save him in this life. Sometimes we pray for a healing that does not come or for a release that is not granted. Then we are called to that high and difficult faith of believing in Jesus as the Savior, as our Savior, even when we are not saved in the way we want to be saved from whatever afflicts us. This is very hard.

How did John do this? Think about the deeper answer Jesus gives him. John went before Jesus, and Jesus followed him in what he did. John comes preaching, Jesus comes preaching. John is arrested, Jesus is arrested. John is executed, and by then we know that Jesus is going to be executed. When John sends his disciples to question Jesus, it is not an academic question. It is not a detached and uninterested question. It is a question of faith, and it is a plea for help. "If you are the one who is to come, save me! Get me out of here! I do not want to die!" And Jesus told him, in effect, "No, I am not getting you out. But move over, I am coming in with you!" No, he did not join John in the same prison cell. John was executed before Jesus was arrested. But across the course of his life and his death, Jesus did join John in both in his arrest and in his execution. Jesus did not avoid the suffering, the pain, the loneliness, the abandonment, or even the death that John experienced. Jesus went through it all. It may appear that he abandoned John to death, but on a deeper level he did not abandon John. He joined John in death, and so he joins even us in all the depths of human suffering. On some days we have a hard time finding Jesus in our lives. But we have a Savior who is right here with us in the middle of the worst hardships of our lives.

This reminds me of a powerful spiritual: "I asked the Lord to take away my troubles, instead he gave me strength; I asked the Lord to move the mountain, instead he gave me faith." Even when we are not rescued out of all our problems, we have a salvation that is more than rescue, a salvation that includes the presence of God with us in Jesus Christ, a salvation that extends beyond this life and into the life that is to come. Thanks be to God!

Given this salvation, consider again the command given in the answer of Jesus to John's disciples: "*Go and tell* John what you have seen and heard: the blind receive their sight, the lame walk, lepers are cleansed, and the deaf hear, the dead are raised up, the poor have good news preached to them. And blessed is the one who takes no offense at me." This answer points the way to the application of this good news in our lives yet today. *Go and tell* what you have seen and heard. Here is the work of the Christ. *Go and tell*. This is part of who we are. This is part of what it means to be Christian. We do not keep Jesus to ourselves. We do not keep the gospel a secret. We go and tell. Tell the world. Tell the children. Tell your next-door neighbor. Tell the children. Tell your husband or wife. And most all, tell the children what we see and hear. It is God who made us, so we belong to God. It is God who saved us, so we belong to God. It is God who sent Jesus Christ to us, so we belong to God. It is God to whom we go, so we shall always belong to God. Go and tell all who will listen, and bring them here to church to hear the gospel preached every Sunday and so to worship God.

As we come to believe in Jesus as the Christ of God, and as we go and tell what we have seen and heard, we shall also be led to follow, to obey, to imitate, and so to extend the ministry of Jesus Christ today as far as we are able. That is why we—the church of Jesus Christ—build hospitals around the world, and feed the hungry, and give drink to the thirsty, and clothe the naked, and house the homeless, and visit those who are sick, and befriend the friendless. That is why we receive the Five-Cents-Per-Meal offering each month, to feed the hungry in Amelia County and around the world. That is why we give money for world missions to go farther around the world than we can go ourselves, helping others. We do this in the name of Jesus Christ, because he has first helped us. We do it in the name of Jesus Christ so that others might see and hear what he has done and taught. We do it in the name of Jesus Christ so that the mercy of God in his gospel might be proclaimed to the ends of the earth. And sometimes, when we cannot rescue people, when we cannot help them, when we cannot heal them, when we cannot get them out of prison, when we cannot save them, sometimes all we can say and do is, "Move over; we are coming in with you, in the name of Jesus Christ." God help us!

"Are you the one who is to come, or shall we look for another?" That is, Are you the one in whom we are to believe, or shall we look for another? Are you the one we are to trust, or shall we look for another? Are you the one we are to obey and to follow, or shall we look for another? Are you the one on whom we are to stake our lives, all that we are and all that we have? Or shall we look for another? Are you the one? Jesus says, "Go and tell . . . what you have seen and heard."

To God be the glory forever and ever! Amen.

22

Who Forgives Sins?

LUKE 7:36–50; 2 SAMUEL 12:1–7A

"WHO IS THIS, WHO even forgives sins?" "Who is this, who . . . forgives sins?" "Who . . . forgives sins?" Therein lies the question. This is the question of our lives. This is the question for which Easter provides the answer. Who forgives? Forgiveness is a grand and wonderful thing. Forgiveness is the one good hope you and I have. Forgiveness is the only way we can make it in this life or the next. Deep down, we all know that. It may be hard to face. It may be hard to admit. It may be hard to articulate. But deep down, we know that it is true. We cannot make it on our own. "We have left undone those things which we ought to have done; and we have done those things which we ought not to have done."[1] And we cannot undo the past. What we might do in the future or even the present is not clear. But even if we never sin again—which is not going to happen—we cannot undo the past. We can and should make amends as best we can, but we cannot pay our debt for the wrong we have already done. So we need forgiveness. We need forgiveness more than we need food. We need forgiveness more than we need water. We need forgiveness more than we need air. We need forgiveness in order to live today and tomorrow. You and I need forgiveness for this life and the next. Who forgives?

This is the situation. This is our situation, into which Jesus said to the woman of the city, "Your sins are forgiven." Not condemned. Not forgotten. Not condoned. Not denied. Not celebrated. Not ignored. "Your sins are forgiven." These are words of life. These are words of hope. These are words of health and restoration. These are words of new beginnings. These are heavenly words. In fact, these are divine words. These are words that no mere human has the authority to speak. "Your sins are forgiven."

1. Presbyterian Church, *Book of Common Worship*, 87.

No wonder that when Jesus spoke to her, those who were at table with him began to say among themselves, "Who is this, who even forgives sins?" "Who is this, who . . . forgives sins?" "Who . . . forgives sins?" Therein lies the question. And we have seen throughout Luke that the questions direct us to the main point of the passage.

We have two announcements of good news here. One is that sin is forgiven. The other is that Jesus forgives sin. In fact, the two are inseparable and even indistinguishable. Without Jesus there is no forgiveness. So, Jesus forgives sin. And therefore, sin is forgiven. Only in and by and through him is sin forgiven. It may be that forgiveness appears first. It is the visible reality, the presenting phenomenon. It is what we see and hear and know. But the identity of Jesus who does the forgiving is the underlying and prior reality. So let us tend to it first.

"Who is this, who even forgives sins?" "Who is this, who . . . forgives sins?" "Who . . . forgives sins?" Therein lies the question. Sin is an offense against God. We do many things to offend, hurt, and injure each other, but sin is an offense against God. As it is written in Psalm 51:1–4a:

> Have mercy on me, O God,
>> according to your steadfast love;
> according to your abundant mercy
>> blot out my transgressions.
> Wash me thoroughly from my iniquity,
>> and cleanse me from my sin!
>
> For I know my transgressions,
>> and my sin is ever before me.
> Against you, you only have I sinned
>> and done what is evil in your sight.

And as the Westminster Shorter Catechism asks and answers (Question 14), "What is sin? Sin is any want of conformity unto, or transgression of, the law of God."[2] So, sin is an offense against God. And in that sin is an offense against God, the forgiveness of sin is the prerogative of God alone. It belongs to God alone to forgive sin against him. It belongs to God alone to forgive sin. It belongs to God to forgive. We know that. Somehow, deep down, we know that. It belongs to God to forgive.

Somehow, deep down, even the people who were at table with Jesus in the home of Simon the Pharisee knew that. That is, in fact, the point of their question. That is why they asked it. "Who is this, who even forgives sins?" "Who is this, who . . . forgives sins?" "Who . . . forgives sins?" Well, of course, God forgives sin. We know that. So, then, who is this? Who is Jesus? Is he a madman? Is he a charlatan? Or does he possibly speak for God? Does he somehow speak on behalf of God? Does he speak the very word of God? Does he pronounce forgiveness on behalf of God? Does he speak as God? Could it be that Jesus is the long-awaited Christ of God? Could it be that he is

---

2. Presbyterian Church, *Book of Confessions*, 176.

the Son of God? Could it be that Jesus is God himself with us, among us, and for us? Therein lies the question.

Consider the possible answers. There is no evidence that Jesus is a madman or a fool. Can anyone make a case for that? No. There is no evidence that he is a charlatan or a liar. Do you have any reason to believe that? No. The one remaining possibility— the one raised by the questioners at the table, the one presented to us by the Gospel according to Luke, the one carried forward in the faith of the church, the only one which means life to you and me—is that Jesus is the one who forgives sin, that Jesus is the Christ of God, that Jesus is the Son of God, that Jesus is God himself with us, among us, and for us. Thanks be to God!

This is the deep and underlying reality of today's reading and of the gospel. This is the prior truth. And this leads to the next, more visible truth: In that Jesus is God himself with us, among us, and for us, in that Jesus is the Son of God, and in that Jesus is the Christ of God, he is also the one who forgives sin—even our sin, yours and mine, yet today. This is where the reality of Easter begins to come into play. Jesus, who lived then and was crucified, was also raised and continues to live today. He still forgives our sin. Thanks be to God! Yes, Jesus is the one who forgives sin. This is the faint glimmer of realization that began to dawn on those at table with Jesus. This is the full gospel of salvation that shone forth on the woman of the city. "Your sins are forgiven." "Your faith has saved you; go in peace." That Jesus accepted her then gives us the courage to realize that he accepts us now! This is the good news that comes down from heaven, through the centuries, all the way to us today. "Your sins are forgiven." "Your faith has saved you; go in peace."

What does it mean that sin is forgiven? What does it mean that our sin is forgiven? It is not condemned. It is not forgotten. It is not condoned. It is not denied. It is not celebrated. It is not ignored. It is forgiven. For sin to be forgiven means that God has absorbed the wrong, received the injury, suffered the offense, taken the insult, borne the pain, undergone the brokenness, and carried the alienation all into himself, all into his being, all into his heart. For sin to be forgiven means that God takes it upon himself to correct the damage we have done to our relationship with God, the damage that is our doing, the damage that is our responsibility, but the damage that is beyond our ability to correct, to repair, or to undo. God does for us what we cannot do for ourselves. For sin to be forgiven means that God does not forget or ignore what we have done, but that instead he takes it so seriously that he takes its effects upon himself in order to shield us from them. For sin to be forgiven means not that sin does not matter, but instead that sin matters so much that God has paid the terrible price which gives him the right to forgive our sin. And for sin to be forgiven means that God has done all of this, God has made all of this both real and obvious, in the life, death, and Easter resurrection of his Son, his Christ, our Lord and Savior, Jesus. Jesus forgives our sin. It is done.

Given the gospel that God in Jesus Christ forgives our sin, how are we to live? How are we to respond? What are we to do? What is the application? Consider the extraordinary account of the woman in today's reading, and consider the example she provides for us:

> A woman of the city, who was a sinner, when she learned that he [Jesus] was reclining at table in the Pharisee's house, brought an alabaster flask of ointment, and standing behind him at his feet, weeping, she began to wet his feet with her tears and wiped them with the hair of her head and kissed his feet and anointed them with the ointment.

That caused no little consternation for the host. And it is certainly nothing that we can do. How did Jesus understand it?

> He said to Simon, "Do you see this woman? I entered your house; you gave me no water for my feet, but she has wet my feet with her tears and wiped them with her hair. You gave me no kiss, but from the time I came in she has not ceased to kiss my feet. You did not anoint my head with oil, but she has anointed my feet with ointment. Therefore I tell you, her sins, which are many, are forgiven—for she loved much."

That is to say, she was grateful. She not only poured out the ointment, but she also poured out herself in gratitude. There was a deep and uncontainable joy welling up from within her. She risked much to show her love for Jesus. The point here is not that because of her great love her sins were forgiven. Not at all. That would not be forgiveness, and that would run against the whole rest of the Bible. The point here, instead, as is made clear by the parable that Jesus tells about debts and debtors, is exactly the other way around: that her great love is demonstrative of her prior forgiveness. Her great love is evidence of her prior forgiveness. Her great love is the result of her prior forgiveness. Her great love is the new life into which her prior forgiveness propelled her. Her great love points back unfailingly to her prior great forgiveness of her admittedly great sin. She was made new and different. Her sin was forgiven. Her faith had saved her. She could go in peace. Her life was changed forever. Is this of interest to you? Because this is what Easter is all about—new and eternal life.

This woman's great love also points ahead to the pattern of the Christian life, of our lives. No, we cannot anoint the feet of Jesus. But as she believed and was saved, so can we believe and be saved. As she loved Jesus, so we can love God, and we can love our neighbor. We can love God in true and exuberant worship, and we can love our neighbor in true and exuberant service. We can hear the good news of God, and we can share the good news of God. We can sing of our joy here, and we can share the joy with those around us, bringing visitors to church to hear the good news of Jesus Christ for themselves. As God pours out his grace upon us, we can respond with gratitude toward God and with graciousness toward each other. Having been forgiven, we can be forgiving. We can worship God gladly, and we can serve our neighbor gladly. And when we do, all the world will wonder what is happening. All the world will be shocked and even scandalized. All the world will ask what is going on.

"Who is this, who even forgives sins?" "Who is this, who . . . forgives sins?" "Who . . . forgives sins?" Therein lies the question. Forgiveness is a grand and wonderful thing. Forgiveness is the one good hope we have. Forgiveness is the only way we can make it in this life or the next. "Who . . . forgives sins?" Jesus is the one who forgives sin. Jesus is the Christ of God. Jesus is the Son of God. Jesus is God himself with us, among us, and for us, now and forever.

To God be the glory forever and ever! Amen.

23

Take Care How You Hear!

LUKE 8:1–21; ISAIAH 6:1–13

"HE WHO HAS EARS to hear, let him hear." Thus Jesus called out to the great crowd at the conclusion of his parable of the sower. When his disciples inquired about his parable, he explained it to them and then concluded, "Take care then how you hear, for to the one who has, more will be given, and from the one who has not, even what he thinks that he has will be taken away." And when he was told that his mother and brothers desired to see him, he answered, "My mother and my brothers are those who hear the word of God and do it." So, (1) "He who has ears to hear, let him hear"; (2) "Take care then how you hear"; and (3) "Hear the word of God and do it."

These first two imperatives, and the third, which is an implied imperative, carry the good news of Jesus Christ all the way to us and urge us to receive it. We would do well to heed them carefully. First (1), then, Jesus called out to the great crowd, and so to us, "He who has ears to hear, let him hear." This raises two possibilities. One is the terrible, negative possibility that we do not have ears and therefore will not hear. That is too horrible to contemplate. How could the Creator speak and the creature not hear? How could the Author of life address us and we not notice or acknowledge him? How could the Redeemer call out and the object of his love not respond? How could the Judge warn us and we continue on our way? That makes no sense. But it seems to represent the terrible, negative possibility of human life that is lost, wandering, or running away.

At the same time, and even more powerfully, this first imperative establishes additionally not only the possibility but also the grace-filled reality that at least some people do have ears and therefore will hear. "He who has ears to hear, let him hear." That is to say, there are people with ears. We are made to hear the word of God. That is who we are. That is what we do. That is what we are all about. That is why God made us. Thanks be to God! More than cogs in the wheels of the great economy, more than citizens in the great nation, more than ingredients in the great melting pot, more than participants in the great society, more than fodder for the cannon, more than numbers in the census, we are creatures created to hear our Creator. That is how he set it up. We know this. Deep down, we know this. And this is very, very good.

What Jesus has said here, in the presupposition of this first imperative, names the human reality that we are: we have ears to hear. Moreover, the content of the first imperative itself provides a surge of energy that powers up this prior reality that turns on the system, that makes things begin to happen. Before this word is spoken, we are only ears without hearing. We know not who or what we are. But when, and only when, this word is first spoken, "Let him hear," true sound first fills our ears, our hearing comes into play, and suddenly we do hear the word of God—not by our own strength, but because God has spoken. Jesus says, "Let him hear," and so we do. We hear. We hear because the word of God, this word of God, creates its own hearing.

What is it that we are supposed to hear? Jesus had just told the great crowd that strange teaching we know as the Parable of the Sower, a parable being a particular kind of teaching that calls not only for understanding but also for response and involvement:

> A sower went out to sow his seed. And as he sowed, some fell along the path and was trampled underfoot, and the birds of the air devoured it. And some fell on the rock, and as it grew up, it withered away, because it had no moisture. And some fell among thorns, and the thorns grew up with it and choked it. And some fell into good soil and grew and yielded a hundredfold.

How very peculiar. The great crowd knew about birds and rocks and thorns. They probably never had heard of a hundredfold yield. That would have seemed fantastic. And yet, as Jesus said these things to them, he called out, "He who has ears to hear, let him hear." This is the first imperative. Let us hear!

Second (2), when his disciples inquired about his parable, Jesus explained it to them and so to us, and then he concluded, "Take care then how you hear, for to the one who has, more will be given, and from the one who has not, even what he thinks that he has will be taken away." Now, while the first imperative raises the negative possibility of not hearing at all and establishes the positive reality of actually hearing the word of God, this second imperative assumes some kind of hearing and points to multiple ways of hearing. "Take care then how you hear." There is faithful hearing, and there is faithless hearing. There is shallow hearing, and there is deep hearing. There is good hearing, and there is not so good hearing. There is careful hearing, and there is careless hearing. There is insignificant hearing, and there is fruitful hearing. This forms the content of the explanation of the parable. There are different ways of hearing.

What is this explanation?

> The seed is the word of God. The ones along the path are those who have heard. Then the devil comes and takes away the word from their hearts, so that they may not believe and be saved. And the ones on the rock are those who, when they hear the word, receive it with joy. But these have no root; they believe for a while, and in time of testing fall away. And as for what fell among the thorns, they are those who hear, but as they go on their way they are choked by the cares and riches and pleasures of life, and their fruit does not mature. As for that in the good soil, they are those who, hearing the word, hold it fast in an honest and good heart, and bear fruit with patience.

All of these heard, but they all heard differently. As Jesus said to his disciples and so to us, with a quotation from Isaiah, "To you it has been given to know the secrets of the kingdom of God, but for others they are in parables, so that seeing they may not see, and hearing they may not understand." Hence the warning in the second imperative, "Take care then how you hear, for to the one who has, more will be given, and from the one who has not, even what he thinks that he has will be taken away." There are different ways of hearing. The wrong ways result in terrible losses.

How shall we hear? Therein lies the question for us today. This is the point of the parable, this is the point of the explanation, and this is the point of all of the imperatives. How shall we hear? Shall we hear but not believe and so not be saved? Surely not that. God help us not to be unbelievers. I saw a bumper sticker some years ago that read, "Happy Heathen." I take it that they were bragging about their lack of faith. It also occurs to me to wonder whom they were trying to convince—us or themselves. Unbelief shall not be happy for long.

How shall we hear? Shall we hear with initial enthusiasm and joy only to fall away in the time of testing? Surely the testing has come and will come again. That is the nature of life. God help us not to be fair weather believers. How shall we hear? Shall we hear but then be distracted by the cares of the world? Surely this is a terrible temptation. We all have cares. We all have worries. We all have demands on our attention. Everyone has issues. God help us not to be distracted hearers.

How shall we hear? Shall we hear the word of God, "hold it fast in an honest and good heart, and bear fruit with patience"? Can we do that? Might God pour out that much grace upon us? Can we consume the word of God, and cherish it, and honor it? Can we read and consult it often, pray through it, learn it, memorize it, and absorb it? Can we get it into our hearts and down into our bones, so that no one can take it away? When the master returns for the harvest—and he is coming back—what kind of harvest shall we have for him? A hundredfold? God help us to be good and faithful hearers of his word.

How shall we hear? John Calvin defines the church by this hearing: "Wherever we see the Word of God purely preached and heard, and the sacraments administered according to Christ's institution, there, it is not to be doubted, a church of God exists."[1] The foundation of our faithful hearing of the word of God will be the faithful reading and preaching of the word of God. That is where we start. Only then can we hear at all. Then hearing the word, let us "hold it fast in an honest and good heart, and bear fruit with patience." That is the way to hear rightly. That is the way we want to hear. That is the burden of the second imperative. "Take care then how you hear."

Third (3), when Jesus was told that his mother and brothers desired to see him, he answered to them and so to us, "My mother and my brothers are those who hear the word of God and do it." Not only are we (1) created to use our ears to hear, and not only are we (2) encouraged to hear appropriately, but now also we are (3) urged to hear and to obey. "Hear the word of God and do it." Hearing is not an academic exercise. This is real life, and the right hearing of the word of God has practical implications in our lives and in the world. What has he already told us, in the earlier chapters of Luke?

> I say to you who hear, Love your enemies, do good to those who hate you, bless those who curse you, pray for those who abuse you. To one who strikes you on the cheek, offer the other also, and from one who takes away your cloak do not withhold your tunic either. Give to everyone who begs from you, and from one who takes away your goods do not demand them back. And as you wish that others would do to you, do so to them. (Luke 6:27–31)

What else has he already told us? "Love your enemies, and do good, and lend, expecting nothing in return" (6:35a). What else has he already told us? "Be merciful, even as your Father is merciful. Judge not, and you will not be judged; condemn not, and you will not be condemned; forgive, and you will be forgiven; give, and it will be given to you" (6:37–38). Could hearing and doing this open our hearts to fellowship with one another? Could hearing and doing this open our hearts to evangelism to those who are not here? Could hearing and doing this open our hearts to mission in this county and around the world? Could hearing and doing this open our hearts to open our wallets to faithful stewardship of our resources? Could hearing and doing this open our hearts to compassion for all those in need, here and around the world?

Consider "Mary, called Magdalene, from whom seven demons had gone out, and Joanna, the wife of Chuza, Herod's household manager, and Susanna, and many others, who provided for them out of their means." These women provided for the ministry of Jesus and that of his twelve disciples. These women gave of their substance so that the gospel could be preached, the word of God could be taught, the sick could be healed, and the poor could have good news preached to them. For what does our giving provide today?

Those who do the things commanded by Jesus Christ are recognized by him as his own mother and his own brothers. That is amazing. It is imperative for us to hear. It is also imperative for us to hear correctly. And it is even more wonderful both to

---

1. Calvin, *Institutes*, IV.1.9, 2:1023.

hear correctly and then to obey, for those who do such are acknowledged as being members of the family of the very Son of God. Is this of interest to you?

So (1), "He who has ears to hear, let him hear"; (2) "Take care then how you hear"; and (3) "Hear the word of God and do it." These first two imperatives and the third, implied imperative carry the good news of Jesus Christ all the way to us and urge us to receive it. We would do well to heed them carefully. First (1), "He who has ears to hear, let him hear." Thus Jesus called out to the great crowd at the conclusion of his Parable of the Sower. So let us hear. This is the necessary starting point. Second (2), when his disciples inquired about his parable, Jesus explained it to them and then concluded, "Take care then how you hear, for to the one who has, more will be given, and from the one who has not, even what he thinks that he has will be taken away." So let us hear correctly. This is the only way to grow. And third (3), when he was told that his mother and brothers desired to see him, Jesus answered, "My mother and my brothers are those who hear the word of God and do it." So let us hear and obey. This is the only way to live.

To God be the glory forever and ever! Amen.

24

Who Commands Winds and Water?

LUKE 8:22–39; PSALM 107:1–3, 23–32

"WHO THEN IS THIS, that he commands even winds and water, and they obey him?" "Who . . . is this, that he commands even winds and water?" "Who . . . is this?" No wonder the disciples were afraid! Yes, they kept following Jesus. But they were afraid, and with good reason. Who is Jesus? Therein lies the question. This is a question of identity, reality, and truth. This is *the* question of our lives. Note that this first question is not "Who do you think Jesus is?" This first question is not even "Who do you believe Jesus is?" Those questions are not unimportant, but they are secondary. We shall get to them in a moment. Correct answers to those secondary questions depend upon a correct answer to this prior question. So, let us deal with first things first.

"Who then is this, that he commands even winds and water, and they obey him?" "Who . . . is this, that he commands even winds and water?" "Who . . . is this?" Who is Jesus? Therein lies the first question. Again, this is a question of identity, reality, and truth. This is *the* question of our lives. That is to say, the correct answer to the question of his identity will give us the correct answer to the question of our identity, of who we are, what we are about, what we are doing, and where we are going. The correct answer to the question of his identity will give us the correct answer to the questions of reality and truth, of what is real and true, of what is dependable and trustworthy. This is the question of our lives.

"Who then is this, that he commands even winds and water, and they obey him?" "Who . . . is this, that he commands even winds and water?" "Who . . . is this?" Who is Jesus? For starters, for the premise of the question, he is the one who commands even the wind and the water, and they obey him. What does this mean? Anyone who has read the book of Genesis or even the first chapter of the book of Genesis would know that God created heaven and earth and all that is in them by the sheer power of his word. Anyone who has read the book of Job would know that the Lord controls the wind and water by the sheer power of his word, and that no mere man could do so. Anyone who has read and sung the Psalms, especially Psalm 107, which we read today, would know that the Lord commands the wind and water, both to storm and to calm, by the sheer power of his word, and that the Lord also delivers his people by the same means. So the Scriptures are clear that the wind and water obey God and that they obey God alone. God commands them through his word. In that Jesus Christ does the same—commanding the wind and the water with his word so that they obey him—there is no other conclusion than that Jesus is God. Jesus is God himself with us, Jesus is God himself for us. That is who Jesus is.

This is the answer. This is the right answer. This is right knowledge. But even this right knowledge is not yet faith. It is not saving faith. Here is where we begin to make the transition from the primary question to the secondary questions. Knowing is important. Knowing is necessary. But knowing is not enough. The second part of today's reading makes that clear:

> They sailed to the country of the Gerasenes, which is opposite Galilee. When Jesus had stepped out on land, there met him a man from the city who had demons. For a long time he had worn no clothes, and he had not lived in a house but among the tombs. When he saw Jesus, he cried out and fell down before him and said with a loud voice, "What have you to do with me, Jesus, Son of the Most High God?"

That is to say, the demons knew exactly who Jesus was. The forces of evil had completely correct knowledge of his identity. But right knowledge did not help them. Right knowledge did not save them. Right knowledge did not make them good. It was not enough. It was not enough for them then; it cannot be enough for us today.

How then do we move from knowledge to faith? Obviously, we have to start with knowledge. We cannot move from knowledge to faith without having knowledge, without knowing the truth. So we have to start with knowledge. This is important, because Christian faith is *not* a matter of believing in what we do not know. We do not worship "Whom It May Concern." We do not worship the great spirit in the sky. Instead, we worship the God and Father of Jesus Christ. That is to say, we know that God is the Father of Jesus Christ, and we know that Jesus Christ is the Son of God. And to say that Jesus is the Son of God is another way of saying that he *is* God. We know that God is eternally the Father of the Son, and that the Son is eternally the Son of the Father. Jesus is God with us and for us. This we know. It is a special kind of knowing. But it is a real knowing. Without this knowing there is no Christian faith. Without this knowing there is no Christianity. Without this knowing there is no salvation.

How do we move from this knowledge to faith? The move from knowledge to faith is both the work of the Holy Spirit and the act of the human will. The move from knowledge to faith is the work of the Holy Spirit, which is to say that it is the result of the power of God at work within us, because faith is not a simple human possibility, and faith is not a mere human accomplishment. Faith is, in fact, a gift from God. At the same time, and viewed from another perspective, the move from knowledge to faith is an act of the human will, which is to say that God does not treat us like sticks and stones or wind and water. He does not force us to believe. Instead, God invites us to believe. He encourages us to believe. He entices us to believe. He woos us to believe. He calls us to believe. He loves us to believe. God gives himself to us in Jesus Christ so that we might believe. So, we are back to faith as a gift. It is not something we can accomplish on our own. It is not something for which we can claim credit. And yet, it is the deepest possible act of the self, an acknowledgment of reality, an act of worship, a commitment of trust. God gives this faith to us by eliciting this faith from us.

What is this faith to which we are called, to which we are invited, to which we are summoned, to which we are drawn, and which, finally, we are given? John Calvin defines faith as "a firm and certain knowledge of God's benevolence toward us, founded upon the truth of the freely given promise in Christ, both revealed to our minds and sealed upon our hearts through the Holy Spirit."[1] Faith is not only knowing that Jesus is God, but it is also knowing in Jesus that God is good toward us and for us, doing for us that which we cannot do for ourselves. The content of this knowing of the benevolence of God is the gospel, "the freely given promise in Christ," which is to say that the gospel provides the content of this knowing, so that the gospel leads us to faith. Faith, then, is not only a kind of knowing held in the mind but also a kind of knowing held and cherished in the heart. Faith is not a disinterested knowledge or a neutral point of view upon which all would agree. Instead, faith is passionate knowledge, love, trust, appreciation, and commitment, available only to those to whom the Holy Spirit has revealed God in Jesus Christ. This is the saving faith toward which this knowledge is headed.

"Who then is this, that he commands even winds and water, and they obey him?" "Who . . . is this, that he commands even winds and water?" "Who . . . is this?" Who is Jesus? The disciples asked the right question, but they could not yet put together the right answer. "What have you to do with me, Jesus, Son of the Most High God?'" The demons had the right information, and in that sense the right answer, but they had the wrong question and the wrong attitude. We, by way of contrast, are in the privileged position of overhearing from both the disciples and the demons both the right question and the right answer. Of course, the danger is that we will learn from the disciples and the demons only their wrong answer and their wrong question, their ignorance and their bad attitude, the worst of each. For instance, the Gerasenes, who saw what Jesus had done to the man who had the demons, were afraid, and they asked Jesus to leave. They failed to believe. They failed to obey. They failed to follow. They sided with the demons. That is *not* what we want to do. But the blessed opportunity,

---

1. Calvin, *Institutes*, III.2.7, 1:551.

the wonderful possibility, the invitation being held out to us is that we receive both the right question and the right answer, both the right knowledge and the right attitude, both knowing that Jesus is Son of the Most High God and also standing in awe of him—or, even better, falling down to worship him, in wonder and in awe at who he is. To know both that Jesus is God and also that God is with us and for us in Jesus is a powerful, joyful, life-changing kind of knowing. To know both that Jesus is God and also that God is with us and for us in Jesus is saving faith. To know both that Jesus is God and also that God is with us and for us in Jesus is both to believe what the Bible says and also to act upon that belief. To know both that Jesus is God and also that God is with us and for us is for us not merely to be students of religion but actually to become followers of Jesus Christ. Thanks be to God!

From time to time, people come before the elders of these congregations and then stand before the congregations in worship and profess for the first time their faith in Jesus Christ as Lord and Savior, or reaffirm their faith, or present a child for baptism. In acknowledgment of the prior work of the Holy Spirit within them, people commit their lives to Jesus Christ and commit their children to Jesus Christ. Let me tell you, there is no better reason to live. There is no better way to live. And in and by such public professions of faith, the people making them also give to all the rest of us a gift of which they may be unaware: the gift of an opportunity for all of us to reaffirm our own faith, to say again in our own hearts that we believe in Jesus Christ as Lord and Savior. When this happens, do not let the opportunity pass you by.

"Who then is this, that he commands even winds and water, and they obey him?" "Who . . . is this, that he commands even winds and water?" "Who . . . is this?" Who is Jesus? This is *the* question of our lives. Jesus is the Son of the Most High God. Jesus is God with us and for us. This is the high and sacred knowledge that we have received from today's reading and that we proclaim to all the world. Who, then, are we? Who are we in light of this knowledge, in light of this identity, in light of this truth and this reality? We are the ones to whom Jesus has come. We are the ones to whom God has come. We are the ones with whom God is and for whom God is. We are the ones for whom Jesus suffered and died. We are the ones for whom God raised him from the dead. We are the ones called to faith. We are the ones called to life. We are the ones called to follow Jesus. Of course we are afraid! But let us not fail to follow.

To God be the glory forever and ever! Amen.

25

Only Believe!

Luke 8:40–56; Ezekiel 34:1–16

"Do not fear; only believe." What good news stands behind and underneath these two brave imperatives? And does that good news speak to us yet today? "Do not fear; only believe." What great gospel undergirds these two directives? And is that gospel of interest to you? "Do not fear; only believe." What firm foundation upholds these two commands? And can you and I build our lives upon that foundation? "Do not fear; only believe." We shall get to the implications of these imperatives in a moment. But let us deal first with these prior questions. How can these imperatives be spoken? Who can say these words? Who has the right and the authority to say them? What does it mean that Jesus said, then and now, to them and so to us, "Do not fear; only believe"?

For starters, Jesus Christ is the one who healed the woman and raised the little girl from the dead. That is what the gospel says. Jesus healed the woman whom no one else could heal, and he restored to life the little girl whom everyone else believed to be irretrievably dead. That is who he is. That is what he did. That is why he has the right and the authority to say, "Do not fear; only believe." There is a cumulative effect to what we read here in the Gospel according to Luke and to what we are taught here as we continue to work through it chapter by chapter and verse by verse. The one who forgives sins, the one who calls disciples and names apostles, the one who teaches love of enemy, the one who commands the winds and the water and they obey him, the one who casts out demons is now also the one who heals a woman of an otherwise incurable malady and who even raises a little girl from the dead.

After all, there were witnesses! The poor impoverished woman who had exhausted her resources and had nothing left to do other than turn to Jesus had to be known to her neighbors. The gospel says explicitly that she "declared in the presence of all the people why she had touched him, and how she had been immediately healed." This could not have been made up in contradiction of the living memory of the people. And what is more, it could not be suppressed. She could not fail to tell it. They could not keep it quiet. So, why would anyone dare to contradict the word of this poor woman? Jesus healed her when no one else could.

Jairus, the ruler of the synagogue, was much more prominent and better known. By the time Jesus arrived, the mourners had gathered and were weeping at their loss. The little girl was dead. They all knew it. They knew it so well that they laughed at Jesus. By the way, when the gospel says that Jesus said that the girl was "sleeping," that is a figure of speech. The point of the story is not that Jesus woke her up. Anyone could have done that. It says explicitly that "her spirit returned," which means, of course, that it had already left her. The point of the story is that when Jesus speaks even the dead listen. When Jesus calls, even the dead obey. It is not the case that the dead are capable of hearing. It is the case, instead, that the word of God creates its own hearing, makes itself heard.

And this means that there is hope even for us, not hope in us or on our own, but hope for us and from beyond us, that God will so speak to us and so raise even us to new life. Do you think it made an impression on the mourners that there was no funeral that day or the next? Do you think they noticed? Do you think they quit laughing? Do you think they began to fear the one who said, "Do not fear"? More to the point for us, do you think the ones whose laughter was silenced would have allowed the story to be told this way if it had not happened this way? There were witnesses! It was incontrovertible. Jesus raised the little girl from the dead. That is who he is. That is what he did. It is up to us to deal with it.

In addition to his power in these matters, it is also his persistence in seeking out those whom he helped that is of significance. After the woman touched the fringe of his garment, Jesus sought out the woman from the crowd and refused to take no for an answer, despite Peter's protests. Jesus sought out the woman from the crowd, and he was not satisfied until she spoke to him and he spoke to her. Jesus sought out the woman from the crowd so that he not only healed her but also brought her into conversation with himself and therefore into communion with himself. That was even more important than the healing.

And "while he was still speaking" to her, news arrived that the little girl had died. Jesus did not let bad news dissuade him. He did not let bad news turn him around. He did not let the doomsayers stop him. He did not let laughter shame him. Indeed, it was precisely in the face of bad news, just as soon as he heard it, that he said to Jairus, "Do not fear; only believe." Jesus was determined to help that girl, and the bad news was not going to stop him. The mourners were not going to stop him. The father was not going to stop him. Death itself was not going to stop him. In fact, her death became the occasion for help even greater than healing. Jesus brought her back to life. Thanks be to God!

Jesus' power and persistence combine to bring us to an even greater conclusion. No one but God can heal an incurable disease. No one but God can raise someone from the dead. No one! The fact that Jesus did both of these can mean nothing else than that God is present with and for us in Jesus Christ. This is the good news behind the imperatives. This is gospel undergirding these directives. This is the firm foundation upholding these two commands. God himself is present with and for us in Jesus Christ. This is who Jesus is, God himself present with us and for us. This is what these stories mean. This is how and why he can say, then and now, to them and so to us, "Do not fear; only believe." "Do not fear; only believe." If I were to say this to you, it would mean very little. I cannot thus take away your fear or your faithlessness. But when Jesus says it to us, and he does, it means everything. "Do not fear; only believe." Jesus has the right and the authority to say it, and he has the power to make it so. "Do not fear; only believe."

Let me be entirely clear here. I believe that what Jesus did that day was in perfect fulfillment of the ancient prophecy we have read from Ezekiel:

> For thus says the Lord GOD: Behold, I, I myself will search for my sheep and will seek them out. As a shepherd seeks out his flock when he is among his sheep that have been scattered, so will I seek out my sheep, and I will rescue them from all places where they have been scattered on a day of clouds and thick darkness. . . . I myself will be the shepherd of my sheep, and I myself will make them lie down, declares the Lord GOD. I will seek the lost, and I will bring back the strayed, and I will bind up the injured, and I will strengthen the weak. (Ezekiel 34:11–12, 15–16a)

It all came true! It all came true in Jesus. God himself came in Jesus Christ to care for his people, seeking and saving the lost, healing the sick, raising the dead, comforting the distraught, giving faith to the doubting. That is who he is. That is what he does. And it is still true today. "Do not fear; only believe."

At this point, I must make an important, painful, and yet also hopeful distinction. I know this is hard for some of us to hear. The gospel we have read today is not a general promise of healing and life, at least not here in this world. The healing of the woman and the raising of the girl were particular actions indicating the power, authority, and therefore the identity of Jesus Christ. They are a way of telling us who he is. There were bound to have been other people that same day who were sick but were not healed. There were bound to have been other people that same day who died but were not raised. So the good news cannot possibly be that all sickness here will be healed or that all who die will be restored to this life. That is not what he did. We might wish that were the case, but that is not the case. That is not what is being said here. That is the painful part. But the good news here—demonstrated by this particular healing and this particular raising from the dead—is instead that God himself is with us and for us in Jesus Christ. This is the truth. This is the important part.

And it is on the basis of this important part that we come now to the hopeful part. In that God is with us and for us in Jesus Christ, Jesus Christ is the one who can and does heal us of our greatest sickness, the sickness of our sin. He seeks us out, he finds us, and he restores us to relationship with himself. Moreover, in that God is with us and for us in Jesus Christ, Jesus Christ is also the one who can and does raise us from the dead, promising us eternal life not in this world but in the next. He seeks us out, he finds us, and he restores us to life forever beyond the power of death. Forgiveness of sin and eternal life might not be exactly what we first wanted. But forgiveness of sin and eternal life are exactly what we most desperately need. Surely we realize that now. That God in Jesus Christ does in fact provide them to us is good news beyond our deserving, beyond our dreams, beyond our imagination. Disease and death do not have the final word about us, or about our loved ones, or about who we are. God has purposes for us beyond our life in this world. There is life beyond death in this world. There is community beyond the brokenness we all know. Thanks be to God!

"Do not fear; only believe." Given the important, painful, and hopeful distinction we have just made, and given the gospel we have affirmed, now let us turn to the implications of these imperatives for us. What do these mean for us today?

"Do not fear." The one who can and does forgive our sin urges us to face life with confidence, poise, and equanimity. The one who can and does forgive our sin tells us to live without fear. More than that, the one who has the authority to tell us this also, by this very telling, actually gives us the courage that he commands. If I were to tell you that, it would mean very little. I cannot take away your fear. But when Jesus tells us that, he gives what he commands. He relieves our fear. Fear eats away at our lives. Gospel courage, which we might also understand as faith, makes is possible for us to live. This is good news.

"Only believe." The one who can and does promise us eternal life urges us to face the future with faith, trust, and commitment. The one who can and does promise us eternal life tells us to believe. More than that, the one who has the authority to tell us this also, by this very telling, actually gives us the faith that he commands. If I were to tell you that, it would mean very little. I cannot give you faith. But when Jesus tells us that, he gives what he commands. He engenders faith. Fear and doubt eat away at our lives. But gospel faith, "a firm and certain knowledge of God's benevolence toward us, founded upon the truth of the freely given promise in Christ, both revealed to our minds and sealed upon our hearts through the Holy Spirit,"[1] makes is possible for us to live. This too is good news.

"Do not fear; only believe." We have heard the good news that stands behind and underneath these two brave imperatives. "Do not fear; only believe." We have heard the great gospel that undergirds these two directives. "Do not fear; only believe." We have seen the firm foundation that upholds these two commands. So now, can you and I build our lives upon this good news, upon this gospel, and upon this foundation?

1. Calvin, *Institutes*, III.2.7, 1:551.

"Do not fear; only believe." We have answered the prior questions. We have learned how these imperatives can be spoken. We have learned who can say them. We have met the one who has the right and the authority to say them. As Jesus Christ said to Jairus then, so also does he say to us yet today, with the forgiveness of sin and the promise of eternal life, "Do not fear; only believe."

To God be the glory forever and ever! Amen.

26

Who Is This?

LUKE 9:1–17; JOB 19:23–27

"JOHN I BEHEADED, BUT who is this about whom I hear such things?" "Who is this?" Already during the earthly life of Jesus Christ, questions were being raised about his identity, about who he was, and already during his earthly life answers were being given in terms of life, death, and new life. For instance, "It was said by some that John had been raised from the dead, by some that Elijah had appeared, and by others that one of the prophets of old had risen." So even before Easter, even before the crucifixion, the categories of Easter, of death and resurrection, were being used to understand who Jesus is. They *mis*understood him at that time, thinking he was someone else. We know that now. But in a way they were on the right track. Jesus does have to do with life, death, and new life, and he cannot be understood apart from that.

Herod said, "John I beheaded, but who is this about whom I hear such things?" Soon enough, Herod would cooperate with Pontius Pilate in the crucifixion of Jesus Christ, still not knowing the answer to his own question. "Who is this?" Surely his question then is our question today. That is why Luke recorded it for us. "Who is this?" There could be no more important question in our lives. Living on this side of Easter, after Easter, we can know the right answer. Living on this side of Easter, we can know who he is. Living on this side of Easter, we can know who we are in relation to who Jesus is. Living on this side of Easter, we can hear the full gospel proclaimed as it could not be before his death and resurrection. So let us pursue the Easter answer to Herod's admittedly pre-Easter question.

"John I beheaded, but who is this about whom I hear such things?" Luke has already told us who Jesus is. Jesus is the son of King David—understanding, of course, that many generations of "greats" and "grands" have been left out of this expression—Jesus is in fact the son of Father Abraham, even the son of Adam, and, infinitely more importantly, the Son of the Most High God. I rehearse these simply to remind us that the other answers available to Herod were wrong. "Who is this?" "It was said by some that John had been raised from the dead, by some that Elijah had appeared, and by others that one of the prophets of old had risen." But even these wrong answers are helpful to us, so that we can rule them out.

For instance, as we pursue the Easter answer to Herod's question, it is good for us to know that Jesus is *not* John the Baptist. John came before Jesus. John prepared the way for Jesus. John preached good news to the people. John suffered and died before Jesus, pointing ahead to the suffering and death of Jesus. But Jesus was *not* John.

It is also good for us to know also that Jesus is *not* Elijah. Elijah was the great prophet of the Old Testament, a mighty contender against paganism and evil kings. Elijah did not even die, but was carried away into heaven in a chariot of fire. His return was prophesied and expected before the great and awesome day of the Lord. But Jesus was not Elijah. Instead, John was Elijah, as it were, so that his arrival before the day of the Lord indicates clearly that Jesus is Lord. We shall return to that in a moment. For now, we know that Jesus was *not* Elijah.

It is also good for us to know also that Jesus is *not* any one of the prophets of old. He was not Elisha. He was not Isaiah. He was not Jeremiah. He was not Ezekiel. He was not Daniel or any of the others. The list of the prophets of old is long. Their work in speaking the word of God to the people of God was worthy. But Jesus was *not* one of them.

"Who is this about whom I hear such things?" We know, of course, that Jesus preached and taught and healed. We know that he commissioned others to preach and heal. We know that he attracted large crowds, which was troublesome to the rulers. We know that he fed the five thousand. But living on this side of Easter, after Easter, we know even more. We have already seen that even during the earthly life of Jesus, as questions were being raised about his identity, answers were being given in terms of life, death, and new life. And now we know that those are the right categories and that he has fulfilled them as never before. Jesus, Son of the Most High God—which is another way of saying that he is God—came and lived among us, with us and for us, as one of us. Jesus, born of the virgin Mary—which is another way of saying that he is human—suffered under Pontius Pilate, was crucified, dead, and buried. And let me say here that the military forces of the Roman Empire were very good at killing people. There can be no serious doubt about the truth and reality of the death of Jesus Christ.

And now, for the Easter part of this, Jesus, the crucified one—which is another was of saying that he gave himself for us and so was wrongly executed though he had done no wrong—was raised bodily from the dead, though not simply restored to this life but elevated to an even greater life forever beyond the power of death. Alleluia! This is who he is. Again, this explicitly does not mean that Jesus was simply resuscitated or restored to this life. For we understand that he was beyond pain, decay, disease, and death. If he had been only resuscitated to this life, he would have had to die again. So, it was not a simple resuscitation. But the bodily resurrection does mean that the tomb was empty so that the body that had been there was somehow taken up into whatever his resurrected body was and still is. This sets the Christian faith apart from every other faith, from every other commitment, and from every other way of looking at the world. And this provides the indispensable basis for the rest of what I want to say.

"Who is this about whom I hear such things?" Jesus, who is the crucified one, is now also the resurrected one, so he is the living one, the one who now lives eternally with his Father. Herod had no idea. Herod had no clue. But we have the whole truth. So we have the answer to his question. Thanks be to God!

We mentioned earlier that John the Baptist's fulfillment of the prophesied and expected return of Elijah pointed ahead to Jesus as being the Lord. And the crucifixion and resurrection of Jesus fulfill and confirm his lordship. Jesus is Lord! Jesus is God with us and for us. Jesus is the ruler of the universe. Jesus is the ruler of our lives. Part of the Easter answer to Herod's question is that Jesus the living one is also the Lord. The preacher, teacher, healer about whom he heard, the one who commissioned his followers to preach, the one who was drawing crowds, the one who fed the five thousand, is also the Lord of the universe. This is more than Herod the tetrarch bargained for. This is, undoubtedly, more than we would have expected. But it is who Jesus is. And this points the way forward to the answer to the question of who we are.

Given the Easter gospel that Jesus the risen and living one is also Lord of the universe, we are made to realize that we are *not* lord of the universe. That is not our responsibility. Moreover, those who would presume to lord it over us are *not* lord of the universe. That is not their prerogative. Given the Easter gospel that Jesus the risen and living one is Lord of the universe, we are set free from all the false claimants to that throne, including both ourselves and also our enemies. Given the Easter gospel that Jesus the risen and living one is Lord of the universe, we are bound to him, bound tighter than death, bound to him forever. Jesus is our Lord, and therefore we are his servants, and this is our greatest good, our highest joy, our only reason for life and being. Jesus is our Easter Lord, and we are his Easter people. Thanks be to God!

There is at least one more piece of this Easter gospel that we certainly want to share. When God raised Jesus Christ from the dead, he defeated the power of death not for Jesus alone but also for us. When God raised Jesus Christ from the dead, he did so not only to make Jesus alive again but also to provide for us the promise and the assurance of bodily resurrection to eternal life on the other side of death. The one who raised Jesus Christ from the dead can and will also raise us from the dead. The power of death has been defeated. We are given good hope to look forward to the life beyond.

Thus, this Easter reality of the resurrection of the body rules out the fearful prospect of the sheer annihilation of humanity. One possibility for the end of human life is that we disappear into oblivion, that we cease to exist, that we dissolve into nothingness, that nothing we have said or done means anything, that though we were, we are no longer. That would be horrible. That is one of the great fears of humanity. But the Easter resurrection of Jesus Christ rules that out. The resurrection of the body of the one person of Jesus Christ means that we are not simply annihilated, that we do not slip away into oblivion, that human life does not end in nothingness, that who we are, what we say, and what we do are not forgotten. The resurrection eliminates that terror of nihilism and thus begins to provide for us the basis for meaning and purpose in this life.

Indeed, the very promise of the life beyond increases the value of life here. If there were no life beyond, it would not matter very much how badly we treat each other. Enemies could be killed with impunity. The poor could be eradicated. The sick and weak could be allowed to die, as we are seeing in our own day. Why would it matter? But the fact that you and I are building relationships here that will last forever puts everything in a totally different light. The fact that people are of eternal significance to God certainly suggests that they should be of great significance to us. So our great hope for the life to come does not mean that this life does not matter, but means instead precisely that this life matters even more than it would have otherwise. Of course, there are things in this life that we will be grateful to leave behind. But as servants of the living Lord of life, we are eager to do good to one another even here.

From time to time, people stand before these congregations and profess their faith in Jesus Christ as Lord and Savior, or reaffirm their faith in Jesus Christ as Lord and Savior. In so doing, they do not make Jesus their Lord and Savior, but they instead acknowledge what is already an eternal truth: that Jesus Christ is *the* Lord and Savior. In so doing, they not only bind themselves to the church of Jesus Christ—for that church relationship cannot be separated from making a profession of faith in Jesus Christ—but they also bind themselves to the lordship of Jesus Christ, willingly embracing the reality of their lives as servants of Jesus Christ, which alone is good reason to live. In fact, the affirmations of faith they make are far more important than marriage vows. They are far more important than citizenship vows. These are matters of life, death, and new life. These are Easter affirmations of an Easter people to our Easter Lord. And we all rejoice with them, reaffirming our own faith, recommitting ourselves to the living Lord of life, becoming an Easter people yet again.

"John I beheaded, but who is this about whom I hear such things?" "It was said by some that John had been raised from the dead, by some that Elijah had appeared, and by others that one of the prophets of old had risen." "Who is this?" Jesus, who is the crucified one, is now also the resurrected one, and so he is the living one, Lord of the universe, who lives eternally with his Father. And we are his people. Thanks be to God!

To God be the glory forever and ever! Amen.

27

Who Do You Say That I Am?

"WHO DO YOU SAY that I am?" Here is where the gospel gets personal. "Who do you say that I am?" There are other questions. "Who do the crowds say that I am?" Who do the history books say that I am? Who do the powers that be say that I am? Who do the trendsetters say that I am? Who do the professors say that I am? These may be interesting. They may be important. But this question is personal: "Who do you say that I am?" And Luke has recorded it not only for its historical value, which is significant, but also and especially for its gospel value for you and me today. "Who do you say that I am?" We have read enough and have heard enough that we have reached a point calling for self-declaration. "Who do you say that I am?" Indeed, Jesus himself looks out from the pages of the gospel right into your eyes and mine, and Jesus himself looks down from heaven right into your heart and mine and asks us today, "Who do you say that I am?" This question cannot be avoided.

Luke, of course, provides an answer for Theophilus, for whom he wrote this gospel, and so he provides an answer for us, to whom this gospel has now come. Peter answered, "The Christ of God." That is who Peter says Jesus is. That is who Luke says Jesus is. The question for each of us is, "Who do you say that I am?" We have to answer that for ourselves. Can we be helped by those who have gone before us?

Peter answered (1), "The *Christ* of God." What does "Christ" mean? It means "Anointed One." In ancient Israel, kings were anointed to their office, with oil being poured over their head. Then, after Israel was defeated and the monarchy was ended, the people expected God to send someone else to save them—a new king, a better king, a stronger king. They called this anticipated redeemer the Anointed One. So, for Peter to call Jesus the Christ was for him to recognize that Jesus fulfilled this ancient prophecy of the word of God. Peter believed that Jesus was the one sent by God and from God to save his people. Can we confess this faith as our own?

Again, Peter answered (2), "The Christ of *God.*" For him to say "of God" was also for him to realize that God did not choose just anyone to be the Christ. Jesus was not merely one more human being, one more prophet, one more priest, or even one more king. Neither was Jesus an angel or a messenger from God. Instead, God sent his only Son. God sent the only one who shares his godliness. In Jesus, God himself is with us. Peter answered, "The Christ of *God.*" Can we confess this faith as our own?

It is absolutely crucial to realize that in direct response to Peter's answer Jesus immediately redefined what "Christ" means and therefore redefined his own life and mission. He did so using four verbs. "And he [Jesus] strictly charged and commanded them to tell this to no one, saying, 'The Son of Man must [1] suffer many things and [2] be rejected by the elders and chief priests and scribes, and [3] be killed, and on the third day [4] be raised.'" With this hard lesson, we have come to the heart of the gospel. It is not pretty, it is not easy, it is not soft, and it is not gentle. But it is the truth. Here, for the first time, Jesus tells us that he will (1) suffer, (2) be rejected, (3) be killed, and (4) be raised again, all on our account. This is for us.

Jesus (1) suffered because all of humanity is opposed to God. We could not tolerate God living among us. He came anyway. Our contempt could not keep him away. But he paid a terrible price for coming here. God took the initiative to enter into relationship with us when we would not and could not take the initiative to enter into relationship with him. He came to us because we do not and cannot go to him. He came as the embodiment and expression of grace. And his willingness to come despite the suffering, his intention to overcome the opposition by suffering, is good news for us. For Jesus suffered willingly and without complaint in order to defeat the powers of evil which inflict suffering. If he had struck back, evil would have won. Only by patient, long suffering could he and did win the victory for us. He suffered for us not so that we would never suffer, but in order to defeat suffering and evil, so that we might live in glory with God.

Jesus (2) was rejected also because of our stubborn opposition to God. The elders, chief priests, and scribes represented the highest religious aspirations of the human race. Yet they could not see, accept, or understand that Jesus was God among us. Part of the reality of what was going on is that Jesus was not simply *a* way to God, but instead he was and is *the* way to God. The significance of his uniqueness is that we have rejected the very one who came to us despite our rejection of him. Jesus willingly suffered rejection by humanity in order that we might be accepted by God.

In the same way, Jesus (3) was killed. Betrayed by one of his disciples, deserted by the rest, falsely accused by the Jewish authorities, and wrongly convicted by the Roman Empire, he was killed not simply by their actions but also in fulfillment of God's plan for our salvation. Jesus took on the sin of the world and paid the price for it in order that we might be forgiven and *not* spend eternity in hell. He died that day in order that we might live forever. Thanks be to God!

So, Jesus did not win a cheap and easy victory for us. He won a hard and painful victory, suffering abandonment by his disciples, accusation by the religious leaders of his day, condemnation by the legal powers of the Roman Empire, and death by crucifixion. Our forgiveness comes through Christ accepting our condemnation. Our victory comes through his defeat. Our comfort comes through his suffering. Our blessing comes through his being cursed. Our very life comes through his death.

In addition to suffering, being rejected, and being killed, Jesus (4) was raised from the dead. He was brought back to life, forever beyond the power of death. God vindicated his suffering, rejection, and death. The resurrection does not come without the suffering, rejection, and death. But suffering, rejection, and death do not have the final word. After they had done their worst and spent themselves, God raised Jesus from the dead. This is the fourth and final verb with which Jesus defined himself.

Jesus asked, "'Who do you say that I am?' Peter answered, "The Christ of God." We have heard at least part of what this means. It is worth asking what it does not mean. It does not mean whatever we want it to mean. It does not mean that we are the ones who get to define the term. It is significant that Jesus began this first hard teaching of his good news only after the first profession of faith that he was the Christ. At least one consequence of this profession is that when you acknowledge someone as the Christ, you have to yield to *that* person the right to define what is meant by "the Christ." And that is the prerogative that Jesus claimed when "he strictly charged and commanded them to tell this to no one," not until he could lead them to deeper understanding, insight, and faith.

"Who do you say that I am?" Peter answered, "The Christ of God." Can that be our answer too? What are the implications for those who would follow Jesus, believe in him, and bear his name? "If anyone would come after me, let him deny himself and take up his cross daily and follow me. For whoever would save his life will lose it, but whoever loses his life for my sake will save it." This runs against everything else we think we know. This runs against every instinct for self-preservation. This runs against every encouragement of the world for us to seek self-fulfillment. But what Jesus is telling us is that every instinct for self-protection leads to death, while true life is found and saved only by following him to the cross, only by dying to self, only by living not for ourselves but for him alone. Life is not and cannot be fulfilled in selfish self-fulfillment; life is fulfilled only in selfless self-emptying and self-denial all in the name of, and for the sake of, Jesus Christ. That may sound backward to us, but that is the way it is. Nobody asked whether we liked it, but this is reality. If we profess Jesus as Christ and so Lord, we have to abandon all claims to being our own lords. We cannot have it both ways. The Christian faith is not about human potential. It is about the grace of God.

It is interesting, since Jesus defined his own role with four verbs, that he also defined his followers with four verbs: "If anyone would [1] come after me, let him [2] deny himself and [3] take up his cross daily and [4] follow me." The Christian life begins with (1) going after Jesus, who is known in and through his word and gospel. It continues with (2) self-denial, the setting aside of all self-centeredness and all self-serving in order to become God-centered and God-serving. It matures with (3) taking up one's cross daily, willingly dying to self and living to Christ. And all of this culminates in (4) following Jesus. Our very lives are not ours to keep, but to give. To keep one's life to one's self is to forfeit life. But to pour out one's life for God and for others is to find true life. Christ has not taken a journey for us so that we do not have to journey. He has gone before us to show us the way. He calls us to follow the path that he has traveled, so we can be with him. Jesus Christ gave away his life in order that we might live.

We realize from everyday experience that individual human life is designed and meant to be part of something larger than itself. We are gathered into families, communities, and nations. We share languages, histories, and cultures. We cooperate in companies and economies. Human life best expresses itself by placing the energies of the self at the service of things larger than the self. This is why loyalties to schools and teams are so strong. It is part of the reason patriotism is so powerful. Yet none of these human realities exhausts the need of the self to be part of something more. Why? Because God designed us to be in fellowship with him, and nothing less will satisfy us. We are meant to be here, in church, singing our songs of praise to God, joining our voices with those of the angels and of the saints who have gone before us, for they already worship God eternally. How do we hear and join the distant song of angels? By dying to the urge to sing our own praises and learning to sing God's praises instead.

Jesus did not win a cheap and easy victory for us. And there is no cheap and easy discipleship. Christ leads the way. Christ sets the example. Christ promises to be with us. He will never ask us to do or to suffer anything that he has not done or suffered. Do we want (1) to go after him? Are we ready (2) to deny ourselves? Are we willing (3) to take up our cross, the means of our execution, the death of the self? Are we able (4) to follow Jesus through the day and through the night, across all the years of our lives? Are we willing to give our best and our all to the service of Christ?

All of human life is lived by some faith. We may believe in ourselves. We may believe in our country. We may believe in the economy. We may believe in the structures and patterns of the natural world. The question is whether we can believe in the God and Father of Jesus Christ, the God who made the world as an arena within which for us to love God and one another, the living God who is revealed through Jesus his Son. And this faith begins with our answer to the question Jesus asks each of us today, "Who do you say that I am?"

We have an advantage in this regard over Peter and the first disciples. We can learn from their hard lessons. We can learn from their mistakes. Moreover, we live after both the crucifixion and resurrection. We know that Jesus was the Christ by being the suffering servant, and that he was the suffering servant because he was the Christ. Nevertheless, knowing it is different from believing it, professing it, and actually living it. So it is that Jesus still asks the faith question of us today, you and me, calling for our answer, waiting for our response: "Who do you say that I am?"

To God be the glory forever and ever! Amen.

28

Who Is the Greatest?

LUKE 9:28–50; EXODUS 34:29–35

WHO IS THE GREATEST among us? It is not I. I am sure that none of you thought that anyway, but I wanted to be sure that all of you knew that I did not think that either. Who is the greatest among us? It is not I. It is probably not one of the elders. It may not even be an adult. Who is the greatest among us? Jesus said, "He who is least among you all is the one who is great." How very strange and backwards! Jesus has a way of standing things on their head. In our case, the greatest among us may be a child or even an infant, the least among us all.

We have been pursuing the questions and answers posed and given in the Gospel according to Luke. In many ways it reads like a catechism, with a learned instructor posing good and important questions of the faith, then leading us to the right answers. In today's reading, a question is posed near the end of the reading in this way: "An argument arose among them as to which of them was the greatest." Sad to say, "them" refers to the disciples. Yes, the followers of Jesus Christ were having an unseemly argument about which one of them was the greatest. Can you imagine? It would not be a bad question for someone else to ask about them. It would have been an interesting question a few years later, after they had fallen to the depths of betrayal, denial, and desertion, and then subsequently grown into true greatness. After all, we are talking about Peter and John and James and all the rest of the disciples who eventually became apostles, carrying the gospel of Christ into all the world.

But on that day, so early in their discipleship, and at the foot of the mountain where they had heard the very voice of God, and in this gospel, about Jesus the son of David and the Son of God, the question about their greatness is so ridiculous and so out of place that it must point beyond itself to something else. "An argument arose

129

among them as to which of them was the greatest." Can you imagine? To what else does this question point? To what else does this question point us yet today? Let me suggest that a clue is to be found in the context of this argument, or actually in the several contexts of this argument. Each contributes something different. So let us start with (1) the smallest and most immediate context of this question, near the end of the reading, and then work our way out into (2) larger contexts and so back to (3) the beginning of the reading, which provides the largest context. Then we will know to what else this question points, and so then we will know the answer to the question.

"An argument arose among them as to which of them was the greatest." Startlingly enough, this perverse argument and its inherent question arose within (1) the immediate context of the second prediction of the crucifixion of Jesus Christ. Jesus said to his disciples, "Let these words sink into your ears: The Son of Man is about to be delivered into the hands of men." And as if to prove that they did not and would not let those words sink into their ears, hearts, minds, and souls, "An argument arose among them as to which of them was the greatest." Instead of weeping for their Lord, instead of fearing for their lives, instead of praying for the people, instead of worshiping God, "An argument arose among them as to which of them was the greatest." Jesus, the Son of God, without sin, has told them that he is going to give his life for the sin of the world, including theirs and ours, and they shrug it off. No big deal! They hurry on to important matters having to do with their own supposed greatness.

The imbalance is dizzying! This immediate context of their question immediately suggests to us that the greatest one among the disciples is not one of the disciples but is their one Lord, Master, and Savior. This immediate context of their question immediately suggests to us that the greatest one among the church is not one of our members but is, of course, our one Lord, Master, and Savior. No wonder "Jesus, knowing the reasoning of their hearts, took a child and put him by his side and said to them, 'Whoever receives this child in my name receives me, and whoever receives me receives him who sent me. For he who is least among you all is the one who is great.'" This is not to say that Jesus is a child or that a child is Jesus. But it is to say that a man hanging on a cross outside Jerusalem is the very least of the least of all, and therefore is the greatest of all.

As if this were not enough, the second (2) and intermediate context of the disciples' discussion of their own supposed greatness is one of their own abject failure. Consider what happened immediately prior to Jesus' prediction of his crucifixion:

> Behold, a man from the crowd cried out, "Teacher, I beg you to look at my son, for he is my only child. And behold, a spirit seizes him, and he suddenly cries out. It convulses him so that he foams at the mouth; and shatters him, and will hardly leave him. And I begged your disciples to cast it out, but they could not."

"I begged your disciples to cast it out, but they could not." That is the charge against them. They do not dispute it. Does this seem to you an appropriate time for them to discuss their own supposed greatness?

The contrast is appalling! How in the world could they make that move? How in the world can we, in the midst of our own abject failures in the church, so quickly become self-absorbed? Is not such self-centeredness the very nature of the sin for which Christ died to forgive us? How easily we forget! Is not such self-centeredness the very nature of the sin for which Christ rose to lead us out of it and into newness of life? How quickly we revert! The very act of raising the question of our own supposed greatness indicates the presence of the opposite of greatness and confirms our need for salvation. To top it all off, John tried the classic strategy of diversion and "answered" Jesus—that is startling, in and of itself, since Jesus had just given them a teaching, not asked for a response. John "answered" Jesus by pointing away to someone else. "Master, we saw someone casting out demons in your name, and we tried to stop him, because he does not follow with us." It is as if to say, "At least we are better than someone else." Have you ever tried that ploy? We can almost see Jesus shaking his head. These guys are hopeless! Jesus said to John, "Do not stop him, for the one who is not against you is for you."

Now it is time for us to look beyond (1) Jesus' second prediction of his crucifixion and beyond (2) the failure of the disciples to help those about them to the larger and even more remarkable context of the disciples' argument about their supposed greatness, and that is (3) the transfiguration of Jesus Christ:

> He took with him Peter and John and James and went up on the mountain to pray. And as he was praying, the appearance of his face was altered, and his clothing became dazzling white. And behold, two men were talking with him, Moses and Elijah, who appeared in glory and spoke of his departure, which he was about to accomplish at Jerusalem. . . . A cloud came and overshadowed them, and they were afraid as they entered the cloud. And a voice came out of the cloud, saying, "This is my Son, my Chosen One; listen to him!" And when the voice had spoken, Jesus was found alone.

Then they came down off the mountain, that very mountain, and "an argument arose among them"—yes, among the disciples—"as to which of them was the greatest."

It is hard to believe, and yet it is not hard to believe. It is incredible but not implausible. It is disappointing but not surprising. It was the wrong question or at least the wrong application of the right question. Do you think they could have applied it to the three men on the mountain—not to the three disciples, Peter and John and James—but to the other three men? Moses, Elijah, and Jesus: "Which of them is the greatest?" Now there is a good question. The Law, the Prophets, and the Gospel; these are what these three proponents represented. "Which of them is the greatest?" There is an intriguing question. Moses delivered the Ten Commandments to the people. Elijah was the greatest prophet of the Old Testament. Jesus was bringing the gospel to the people. "Which of them is the greatest?" The Law was the will of God for the people of God. The Prophets spoke the word of God to the people of God. The Gospel is the forgiveness of God for the people of God. Which of these is the greatest? There is a worthy question. There is something to study. There is something to ponder. There is something to discuss. There is something into which to sink one's teeth. But the disciples? How could they think only about themselves?

Moses, Elijah, and Jesus: "Which of them is the greatest?" Here is a question that Luke poses for us yet today. Do we intend to live our lives only in obedience to the Law? That might be a good and worthy goal, except that all of us would fail. Do we intend to live our lives under the prophetic cries for social justice as if we were capable of building a better world here? That might be a good and worthy goal, except that it has been superseded. Do we intend to live our lives in grateful confession of our sin and in confident hope for renewal both here and in the world to come? That is the good and worthy reality of our lives. Which of these is the greatest?

It has occurred to me that the question of the transfiguration is not such an ancient one as we may think. I do not know in what regard the Jewish faith of today holds the Prophets. It may be very high. I simply do not know. I do know that they continue to hold the Law in very high regard. But there has been another prophet of another faith, an alien faith, and if we were to substitute his name for the name of the prophet Elijah, suddenly the question would become contemporary, vital, and important. Moses, *Mohammed*, and Jesus: "Which of them is the greatest?" Judaism, *Islam*, and Christianity: Which of them is the true way? Now do you see the significance of this ancient question? Do you see it any better after September 11, 2001? This question has played itself out across the centuries, and it will continue to do so. It is not what some would call merely an academic question, a matter for disinterested research. It is a question of faith, life, truth, reality, passion, commitment, politics, and the rise and fall of nations and peoples. It may be *the* question of this century. We need to stand ready to answer it and to answer it well.

Hear again the answer to the question given by the very voice of God and recorded for us by Luke: "A cloud came and overshadowed them, and they were afraid as they entered the cloud. And a voice came out of the cloud, saying, 'This is my Son, my Chosen One; listen to him!' And when the voice had spoken, Jesus was found alone." The voice of God said, "This is my Son, my Chosen One; listen to him!" Moses disappeared. Elijah disappeared. Their role on the mountain, indeed their role in life, was to point to Jesus. So Jesus was left there alone. Who is the greatest? The only one left standing, the very Son of God, God's Chosen One.

Who is the greatest? As the church eventually learned from this gospel and has answered through the centuries in the Nicene Creed, the greatest is the one Lord Jesus Christ:

The only-begotten Son of God, begotten of the Father before all worlds, God of God, Light of Light, Very God of Very God, begotten, not made, being of one substance with the Father; by whom all things were made; who for us men, and for our salvation, came down from heaven, and was incarnate by the Holy Spirit of the Virgin Mary, and was made man, and was crucified also for us under Pontius Pilate. He suffered and was buried, and the third day he rose again according to the scriptures, and ascended into heaven, and sitteth on the right hand of the Father. And he shall come again with glory to judge both the quick and the dead, whose kingdom shall have no end.

Who is the greatest? Let me dare to proclaim to us all yet today, nearly two-thousand years after the transfiguration, that Jesus Christ is still the greatest, that Jesus Christ always has been the greatest, that Jesus Christ always will be the greatest, and that none do now or ever shall equal him. He stands alone. There shall be many pretenders. There shall be many false prophets. There shall be powerful voices of despair, negativity, and defeat. There shall be proponents of greed and of false ambition. But do not be deceived. Do not be disturbed. Do not listen to them. Do not be taken in by them. There is one Lord, Jesus Christ, who is greater than them all.

When the night grows dark, and the air falls still, and your friends are gone, and you are forced into the loneliness of your heart, to what voices do you listen then? What suggestions do you follow? In whom do you place your trust and confidence? Upon what foundation do you build your life? What are your guides, your markers, your signs along the way? In the busyness of life, and in the failures, the contradictions, and the frustrations, upon what do you rely? And on those happy days, to whom do you give the thanks, the praise, and the glory?

We all hear the other voices. One says, with a snarl, "Look out for yourself; no one else is going to!" How much of my poor, misguided life have I marched in willing obedience to this bad advice! Another voice says, with a smile, "Do whatever you want; no one is watching; no one will see; no one will ever know." Sometimes it makes me forget that I will always know, let alone that the Lord will know. Another voice cries, "Grab all you can, while you can, when you can, for life consists in the abundance of possessions." Strange that almost nothing I ever owned lived up to the joy or satisfaction I expected. Another voice whispers in the wind, "You fool, you fool, you fool; all is vanity; all is death; all is dying; why do you struggle so?" Can I find the strength to refuse to yield to that lying voice? We all hear the other voices. To which voice do we listen? What do we believe? Whom do we obey?

The voice of God said, "This is my Son, my Chosen One; listen to him!" "Listen to him!" What shall we do? We cannot see Jesus Christ anymore. He has ascended into heaven. We cannot touch him anymore. He is seated at the right hand of the Father. But we can listen to him. We do have his words. We do have his gospel. We do have the Scriptures. We do have the Bible. "Listen to him!" Therein are life, faith, and hope. How can we do any other?

An argument arose among them as to which of them was the greatest. But Jesus, knowing the reasoning of their hearts, took a child and put him by his side and said to them, "Whoever receives this child in my name receives me, and whoever receives me receives him who sent me. For he who is least among you all is the one who is great."

It is fascinating that he did not reprimand them for seeking greatness. There is nothing wrong about wanting to be great. In fact, Jesus commended and encouraged it in this very reading. At the same time, he redefined it. If you want to be great—and we should—listen to Jesus, believe in him and his gospel, obey his will and his commandments, receive and accept his gracious service to us both on the cross and in being raised from the tomb, and so become a servant like him, loving and caring for one another, even those of no account to the world. Thus even the Law is obeyed. Thus even the Prophets are rightly honored. And thus alone the gospel itself is finally fulfilled in our lives.

To God be the glory forever and ever! Amen.

29

How Shall We Follow?

LUKE 9:51–62; 1 KINGS 19:15–21

"NO ONE WHO PUTS his hand to the plow and looks back is fit for the kingdom of God." These are startling words from Jesus. "No one who puts his hand to the plow and looks back is fit for the kingdom of God." They do at least raise the possibility that someone may *not* look back and thus may *be* fit for the kingdom of God. We shall return to that possibility in a moment. But for now we need to realize that these words come at the end of a series of problematic engagements with three would-be followers. Taken together, these three problematic engagements raise the question for us, how shall we follow Jesus Christ? Wholeheartedly? Or halfheartedly? Fervently? Or distractedly? Eagerly? Or with hand to the plow and looking back? How shall we follow?

"No one who puts his hand to the plow and looks back is fit for the kingdom of God." These words always remind me of how I learned to plow a straight row when I was a little boy. We would go to my grandmother Goodloe's house on her farm, which was named Twin Trees, in La Vergne, Tennessee, outside of Nashville. Out the back door of her house, to the left, off the porch, across the yard, past the limestone slab table where we always made ice cream, past the cherry trees on the right, and through the gate—there was her garden. And just inside the gate, to the right, under a piece of metal roof, were her ancient garden tools: a hoe and a rake and a plow. The plow had two long, weather-beaten wooden handles. Up front it had a metal wheel that wobbled so badly I never could figure out how it worked at all. And just behind that was a single metal blade, the size of my hand, to open the ground for seed.

My father must have already plowed the garden with the little Ford tractor and run the disk over it, though I cannot now remember him doing that. I would start at one end of the large garden, looking down intently at the ground before me, and the more slowly and carefully I walked and pushed, the worse the loose wheel wobbled, and the more I would lead the blade on a crooked and winding path. Then after a while of doing this, I would look back over my shoulder to survey the results or the damages, and of course that only made matters worse, because I would veer farther off to the left or the right, depending on which shoulder I looked over. It must have been a sight to behold.

My father, not wanting the rows to be so crooked as to be impossible to cultivate later, would have to take the plow in his own hands and redo them. He would step out confidently and quickly, and he made a straight row every time. And in so doing, he taught me not to look at the ground in front of me so intently that I saw nothing else. He especially taught me not to look back over my shoulder while I was trying to go forward. And best of all, he taught me to look at a distant target—a fence post at the far end of the garden or even a tree in the woods beyond the garden—and having set my sights on that target to walk straight toward it, confidently pushing the plow along at the same time, and at least usually creating an acceptably straight furrow.

"No one who puts his hand to the plow and looks back is fit for the kingdom of God." What my father taught me about using that rickety old plow applies to a lot of situations in life, and it especially helps me to understand these words of Jesus Christ to us yet today. If we look down and become absorbed and swamped in the immediate details of the present, we will be hopelessly lost. If we look back and remain fascinated by, attached to, and committed to the past, in either its glories or its abysmal failures, we will be worse than worthless. Only as we lift our eyes to the horizon before us and set our sights firmly on the distant goal of the kingdom of God shall we be able to travel through the day and through our lives on the commanded, straight, and narrow path toward that kingdom. Of course, we rejoice that even today our heavenly Father can and does straighten the crooked paths of our lives. We could not live without that help. And yet we also know that the reason God forgives, teaches, and guides us is not to encourage us to continue to wander and so to mess up the garden even more, but is instead to point us in the right direction, to set us on the right path, and so to start us surely on the way of discipleship, faith, and obedience. How shall we follow?

Now, in order better to understand this teaching of Christ for us as his disciples, let us first look at what he accomplished in his own life and death and so at the example he gave with his own life and death. As today's reading from the Gospel according to Luke begins, the time had grown near for Jesus to be crucified. The climax of his obedience, the height of his absolute trust in and dependence upon God, would come at the moment of a painful, shameful, and apparently God-forsaken death on a cross outside Jerusalem. At that moment he did *not* hate those who persecuted him, but instead he continued loving them until the end. At that moment he did *not* ask to escape death miraculously, but continued to trust that God was greater than death. At that moment he did *not* seek to save himself, but continued to obey God. It was that terrible moment that Jesus anticipated and accepted in today's reading, when he made up his mind and "set his face to go to Jerusalem."

Nothing would distract him now. Nothing would turn him aside. Nothing would hold him back. Jesus marched boldly to Jerusalem and so to his death for our sake, yours and mine. What we see here is the determination of God, in the absolute commitment of Jesus Christ, to save us at any cost. And the cost was supreme. The cost was the life of the Son of God. And yet, he paid it willingly. This is the good news, this is the gospel in today's reading: that God in Jesus Christ is absolutely determined to do what it takes to win us back to God. We who have been lost are found. We who have been dead are alive again. We who have wandered have been regathered. We who were destitute have been restored. Nothing is going to stop, or stand in the way of, our Lord and Savior. How shall we follow?

It is in this context of Christ's commitment and determination that three would-be followers appear on the scene, surely remembered as warnings to would-be followers today. One (1) volunteers too enthusiastically, apparently without any anticipation or realistic knowledge of the difficulties and sacrifices involved. Jesus said to him, "Foxes have holes, and birds of the air have nests, but the Son of Man has nowhere to lay his head." How he could have missed this, when Jesus was on his way to Jerusalem to die, is hard to understand, except when we remember that we too started out as enthusiastic Christians, maybe when we were young and before life had shoved us around more than a little, and when we remember that we have backed away from some of the difficult demands placed before us: faith and faithfulness, trust and obedience, worship, prayer, tithing, ministry, mission, evangelism, witnessing, sharing the good news of Jesus Christ with those about us, feeding the hungry, clothing the naked, visiting the lonely, the sick, and those in prison, and on and on and on. It is harder than we thought when we first started. But if the Son of God was crucified, why should we who would follow him expect any better?

A second (2) would-be follower actually represents the only occasion, so far as we know, that Jesus called someone, saying, "Follow me," and that person did *not* follow him. In every other instance, we are clearly told that Christ's very call to someone to be his disciple effectively created that person as a new disciple. We are not told that here. This poor fellow seems to have a good excuse: "Lord, let me first go and bury my father." But Jesus offers him a strange answer: "Leave the dead to bury their own dead. But as for you, go and proclaim the kingdom of God." That is, the call of God has first claim upon us, and any other conflicting claims, even if good in and of themselves, are to be set aside.

A third (3) would-be follower volunteers to follow Jesus, but asks first to go home and say farewell to his family. We are not told what the first, second, or even this third would-be follower did, but the way this one disqualifies himself strongly suggests that none of the three followed Jesus on his way to Jerusalem. For it is to this suggestion of settling things with one's family before following Christ that Jesus responded with the hard teaching, "No one who puts his hand to the plow and looks back is fit for the kingdom of God." This does not mean that family is unimportant. But it does mean that family is not absolute. Family is not to be worshiped. Simply put, family does not save us. Undue and inappropriate love of family can thwart our faith and block our relationship with God. These are hard and startling teachings, perhaps especially so here in Virginia, where we know the importance of family. But these hard teachings show us, by sharp contrasts, the seriousness of the claims that God makes upon us and the importance of our faith, commitment, and obedience. Jesus "set his face to go to Jerusalem," and he calls on us to set our face toward the kingdom of God. If we do not do so, we shall never get there. How shall we follow?

How does all of this gospel teaching apply to our life together here and now as Mattoax and Pine Grove Presbyterian Churches? First of all (1), and most obviously, we rejoice in and give thanks to God for God's determination in Jesus Christ to save us, to reclaim us, and to regather us as God's own, whatever the cost. This is our life. This is our salvation. This is our one sure and strong hope for the future. We praise and thank God for the life, death, and resurrection of Jesus Christ, for all that Christ has done, is doing, and will do for us. We are a community of worship, a people of praise, a gathering of givers of thanks. One of the names for the Lord's Supper is Eucharist, which means to give thanks. This is what we do first: acknowledge and receive what God has done for us that we could not do for ourselves.

Second (2), immediately and inseparably from the first, we set our sights on the distant goal of the kingdom of God. We lift our eyes beyond the wobbly wheel at the end of the old plow, beyond the fencepost at the far end of the garden, even beyond the tree in the woods past the end of the garden, all the way to that mountain on the horizon, and we walk, live, and work straight toward it all the days of our lives. This is not easy. It is not automatic. We do not always live up to it. But this is what we are called to do. We are called to be faithful followers of our Lord and Savior Jesus Christ.

What could prevent us from fulfilling this? One easy mistake to make is to get so involved in the issue and the emotion of the moment, whatever that might be, that we lose sight of the distant goal of the kingdom of God and become overwhelmed by the present, with its harsh slavery to immediate goals and problems. There is always something that can be stirred up to distract us from faithfulness, discipleship and mission. That is definitely a recipe for going in circles, wasting time and energy, and accomplishing nothing. Let us strive to avoid it.

Perhaps the greatest temptation for any church, and the worst thing to do, is to look back over the shoulder to our past. That is deadly for Christian discipleship. I ran across a book one time that posed some interesting questions for churches: Do we believe that some of our best years in mission are before us? Or, do we believe that our best years as a church are behind us? It is an extremely important matter of attitude and perspective. There are voices in every congregation that would tell us that the entire mission of the church is to preserve what has always been. But we need at the very least to raise the question as to whether those voices serve us well. Do they not fairly obviously run the risk of looking backward instead of forward? Do they not represent a clear and present danger to the life and faithfulness of the Christian church?

I invite and urge us all instead to set our sights on the distant goal of the future kingdom of God, that mountain on the horizon ahead of us, and to walk, to live, and to work straight toward it all the days of our lives. That is where our faithfulness and obedience lie. The past is not our goal. The past is prelude to the future. God placed Mattoax and Pine Grove Presbyterian Churches here many years ago, not only to accomplish the mission that now has already been completed, not only to gather and minister to this community that is now already here, but also and especially to have us in place, trained, and ready to go for the great and future mission that is yet ahead of us. There are more people living within a ten-mile radius of these churches than we can count or even imagine. There are more people who need to hear the good news about God, the gospel of Jesus Christ, the good words of redemption, forgiveness, and release, than we have ever met before. And the challenge before us will not be to maintain without change the Mattoax and Pine Grove of the past, but to build upon that past as foundation and to grow into something new and different from what we have ever been before: the Mattoax and Pine Grove of the future.

How shall we follow? We have already put our hand to the plow. We have already started down this row. Now is not the time to look back! Now is not the time for Jesus to declare us unfit for the kingdom of God! We want to push ahead to the distant goal. Jesus calls us to be as single-minded, devoted, determined, and committed as he is. Mattoax and Pine Grove can have a vast and far reaching ministry to this community, a ministry that is Christ centered and biblically based. We can have simple, sturdy worship services, reading and preaching the word of God, singing his praises, offering our prayers and our selves, gathering people from this community and the surrounding counties and cities, all to the glory of God. We can have educational programs for children, youth, and adults, and multiple fellowship groups organized around different interests. We can have missions of caring, compassion, and justice, of which we have not yet dreamed but for which some day soon we shall perceive the need. We will need to move beyond the point where only a few families see tithing (tithing means giving 10 percent of one's income to the church) even as an idealistic goal to the point where the vast majority of families see tithing as a realistic starting point and in fact move out in faith way beyond tithing in their giving. That is the only way to go for a community of people who worship the Christ who gave his very life for us. How shall we follow?

None of this will be easy. It will take the best we have, and then some—a lot. But how can we do any less? The kingdom of God is not for shallow or ill-prepared enthusiasts. It is not for those of divided loyalties. It is not for the hesitant or the backward looking. It is not for the faint of heart. Jesus "set his face to go to Jerusalem" to die for us. And then he said to those who would follow him, to us who would bear his name as Christians, "No one who puts his hand to the plow and looks back is fit for the kingdom of God."

To God be the glory forever and ever! Amen.

30

Who Hears You?

LUKE 10:1–24; NUMBERS 11:16–30

"THE ONE WHO HEARS you hears me, and the one who rejects you rejects me, and the one who rejects me rejects him who sent me." These strange words stand at the end of the commission that Jesus gave to the "seventy-two others," that larger circle of disciples reaching beyond the inner circle of twelve disciples with whom we are more familiar, the "seventy-two others" whom Jesus "appointed" and "sent on ahead of him, two by two, into every town and place where he himself was about to go." These strange words contain (1) the very gospel of Jesus Christ, valid then and now, words of truth and life for them and so for us. We rejoice to hear that again. We shall explore that first. At the same time, these strange words pose (2) a tremendous question, both then and now, as to who does and who does not hear the gospel of Jesus Christ. We shall turn to that second.

"The one who hears you hears me, and the one who rejects you rejects me, and the one who rejects me rejects him who sent me." Here is (1) the good news of Jesus Christ: God has not abandoned us. God has not deserted us. God has not remained silent or hidden. God is not a puzzle or a riddle. God is not inaccessible. God has not left us behind. Instead, God has drawn near to us and come to us in the person, work, life, death, resurrection, and words of Jesus Christ. God is in Christ. God has come to us in Christ. God makes himself known in Christ. God draws us to himself in Christ. God reclaims us as his own in Christ. To know Christ is to know God. To hear the word of Christ is to hear the word of God. To love Christ is to love God. The two are one and the same.

This is good news beyond our wildest imagining. Kings and nobles have sought such knowledge. Wise men have sought such wisdom. Prophets have sought such surety. Mystics have sought such vision. And now it has been given to us. It has been given to us that God Almighty, Creator of the universe, Ruler of the world and all that is in it, Sustainer of our lives, Judge of all who are and ever will be, has come to us in Jesus Christ, both to be with us and also to be for us. What more could we ask? In him our alienation has been overcome, our gone-wrongness has been set right, our sin has been forgiven, our lives have been turned around, our deepest wound has been healed, our brokenness has been made whole, and our very death has been turned into life. Thanks be to God!

Think together with me about what this means, line by line. The first line (A) reads, "The one who hears you hears me." The one who hears the proclamation of Jesus Christ yet today hears the very word and voice of Jesus Christ himself. The gospel of Jesus Christ is communicated in the preaching of the gospel of Jesus Christ. The good news of Jesus Christ is communicated in the preaching of the gospel of Jesus Christ. The person of Jesus Christ is communicated in the preaching of the gospel of Jesus Christ. The presence of Jesus Christ is communicated in the preaching of the gospel of Jesus Christ. The reality of Jesus Christ is communicated in the preaching of the gospel of Jesus Christ. The work of Jesus Christ is communicated in the preaching of the gospel of Jesus Christ. The love of Jesus Christ is communicated in the preaching of the gospel of Jesus Christ. The forgiveness of Jesus Christ is communicated in the preaching of the gospel of Jesus Christ. The glory of Jesus Christ is communicated in the preaching of the gospel of Jesus Christ. "The one who hears you hears me." Do you realize what that means for the importance of our worship together, the importance of my preparation, and the importance of our attendance, participation, and hearing? Its value is incalculable. And it is promised to us.

The second line (B) reads, "the one who rejects you rejects me." Jesus here shows us the importance of what we have just said by revealing the significance of its opposite. The one who refuses to hear the proclamation of Jesus Christ refuses to hear the very word and voice of Jesus Christ himself. The gospel of Jesus Christ is rejected in rejecting the preaching of the gospel of Jesus Christ. The good news of Jesus Christ is rejected in rejecting the preaching of the gospel of Jesus Christ. The person of Jesus Christ is rejected in rejecting the preaching of the gospel of Jesus Christ. The presence of Jesus Christ is rejected in rejecting the preaching of the gospel of Jesus Christ. The reality of Jesus Christ is rejected in rejecting the preaching of the gospel of Jesus Christ. The work of Jesus Christ is rejected in rejecting the preaching of the gospel of Jesus Christ. The love of Jesus Christ is rejected in rejecting the preaching of the gospel of Jesus Christ. The forgiveness of Jesus Christ is rejected in rejecting the preaching of the gospel of Jesus Christ. The glory of Jesus Christ is rejected in rejecting the preaching of the gospel of Jesus Christ. "The one who rejects you rejects me." Do you realize what that means for the importance of our worship together, the importance of my preparation, and the importance of our attendance, participation, and hearing? Again, its value is incalculable.

Now, on the outside chance that even this strengthened point has been missed, Jesus takes it up to a higher level in the third line (C): "The one who rejects me rejects him who sent me." In that God himself is present with us and for us in Jesus Christ, the rejection of Jesus Christ constitutes the very rejection of God himself. The rejection of Jesus Christ is the rejection of God Almighty. The rejection of Jesus Christ is the rejection of the Creator of the universe. The rejection of Jesus Christ is the rejection of the Ruler of the world and of all that is in it. The rejection of Jesus Christ is the rejection of the Sustainer of our lives. The rejection of Jesus Christ is the rejection of the Judge of all who are and ever will be. In such rejection of God our alienation would reign supreme, our gone-wrongness would continue its course, our sin would not be forgiven, our lives would not be turned around, our deepest wound would be left unhealed, our brokenness would be increased, and any remaining life would be turned into death.

We must be entirely clear about this. The rejection of Jesus Christ in and of itself constitutes nothing less than, and nothing other than, the very rejection of God himself. "All things have been handed over to me by my Father, and no one knows who the Son is except the Father, or who the Father is except the Son and anyone to whom the Son chooses to reveal him." It is a matter of revelation. There is no mention here of another way to God. Any other way is ruled out. This is not fun and games. This is deadly serious business. This is real. This is life and death. "Whenever you enter a town and they do not receive you, go into its streets and say, 'Even the dust of your town that clings to our feet we wipe off against you. Nevertheless know this, that the kingdom of God has come near.' I tell you, it will be more bearable on that day for Sodom than for that town." That is to say, even the sin of the Sodomites, as great as it was, and as explicitly condemned as it is here, was not as great as the sin of rejecting the preaching of the gospel, rejecting the gospel, rejecting God's Christ, and so rejecting God Almighty himself. Thus is the gospel of Jesus Christ both positively stated in terms of the real presence of God in Christ, in the gospel, and in the preaching of the gospel, and also accentuated by the specification of the negative consequences.

Now for (2) the implied question: "The one who hears you hears me, and the one who rejects you rejects me, and the one who rejects me rejects him who sent me." These strange words convey to us the very gospel of Jesus Christ, as much so today as two thousand years ago. At the same time, these strange words pose a tremendous question as to who does and who does not hear the gospel of Jesus Christ, still now as well as then. This question continues to have implications for us as individuals, for us as the church, and for the world in which we live. Here it is: In that we who would be followers of Jesus Christ are sent forth to live and share the gospel, who hears us? Who hears you? Who listens to you? We live in a world intent upon finding its own way, apart from any guidance by God. We live in a society that prides itself on its secularism, as if that were some great wisdom. So the question is raised for those of us who would follow Jesus Christ, who hears us? Who hears you? Who listens to you? These questions continue to have implications for us as individuals, for us as the church, and for the world in which we live.

Let me make some observations and suggestions in this regard. It is (A) likely the case for most of us that those of us here in church today as adults were brought to church by our parents. This is not the case for all of us, and I will get to that in a moment, but it is likely the case for most of us. That is to say it is most likely that we heard the gospel of the love of God in Jesus Christ from our parents, who brought us to church. On the one hand, this becomes an occasion for gratitude. The most important thing in the world our mothers and fathers could give us is the good news of Jesus Christ. On the other hand, this becomes an occasion for responsibility and an opportunity for obedience. The most important thing in the world that we can give our children is the good news of Jesus Christ. This is one group of people who hear us. This is one group of people who listen to us. This is one group of people for whom we have special responsibility, the highest responsibility, and this is one group of people whom we most especially do not want to fail.

If you are not here in church today because of your parents, or if you have come back to church after some long absence, it is (B) likely that you are here because some other family member, or perhaps a friend or neighbor, invited you and brought you to church. That is to say, someone whom you know and respect is probably responsible for speaking a word to you that helped to bring you here today. Again, on the one hand, this becomes an occasion for gratitude. The single most important thing in the world that our relatives, friends, and neighbors could give us is the good news of Jesus Christ. And on the other hand, this becomes an occasion for responsibility and an opportunity for obedience. The single most important thing in the world that we can give our relatives, friends, and neighbors is the good news of Jesus Christ. This is another group of people who hear us. This is another group of people who listen to us. This is, therefore, another group of people for whom we have special responsibility. Who hears us? Who hears you? Who listens to you? The people whom you already know are the ones most likely to hear you. The people whom you already know are the ones most likely to listen to you. The people whom you already know are the ones most likely to respond positively to your invitation to church. There may not be anyone else here who knows the people whom you know. It is up to you to speak a good word for these people to hear. There are people in the village, people in Amelia County, people in Powhatan County, people in Chesterfield County, people in Richmond and beyond, who need to hear the gospel of Jesus Christ. And they need to hear it from us. These two congregations include a very small percentage of the people living within a five-mile radius of the churches. I submit to you that God put Mattoax and Pine Grove Presbyterian Churches here for us to tell the other 99 percent of those people the gospel of Jesus Christ, to share with them the forgiveness of sin, and to love them with the love of God.

Beyond this, there are (C) people around the world who have heard the good word about Jesus Christ because of the mission work of the Christian church. There are people around the world whom you and I have never met who know the gospel of Jesus Christ today because of the mission work of the Christian church. If you think about it, all of us here today are children of a church started by missionaries. The church did not start in the United States. The church did not start in Europe. The church started closer to that part of the world served by the early seventy-two missionaries of Jesus Christ about whom we have read today. All of us here today are children of a church started by missionaries. Again, on the one hand, this becomes an occasion for gratitude. We are grateful to God for the missionaries of times past who brought to us the good news of Jesus Christ. And on the other hand, this becomes an occasion for responsibility and an opportunity for obedience. The single most important thing in all the world that we can give to all the world is the good news of Jesus Christ. If we cannot go as missionaries ourselves, we can at least support the mission of the church through our tithing, giving ten percent of our income to the work of the church. There are people around the world needing to hear, wanting to hear, and waiting to hear a good word about God. "The harvest is plentiful, but the laborers are few. Therefore pray earnestly to the Lord of the harvest to send out laborers into his harvest." Let us not fail in this opportunity and responsibility.

It is significant that Jesus gave this commission to his second string, that larger circle of disciples. We do not even know their names. These were not the twelve starters. But even this B-team received the promise and the gospel inherent in this commission. It was not limited to the elite. And even this B-team understood the importance of the question for their mission. Consider the joyous response of Jesus himself to their first report back to him of their ministry: "I saw Satan fall like lightning from heaven." So Jesus commissions even you and me, even the church yet today, even Mattoax and Pine Grove, sending us out into the world—his world—and saying to us, "The one who hears you hears me, and the one who rejects you rejects me, and the one who rejects me rejects him who sent me."

To God be the glory forever and ever! Amen.

31

What Shall I Do?

LUKE 10:25–42; DEUTERONOMY 6:4–9; LEVITICUS 19:1–2, 17–18

"TEACHER, WHAT SHALL I do to inherit eternal life?" Therein lies the question. "What shall I do to inherit eternal life?" The lawyer's question is recorded here not so much as a lesson in ancient history as an encouragement for you and me today to take it up as our very own. The questions we ask have a great deal to do with the answers we get. This question may be the most important one of our lives. There are other questions: What shall we wear? What shall we eat? What shall we drink? Where shall we be this time next year? These are important in their own way. But none is as important as this question: "What shall I do to inherit eternal life?" We would do well to make this question our very own. Today's reading gives two answers to this question. One is terrifying. The other is full of grace and mercy. We shall get to those answers in a moment. For now, let us consider the question itself.

I.

"What shall I do to inherit eternal life?" Part (A) of the good news of today's reading, embedded in this very question, is that there is in fact eternal life for us. There is life beyond this life. There is life beyond death. There is life for us beyond the ravages of time, decay, decline, disease, and death. There is another world beyond this one, where wrongs of this world are righted, where the incompletenesses are made whole, and where the mysteries are clarified. In fact, it is only in the hope of that world that the moral ambiguities of this world can be tolerated, that insults can be borne, and that forgiveness can be sought. It is only in the hope of that world that we can dare to believe that the one who made us for himself shall one day regather us all to himself. So the gospel of Jesus Christ affirms that there is eternal life, that God does hold us dear, and that he has plans and purposes for us that go far beyond this life and this world. Thanks be to God!

Some would think that such otherworldly faith diminishes this life. They reason that if the next life is held to be so wonderful, then this one must be reduced to insignificance and therefore be unimportant. But that is wrong. Setting this brief life within the context of eternal life shows just how important this life is. What we do here matters forever. The relationships we form here are part of eternity. The growth in maturity and character we accomplish here will be with us forever. So the hope of eternal life does not diminish this temporal life. In fact, it provides the only possible context for its true importance. To see this from the other way around, if there were no hope for eternal life, it really would not matter what we do here. We could hate, steal, lie, and cheat with impunity. We could do whatever we pleased precisely because there would be no long-term consequences. So let us be clear that the hope for eternal life does not at all diminish this temporal life. Instead, quite the opposite: only the hope for eternal life elevates this temporal life to its true importance.

"What shall I do to inherit eternal life?" The urgency (B) of today's reading, also embedded in this very question, is the realization that there is also the opposite to eternal life. That is to say, there is also eternal death. There is beyond this life and death an everlasting death, an eternal separation from God, where there is weeping and gnashing of teeth. So the inheritance of eternal life is not automatic. The very question of what to do to inherit eternal life would make no sense apart from this realization that it is entirely possible to go the other direction. The gospel of Jesus Christ acknowledges this terrible, negative possibility that human life here may reach its end continuing in willful alienation from God and that such a horrible end may also be the eternal disposition of the self. Surely we want to do everything we can to avoid that. Indeed, we would do well to use this life we have been given here to seek that which leads to the life beyond and not to follow that which leads to eternal death. So the lawyer's concern was pertinent. His question was appropriate. There are other questions: What shall we wear? What shall we eat? What shall we drink? Where shall we be this time next year? These are important in their own way. But none is nearly as important or as urgent as this question: "What shall I do to inherit eternal life?" We would do well to make this question our very own.

II.

So, given the question of how to inherit eternal life, and given both the good news that the question contains and the urgent warning to which it alludes, what is the answer, or what are the answers? First (A), Jesus said to the lawyer, "What is written in the Law? How do you read it?" And the lawyer answered, "You shall love the Lord your God with all your heart and with all your soul and with all your strength and with all your mind, and your neighbor as yourself." And Jesus said to him, "You have answered correctly; do this, and you will live." This first answer is the one that terrifies me: "Do this, and you will live." Obey the law of God, and you will live forever. Obey the Ten Commandments, and you will have eternal life. Do perfectly everything that God says, and you will have eternal life. This answer is, of course, entirely correct. Jesus spoke no lie. And we always want to acknowledge that behind the commandments to love God and neighbor stands the always prior good news that God has already loved us, apart from which good news the commandments make no sense. And yet, by itself this answer terrifies me. This answer brings me low, because I know that already I have not obeyed God, and I hear the door to life closing. I know that I have not obeyed the law in the past, and I realize that I cannot obey the law in the present or in the future, so I know that I cannot earn eternal life. Yes, one person obeyed the law perfectly—Jesus Christ our Lord and Savior, and we shall return to that in a moment—but none of the rest of us can do that. So this entirely correct answer, that obedience leads to life and that perfect obedience leads to eternal life, by itself leaves me cold and scared. It is no comfort at all.

There is a second answer (B), and it is full of grace and mercy. The second answer comes in what appears to be the next story, or in what I had always taken to be the next story, but which I now think it is part of the same story because it gives another answer to the same question. "What shall I do to inherit eternal life?" "Martha, Martha, you are anxious and troubled about many things, but one thing is necessary. Mary has chosen the good portion, which will not be taken away from her." "What shall I do to inherit eternal life?" "One thing is necessary." What did Mary do? Mary "sat at the Lord's feet and listened to his teaching." Ah! There is the answer. Mary listened to the gospel of Jesus Christ. That is the one thing necessary. That is the good portion to be chosen. That will not be taken away, ever, which means it leads to eternal life. Thanks be to God!

Mary "sat at the Lord's feet and listened to his teaching." And that is exactly what we are doing today. I am not the one who teaches. It is the Lord who teaches through me. Otherwise, what I say would be worth nothing. Let me say this as clearly as possible: If you do not hear the voice of Jesus in my words, you need to find a preacher in whose words you do hear his voice. But if you do hear the voice of Jesus in my words, or in any preacher's words, you have to realize that what is being preached is the very word of God. There is not a preacher in the world who is smart enough on his or her own to have anything to say to you that is worth hearing. The word of God alone is what we need to hear. "One thing is necessary."

That, by the way, is what Pentecost is all about: God sent his Holy Spirit to work in and through the preachers of the gospel so that their words would be his words; and God sent his Holy Spirit to work in and through the hearts of the hearers so that hearing they might believe, and believing they might be saved. That is what the Holy Spirit does: communicate God's word to us and work saving faith within us. Again, Mary listened to the gospel of Jesus Christ. And, by the grace of God and the power of the Holy Spirit, that is what we are doing yet today, for the stumbling words I offer are graciously and miraculously changed into the one thing that is necessary, the good portion that will not be taken away, ever. And so in hearing the gospel we inherit eternal life.

There are other ways of talking about this. You would be familiar with the language if I were to say, "You shall not be saved through works of the law." Well, we could be if we could and would obey the law, but, as a matter of fact, neither you nor I shall be saved through our works of the law. You would also be familiar with the language if I were to say, "You shall be saved by grace through faith." Now, that is the gospel, and that is our only hope. The grace of God, enacted particularly in the life, death, and resurrection of Jesus Christ and poured out upon us in the preaching of the gospel, is what saves us.

In a way, this gets us back to the first answer, that obedience leads to life, except that here we realize that it is Jesus Christ's perfect obedience that has been credited to our account. That is sheer, undeserved grace. So the cross fulfills the first answer. And we receive this grace of God through faith, through hearing the gospel of grace, through believing the gospel of grace, through trusting the gospel of grace, and through relying upon the gospel of grace. Such faith is not another work on our part. Faith is the special knowledge—an acknowledgment—that in Jesus Christ God has done for us the work we could not do for ourselves. We would continue to be lost if we harbored any hope of saving ourselves. But we are saved precisely in the realization that God alone has saved us.

So this good news is the second answer to the question. A lawyer asked, "Teacher, what shall I do to inherit eternal life?" The first answer was: "Obey the law, and you shall live." That is terrifying in and of itself. But the second answer is: "Hear and believe the gospel of Jesus Christ, and you shall live forever." That is wonderful. That is full of joy and life. That is something we are doing right now, right here, hearing and believing the gospel, rejoicing in the goodness of God, and receiving the blessing of Jesus Christ, all by the work of the Holy Spirit. Thus eternal life begins.

III.

What now? What shall we do? How shall we live? What about the rest of this life before we enter into the fullness of the next life? Having heard the gospel, how shall we live the Christian life? At this point, it seems, it would helpful to return to what Jesus and the lawyer had to say to each other. After that absolutely brilliant answer, summing up the entire Old Testament in one sentence—love God and neighbor—the lawyer realized that he was in trouble, and he began to backpedal and to seek a way out. "Who is my neighbor?" The point was, of course, "Who is *not* my neighbor?" That is, "From whom may I legally withhold love?" That was not very becoming. But the answer that Jesus gave him sets a wonderful standard for living the Christian life:

> "A man was going down from Jerusalem to Jericho, and he fell among robbers,
> who stripped him and beat him and departed, leaving him half dead. Now by

chance a priest was going down that road, and when he saw him he passed by on the other side. So likewise a Levite, when he came to the place and saw him, passed by on the other side. But a Samaritan, as he journeyed, came to where he was, and when he saw him, he had compassion. He went to him and bound up his wounds, pouring on oil and wine. Then he set him on his own animal and brought him to an inn and took care of him. And the next day he took out two denarii and gave them to the innkeeper, saying, 'Take care of him, and whatever more you spend, I will repay you when I come back.' Which of these three, do you think, proved to be a neighbor to the man who fell among the robbers?" The lawyer said, "The one who showed him mercy." And Jesus said to him, "You go, and do likewise."

Jesus did not say, this time, "Do this, and you will live." He said, instead, "You go, and do likewise." That is to say, doing this does not earn eternal life. However, this is the kind of life that our Lord wills for us to live, so it is of special significance to those of us who have heard and believed the gospel. It is an expression of gratitude and obedience. It is not up to us to define who is and who is not our neighbor. It is, instead, up to us to be a neighbor, to see the needy, to have compassion, to bind up wounds, and to take care of those beaten down by the world. There is nothing specifically religious about such activity. The religious part of life is hearing the gospel in the context of praising and worshiping God. That is what we are doing here and now. But the life of compassion out there in the world is the direct result of the religious part of life in here. The Christian life there is the fruit of the gospel here and the consequence of grace here. It is only because we learn here of the always-prior love of God for us in Jesus Christ that we are made able to love God and to love neighbor there.

That is to say again, the grace of God to us elicits from us both our gratitude to God, which we express in worship here and work beyond here, and also in our graciousness toward each other, which we model here and live in the Christian life beyond here. It is this graciousness, this life of compassion, which this parable seeks to elicit from us. Are we ready to do this, individually and as a church? We do this through our tithes and alms. We do this through feeding the hungry, including through our Five-Cents-per-Meal offering. We do this through supporting the mission of the church around the world. "Which . . . proved to be a neighbor?" "The one who showed him mercy." "You go, and do likewise." That is how to live the Christian life. God help us!

Of course, prior to living the Christian life, it is necessary to become a Christian, to become a believer, so that brings us back to the beginning: "Teacher, what shall I do to inherit eternal life?" Therein lies the question, and it is indeed our question yet today. I still like the second answer the best by far: "One thing is necessary. Mary has chosen the good portion, which will not be taken away from her." What did Mary do? Mary "sat at the Lord's feet and listened to his teaching." Shall we do the same?

To God be the glory forever and ever! Amen.

32

How Much More!

LUKE 11:1–13; EZEKIEL 36:22–32

"IF YOU THEN, WHO are evil, know how to give good gifts to your children, how much more will the heavenly Father give the Holy Spirit to those who ask him!" "How much more will the heavenly Father give the Holy Spirit to those who ask him!" "How much more!" By this comparison and exclamation Jesus Christ communicates to all of us yet today the overflowing grace and goodness of God Almighty. First (1), Jesus tells us that God is our heavenly Father. Even a little child knows his or her father and can begin to realize how close God is. Second, (2) Jesus tells us that God is the Giver of all good gifts. Even a little child appreciates good gifts and can begin to know whence they come. Third (3), Jesus tells us that the Holy Spirit is the greatest gift. Even a little child can receive the Holy Spirit and can begin to rejoice in the goodness of God. And the very telling of this good news is nothing other than the giving of his grace to you and to me, young and old, male and female, rich and poor, whatever our race may be. So come today and hear again the words that give us life, the words that give us hope, the words that give us faith, comfort, and courage. Come and hear the gospel of Jesus Christ.

"If you then, who are evil, know how to give good gifts to your children, how much more will the heavenly Father give the Holy Spirit to those who ask him!" With these words, the first thing (1) that Jesus tells us is that God is our heavenly Father. God Almighty, the Creator of the universe and all that is in it, the Sustainer of all life, the Judge of all sin, the Redeemer of the elect, and the God and Father of Jesus Christ, is also the heavenly Father of the hearers of Jesus Christ, the heavenly Father to whom we are to pray, the heavenly Father from whom we receive good gifts, and the heavenly Father who gives us the Holy Spirit. This may seem simple and familiar to us, but it is also profound and radical. For instance, it says that God is one: "the heavenly Father." Some have thought that there were two heavenly Fathers, one good and one evil, being the source of good and evil people in the world. Others have thought there were thousands of gods, for thousands of causes, all competing for our hearts, minds, souls, and allegiances. But it is the witness of Jesus Christ that there is one God with whom we have to do, and that God is our Father.

Not only is God one, but also God the Father is knowable and accessible. Others have thought that God was the great unknown. Others have thought that God was distant, hidden, and absent. But this familial language used by Jesus Christ shows us that God the Father has drawn near to us in him and that God has made himself known to us in him. God the Father makes himself known to us in and through Jesus Christ his Son. This is not empty language. This is not abstract language. This is language shown to be true and real in the life, death, and resurrection of Jesus Christ. Jesus did not put a name on something he did not know. Instead, he named for us the One whom he knew intimately, the One from whom he came and to whom he went, the One to whom he prayed constantly. And, by identifying God as our Father, he opens heaven for us and opens us to heaven. He reveals that God is our heavenly Father and teaches us that we are his children. This is who God is, and this is who we are, and it is a great joy in our lives to know and to acknowledge God as our Father.

Not only is God one, and not only is God the Father knowable and accessible, but also we are taught even to address God as Father. The exclamation we have quoted is not the only basis for this. It is also included explicitly in the teachings of Jesus Christ. "Jesus was praying in a certain place, and when he finished, one of his disciples said to him, 'Lord, teach us to pray, as John taught his disciples.' And he said to them, 'When you pray, say: "Father, hallowed be your name."'" "When you pray, say: 'Father.'" It is that simple. Of all the possible titles—Lord God Almighty, Creator of heaven and earth, God of Abraham, God of Isaac, God of Jacob, God of Moses, God of the prophets, God of the apostles—the one we are taught to use, the one we are permitted to use, indeed, the one we are commanded to use, is "Father." None other suffices. None other captures the joy, the wonder, and the awe. None other thus opens our hearts to the heart of the Father.

We have been thinking about this from the perspective of a child. Dr. John A. Redhead, one-time pastor of First Presbyterian Church, Greensboro, North Carolina, preaching from this passage more than fifty years ago, realized from his own experience as a father to his children—including the love that he had for them and also the impossibility of his turning them away—that in the very word "Father" we have a charter that guarantees God's benevolence and that bids us come before his throne to make our wants and wishes known.[1] That is to say, from what we know about fatherly love for children, the very permission we have from Christ to address God as Father

---

1. Redhead, *Learning to Have Faith*, 39–45.

gives us joy and confidence in his love so that we can approach God in prayer as his children. What a comfort this is!

Let me say again that of all the possible titles for God, the one we are taught to use, the one we are permitted to use, indeed the one we are commanded to use, is "Father." This is especially significant today because some people are uncomfortable with this word, some people are reluctant to use this word, some people refuse to use this word, and some people even condemn those who do use this word. That is to say, there are congregations that do not recite the Apostles' Creed, do not pray the Lord's Prayer, and do not use the words of baptism all to avoid speaking this dreaded name of "Father." Such stubbornness and reticence is incomprehensible. That is not inclusive. That is not tolerant. That is not progressive. That is not intelligent. That is, instead, simply disobedient, stupid, arrogant, and, worst of all, ungrateful. We need to be entirely clear about this.

The church did not invent the language of "Father." It comes straight from Jesus Christ. It is not within our authority to abandon it. To refuse to use the word Father is to disavow this explicit teaching of our Lord. To refuse to use the word Father is to presume explicitly to know better than Jesus how to address God and to know better than Jesus and how to pray. That is frightening! To refuse to use the word Father is to forfeit the most wonderful access we have been given to our Father in heaven. There is hope for unbelief. The unbeliever may yet be converted. But there is no hope for sheer stupidity. Today's service, as every Sunday service here, includes not only the Creed and the Prayer but also the Gloria and the doxology, which praise God by name as "Father." We do not do this to be stubborn or backwards. We do this to be obedient and faithful. Do you not see how wonderful this permission is? Jesus tells us that God is our heavenly Father. Even a little child knows his or her father and can begin to realize how close God is.

"If you then, who are evil, know how to give good gifts to your children, how much more will the heavenly Father give the Holy Spirit to those who ask him!" With these words, the second thing (2)that Jesus tells us is that God the Father is the Giver of all good gifts. "What father among you, if his son asks for a fish, will instead of a fish give him a serpent; or if he asks for an egg, will give him a scorpion?" That would be horrible! No one is that bad of a parent. We could even ask the children who are here. If you asked your parents for something to eat, they would not give you something that would hurt you, would they? No! Of course not. They would not give you poison, would they? No! Of course not. They would give you something to eat. They would give you something good. You know that, and we know that, and Jesus knew that. That is what parents do.

Now, his point was not that we are such good parents, but that God is an even better parent. "If you then, who are evil, know how to give good gifts to your children, how much more will the heavenly Father give the Holy Spirit to those who ask him!" This argument is from less to more. "How much more will the heavenly Father give the Holy Spirit to those who ask him!" "How much more!" If it is of the essence of parenting to be a gift giver, how much more is the heavenly Father the Giver of all good gifts!

Life itself is a gift. We did not come here of our own volition. We are here because God called us by name and gave us life. Love is a gift. Family is a gift. Children are gifts. Community is a gift. Church is a gift. Language is a gift. Music is a gift. If we are perceptive at all, and if we are honest at all, we have to realize and to admit that there is a tremendous givenness to all of life. We have not made ourselves. We have not gathered ourselves here. We have not invented our language. There is a tremendous givenness to all of life. And what Jesus is teaching us here is that God the Father is the Giver of all good gifts. Even a little child appreciates good gifts and can begin to know whence they come. Moreover, the Giver of all good gifts is to be trusted. He gives us what we need, even if it is not always what we want.

"If you then, who are evil, know how to give good gifts to your children, how much more will the heavenly Father give the Holy Spirit to those who ask him!" With these words, the third thing (3) that Jesus tells us is that the Holy Spirit is the greatest gift. Of all the things God gives us—food and drink, life and breath, clothing and shelter, family and friends—the greatest gift is the Holy Spirit. The greatest gift God has, the greatest gift God gives, is none other than the Holy Spirit. What does this possibly mean? The Holy Spirit is none other than the presence and power of God. For God to give us the Holy Spirit is for God to give us himself. That is why it is the greatest gift. For God to give us the Holy Spirit is for God to give us Jesus Christ. That is how he applies Jesus to us and to our lives today. For God to give us the Holy Spirit is for God himself to come down out of heaven and to work within our very hearts and souls. That is what this means.

What does this accomplish for us? The great work of the Holy Spirit is faith. Believing in God is not a simple human possibility. Believing in God is a gift, a miracle worked within us by the Holy Spirit. Worshiping God is not a simple human possibility. That is why our worship begins with a prayer of invocation asking for God's help for us to worship him rightly. Worshiping God is a gift, a miracle worked within us by the Holy Spirit. Even a little child can receive this wonderful gift. Living the Christian life is not a simple human possibility. It takes a lifetime of effort. And yet, living the Christian life is a gift, a miracle worked within us by the Holy Spirit.

Surely this is what the ancient prophet Ezekiel meant, when he spoke to the people of Israel while they were still in exile in faraway Babylon:

> Thus says the Lord God . . . I will give you a new heart, and a new spirit I will put within you. And I will remove the heart of stone from your flesh and give you a heart of flesh. And I will put my Spirit within you, and cause you to walk in my statutes and be careful to obey my rules. You shall dwell in the land that I gave to your fathers, and you shall be my people, and I will be your God. (Ezekiel 36:22a, 26–28)

Here then are the words that give us life, the words that give us hope, the words that give us faith, courage, and comfort. Indeed, this is the gospel of Jesus Christ. God is (1) our heavenly Father. Even a little child knows his or her father and can begin to realize how close God is. God is (2) the Giver of all good gifts. Even a little child appreciates good gifts and can begin to know whence they come. The Holy Spirit is (3) the greatest gift. Even a little child can receive the Holy Spirit and can begin to rejoice in the goodness of God. By this comparison and exclamation, Jesus Christ communicates to all of us yet today the overflowing grace and goodness of God Almighty: "If you then, who are evil, know how to give good gifts to your children, how much more will the heavenly Father give the Holy Spirit to those who ask him!"

To God be the glory forever and ever! Amen.

33

How Will His Kingdom Stand?

"Every kingdom divided against itself is laid waste, and a divided household falls. And if Satan also is divided against himself, how will his kingdom stand?" "How will his kingdom stand?" Therein lies a fascinating question. It functions on several levels at once, reaching all the way from then to now, from Jesus to us and beyond. "How will his kingdom stand?" First (1), and most obviously, this establishes that the kingdom of Satan is not divided. That would be stupid. Satan is evil, and he is devious, but he is not stupid. So his kingdom is not divided. He does not work against himself. It is a simple law of nature, of history, and of all reality: "Every kingdom divided against itself is laid waste, and a divided household falls." This reality is the basis of the military strategy of divide-and-conquer. This is also a basic skill of parenting. If children are misbehaving, separate them and the level of mischief will drop significantly. Even Satan cannot avoid that reality. So, "if Satan also is divided against himself, how will his kingdom stand?"

Now, while it is sobering to realize that Satan is not stupid and that his kingdom is not divided, it is not really all that important in the great scheme of things, especially not in light of the gospel. So this first point leads quickly to the second point (2), the most immediate and pressing point being made: that Jesus Christ—who casts out demons, who heals the sick, who speaks the truth, who lifts up the poor, who forgives sin, and who saves his people—is not, and by definition cannot be, a part of the kingdom of Satan. That would be ridiculous. The very suggestion is insulting. And most importantly, it is wrong.

Everyone is entitled to his or her opinion, but not every opinion is correct. Not every opinion is right. Not every opinion is good. Not every opinion is valid. The

Christian faith is not open to every belief. The Bible is not open to every interpretation. The gospel cannot be bent to every whim. Jesus reacted vigorously against this wrongheaded accusation that he was satanic. Satan has his kingdom, and his kingdom is not divided. Jesus stands and works against Satan, and therefore he is not of Satan. This confirms that, as we might say today, theology matters. It is our responsibility to seek out and learn the faith that the church has always believed. Indeed, that is the purpose of the Gospel according to Luke, and that is why it was written as a catechism, a series of questions and answers instructing us in the faith. We are not free to say anything we want about Jesus Christ. We are not free to make Jesus Christ say anything we want him to say.

This second point needs to be expanded upon a little. Satan's kingdom is not divided, and therefore Jesus Christ, his opponent, is not of Satan's kingdom. But Jesus is more than *an* opponent. He is *the* opponent, the conquering opponent, the one who takes on and defeats Satan. So, not only is Jesus not of Satan, and not only is he absolutely opposed to Satan, but also he is successfully and victoriously opposed to Satan. "When a strong man, fully armed, guards his own palace, his goods are safe; but when one stronger than he attacks him and overcomes him, he takes away his armor in which he trusted and divides his spoil." Yes, Satan is a strong man. He is stronger than you or I. We cannot defeat him. If we could, we would not need a savior. But Jesus is the stronger man who attacks and overcomes Satan, takes away his defenses, and takes away from him those whom he has captured. Jesus Christ is the Savior. "Behold, something greater than Solomon is here." "Behold, something greater than Jonah is here." And behold, someone even stronger than Satan is here in the person, work, life, death, and resurrection of Jesus Christ. Shame on us if we do not come from the ends of the earth to hear his wisdom. Shame on us if we do not repent at his preaching. Shame on us if we do not believe his gospel, rejoice in his goodness, and live in his grace.

Do you see how Jesus wins this victory? He does not do this on his own. Rather, he does this (3) on the basis of another kingdom, a greater power, the One to whom he does belong. "For you say that I cast out demons by Beelzebul. And if I cast out demons by Beelzebul, by whom do your sons cast them out? Therefore they will be your judges. But if it is by the finger of God that I cast out demons, then the kingdom of God has come upon you." "If it is by the finger of God that I cast out demons, then the kingdom of God has come upon you." This is the third point based on the indivisibility of Satan's kingdom.

Satan's kingdom is not divided, so Jesus is not of Satan's kingdom. Instead, Jesus is both opposed to and stronger than Satan, because—and this is the third point—Jesus is of the kingdom of God. Where Jesus is, the kingdom of God is. Where Jesus is, God is. In fact, Jesus is God, with us and for us. Thanks be to God! Here is the great affirmation about Jesus Christ embedded in his observation about Satan. Where Jesus is, the kingdom of God is. Where Jesus is, God is. In fact, Jesus is God, with us and for us.

This brings me to a final point. We started with a question about Satan's kingdom. "If Satan also is divided against himself, how will his kingdom stand?" By extension, this applies to God's kingdom, also. If Jesus is divided against himself, how will his kingdom stand? If God is divided against himself, how will his kingdom stand? "How will his kingdom stand?" Therein lies a fascinating question. It functions on several levels at once, reaching all the way from then to now, from Jesus to us and beyond. It is a simple law of nature, of history, and of all reality: "Every kingdom divided against itself is laid waste, and a divided household falls."

So, finally (4), even the kingdom of God is not, and cannot be, divided. The kingdom of God is one, not manifold; it is united, not divided; and it is single, not multiple. It is of single purpose and direction. Or, as Jesus said, "Whoever is not with me is against me, and whoever does not gather with me scatters." The kingdom of God is not multiple. It cannot mean many different and opposing things. It cannot be going in opposite directions at once. Thus, the church of Jesus Christ cannot be divided. If the church of Jesus Christ were to be divided, it would no longer be the church. The church is, by definition and necessity, one. It can be no other. It cannot mean many different and opposing things. It cannot be going in opposite directions at once. "How will his kingdom stand?" Beware those who would tell us any differently.

Now this comes all the way down to us, to you and me. "Whoever is not with me is against me, and whoever does not gather with me scatters." Are we with Jesus or are we against him? How do we know? Do we gather with him or do we scatter? Do we build up his church or do we tear it down? As I told the children, "Blessed . . . are those who hear the word of God and keep it!" It is imperative for us to know the gospel of our Lord. It is imperative for us to know the word of God. It is incumbent upon us to receive the Holy Spirit. It is given to us to believe. God has called us by name and gathered us into his people. Jesus Christ has won the victory. He has redeemed us as his own. And as we hear his word, as we praise his name, as we rejoice in his redemption, as we live in the Spirit, as we love and comfort each other, as we eat and drink together, as we bring others here with us, we are the church, and we do gather with him, and we are with him, and we are of his glorious kingdom.

"How will his kingdom stand?" The kingdom of God will stand by the victory of Jesus Christ. "Then the kingdom of God has come upon you." In the preaching of the gospel of Jesus Christ, in the singing of his praises, in the forgiveness of our sin, in our prayers of thanksgiving, the kingdom of God has come even upon us, even upon us today. "Whoever is not with me is against me, and whoever does not gather with me scatters." So let us receive this gift gladly, cherish this treasure, and live this new life. "Blessed . . . are those who hear the word of God and keep it!"

To God be the glory forever and ever! Amen.

34

Did Not He Make You?

LUKE 11:37–54; JOB 40:1–14

"Now you Pharisees cleanse the outside of the cup and of the dish, but inside you are full of greed and wickedness. You fools! Did not he who made the outside make the inside also? But give as alms those things that are within, and behold, everything is clean for you." Let us remember that such historical criticisms of the Pharisees have been remembered in the Scriptures not as condemnations of the Jews but as warnings for all the generations of Christians who have read this, who are reading this, or who ever will read this, including even us yet today. That is to say, this warning and this exhortation are for us, here and now.

"You . . . cleanse the outside of the cup and of the dish, but inside you are full of greed and wickedness. You fools! Did not he who made the outside make the inside also? But give as alms those things that are within, and behold, everything is clean for you." Let us also remember that so far in our reading of the Gospel according to Luke we have found it to function as a catechism, a question-and-answer teaching device intended to communicate the gospel and to explicate the Christian faith, in order that we might have certainty concerning the things we have been taught (Luke 1:4). That is to say, the questions in the text have almost always pointed us to the major affirmations of the text. And this is the only question in today's reading from Luke: "Did not he who made the outside make the inside also?"

The first (1) and most obvious point being made here—and this point has three parts—is that (a) the interior life is as important as the exterior life, that (b) the spiritual is as important as the bodily, and that (c) faith is as important as obedience. In fact, even to say it this way may overstate the distinctions, for we cannot have the interior life without the exterior life, we cannot have the spiritual without the bodily, and we cannot have faith without obedience. We shall return to that in a moment.

For now, in a world in which we are tempted to emphasize the exterior life more than the interior life, to value the bodily more than the spiritual, and to champion action more than faith, the first and most obvious point Jesus is making to us here is that the interior life is at least as important as the exterior life, that the spiritual is at least as important as the bodily, and that faith is at least as important as obedience. "Did not he who made the outside make the inside also?" Well, yes, he did. So we need to pay attention to the inside, also. The Christian life includes at least something of (a) the interior, of (b) the spiritual, and of (c) faith. Perhaps we should take up these three one at a time.

The interior life (a) is at least as important as the exterior life. That is to say, the Christian life is more than exterior behavior. It includes exterior behavior, but it goes beyond that. In addition to coming to church, we are actually to worship God Almighty. In addition to confessing our sins, we are to repent of our sins. In addition to reading the Bible, we are inwardly to absorb and digest it. In addition to giving of our treasures, we are to give of our very selves. In addition to feeding the hungry, we are actually to love the hungry. In addition to housing the homeless, we are actually to love the homeless. In addition to welcoming the stranger, we are actually to love the stranger. In addition to sponsoring the refugee, we are actually to love the refugee. In addition to praying for our enemy, we are actually to love our enemy. To have the outward alone, without the inner reality, would be a sham. And there are a lot of shams in the world. We do not want any here in church. So, for the Christian life, the interior life is at least as important as the exterior life.

Also, the spiritual (b) is at least as important as the bodily. Every day of the week, and every Sunday morning, I see people walking and running as I come to church. They are not going anywhere, of course. They are walking or running in circles, large or small, in order to get exercise. Walking and running are good in and of themselves. I need to do more of that myself. But the zeal, the effort, and the dedication that I see poured into them do raise certain questions. Do we pray as much as we exercise, minute for minute and hour for hour? Do we worship God as much as we exercise, week in and week out, year after year? Do we even read the Bible as much as we exercise, listening to the word of the living God and being shaped on that anvil as much as we try to sculpt our bodies? For the Christian life, the spiritual is at least as important as the bodily. If we know that we need to exercise our hearts and lungs, our arms and legs—and we do need to do that—then it is important for us to realize that we need to exercise our hearts and souls also, as well as our minds and spirits.

And faith (c) is at least as important as obedience. Here we come to the gist of it all. Jesus was speaking then to a group of people who emphasized outward, visible obedience more than inner faith. We may or may not think that that is our problem, but the tendency toward attempting self-justification runs very deep in the human race. So we would do well to appreciate this distinction and to learn this lesson. After all, justification comes from God, not from our own efforts. When we think about obedience, we think about the law of God that is to be obeyed. The law of God is summarized in the Ten Commandments. That is to say, the Ten Commandments express the will of God for the people of God. Everything they say to do is very good. But one of the problems that the people of God frequently have is the assumption that we can obey and fulfill the will of God without God's help. But if we were good enough to do that, we would not need to be saved by Jesus Christ. Think about it. If we were good enough to obey the will of God, we would not need to be saved by Jesus Christ.

Since we do need to be saved by Jesus Christ, since he has already come and died on our behalf, since he has provided for the forgiveness of our sin, it should be clear that we are not good enough to obey and fulfill the will of God without God's help. We need God's help. So, in addition to our efforts at outward obedience, we need that inner assurance of our forgiveness in Christ, that confidence in the goodness of God toward us, sealed upon our hearts by the Holy Spirit. That is to say, we need grace, and we need faith. Jesus said, "Give as alms those things that are within, and behold, everything is clean for you." Yield up your inner faith to God, and only then will your outer obedience be correct too. So, the first and most obvious point being made here—and this point has three parts—is that (a) the interior life is as important as the exterior life, that (b) the spiritual is as important as the bodily, and that (c) faith is as important as obedience. But that is not the only point.

A second (2) and less obvious point being made here—and this point has three parts also—a point included in the very presupposition of the question, is that (a) the exterior life is still important, that (b) the bodily is still important, and that (c) obedience is still important. To emphasize the interior, the spiritual, and faith is not to belittle the exterior, the bodily, and obedience. Quite the opposite: the very way the question is phrased maintains an emphasis upon these. "Did not he who made the outside make the inside also?" In a way, this is a secondary emphasis of this text, but it is an important one. Jesus never said *not* to be obedient. He said to have an inner faith to match and undergird the outward obedience. So yes, worship God, pray, and love your enemy, and continue to do so within the outward context of coming to church, giving our tithes and alms, and feeding the hungry.

As Jesus said to the Pharisees, "You tithe mint and rue and every herb, and neglect justice and the love of God. These you ought to have done, without neglecting the others." He did not tell them to promote justice and the love of God *instead* of tithing. Tithing was not a problem in and of itself. The problem was that they wanted to stop at tithing and not give their hearts also to God. So, Jesus tells us to promote justice and the love of God in addition to tithing. That makes a big difference. So, the second point (2) is that (a) the exterior life is still important, that (b) the bodily is still important, and that (c) obedience is still important.

A third (3) and deeper point being made here—and this point also has three parts—a third point in the very conjunction of the outside and the inside, is that (a) God made both the exterior and the interior, that (b) God made both the bodily and the spiritual, and that (c) God calls for both obedience and faith. As we said earlier, even to contrast these may overstate the distinctions, for we cannot have the interior life without the exterior life, we cannot have the spiritual without the bodily, and we cannot have faith without obedience. "Did not he who made the outside make the inside also?" Well, yes, he did. But the significance of this is not that he made the inside *instead* of the outside. The significance of this is that he made *both*. Perhaps we could helpfully combine both the presupposition and the main part of the question into a single question: Did not he make you, inside and out, body and soul? Yes, he did. That is to say, God is our Creator. God is our Father. God is not a remote and arbitrary lawgiver. God is not a distant and angry judge. God is the One who made us, inside and out, for himself, for his own good pleasure, that we might forever know, love, and enjoy him.

The upshot of this third point is that while God does not want obedience without faith, neither does he want faith without obedience. There is one God. He has made us as unified human beings. And he wants both faith and obedience from us. In fact, these two are even closer than that. Faith is obedience. The first thing God wants from us is for us to believe in him and in his goodness toward us, embodied and revealed in Jesus Christ. To believe in him is to obey this call to faith. At the same time, obedience flows out of faith. If outer action apart from the love of God is not and cannot be pleasing, outer action flowing from of the love of God is obedience as an expression of faith. Indeed, faith leads to obedience. If there were no obedience, the question would have to be asked as to whether there is any faith. These two go together, and God is the God of both. So (3), God made (a) both the exterior and the interior, God made (b) both the bodily and the spiritual, and God calls for (c) both obedience and faith.

The fourth (4) and final point being made here—perhaps somewhat of an abstraction from the other three, but actually the one great truth underlying them all—is that in all of life it is God with whom we have to deal. What this meant for the Pharisees then was that it was not only the law with which they had to deal but also the very Giver of the law with whom they had to deal. He was far more important. So also for us, in all of life, it is God with whom we have to deal. In (a) the exterior life as well as the interior, in (b) the bodily as well as the spiritual, and in (c) matters of obedience as well as matters of faith it is God with whom we have to deal. "Did not he who made the outside make the inside also?" Did not he make you? Well, yes, he did. In all of life, it is God with whom we have to deal.

We may think we are dealing with a rude neighbor. It is God with whom we have to deal. We may think we are dealing with a hurricane. It is God with whom we have to deal. We may think we are dealing disease, decay, decline, and death. It is God with whom we have to deal. We may think we are dealing with an enemy. It is God with whom we have to deal. We may think we are dealing with a beloved family member. It is God with whom we have to deal. In all of life, it is God with whom we have to deal. No matter what the presenting realities, no matter what our supposed accomplishments, no matter what struggles we have or hardships we endure, the one great truth behind them all, the liberating truth of our lives, is that in all of life it is God with whom we have to deal.

This is what Job learned the hard way. Having lost almost everything, he demanded his day in court. He got it. And as Job finally stood before God Almighty, he fell silent. All of his self-justification fell away. He realized as never before that it was God with whom he had to deal. It was not just his own suffering with which he had to deal, as terrible as it was. It was God with whom he had to deal. That changed everything. Job's horrible losses are remembered for us in the hope that we might learn his lesson easier and earlier. And I submit to you that the living Lord Jesus Christ continues to teach us the same lesson today about God his Father. Did not he make you? Is it not the case that in all things we are dealing with him?

John Calvin, one of the leading Reformers of the 1500s, taught this same lesson throughout his life. He wrote in a commentary on this very passage from Luke that man's chief error is failing to realize that we have to deal with God.[1] What this means for us is that in our faith, in our obedience, in our worship, and in our life it is God with whom we have to deal. In both the routine and in the spectacular, in the good and in the bad, in what sustains us and in what crushes us, it is God with whom we have to deal. To remember this, to hold this close, and to keep this perspective on life is a powerful thing. Calvin also wrote of this reality more generally in his *Institutes of the Christian Religion*:

> Therefore no one will weigh God's providence properly and profitably but him who considers that his business is with his Maker and the Framer of the universe, and with becoming humility submits himself to fear and reverence. . . .
>
> Accordingly, the Christian must surely be so disposed and minded that he feels within himself it is with God he has to deal throughout his life.[2]

So (1), the interior life (a) is as important as the exterior, the spiritual (b) is as important as the bodily, and faith (c) is as important as obedience. At the same time (2), the exterior life (a) is still important, the bodily (b) is still important, and obedience (c) is still important. Indeed (3), God made (a) both the exterior and the interior, God made (b) both the bodily and the spiritual, and God calls for (c) both obedience and faith. So (4) in all of life, in (a) the exterior life as well as the interior, in (b) the bodily as well as the spiritual, and in (c) matters of obedience as well as matters of faith, it is God with whom we have to deal. "You . . . cleanse the outside of the cup and of the dish, but inside you are full of greed and wickedness. You fools! Did not he who made the outside make the inside also? But give as alms those things that are within, and behold, everything is clean for you."

To God be the glory forever and ever! Amen.

1. Calvin, *Harmony of the Gospels*, 2:101.
2. Calvin, *Institutes*, I.17.2, 1.212; and III.7.2, 1.691.

35

Fear Not!

"I TELL YOU, MY friends, do not fear those who kill the body, and after that have nothing more that they can do. But I will warn you whom to fear: fear him who, after he has killed, has authority to cast into hell. Yes, I tell you, fear him! Are not five sparrows sold for two pennies? And not one of them is forgotten before God. Why, even the hairs of your head are all numbered. Fear not; you are of more value than many sparrows." So Jesus said, in quick succession, (1) "Do not fear," (2) "Fear," and (3) "Fear not." When said this succinctly, these three form an odd series of apparently contradictory imperatives: (1) "Do not fear," (2) "Fear," and (3) "Fear not." We would do well to ask what each of these three imperatives means and how each of them applies to us. Let me say now also that these do have a cumulative effect so that it will be important to hear all three in order to appreciate each one.

First (1), Jesus says, "Do not fear those who kill the body, and after that have nothing more that they can do." And this is what he told his "friends." This is what he is still telling us. "Do not fear those who kill the body"? "After that [they] have nothing more that they can do"? This is very strange, indeed. What in the world stands behind this teaching? What good news can be hidden here? Initially (a), there is an acknowledgment of the reality of evil in the world, and yet (b) there is also a limiting context to that evil. These two are held together, and we would not want to consider (a) the reality of evil without considering (b) the limits to evil. That is to say (a), there *are* (i) terrible people in the world, people who seek to do us harm, both criminals and enemies. As Christians, we acknowledge that. We do not pretend to live in a world where that is not the case. And yet, we are told (b), "Do not fear those who kill the body, and after that have nothing more that they can do." We shall deal more with these limits in just a moment.

To expand initially upon the reality of evil (a), we acknowledge also that there *are* (ii) evil forces in the world, forces that seek to undo the good that God has done. We are told not to fear them, either. It does not say not to take reasonable precautions against them, but we are not to fear them absolutely. And in addition to those people and forces that work against us, we all face (iii) disease, decay, decline, and death. And again, we are told not to fear them. All of this is to say on the one hand that all who are alive now will face in this world a day of death. We admit that. We are told not to fear it. We are all limited in time. We all had a beginning in this world and in this life. We all shall have an end in this world and in this life, whether it comes early or late. That is part of the reality of our lives. We are told not to fear that. So, with this first imperative there is an acknowledgment (a) of the reality of evil in the world and yet, at the same time, (b) we are told not to fear those forces of evil. And this is very important. The very fact that we are told not to fear those forces of evil means that there is a limiting context to that evil.

The fact that there is a limiting context to evil means, additionally, that (c) the power of evil is not absolute. Thus, we do not belong to the powers of evil. Our bodies do not belong to the powers of evil. Our lives do not belong to the powers of evil. We ourselves do not belong to the powers of evil. Evil does not have the final word about us. Instead, the very facts that we are born, that we die, and that something *can* be done to us after we die, even if the forces of evil are not capable of doing it, these very facts mean that we belong to Another, to a greater One, to One who does have purposes for us beyond this life. We belong to Another, and this One is our Creator, the God and Father of Jesus Christ. We belong to Another, and this One, our Creator, has set a limit to the powers of evil to destroy. We belong to Another, the One who made us for himself, and this means that even the day of death that we all face here will not be the end for us.

This teaching we have received from Jesus Christ is not unlike the faith exuded by the prophet Jeremiah, who was confident that God conquers evil:

> But the LORD is with me as a dread warrior;
>> therefore my persecutors will stumble;
>> they will not overcome me.
> They will be greatly shamed,
>> for they will not succeed.
> Their eternal dishonor
>> will never be forgotten.
> O LORD of hosts, who tests the righteous,
>> who sees the heart and the mind,
> let me see your vengeance upon them,
>> for to you have I committed my cause. (Jeremiah 20:11–12)

165

Moreover, this teaching we have received from Jesus Christ and the prophecy we have received from Jeremiah are not unlike the great hymn of praise we hear in Psalm 92:

> How great are your works, O Lord!
>> Your thoughts are very deep!
> The stupid man cannot know;
>> the fool cannot understand this:
> that though the wicked sprout like grass
>> and all evildoers flourish,
> they are doomed to destruction forever;
>> but you, O Lord, are on high forever.
> For behold, your enemies, O Lord,
>> for behold, your enemies shall perish;
>> all evildoers shall be scattered. (vv. 5–9)

Therefore Jesus tells us, "Do not fear those who kill the body, and after that have nothing more that they can do." We belong to Another. We belong to our Creator. Therefore we are not to fear even those who can kill us.

Second (2), Jesus says, "But I will warn you whom to fear: fear him who, after he has killed, has authority to cast into hell. Yes, I tell you, fear him!" Here we begin to notice the odd juxtaposition of apparently contradictory imperatives: (1) "Do not fear" and (2) "Fear." With this we have been carried beyond the reach of the powers of evil and placed directly before the power of good. Here is the larger, limiting context. Here we are taught here that the power of evil to destroy the good is nothing compared to the power of good to destroy the evil. There is One who is greater than the forces of evil. There is One who is greater than the power of death. There is One whom we shall face beyond the end of this life. That is to say, not only is there a day of death here, but also there is a day of judgment beyond here. On that day we shall face the Judge. The Judge is none other than our Creator. He made us for himself. And he has very high standards and expectations. He wants us to be righteous and holy. So, we have much more reason to fear him than we have to fear the agents of death. But even this is not the last word, either.

Third (3), Jesus says, "Are not five sparrows sold for two pennies? And not one of them is forgotten before God. Why, even the hairs of your head are all numbered. Fear not; you are of more value than many sparrows." So now we have all three imperatives: (1) "Do not fear," (2) "Fear," and (3) "Fear not." (1) God is our Creator, who has purposes for us beyond this world, so that we are not to fear the forces of evil. (2) God is also our Judge, beyond life and death, and who as such is rightfully worthy of our fear. (3) And yet, Jesus now carries us to a third level, "Fear not." How can this be? Not only is there (1) a day of death, and not only is there (2) a day of judgment, but also there is (3) a day of grace, and that grace spills back into this life. That is to say, (1) our

Creator and (2) Judge is also (3) our Redeemer. There is no other way to account for this final prohibition of fear. Of course we have every reason to fear the Judge on our own. The fact that finally we are not to fear means and can only mean that he himself has provided for our well-being. Precisely in the life, death, and resurrection of Jesus Christ, God has redeemed us. God has saved us for himself. Thanks be to God!

It is this gospel of Jesus Christ, this good news of God's favor upon us, this teaching of life beyond death, that gives us courage for the living of our lives here. Dr. James M. McPherson, Professor of History at Princeton University and a Presbyterian elder, has noted from reading letters of Civil War soldiers on both sides of the conflict that the belief in eternal life gave them comfort, courage, and the ability to do their duty.[1] General Thomas "Stonewall" Jackson, Professor of Artillery Tactics and Natural Philosophy at the Virginia Military Institute and a Presbyterian deacon, is a well-known example of this. When asked by one of his officers how he kept his calm, standing bravely on the battlefield even while bullets were flying all around him,

> He instantly became grave and reverential in his manner, and answered, in a low tone of great earnestness: "Captain, my religious belief teaches me to feel as safe in battle as in bed. God has fixed the time for my death. I do not concern myself about that, but to be always ready, no matter when it may overtake me." He added, after a pause . . . : "That is the way all men should live, and then all would be equally brave."[2]

If soldiers can find in the Christian faith courage for the fields of battle, surely the rest of us can find in the Christian faith courage for the living of our daily lives! Jesus said, finally (3), "Fear not."

This third teaching (3), "Fear not," applies not only to the faith and lives of individuals but also to the faith and life of the church as a whole. As Dr. Thomas C. Oden, Professor of Theology at Drew University, has written in *The Rebirth of Orthodoxy*:

> The one holy catholic and apostolic church the world over is promised imperishable continuance, even if particular associations and groupings of apostate believers languish, falter, or atrophy. The covenant of God with Israel [and, by extension, with the church] is not threatened by human faithlessness. It is an *eternal* covenant, not limited to any particular time or ethos. It is held together by God's own sovereign will.[3]

That is to say, again, the basis for our not fearing does not lie in our own supposed strength, wisdom, or goodness, but in the strength, wisdom, and goodness of God alone, in the grace of God alone, in the redemption God has worked for us in the life, death, and resurrection of Jesus Christ alone.

1. McPherson, *For Cause and Comrades.*
2. Jackson, "Stonewall Jackson."
3. Oden, *Rebirth of Orthodoxy*, 42.

This faith in God, this confidence, and this reassurance have all been well embodied at a very personal level in the first question and answer of the Heidelberg Catechism, which we would all do well to learn and to hold close:

> Q. 1. What is your only comfort, in life and in death?

> A. That I belong—body and soul, in life and in death—not to myself but to my faithful Savior, Jesus Christ, who at the cost of his own blood has fully paid for all my sins and has completely freed me from the dominion of the devil; that he protects me so well that without the will of my Father in heaven not a hair can fall from my head; indeed, that everything must fit his purpose for my salvation. Therefore, by his Holy Spirit, he also assures me of eternal life, and makes me wholeheartedly willing and ready from now on to live for him.

In this way these teachings of Jesus Christ have been brought forward into the teachings of the church. It would behoove us all to learn them by heart, to absorb them, to let them become our very own, and to let them get down into our bones where no one can ever take them away from us.

So, first (1), "Do not fear those who kill the body, and after that have nothing more that they can do." Second (2), "Fear him who, after he has killed, has authority to cast into hell." Third (3), "Fear not; you are of more value than many sparrows." Here is a quick succession of three apparently contradictory imperatives. What do these three mean for us? God is (1) our Creator. God is also (2) our Judge. And, finally, God is (3) our Redeemer. Therefore, "Fear not"!

To God be the glory forever and ever! Amen.

36

Why Are You Anxious?

LUKE 12:13–34; ECCLESIASTES 1:1–2; 2:18–26

"THEREFORE I TELL YOU, do not be anxious about your life, what you will eat, nor about your body, what you will put on. For life is more than food, and the body more than clothing. . . . And which of you by being anxious can add a single hour to his span of life? If then you are not able to do as small a thing as that, why are you anxious about the rest?" "Why are you anxious?" Jesus addressed this question directly to his disciples and so to us yet today. "Why are you anxious?" Clearly, the implication is that we should not be anxious. And yet, one of the most ironic things about this exhortation is that preachers preaching about not being anxious themselves become anxious about whether the congregations will hear the message that we are not supposed to be anxious. Noting that irony and setting it aside, let us hear what Jesus has to say to each of us today, including me.

"Therefore I tell you, do not be anxious about your life, what you will eat, nor about your body, what you will put on. . . . Which of you by being anxious can add a single hour to his span of life? If then you are not able to do as small a thing as that, why are you anxious about the rest?" "Why are you anxious?" We have seen again and again in the Gospel according to Luke that the questions have pointed us toward the major affirmations being made, to the gospel being proclaimed, to the faith being taught. And of the several questions in today's readings, this is the main one: "Why are you anxious?" Let me suggest that this question functions on at least four levels of increasing depth and importance, leading us to the gospel of Jesus Christ and so leading us into the very kingdom of God. Join me, and let us explore these together, and so let us seek God's good will for our lives.

"Why are you anxious?" First of all (1), this simple question seems to function as a request for information. "Why are you anxious?" What is it about your life that leads to anxiety? Food, drink, clothing, and shelter, disease, decay, decline, and death, parents, spouses, children, and neighbors, work and leisure, wealth and poverty, disagreements, politics, war, and terrorism, the evening news, fear of the great unknowns, fear of what is known, and the ongoing realities of sin and guilt. Why are we anxious? We might ask in reply, "Why should we not be anxious?" We shall get to that in a moment. The question that Jesus asks us seems an odd one. For now, let us acknowledge that there are many, many things about life itself that cause us great anxiety.

"Why are you anxious?" Second (2), beyond a simple request for information, this question serves also as an invitation to insight. This is an invitation to insight into life. "For life is more than food, and the body more than clothing. Consider the ravens: they neither sow nor reap, they have neither storehouse nor barn, and yet God feeds them. Of how much more value are you than the birds! . . . Consider the lilies, how they grow: they neither toil nor spin, yet I tell you, even Solomon in all his glory was not arrayed like one of these. If God so clothes the grass, which is alive in the field today, and tomorrow is thrown into the oven, how much more will he clothe you, O you of little faith!" Of all the things about which we are anxious, food and clothing are near the top of the list. And if by food we might understand all matters of health and by clothing we might understand all matters of wealth, then these two would encompass most of our concerns.

And yet, "life is more than food, and the body more than clothing." This is the insight to which Jesus invites us. In our age of spectacular consumption, it seems very odd, indeed. This would be a hard saying, though a hopeful one, to those who are hungry and not well dressed. Might it also be possible for the rest of us, even when our appetites are sated and our closets are full, still to yearn for something more, still to seek that which is greater? Lord, help us! "For life is more than food, and the body more than clothing." Thanks be to God! Life is, finally, knowing God and knowing his Jesus Christ (John 17:3). Life is being in relationship with God through his word and through his Holy Spirit. Life is acknowledging God as our Creator, standing before him as our Judge, and rejoicing in him as our Redeemer.

These things are more than food. These things are more than clothing. These things are beyond even disease, decay, decline, and death. These things are beyond anxiety, and so they relieve us of the burden of being anxious. Consider the birds of the air: they do not plant or harvest, they do not have warehouses, and they do not even go to the grocery store, and yet they eat. They eat because God provides. Consider the flowers of the field: they neither toil nor fret, and yet their blossoms are more beautiful than our finest clothes, so that when we want to improve what we are wearing, we add a flower. God provides sun and rain, and so the flowers prosper. God has given us life. And God provides what we need for life. The Bible does not tell us not to work. But it does tell us not to worry.

Consider also the rich man whose land produced bountifully so that he thought he needed bigger barns. He was not criminal. He was not unjust. He did not come by his wealth in an evil way. And yet, he made a very serious mistake. It somehow seemed to him that life consists in the abundance of possessions. But that is exactly wrong. Life does not consist in the abundance of possessions. Life is more than that and other than that. And to focus on the abundance of possessions is to run the severe risk of missing life itself. Possessions are not bad things in and of themselves. But they are not as wonderful as they might seem, either. They are very dangerous. They are dangerous because they are distracting. It is possible that possessions can lure us away from love of God and love of neighbor. It would be far better for us to use them to serve God and to serve neighbor.

Consider also the despair of Ecclesiastes: "a person who has toiled with wisdom and knowledge and skill must leave everything to be enjoyed by someone who did not toil for it" (Ecclesiastes 2:21). That is to say, you cannot take it with you. Worrying about not taking it with you can only create a lot of grief. And yet, that preacher also wrote, "There is nothing better for a person than that he should eat and drink and find enjoyment in his toil. This also, I saw, is from the hand of God, for apart from him who can eat or who can have enjoyment?" (Ecclesiastes 2:24–25). What we do have—what we can eat to our nourishment and what we can wear for our protection and enjoyment—all comes from the will of God to provide it for us, even if God does that through the intermediate means of our own hard labor. It is good for us not only to appreciate but also and especially to enjoy what God has given us.

"Why are you anxious?" Third (3), in addition to being a request for information and to being an invitation to insight into life, this question is also, on the basis of these two prior considerations, an expression of surprise on the part of Jesus. "And which of you by being anxious can add a single hour to his span of life? If then you are not able to do as small a thing as that, why are you anxious about the rest?" It is as if, even as well as he knows us and our shortcomings, he is surprised that we are not doing at least a little better than we are. It is as if he were asking why we have not yet figured out at least the basics. Of course, for the first disciples this was still before the crucifixion and resurrection. But for us, this is not only after the crucifixion and resurrection but also after two thousand years of church history and thought. We should be getting it right by now. Again, it is not that Jesus says for us not to take care for our lives. But he does raise a profound and simple question as to whether anxiety ever added a single hour to our lives or, for that matter, made any hour we did have any better.

"Why are you anxious?" Fourth (4), in addition to being a request for information, to being an invitation to insight into life, and to being an expression of surprise on the part of Jesus, this question is also, and most importantly, an affirmation of the grace of God in and for our lives. That is to say, this very question is gospel. We have touched on this affirmation a little already in terms of insight into life, but we need to explore it here more fully. "Fear not, little flock, for it is your Father's good pleasure

171

to give you the kingdom." "Fear not, little flock, for it is your Father's good pleasure to give you the kingdom." Here it is! God will, and God even delights to, give us his very kingdom. God has called us his very own, and so he has made us his very own.

We can work for food. We can work for clothing. We should not worry over them, but we can work for them, even though the birds and the flowers do not have to do so. But the really important thing in life, the very kingdom of God, is sheer gift. We do not have to work for it, and we cannot work for it. We do not have to worry about it, for we cannot achieve it. The kingdom of God is pure gift. God delights to give it to us. And he does so precisely through the gospel, through the birth, life, ministry, teachings, healings, death, resurrection, ascension, and return of his only Son, our Lord and Savior, Jesus Christ. Thanks be to God!

From time to time, people stand before these congregations of the church of Jesus Christ and profess or reaffirm their faith in Jesus Christ as Lord and Savior. Some are joining the church. Some are presenting their children for the sacrament of baptism. In so doing, they acknowledge the wonderful grace of God who marks us as his very own before we know our own names. And in so doing, they promise before God and these witnesses to teach their children the gospel of Jesus Christ, this very gospel we have heard today, and to do so both at home and at church until such time as their child is able to make his or her own profession of faith. And we too as the congregation are also asked to promise to help them in this grand endeavor. What a high privilege this is, and what a soberingly joyful responsibility!

This affirmation by Jesus Christ of the grace of God in and for our lives, particularly the realization of its anxiety reducing aspects, has certain implications for our lives. For starters (a), "Do not be anxious about your life, what you will eat, nor about your body, what you will put on. For life is more than food, and the body more than clothing." We have already dealt with this to some extent. "Do not be anxious about your life." That anxiety is ruled out of bounds by the gospel. Life is a gift, and the Giver of all good gifts is to be trusted in all things. This is easier to say than to do, but it is important at least to try to do it, and it becomes more and more a part of you the longer you do it. More specifically, "Do not seek what you are to eat and what you are to drink, nor be worried." Again, Jesus never says not to work. Jesus never says for us not to work hard. He does say for us not to worry.

Again (b), "For all the nations of the world seek after these things, and your Father knows that you need them. Instead, seek his kingdom, and these things will be added to you." Now we are moving from the negatives to the positives, from what we are not to do to what we are to do. "Seek his kingdom, and these things will be added to you." We have already said that the Father delights to give us his kingdom. So our seeking his kingdom has nothing to do with our establishing it or, so far as I can tell, with that very popular misconception that somehow we are involved with building the kingdom of God. It is God's kingdom. He establishes it. He builds it. He gives it to us. Our seeking it has to do with our living into it, becoming a part of it by worshiping God and by loving and serving neighbor.

Moreover (c), "Sell your possessions, and give to the needy." We have come a long way today. We started with not worrying about what to eat, drink, or wear. Now we have arrived at disposing of what we do own in order to give to the needy, to help those who do not have. We shall always have the needy among us, to do good to whenever we will (Mark 14:7). Could it be that part of the way God provides for the poor is through us and our gifts?

Finally (d), "Provide yourselves with moneybags that do not grow old, with a treasure in the heavens that does not fail, where no thief approaches and no moth destroys. For where your treasure is, there will your heart be also." Now we are reaching the very farthest. The kingdom of God, which God gives to us, begins here in this world and is very real here in this world. And yet, it has implications far beyond here. It begins to orient us to the next life. It points us beyond the passing realities of this world toward the eternal realities of the next world. If we treasure only what we have here, as did the rich man who built bigger barns, then our hearts will be trapped here and we will die here. But if we treasure what lies beyond, if we thrill to the eternal worship of God, if we long to be in the presence of Jesus Christ, if we ache for love of neighbor unmarred by our selfishness or theirs, if we cherish the love, grace, and mercy of God above all, then our hearts, souls, minds, and bodies are heaven bound. Thanks be to God!

"Therefore I tell you, do not be anxious about your life, what you will eat, nor about your body, what you will put on. For life is more than food, and the body more than clothing. . . . And which of you by being anxious can add a single hour to his span of life? If then you are not able to do as small a thing as that, why are you anxious about the rest?"

To God be the glory forever and ever! Amen.

37

Who Is Faithful?

LUKE 12:35–59; 2 KINGS 17:33–41

"WHO THEN IS THE faithful and wise manager, whom his master will set over his household, to give them their portion of food at the proper time?" "Who . . . is the faithful and wise manager?" In short, "Who is faithful?" Therein lies a very important question not only for Peter and the other disciples, and not only for Luke, and for Theophilus, for whom Luke wrote this book, but also for us yet today. "Who is faithful?" How would we know? What constitutes faithfulness? Why do we want to be faithful? It is fascinating that Jesus poses this question to his disciples instead of them asking him. It is also gratifying that he goes ahead and answers the question himself. Join me in hearing again what our Lord says about who we are in relation to him.

"Who is faithful?" Jesus gives a two-part answer, in what might seem to be a reverse order—more about that in a moment—with each of the two parts having both positive and negative examples. The first part of the answer might be summarized by saying that one is faithful who does the will of God. That is to say (a), one is faithful who is obedient to God. Faithfulness involves obedience. "Who then is the faithful and wise manager, whom his master will set over his household, to give them their portion of food at the proper time? Blessed is that servant whom his master will find so doing when he comes. Truly, I say to you, he will set him over all his possessions." Doing what the master wants is good. Doing what the master wants is important. Doing what the master wants is faithful. Doing what the master wants contributes to the well-being of the household and leads to increased responsibilities. "Who is faithful?" For starters, faithfulness involves obedience.

Conversely (b), being disobedient constitutes unfaithfulness. "If that servant says to himself, 'My master is delayed in coming,' and begins to beat the male and female servants, and to eat and drink and get drunk, the master of that servant will come on a day when he does not expect him and at an hour he does not know, and will cut him in pieces and put him with the unfaithful." The disobedient will be put "with the unfaithful" because disobedience makes one unfaithful. That is not an arbitrary punishment. That is the outcome of disobedience.

An even stronger negative example of disobedience and unfaithfulness may be found in our reading from 2 Kings. The people tried to worship both the Lord God of Israel and also the various gods of the people from whom they came. They hedged their bets. They tried to please multiple gods. They tried to maintain the outer show of their religion but to avoid the inner realities of the faith in order to maintain their religious diversity, inclusivity, tolerance, and pluralism. But the Lord God of Israel does not want to be worshiped as one God among many. The God and Father of Jesus Christ is one, and him alone are we to worship. He is not tolerant of the worship of other gods. He is not tolerant of theological pluralism. He is not tolerant of accommodating the cultural faith of any people. He does not care to be inclusive of other gods, others faiths, other worship, other prayers, or other practices. God is one, and he commands the integrity of single-minded and single-hearted worship. Again, disobedience constitutes unfaithfulness.

"Who is faithful?" The first part (1) of the answer is that one who does the will of God is faithful. This leads, of course, to the second (2) but logically prior part of the answer: that doing the will of God requires knowing the will of God. It would not be possible for one to obey what one did not know, except, perhaps, accidentally, and that would hardly be called obedience and certainly not be called faithfulness. It might be blind, good luck, but it would not be obedience or faithfulness. So, positively (a), doing the will of God requires and involves knowing the will of God. Therefore, part of being faithful is knowing the will of God.

Jesus brought this out in his teaching on the negative (b) side of his presentation in terms of gradations of punishment for various levels of disobedience. "That servant who knew his master's will but did not get ready or act according to his will, will receive a severe beating." That is to say, knowing the will of God but not doing it is very highly blameworthy. Conversely, (a) the clear implication is that knowing the will of God and doing it is very highly praiseworthy. "Who is faithful?" The one who both knows and also does the will of God. "But the one who did not know, and did what deserved a beating, will receive a light beating." The one who did not know the will of God and therefore did what was wrong is still blameworthy but not so much so as the one who knew the will of God and did not do it. Still, for our purposes, the point behind even this lesser punishment is that we are supposed to know the will of God. Knowing the will of God is a necessary prerequisite to knowingly doing the will of God, so both knowing and doing are part of faithfulness.

Now, as a preacher of the gospel of Jesus Christ, the good news of Jesus Christ, I am required to ask what good news stands behind this two-part teaching in answer to the question, "Who is faithful?" And as hearers of the gospel, as a church gathered by and for the gospel of Jesus Christ, we all want to know where the good news is. It is not enough to say that one who knows and does the will of God is faithful. That is true, but it could be oppressive by itself. So, what gospel stands behind it? What good news stands underneath it? What mercy undergirds it and holds it up and transforms it from a two-part answer into words of life and hope?

There are two parts to this underlying gospel, also. First (1), when Jesus Christ teaches us that one is faithful who both knows and does the will of God, the first good news implied and required by this teaching is that God does in fact make his will known. God has not hidden his will from us. We are not left in the dark. We are not reduced to guessing. Instead, God has made his will known to us. And by this, I do not mean simply the Ten Commandments, with duty to God and duty to neighbor, as important as they are. I do not mean simply the Great Commandment of love of God and love of neighbor, as important as that is. Yes, of course, God does will for us to do all these things, and it is good and important for us both to know and to do them. That is true.

But the will of God for us, which God makes known to us, also runs much deeper than that. Finally, it is in the life, death, and resurrection of Jesus Christ that God makes his will known to us, and there we see that God's will is for our good, our ultimate good. To state this more fully, it is in the birth, life, ministry, teachings, healings, sacrifice, death, resurrection, and ascension of Jesus Christ that God has made known his will for us in order that we be saved to and for him. This is what Jesus was talking about when he said, "I have a baptism to be baptized with, and how great is my distress until it is accomplished!" He had already been baptized by John the Baptist in the Jordan River. Now it was time for him to suffer the baptism of death by crucifixion and to do so on our behalf. And so it is that when we are baptized, we are baptized into the death of Jesus Christ, which is to say that we are so united with him that his death counts for us, and our sin is washed away, so that our old self dies and our new self lives with and for him (Romans 6:3–4). Thanks be to God! All of this will of God for us in Christ has been recorded and preserved for us in the Scriptures, the word of God in its written form. It continues to be proclaimed from pulpits around the world. This is how we know it yet today. This, then, is the good news, which God would have us know: it is God's good and gracious will that we belong to him, in and through Jesus Christ, now and forever and ever.

Second (2), when Jesus Christ teaches us that one is faithful who both knows and does the will of God, the second good news implied is that God's will for us is in fact doable, also. We do not always do God's will, so we must always ask for forgiveness, but God's will is doable. God does not mock us. He does not ask us to do what we cannot do. Instead, he asks us whatever he wills to ask us, and he also gives us whatever he asks. Again, it is not only the case that we are called upon to obey the Ten Commandments and the Great Commandment. Of course we are. But those follow upon what I am talking about here. Those have to do with the Christian life. One must first become Christian and be Christian before one can embark upon, and live, the Christian life. For it is also the case, at a far deeper level, in that it is God's prior will to save us in Jesus Christ, that we are first called upon to obey his will for us by believing in him, by having confidence in his good and benevolent will toward us, by trusting him, by committing ourselves to him, and so to receive from him the salvation he has extended to us.

That is to say, we are to have faith, which John Calvin defined as "a firm and certain knowledge of God's benevolence toward us, founded upon the truth of the freely given promise in Christ, both revealed to our minds and sealed upon our hearts through the Holy Spirit."[1] God's will is for our good and for our well-being, and our obedience to his good will includes our gladly accepting all that he gives us. In summary, the good news standing behind and underneath the teaching of Jesus Christ—that one who is faithful both (1) does the will of God and also does so because he or she (2) knows the will of God—is that the will of God for us is, in fact, both (1) knowable and also (2) doable. For all of this, for these words of life and hope, we give God thanks and praise.

This understanding of the gospel and teachings of Jesus Christ is confirmed by his conclusion to this central section of his teaching in today's reading: "Everyone to whom much was given, of him much will be required." We have been given so, so much. We have been given the only Son of God. We have been given salvation. We have been given the knowledge of the will of God. Thus God has poured out his grace upon us. Therefore, much will be required of us, of you and me. You and I are called to faith. We are called to joy. We are called to worship. We are called to prayer. We are called to life. And, yes, of course, we are all called to obedience. How good it is that God has both given so much to us and also therefore expects so much of us! Lord, help us!

"Who then is the faithful and wise manager, whom his master will set over his household, to give them their portion of food at the proper time?" "Who . . . is the faithful and wise manager?" In short, "Who is faithful?" The one who knows and does the will of God, which will is, thank God, both knowable and doable.

To God be the glory forever and ever! Amen.

---

1. Calvin, *Institutes*, III.2.7, 1:551.

38

Worse than All the Others?

LUKE 13:1–17; EXODUS 3:1–15

"Do you think that these Galileans were worse sinners than all the other Galileans, because they suffered in this way? . . . Or those eighteen on whom the tower in Siloam fell and killed them: do you think that they were worse offenders than all the others who lived in Jerusalem?" Suffering. Pain. Death. Loss. Sin. Guilt. Despair. Fear. Presumption of one's own innocence. Jesus is into the thick of it now! This is not about angels in heaven. This is not about ancient rules and regulations. This is not about the niceties of worship. This is about life. This is about life in the rough and tumble world of the Roman Empire, which was not so different from the world in which we live. We still know about murderous tyrants, about contempt for others' religion, and even about falling towers. These teachings of Jesus Christ are about the meaning of life, and they are particularly about the meaning of life precisely when we are brought face to face with the end of life. What does it mean when one day we are here and the next day we are not?

Again and again, we have seen that the questions in the Gospel according to Luke point us toward the truth being taught, toward the affirmation being made, and toward the gospel being proclaimed. The same holds true for today's reading. Jesus asks a question of his hearers. Thus Luke asks the question to Theophilus, for whom he wrote this book. And so Jesus and Luke both ask the same question to us. In fact, the question so important that it is repeated almost word for word to be sure that we get it: "Do you think that these Galileans were worse sinners than all the other Galileans, because they suffered in this way? . . . Or those eighteen on whom the tower in Siloam fell and killed them: do you think that they were worse offenders than all the others who lived in Jerusalem?"

There are three answers to this question, three levels of response. The first answer (1), unstated but assumed, is "Yes." Yes, of course, the hearers thought that the slaughtered Galileans were worse sinners than all the other Galileans and that the eighteen on whom the tower fell were worse than all the others who lived in Jerusalem. That was obvious. Yes, of course, they thought those people were worse, or Jesus would not have posed the question the way he did. He was not looking for information. He knew what they thought. Jesus put their thoughts into the form of a question so that he could provide an alternative answer. We will get to that in a moment. But the first answer, the premise of this whole teaching, is that yes, of course, the hearers did think that the slaughtered Galileans were worse sinners than all the other Galileans and that the eighteen on whom the tower fell were worse than all the others who lived in Jerusalem. Worse than all the others. Worse, of course, than the hearers.

There are a couple of things going on here in this first, affirmative answer to the question. One (a) has to do with self-deception. Never underestimate the power of self-deception. It must have been a means of self-protection that the hearers of such bad news had to tell themselves that they were different from those other people, that those other people must have had something wrong with them, that those other people must have had it coming to them, and that whatever horrible things happened to those other people could not and would not ever happen to them. God forbid! Perhaps at some level they knew that was not true. Perhaps at some level they knew they too had good reason to be afraid of murderous tyrants and falling towers. But they could not face that directly. So they convinced themselves that such bad things happened only to other people, to bad people, to people worse than all the others. Or at least that is what they wanted to believe. Does that sound familiar? Do people still think that way today? Do tsunamis happen only far away? What about earthquakes, hurricanes, fires, and floods?

Beyond the power of individual self-deception, the same thought (b) was enshrined in their religious teachings. That was how they made sense of the world in which they lived. They were convinced that God punished evildoers in this world and that God rewarded the good people in this world. Severe suffering and death were regarded as evidence of divine displeasure and therefore of sin and immorality, while health and wealth were considered evidence of divine blessing and therefore of one's religious and moral superiority. Thus the world was divided simply among the good people and the bad people. And there was no sympathy for the people who suffered, since the system encouraged self-righteousness—the system encouraged not gratitude to God, but self-righteousness—there was no sympathy for the people who suffered on the part of those who did not suffer.

Of course, since the sinless and righteous Jesus Christ himself later "suffered under Pontius Pilate, was crucified, dead, and buried," Christians eventually had to come to question and to reject the simple correlation of suffering in this world with the punishment of God and therefore to question and to reject the simple correlation of ease in this world with the reward of God. And in fact, that rejection is exactly where this teaching is heading. We will get to that in a moment. But the first answer to the question about whether his hearers thought sufferers were worse sinners, an unstated but everywhere assumed answer, was that yes, of course, they thought that. And they did so with a vengeance.

They are not the only ones. It is still a temptation today (c) to think that people deserve the suffering they receive. It is easy to think that people are poor because they are lazy. It is easy to think that people are sick because they misbehave. It is easy to think that people are lost because they want to be, confused because they enjoy it, wandering because they choose it, and on and on. That is to say, it is easy to think that those who suffer are worse sinners than all the rest of us. But just because it is easy to think that does not make it right.

The second answer (2) to the question is the one that Jesus gives, and it is, of course, exactly the opposite of that of his hearers: "Do you think that these Galileans were worse sinners than all the other Galileans, because they suffered in this way? No, I tell you . . . Or those eighteen on whom the tower in Siloam fell and killed them: do you think that they were worse offenders than all the others who lived in Jerusalem? No, I tell you." No. No, no, no, no, no! Not at all. Don't go there. That is not the way it works. According to this explicit teaching of Jesus Christ, even those who suffer horrible deaths, whether by a cruel tyrant or by a seeming accident, are not worse sinners than the rest of us. That false understanding is laid to rest once and for all, forever and ever. That is not the way the world works. That is not the way God works. That is not the way we are to think. The first answer, "Yes," has tremendous staying power, even among us church people yet today. But this second answer, "No," is the truth. This "No" is the explicit teaching of Jesus Christ. This "No" is part of the gospel. This "No" is the answer to which we are to return again and again.

This second answer, this "No," makes the world a much more complicated place. It is not easy to sort out the good people from the bad people. The evidence that provided the grounds for our self-righteousness has been cut out from underneath us. The tendency to separate ourselves from the sufferers has been rejected. And this makes us realize that God is more complex than we thought. Yes, of course, he rewards the good and punishes the evil, but he does not necessarily do so in this world. Sometimes the evildoers prosper here, and we are not to fret over it. Sometimes God allows his chosen ones to suffer here, and we are not to be dismayed by it. Our own presumptions of righteousness are left in shambles, and therefore we are cast back upon the sheer grace, mercy, love, goodness, and righteousness of God Almighty alone. And that, of course, is a good place to be.

Now, there is also a third answer (3) given to the question. It is not so much a verbal answer as an implied action. And it has a real twist to it. "Do you think that these Galileans were worse sinners than all the other Galileans, because they suffered in this way? No, I tell you; but unless you repent, you will all likewise perish. Or those eighteen on whom the tower in Siloam fell and killed them: do you think that they were worse offenders than all the others who lived in Jerusalem? No, I tell you; but unless you repent, you will all likewise perish." Can you believe that? Not only are the sufferers not any worse sinners than all the rest of us, but also we are likely to meet the same terrible end. Moreover, even worse than the horrible deaths those people suffered was the possibility that their sudden deaths had caught them not right with God. Their sudden deaths stand as a warning to all the rest of us to repent of our sin and to turn to God while we still have time and before we die apart from God. It is that simple. That is what Jesus is saying here.

Remember that Jesus was speaking to the people of God and about the people of God. The Galileans from the north had even been slaughtered while they were worshiping God in Jerusalem. So Jesus was not talking about unbelievers. And he was talking to his followers, and so he is talking to us yet today, with his warning to repent. Indeed, our very continuing to be alive is itself evidence of the grace, mercy, and patience of God, who is giving us time to repent.[1] But we should not presume upon this grace of God. We should receive it gratefully and use it for the purpose for which it is given, to repent and return to God. His patience will not last forever. As Jesus taught of the fruitless fig tree, "If it should bear fruit next year, well and good; but if not, you can cut it down." Do not wait.

To repent is both to turn away from sin, to turn away from self-centeredness, to turn away from the presumption of self-righteousness, and also to turn instead to God, who made us for himself, who calls us his very own, and who sent his son to die that we might live. Of course, this is not a simple human possibility. If we were good enough to repent on our own, we would not need to repent. The fact that we do need to repent is indicative of our need for the grace of God. All of this is to say that the order of events is important. It is not the case that we repent first in order to receive the gospel second. It is instead the case that, having heard the gospel first, having received the good news of Jesus Christ first, then we repent second, then we turn away from the gone-wrongness of our lives, and then we turn to God. So repenting is not merely the prelude to the Christian life. Repenting is the content of the Christian life, and we are to continue to do it until the day we die. That is to say, it has less to do with justification and more to do with sanctification.

Yes, this teaching of Jesus Christ is a warning, and thus it is also an invitation. It is a wonderful, gracious, life-giving invitation to follow the loving Jesus Christ who has come to us to make us his very own. And there is an urgency to this gospel invitation. Do not wait until tomorrow to begin to turn ever more fully to God and so to follow Jesus Christ ever more closely. Now even massive human suffering in the

---

1. Compare 2 Peter 3:8–9: "But do not overlook this one fact, beloved, that with the Lord one day is as a thousand years, and a thousand years as one day. The Lord is not slow to fulfill his promise as some count slowness, but is patient toward you, not wishing that any should perish, but that all should reach repentance."

world becomes the occasion not for promoting self-righteousness, self-satisfaction, or a sense of superiority, but instead for self-examination, remorse, and repentance, for commitment to improvement, to obedience, and to righteousness, and for gratitude, graciousness, and the worship of God Almighty.

"Do you think that these Galileans were worse sinners than all the other Galileans, because they suffered in this way? No, I tell you; but unless you repent, you will all likewise perish. Or those eighteen on whom the tower in Siloam fell and killed them: do you think that they were worse offenders than all the others who lived in Jerusalem? No, I tell you; but unless you repent, you will all likewise perish."

To God be the glory forever and ever! Amen.

39

What Is the Kingdom of God?

LUKE 13:18–35; ISAIAH 66:18–24

"WHAT IS THE KINGDOM of God like? And to what shall I compare it?" This repetition and variation of the question emphasizes its importance. Then, to be sure that we catch it, Jesus asks the question yet a third time: "To what shall I compare the kingdom of God?" So this is the thrice asked question that points us toward, and therefore leads us into, the good news in today's reading from Luke: "What is the kingdom of God like?" What is the reign of God like? What is the rule of God like? How shall we recognize it? How shall we enter it? How shall we participate in it? How is it related to this world? How is it related to heaven? What does it mean for our lives? What is the kingdom of God?

There are at least five answers given in today's reading, and we shall get to those in just a moment. But even before we do that, it is worthwhile to reflect a little on the implications of the question itself. "What is the kingdom of God?" For starters, it is that kingdom that belongs to, and therefore is ruled by, none other than God himself. That seems very simple, but one thing it means is that God, and God alone, gets to define the kingdom of God. The kingdom is his; he alone can say what it is. This reality eliminates a lot of speculation on our part. This truth eliminates the role of our imagination. This teaching eliminates the false teachings of those who want to claim the kingdom for their own political goals and purposes. And this also says something about Jesus Christ: the fact that he can and does tell us about the kingdom of God indicates not only that he speaks on behalf of God but also and even more so that Jesus is in fact God himself with us and for us. Jesus Christ defines the kingdom of God. The kingdom of God is his kingdom. He is the king. Jesus is God with us and for us. Thanks be to God!

"What is the kingdom of God like? And to what shall I compare it?" The first (1) answer uses agricultural imagery. "It is like a grain of mustard seed that a man took and sowed in his garden, and it grew and became a tree, and the birds of the air made nests in its branches." How very strange! No kings. No generals. No battles or wars. No borders. No boundaries. No taxes. What kind of kingdom is this? This first agricultural answer emphasizes a tiny, inauspicious beginning, an element of purposefulness on the part of the man planting it, the mystery of growth, and then the wonderfully contrasting ending of a huge tree providing a home and shelter for God's good creatures, the birds of the air. That is to say, the kingdom of God might start with only one lonely teacher and twelve sorry disciples, but we should not despise such small beginnings. That is to say, the kingdom of God may look like two little country churches in Amelia County, Virginia, but we will not be worried by such intermediary manifestations. The kingdom of God, then, (1) grows remarkably, inexplicably, and to great benefit for many throughout the world.

"To what shall I compare the kingdom of God?" The second (2) answer uses food preparation imagery. "It is like leaven that a woman took and hid in three measures of flour, until it was all leavened." Again, how very strange! No men. No rules or rulers. No laws or regulations. No flags. No banners. No trumpets. What kind of kingdom is this? This second food preparation answer emphasizes mystery, silence, hiddenness, and yet a widespread influence on all that it touches. Just a little bit of yeast makes all the dough rise. So the kingdom of God, then, not only (1) grows remarkably, inexplicably, and to great benefit to many throughout the world, but it also (2) works in a hidden and mysterious way to have a tremendous influence on all within its reach. The kingdom is both (1) growing and (2) influential.

What else is there to say about the kingdom of God? The reading indicates that Jesus "went on his way through towns and villages, teaching and journeying toward Jerusalem." Such a geographical signal might indicate that he was changing the subject of his teaching to something else. Moreover, someone asked him what might seem to be a different question: "Lord, will those who are saved be few?" Jesus certainly did not seem to have many followers at that time. On the face of it, this question seems to be about a different topic. And yet, in his answer to this question about the number of people to be saved, Jesus not only turns the question back onto the questioner, calling for his own response to the gospel and therefore calling for our response to the gospel, but he also says three more things about the kingdom of God. And our understanding of what he has to say about that kingdom depends upon our hearing what he has to say in answer to this interjected question about being saved, so we should listen to this first:

> Strive to enter through the narrow door. For many, I tell you, will seek to enter and will not be able. When once the master of the house has risen and shut the door, and you begin to stand outside and to knock at the door, saying, "Lord, open to us," then he will answer you, "I do not know where you come

from." Then you will begin to say, "We ate and drank in your presence, and you taught in our streets." But he will say, "I tell you, I do not know where you come from. Depart from me, all you workers of evil!"

This indicates that there is an urgency to the gospel invitation and that there is a timeliness to our response. There is a time now to enter through the narrow door, a door perhaps as narrow as a cross, but there will be a time in the future when even that narrow door is shut. Do not wait too long! Enter now.

Then Jesus, in his third (3) answer to our primary question, names that future time and place on the other side of that shut door as none other than the kingdom of God. "In that place [outside the door] there will be weeping and gnashing of teeth, when you see Abraham and Isaac and Jacob and all the prophets in the kingdom of God but you yourselves cast out." What kind of kingdom is that? The patriarchs are there, and all the prophets are there, but not all the children of Israel are there. Not all the hearers of the gospel are there. Not all the members of the church are there. To be saved is to be in the kingdom of God. Not to be saved is to be left outside the kingdom of God.

The important question for us is not how many or how few others will be there but whether each of us hearers of the gospel has become a believer of the gospel and a follower of Jesus Christ and so has entered the narrow door of the kingdom. Given that the prophets are inside the kingdom, this strongly suggests that we are to be attentive to the word of God, which is what we are trying to do this very moment, in the reading and preaching of the word of God. Given that the faithful ones are inside the kingdom, this strongly suggests that the narrow door is the door of faith, the door of believing in Jesus Christ, and in Jesus Christ alone, as Lord and Savior. There is no room to carry our own supposed goodness through the narrow door. So the kingdom of God, then, not only (1) grows remarkably, inexplicably, and to great benefit to many, even in this world and time, and not only (2) works in a hidden and mysterious way to have a tremendous influence on all within its reach, even in this world and time, but is also (3) a matter of great urgency, a matter of ultimacy, and a matter calling our for our timely response now, before it is too late.

Then Jesus immediately follows this declaration of urgency with a fourth (4) answer to our question, an answer going in yet another direction, opening even another dimension. "And people will come from east and west, and from north and south, and recline at table in the kingdom of God." Can you imagine? Despite the exclusivity of urgency, people will come from all over the world to eat together at the banquet of the kingdom of God. People of all races, people of all nationalities, people of all ethnicities, people of all languages, people of all colors, people of all circumstances and conditions, people rich and people poor, will all come together to live in, and to be a part of, this wonderful kingdom of God revealed to us in these teachings of our Lord Jesus Christ. Even Gentile people of faith will join the patriarchs and the prophets.

"They shall bring all your brothers from all the nations as an offering to the Lord, on horses and in chariots and in litters and on mules and on dromedaries, to my holy mountain Jerusalem, says the Lord" (Isaiah 66:20). And when they get there, they will all be eating together.

Two Sundays from now is World Communion Sunday. The Lord's Supper which we are about to share then will be not only a memory of the Last Supper of Jesus Christ but also an anticipation of this great heavenly banquet yet to come. So the kingdom of God, then, not only (1) grows remarkably, inexplicably, and to great benefit to many, and not only (2) works in a hidden and mysterious way to have a tremendous influence on all within its reach, and not only (3) is a matter of great urgency, a matter of ultimacy, and a matter calling our for our timely response, but it is also (4) a place of—dare we say it?—a great, wonderful, far-reaching, and almost unimaginable inclusivity, all around a good meal. How can we rest content here and now until we have sent missionaries to all the nations and gathered all the world here around this very table?

And yet, even within that context of inclusivity, there will still be surprises. Jesus gives what I take to be a fifth (5) answer to our question, though the kingdom of God is not named explicitly in this one sentence. It does follow immediately upon what he said about people from everywhere eating together, so surely it is referring to that same reality. "And behold, some are last who will be first, and some are first who will be last." What kind of disorderly kingdom is that? The first are not first. The last are not last. People do not get what they think they deserve. And more importantly, people do not get what they really do deserve. Thanks be to God!

The gospel is not about justice. The gospel is about mercy. If we got what we deserved, we would all go to hell. Whatever you ask for, do not ask for what you deserve. That would be awful. Thanks be to God that God does not give us what we deserve! God gave Jesus Christ what we deserve, and he gives us what Jesus deserves. This is the amazing truth and reality of the gospel. The kingdom of God is a backwards kind of place. It involves tremendous reversals and upheavals. So the kingdom of God, then, not only (1) grows remarkably and inexplicably, and not only (2) works in a hidden and mysterious way with tremendous influence, and not only (3) is a matter of great urgency, and ultimacy, and not only (4) is a place of a great and wonderful inclusivity, but is also (5) a matter of strange and unexpected reversals.

"What is the kingdom of God like? And to what shall I compare it?" It is (1) quietly growing, (2) massively influential, (3) ultimately urgent, (4) wildly inclusive, and (5) startlingly backwards. This we know from the very King of kings and Lord of lords, the one who speaks for God and who is God, the one of whom alone it is proper to say, "Blessed is he who comes in the name of the Lord!" If you realize and know that Jesus Christ is the King of the kingdom, then he is the most important thing in your life. Conversely, if Jesus Christ is not the most important thing in your life, you do not have a clue as to what is going on in the world. So, is this kingdom of interest to you? "Strive to enter through the narrow door." Believe in Jesus Christ as Lord and Savior. It is through such faith that we acknowledge him as King and by this very acknowledgment are thus brought into his kingdom.

To God be the glory forever and ever! Amen.

40

Is It Lawful to Heal?

LUKE 14:1–24; EXODUS 20:8–11

"IS IT LAWFUL TO heal on the Sabbath, or not?" Thus Jesus responded to the carefully watching Pharisees. It strikes me as a very strange question for him to ask. It assumes, of course, the power to heal, either on his part or someone else's. It names the issue, before his detractors articulated it, of the rightness or wrongness of certain activities on the Sabbath. That in turn raises the question of the nature and purpose of the Sabbath itself. And all of this together leads me to ask, what does this ancient question have to do with us? Sabbath keeping seems very esoteric or even quaint. What does this have to do with you and me, on Sunday, October 2, 2011, as we gather for the worship of God?

"Is it lawful to heal on the Sabbath, or not?" Again and again in the Gospel according to Luke, we have found that the questions have pointed us in the right direction and have led us to the good news of Jesus Christ. It is my contention that this question will do the same thing. "Is it lawful to heal on the Sabbath, or not?" The (1) negative assumption here, of course, is that there is reluctance on the part of his hearers for healings to be conducted on the Sabbath. Apparently it was regarded as a form of work. I note for the record that there is not a word in the Ten Commandments forbidding healing on the Sabbath. So these hearers were overzealous and far too strict in their application of the law to the lives of the people, especially other people. That is clearly part of what is going on here. However, I cannot see how that applies to us today. So, let us move on.

"Is it lawful to heal on the Sabbath, or not?" The (2) positive affirmation being made here, the good news toward which this question points, is that the will of God is for human well-being, even when it involves healing on the Sabbath. The will of God, articulated and lived out by Jesus Christ, is for human well-being, for the healing of the gone-wrongness of humanity. This is good news, indeed. It is *good* to know that God is for us and not against us. And it is *news* to find out that God is for us and not against us, because that is not at all obvious when we look around the world. Despite the number of things in the world for us—food and drink, air and light, friends and family—there are a tremendous number of things that work against us—including disease, decay, decline, and death. These last things can tend to make us doubt the goodness of God.

"Is it lawful to heal on the Sabbath, or not?" The positive affirmation being made here, the good news toward which this question points, is that the will of God, articulated and lived out by Jesus Christ, is for human well-being, for the healing of the gone-wrongness of humanity. Since this is not immediately obvious, it is good that Jesus teaches this to us. That is to say, this is something we can learn. This is something we can receive. This is something we can hang on to. This is something we can hold close. The will of God is for human well-being. The will of God is for our well-being. The will of God is for your well-being and for mine, today. And if God is for us, who can be against us (Romans 8:31b)? Now, it may be that God's understanding of what ails us and God's understanding of our well-being are far different from our own. We will get to that in a moment. For now, let us rejoice in the good news that God wills our well-being.

There is more here than the question that points to the good will of God. When no one would answer the question that Jesus asked, he took the sick man who had come among them, healed him, and sent him away. Jesus backed up his words with actions. Jesus backed up his teaching with healing. Jesus backed up the good news of God's good will with the reality of a man made well. One would think this would have convinced them. One would think this would have moved them. One would think this would have impressed them. One would think such a miracle would have led them to faith. But it seems only to have hardened them in their faithlessness. "They remained silent." And Jesus said to them, "Which of you, having a son or an ox that has fallen into a well on a Sabbath day, will not immediately pull him out?" "They remained silent." "They could not reply to these things."

This exchange, or the lack thereof, brings two things to our attention. The first (1) is that the negative example of hardened hearts stands as a warning to all of us today. That is not the right way to respond to Jesus. Distrust, dislike, arrogance, contempt, disdain, the presumption of moral superiority, disregard for human well-being, standoffishness, and stony, hard, cold silence are not the right way to respond to Jesus. We have no interest in belittling the Pharisees two thousand years after the fact. That is not the point here. But the point is that what they did inappropriately continues to stand as a warning even for us, here on the other side of the world, all these centuries later. What a wonderful privilege it is that the gospel of Jesus Christ has been given to us! Let us not squander this gift by acting as if it were of no significance to us.

The second (2) thing brought to our attention by this healing, despite the failure of its witnesses to appreciate it, is that Jesus is the agent of God's good will for us, which is to say that Jesus Christ is God with us and God for us. The question of the lawfulness of healing on the Sabbath, followed by just such a healing conducted by Jesus, leads directly to this good news: Jesus is the agent of God's good will for us, which is to say that Jesus Christ is God with us and God for us. God has not remained silent. God has not remained hidden. God has not remained far away. God has drawn near to us and come to us in the person and work of Jesus Christ, in the life, death, and resurrection of Jesus Christ. God is here! There is no more doubting. There is no more questioning. There is no more wondering or imagining. God has revealed himself to us in Jesus Christ.

At this point, our reading takes an odd twist and turn. Having healed the man and sent him home, Jesus goes right ahead with dinner, observing human behavior and teaching, almost as if nothing had happened. He begins with what has always seemed to me to be his most *un*remarkable teaching. It is good and useful and interesting, but it seems to be based entirely on common sense and so to have no specifically religious content:

> When you are invited by someone to a wedding feast, do not sit down in a place of honor, lest someone more distinguished than you be invited by him, and he who invited you both will come and say to you, "Give your place to this person," and then you will begin with shame to take the lowest place. But when you are invited, go and sit in the lowest place, so that when your host comes he may say to you, "Friend, move up higher." Then you will be honored in the presence of all who sit at table with you.

That makes sense. It is even good advice. But is it good news?

The gospel significance of the teaching is made clear in the two additional concluding lines: "For everyone who exalts himself will be humbled, and he who humbles himself will be exalted." Suddenly we are far beyond the wedding feast. We are far beyond table manners, as good and as important as they are. We are far beyond social strategies of how to be honored instead of embarrassed. Suddenly the teaching has been universalized to apply to all people, including us. And the teaching has been placed within the ultimate context of final judgment, of eternal humiliation or exaltation. Self-exaltation and arrogance here in this world, such as unbelief in, rejection of, and disobedience of God, will be dealt with supremely harshly in the world to come. Self-humbling and service here in this world, such as faith in, acceptance of, and obedience to, Jesus Christ, will be dealt with very graciously in the world to come. The stakes are high. The gospel contains both warning and promise. Which will it be for us?

Then Jesus turned from the guests and offered an even more pointed teaching to their host:

> When you give a dinner or a banquet, do not invite your friends or your broth-
> ers or your relatives or rich neighbors, lest they also invite you in return and
> you be repaid. But when you give a feast, invite the poor, the crippled, the
> lame, the blind, and you will be blessed, because they cannot repay you.

Is this for real? Well, yes, I think it is. And it undercuts the reciprocity that we value so
highly. And yet, the conclusion of this teaching also carries us far beyond this world:
"You will be repaid at the resurrection of the just." There is a context of ultimacy. There
is a teaching from the great world beyond. There is a word here spoken to us from
outside and beyond us. Jesus Christ speaks to us on behalf of, and therefore as, God
himself.

Finally, Jesus builds on his teaching of what a dinner should be to tell a grand
parable of that most wonderful banquet of all, the very kingdom of God. Someone else
brought up the topic: "Blessed is everyone who will eat bread in the kingdom of God!"
But Jesus said to him:

> A man once gave a great banquet and invited many. And at the time for the
> banquet he sent his servant to say to those who had been invited, "Come, for
> everything is now ready." But they all alike began to make excuses. The first
> said to him, "I have bought a field, and I must go out and see it. Please have
> me excused." And another said, "I have bought five yoke of oxen, and I go to
> examine them. Please have me excused." And another said, "I have married a
> wife, and therefore I cannot come." So the servant came and reported these
> things to his master. Then the master of the house became angry.

So far, so good; this makes perfect sense. But it is precisely at this point that common
sense is left behind and a strange, heavenly kind of logic begins to take over:

> Then the master of the house became angry and said to his servant, "Go out
> quickly to the streets and lanes of the city, and bring in the poor and crippled
> and blind and lame." And the servant said, "Sir, what you commanded has
> been done, and still there is room." And the master said to the servant, "Go
> out to the highways and hedges and compel people to come in, that my house
> may be filled. For I tell you, none of those men who were invited shall taste
> my banquet."

And this, I submit to you, is the gospel answer to our initial question. "Is it lawful to
heal on the Sabbath, or not?" "Go out to the highways and hedges and compel people
to come in, that my house may be filled." Thanks be to God!

"Is it lawful to heal on the Sabbath, or not?" That is the question. The positive
affirmation being made here, the good news toward which this question points, is that
the will of God, articulated and lived out by Jesus Christ, is for human well-being, for
the healing of the gone-wrongness of humanity. "Is it lawful to heal on the Sabbath,
or not?" Here is the answer, the concrete form of the positive affirmation: "Go out

quickly to the streets and lanes of the city, and bring in the poor and crippled and blind and lame. . . . Go out to the highways and hedges and compel people to come in, that my house may be filled." The greatest illness from which we all suffer is our horrible estrangement from God. The great banquet that God provides, the very kingdom of God, is a breathtakingly broad, surprising, and startling reconciliation, reaching out to include the least among us and the most unlikely to be invited, and so it is healing for the deepest wound of our estrangement.

Yes, this is the purpose of the Sabbath, a day of rest and remembrance, to bring us close to God. This is why we are here in church today. Yes, this is the content of the gospel, that God has come close to us in Jesus Christ and that God brings us close to himself. This is what we preach. Yes, this is the good news of Jesus Christ, that he is God with us and God for us. He has come to the streets and the lanes of our cities and counties to find even us. He has come to the highways and hedges of our cities and counties to find even us. He is determined that his house shall be full. This gives us good reason to live. This gives us good reason to believe and to obey. This gives us good reason to carry Christ's invitation to all the people of the world. Yes, it is lawful to heal on the Sabbath. And God himself is doing that for us, lifting us out of brokenness and death and restoring us to himself. Let us rejoice in this great goodness of God toward us.

To God be the glory forever and ever! Amen.

41

Do You Not Count the Cost?

LUKE 14:25–35; PROVERBS 24:3–6

"FOR WHICH OF YOU, desiring to build a tower, does not first sit down and count the cost, whether he has enough to complete it?" In short, the question is, "Which of you . . . does not first sit down and count the cost?" In case we did not get it the first time, Jesus and Luke repeat the question for us in a slightly different form: "Or what king, going out to encounter another king in war, will not sit down first and deliberate whether he is able with ten thousand to meet him who comes against him with twenty thousand?" Again, the underlying question is, "Do you not count the cost?" Before you build a house, before you embark on any grand endeavor, do you not count the cost? Do you not determine what the cost will be and whether or not you are able and willing to pay it?

As happens so many times, the question functions on several levels. At the simplest and most basic level (1), it is a request for information. Jesus asked the crowd, and so us, "Before you do anything significant, which of you does not sit down and count the cost?" The way the question was asked, I am sure that the crowd would have answered that none of them would fail to count the cost. That was, in fact, the point of the question. None of them would have failed to count the cost. I suspect the same is true of us today. None of us would fail to count the cost. Oh, we may be careless on frivolous or insignificant things, but on anything of significance or importance, we count the cost. We do the math. We make the calculations. That is the way we are. And that, again, is the initial point of the question. Jesus is pointing out to us the way we are, and he is seeking our acknowledgment of that reality to build a foundation to make his main point.

So, at its simplest level and in its very form, the question is a request for information. Of course, it assumes a particular answer and does not even wait for a reply. So, immediately and even simultaneously, the question also functions at a second level (2) as an affirmation not only of reality but also of a certain practicality in doing things and therefore of the wisdom underlying that. Of course people count the cost before they build. They would be ridiculed if they did not and their building project had to stop half way and stand incomplete. Of course kings deliberate before they go to war. If they did not, they would not live to go to war again or to do anything else. Not only is this the way things are, but also it is good that things are this way, and it is even the case that those who act in this way are wise. They are, after all, fulfilling the ancient proverbs that we have read together from the very word of God.

So, the question is both a request for information and also an affirmation of the goodness and wisdom of the reality toward which it points. "Do you count the cost?" Yes, of course we do. Good, that is what you are supposed to do. That is what God wants you to do. Now, given that—and here comes the kicker, where Jesus takes it up to the third level (3)—given that you are wise enough to count the cost before you build a tower, do you think it might make sense to use the same procedure before you follow me? Do you think that following me might be at least as important as building another tower in the back yard? Do you not realize that I am doing battle with forces far greater than those amassed by any earthly king? Would you at least do me the courtesy of coming into this relationship with your eyes wide open? Beyond information and affirmation, he is asking for consideration. What good is a crowd that carries Jesus to and through Palm Sunday if they thin out and desert him by Good Friday?

Fourth (4), then, the question is not merely about towers and wars. The question is finally about the cost of following Jesus Christ. The question is about the cost of Christian faith and life. The question is about the cost of discipleship. Do you have any idea? Do you know what it will cost to be a disciple? Do you know what it will cost to be a believer in and a follower of Jesus Christ? Do you know what it will cost to give your life to him? And are you willing to consider it? Are you willing to think about it? Are you willing to count up the cost before you jump in all excited but not knowing what you are up to? These strike us, I suspect, as very strange questions. We are accustomed to people trying to talk us into something. This sounds as if Jesus was trying to talk people out of something. But I think he knew that he did not need shallow, uninformed, and therefore uncommitted disciples. They would only fall away later on.

"Which of you . . . does not first sit down and count the cost?" This has now become a deadly serious question. What is the cost of Christian discipleship? And are we willing to consider it? The cost might not have been so obvious to those first hearers. But we have a tremendous advantage over them. And the cost is nothing we have to imagine or speculate about. I submit to you that the answer to the implied question in this passage is found beyond this passage in the rest of the gospel. The answer to the question of the cost of discipleship can only be found in, and determined by, the answer to the prior question of the cost of Christ-ship. The answer to the question of how much it costs to follow Christ can only be found in, and determined by, the answer to the prior question of how much it cost to be Christ. The answer to the question of how much the Christian life costs can only be found in, and determined by, the answer to the prior question of how much the life of Christ cost. And that we know. That we know.

The great, good news, unspoken in today's reading but surely standing behind it, is that Jesus counted the cost for Christ-ship. Jesus paid the price to be the Christ. He paid with his life. The cost for living as the Christ was dying as the Christ. Without the latter, the former would not be. Consider the three things that Jesus did say about discipleship in this passage, and think about how each applies first of all to him. First (1), "If anyone comes to me and does not hate his own father and mother and wife and children and brothers and sisters, yes, and even his own life, he cannot be my disciple." Does this sound harsh? And yet, Jesus himself left his earthly father and mother, as well as his brothers and sisters, in order to do what he did. They all thought he was crazy. Jesus took no wife and had no children in order to do what he did. Jesus gave "even his own life" in order to do what he did. Everything that he asked of his hearers he did himself. Everything that he asks of us he has already done himself. He counted the cost. He paid the price.

Second (2), "Whoever does not bear his own cross and come after me cannot be my disciple." Does this not sound bizarre? "Bear his own cross?" Submit to execution by the Roman Empire? Hang outside the city and die? This teaching makes absolutely no sense apart from the historical reality that Jesus Christ himself did bear his own cross to a hill outside Jerusalem, and did submit to execution by the Roman Empire so that he hanged there and died. He paid the price. He could not ask people to "come after" him to the cross unless he went to the cross himself. And he did.

Third (3), "So therefore, any one of you who does not renounce all that he has cannot be my disciple." All? Does he really mean all? Everything? Well, what did Jesus have left at the end? Absolutely nothing. Not a penny. Not a friend. Not a house. Not a home. Not a breath. Not a drop of blood. Not a heartbeat. Not a stitch of clothing. He gave it all up in order to be who he was. If he had kept any of it, he would have had something, but he would have been nothing. He would not have been the Christ. But he gave it all up. He counted the cost. He paid the price. He paid it for you and me. He built the kingdom. He has won the war. God expected everything from Jesus, and he received it—even his very life. When the way is hard and the night is dark, and when doubt, frustration, weariness, and sadness assail us and threaten to undo and defeat us, it is encouraging to know that Christ has traveled this way before us and travels it with us even now, helping us in our weakness. And so he bids us to come and follow.

Again, I submit to you that it is only within this context of the cost of Christ-ship that we can begin to realize or understand the cost of discipleship. Listen again to the three things he says to us about discipleship, and consider how they apply to us. First

(1), "If anyone comes to me and does not hate his own father and mother and wife and children and brothers and sisters, yes, and even his own life, he cannot be my disciple." Jesus Christ calls for our highest loyalty. With him, it is all or nothing. He will not and cannot take second place to anyone. If you love your father and mother more than you love Jesus Christ, you are not his disciple. If you love your wife and children more than you love Jesus Christ, you are not his disciple. If you love your brothers and sisters more than you love Jesus Christ, you are not his disciple. In fact, if you love your own life more than you love Jesus Christ, you are not his disciple. We cannot have multiple, absolute commitments. Christ calls for our exclusive, absolute commitment. Jesus may or may not ever call us to act on any of these "hatreds," if you will, any of these acknowledgments of lesser loyalty. Most of us have not had to leave father and mother, wife and children, brothers and sisters. Those of us here today have not yet been asked to give our lives. But at the very least, we are asked to be ready to make these sacrifices. We are asked to love Jesus more than we love all of these.

Second (2), "Whoever does not bear his own cross and come after me cannot be my disciple." On the one hand, Christ has gone to the cross for us and done what we could not do for ourselves. On the other hand, we are called to follow him to the cross. This is not suicide. We are not being asked to take our own lives. This is, after all, and finally, a way of life, not a way of death, as such. But we are being asked to give our own lives. And while some are asked to do this literally and physically, so that we should all be prepared for that, all of us are asked to do this internally and spiritually. We all are to die to self in order to live to God. Self-centeredness is the terrible condition of fallen, sinful humanity. The proper condition is God-centeredness. The only cure for our sickness is to die to self in order to live to God. Note carefully that this stands diametrically opposed to the supposed wisdom of our day and our world, which says that low self-esteem is the problem underlying all human misery and that elevating self-esteem is the great solution to all our problems. That is madness! That is sheer madness! Self-esteem is the great malady of humanity. Elevating self-esteem is the strategy of the devil in his efforts to win us over to himself. Our only hope is to esteem self less and less and so to esteem God and his Christ more and more.

Third (3), "So therefore, any one of you who does not renounce all that he has cannot be my disciple." Yes, he said "all." He means everything. That is what he did, and he did it for us. So there are no halfway disciples. How could the Christ who gave his all be followed half-heartedly? That would not make sense. What does it mean to renounce all? It means, among other things, to live in freedom from the world in order to live in freedom for Christ. It means, among other things, to have things as if we did not have them to have no things as if we did have them (Philippians 4:11–12). It means, among other things, to give substantially and even sacrificially for the cause of the gospel and for the proclamation of the good news. In most cases, that means giving to and through the church of Jesus Christ. Think of the local, regional, national, and international mission upon which we could embark with this kind of giving. It is mind-boggling and exciting. Why are we waiting? At the same time, renouncing all means, among other things, realizing that even what we do not give to the church still belongs to God, and that all we are, all we have, and all we spend are still to be used to the glory of God in all aspects of our lives. These three things define the cost of discipleship.

So (1), "Hate his own father and mother," (2) "Bear his own cross," and (3) "Renounce all that he has." These are strong words. But it does not really seem that it is the intent of Jesus Christ to turn and send everyone away. It does seem, instead, that it is his intent to call and gather people to himself. He certainly invites us to follow him. And he invites us to come to him with our eyes wide open to the high cost of discipleship which follows closely upon the high cost of his own Christ-ship.

> For which of you, desiring to build a tower, does not first sit down and count the cost, whether he has enough to complete it? Otherwise, when he has laid a foundation and is not able to finish, all who see it begin to mock him, saying, "This man began to build and was not able to finish." Or what king, going out to encounter another king in war, will not sit down first and deliberate whether he is able with ten thousand to meet him who comes against him with twenty thousand? . . .
>
> . . . He who has ears to hear, let him hear.

To God be the glory forever and ever! Amen.

42

Do You Not Go after the Lost?

LUKE 15:1–32; EXODUS 32:7–14

"WHAT MAN OF YOU, having a hundred sheep, if he has lost one of them, does not leave the ninety-nine in the open country, and go after the one that is lost, until he finds it?" Here is the question in today's reading. As seems to be the case throughout the Gospel according to Luke, the question points to the gospel, to the main emphasis of the passage. Do any of you own sheep? Even those of us who do not can still appreciate the startling and even dubious strategy of leaving the ninety-nine that were not lost in the open country—not safe in the sheepfold, but still exposed in the open country—for the sake of finding the one that was lost. We can still sense the importance attached by that good shepherd to finding one lost sheep. We can still understand what is being asked: Who among you, if you have lost something valuable to you, does not go and look for it until you find it?

Now, just in case we missed that, Jesus repeats the question to his hearers in a slightly different form, and Luke faithfully records it for us to hear again: "Or what woman, having ten silver coins, if she loses one coin, does not light a lamp and sweep the house and seek diligently until she finds it?" Again, this is the question in today's reading. Its repetition confirms and elevates its importance. It does not matter that some of us are not women. All of us can appreciate the urgency of her loss. It does not matter that we do not use oil-burning lamps with wicks, at least not very often. All of us can appreciate the diligence of her search. It does not mean that she did not treasure the other nine coins. But is does mean that she valued and treasured the one she had lost. We can still understand what is being asked even of us today: Who among you, if you have lost something valuable to you, does not go and look for it until you find it?

Given that this is the question being posed, what is the answer? What is the gospel toward which it points? How does it work? What does it mean? Why does he ask it? As is very often the case, the question functions at several levels, and it is important for us to hear each of these. The first (1) level is a very simple request for information: Who among you, if you have lost something valuable to you, does not go and look for it until you find it? The answer, of course, then and now, is "No one." That is the expected answer from the very way the question is written. No one fails to go and look for a valuable lost possession. If there were a failure to go and look, then by definition the lost possession must not have been very valuable. Some things are not worth looking for. The effort would be a waste of time. If, on the other hand, the lost possession was valuable, then no one fails to go and look for it. If a shepherd let his lost sheep go, before long he would not have a flock. If a woman let her lost coin go, before long she would not have any coins. If a medical researcher let a lost experiment go, she would not find the cure for which she was looking. If a writer let a lost word go, he would not be able to express himself eloquently or powerfully. The initial point of the question is to have the crowd nodding in agreement: Yes, that is what we all do when we lose something valuable; we look for it until we find it.

The second (2) level applies that directly to Jesus Christ. "You agree, then," we can just hear him saying, "that a shepherd looks for his lost sheep?" Yes. "You agree, then, that a woman looks for her lost coin?" Yes, of course. "Then open your eyes to what I am doing in your midst! Open your eyes to me! I am what my parables are about. I am what my question is about." We have to remember that today's reading began with accusations and complaints being made against Jesus. "Now the tax collectors and sinners were all drawing near to hear him [Jesus]. And the Pharisees and the scribes grumbled, saying, 'This man receives sinners and eats with them.'" The argument here in the parables, unstated but obvious, is from the lesser to the greater. If you shepherds seek one, pitiful lost sheep, how much more am I going to seek tax collectors and sinners! If you women seek one lost coin, how much more am I going to seek tax collectors and sinners! That is to say, "You understand the everyday illustrations, so apply them to me. I am the one who seeks and finds the lost, the lost people of the world, even tax collectors and sinners." Okay. That makes sense. It may not have convinced the ones complaining, and we will return to that in a moment, but at least the ones being sought and found probably liked it. Jesus is the one who seeks and finds the lost. That is why he received and even ate with sinners. That is probably not unrelated to why they crucified him not too long after this.

Now, there is at least a third level of meaning to the question, and I want to get to that in just a moment. But we need to stay with this second level a little longer. It is not enough to say that Jesus is the one who seeks and finds the lost. He does that, of course, and the parables illustrate and illuminate his actions brilliantly. But this does raise another consideration. Why does he do this? Who is he? Did not his mother teach him to be careful about with whom he ate and with whom he associated? But, you see, to say that Jesus is the one who seeks and finds the lost is also to say that Jesus is the one to whom the lost belong. The seeking Jesus is the one to whom the tax collectors and sinners belong. The finding Jesus is the one to whom the Pharisees and scribes belonged, whether they liked it or not, whether they knew it or not. The seeking and finding Jesus is the one to whom you and I belong, yet today. This is the great truth toward which the question points. "It is he who made us, and we are his; we are his people, and the sheep of his pasture" (Psalm 100:3b, c).

You see, the argument from the lesser to the greater is not only from the sheep to the sinners or from the coin to the sinners, but is also and even more so from the shepherd and the woman to the Son of God. Jesus is not just anyone looking for sinners. A lot of people look for sinners. Some people want to help them sin more! Some people want to take lessons! Jesus looks for sinners not only to find them but also to rescue them, to bring them back to himself. Jesus looks for sinners in that he is the one to whom all sinners belong. He is the one to whom all people belong. That is to say, Jesus is God himself with us and for us. This is the sort of delayed impact of the second level of meaning of the question in today's reading. "Who among you, if you have lost something valuable to you, does not go and look for it until you find it? Not one of you would fail to do that? Then please understand that neither would I. That is why I am here looking for you. You belong to me. I am the Creator. I am also your Redeemer. That is what this is all about."

Now we are ready for the third (3) level of meaning. And we will be helped in finding it by seeing how Jesus builds up to it. Do the math. To lose one sheep of one hundred would be to suffer a one percent loss. To lose one coin of ten would be to suffer a ten percent loss. That is quite a jump. I did not used to understand or to appreciate the significance of this. A dime, after all, is a silver coin. Losing one makes little difference. So what is the big deal? But what if those ten silver coins were all that she had? The parable is not about pocket change. The parable is not about a coin collection. The parable is about her life savings. The one coin was ten percent of her capital, of all that she had. No wonder it was valuable. See how this concern is building?

Then we come to the third parable. "There was a man who had two sons." This very introduction makes us shudder. We have heard the first two parables already, so we know where this third one is going. "There was a man who had two sons." And he lost one of them. Even at a crude, mathematical level we are up to a fifty percent loss, and we all know, of course, that when we are dealing with people we cannot even use such numbers. The loss is incalculable. The loss is too horrible to contemplate. The loss is too much to bear. Many of you—too many—have lost children. I know that. I grieve with and for you. And I do not mean to dwell on that today. But you know best of all the agony of this poor father. "There was a man who had two sons." Suddenly we are not talking about sheep and coins anymore. We are talking about people. We are talking about loved ones. We are talking about children. We are talking about the hard realities of life and death. And we are still talking about the work of God in and through Jesus Christ.

If the first level of meaning is a simple request for information, and if the second level of meaning is an application to the life and ministry of Jesus Christ, indeed an affirmation of his identity, divinity, and saving work, then the third level of meaning comes back on the first hearers of these parables and therefore comes back on us yet today, raising the question of where we stand in relation to this seeking and finding Christ. Are we admittedly lost and found sinners who enjoy his company and appreciate his table fellowship? Or are we the persistently lost righteous ones who disdain his guests and therefore reject even Christ himself? The stakes are high. Where do we stand? Where do you and I stand in relation to Christ?

Again, we can be helped by observing how the parables build in their description of the joy of finding the lost. First (1), "When he [the shepherd] comes home, he calls together his friends and his neighbors, saying to them, 'Rejoice with me, for I have found my sheep that was lost.' Just so, I tell you, there will be more joy in heaven over one sinner who repents than over ninety-nine righteous persons who need no repentance." Second (2), "When she [the woman] has found it [the coin], she calls together her friends and neighbors, saying, 'Rejoice with me, for I have found the coin that I had lost.' Just so, I tell you, there is joy before the angels of God over one sinner who repents." And then third (3), it is as if Jesus said, Let me show you what joy in heaven looks like: "While he was still a long way off, his father saw him and felt compassion, and ran and embraced him and kissed him. . . . The father said to his servants, 'Bring quickly the best robe, and put it on him, and put a ring on his hand, and shoes on his feet. And bring the fattened calf and kill it, and let us eat and celebrate. For this my son was dead, and is alive again; he was lost, and is found.' And they began to celebrate." Now that is joy in heaven! Who cares about the sheep or the coin anymore? Here we have hugs and kisses, robes and rings, eating and celebrating: "There is joy before the angels of God over one sinner who repents."

And here is precisely where the point about our relation to Christ is made. No sooner has the one son come home than the other refuses to set foot in the house. "Now his older son was in the field, and as he came and drew near to the house, he heard music and dancing. And he called one of the servants and asked what these things meant." That is to say, no sooner is the one son found than the other son is even more lost. "And he [the servant] said to him, 'Your brother has come, and your father has killed the fattened calf, because he has received him back safe and sound.' But he was angry and refused to go in." And no sooner is the second son lost than the father leaves the party and goes looking for him.

> His father came out and entreated him, but he answered his father, "Look, these many years I have served you, and I never disobeyed your command, yet you never gave me a young goat, that I might celebrate with my friends. But when this son of yours came, who has devoured your property with prostitutes, you

killed the fattened calf for him!" And he said to him, "Son, you are always with me, and all that is mine is yours. It was fitting to celebrate and be glad, for this your brother was dead, and is alive; he was lost, and is found."

Now, that is a loving father, seeking and finding the lost. Indeed, the great, good news in our reading today is that the relentless love of God pursues us, seeks us out, and always finds us, no matter where we are, no matter how far away we have run, no matter how far down we have fallen, no matter how well we have hidden, no matter how very much we think we do not want or need to be found. The love of God in Christ Jesus our Lord pursues us, seeks us out, and always finds us. Where are we in all of this?

Was there a big party for the prodigal son who repented? Yes, no doubt about it. But I do not think that is the main point of the story. The first parable was about the shepherd finding the sheep, not about the sheep finding its way home. The second parable was about the woman finding the coin, not about the coin finding its way back into her purse. And even though this third parable surely illustrates the joy of heaven, it is not, finally, so much about the one son coming home as it is about the father looking for his son, even the one who was lost right there at home. Let us not glory in our own repentance or even in our supposed strength to repent. Instead, let us glory in God, who seeks us out and always finds us. Note that the parable ends without telling us how the situation ends. Or, I should say, the parable ends with the older brother still standing outside. And yet, his father is with him, so he is not alone. I suppose there would be a way to hear this strange parable as a reprimand. But that would miss the point. This is, instead, a wonderfully gracious invitation. Jesus is saying to each of us, "Come into the house. Come to the table. Come to the party. It is not complete without you. Enter into the joy of heaven."

So I ask again, "What man of you, having a hundred sheep, if he has lost one of them, does not leave the ninety-nine in the open country, and go after the one that is lost, until he finds it?" "Or what woman, having ten silver coins, if she loses one coin, does not light a lamp and sweep the house and seek diligently until she finds it?" Who among you, if you have lost something valuable to you, does not go and look for it until you find it? Even so, do you not know how much more, in and through Jesus Christ, God Almighty is looking for you? Were we not once lost? Are we now found?

To God be the glory forever and ever! Amen.

43

Who Will Entrust to You the True Riches?

LUKE 16:1–18; JOSHUA 24:1–27

"ONE WHO IS FAITHFUL in a very little is also faithful in much, and one who is dishonest in a very little is also dishonest in much. If then you have not been faithful in the unrighteous wealth, who will entrust to you the true riches? And if you have not been faithful in that which is another's, who will give you that which is your own?" Jesus asked these two questions to his disciples, to the Pharisees who overheard him then, and so to us now. The two questions are variations of one question, repeated not only for greater understanding but also for extra emphasis. "If then you have not been faithful in the unrighteous wealth, who will entrust to you the true riches? And if you have not been faithful in that which is another's, who will give you that which is your own?" Despite the way the question is asked with a negative assumption, there is good news embedded here for you and me, and the question leads us to it.

What this question affirms in the very way that it is asked is that (1) far beyond the unrighteous wealth of this world there are "true riches," fabulous wealth not tainted by unrighteousness, true riches waiting to be given to us. That might not be obvious to us in the rough-and-tumble life of the everyday world. That might not be something we could discover on our own. But here, in the teaching and gospel of Jesus Christ, we are told about something wonderful in the great beyond. Again, what this question affirms is that beyond the complicated entanglements of this world where we care for and use things that belong to others there is that which is "our own," our very own, not anyone else's, and it is waiting to be given to us. It can be given to no other, for it belongs to no other. It is waiting to be given to us, if only we will have it. Even though it appears here in a question, the affirmation is made that true riches are to be our very own.

What is this wonderful thing toward which the gospel points us? Given that the wealth with which we are familiar here is a part of this passing world, true riches must be lasting, eternal, permanent, and otherworldly. Given that everything we have here can and will be taken away from us, the one thing that can be our very own is life itself. And taken together, these true riches which are to be our very own are nothing other than eternal life itself. Can you imagine? We live in a world that worships youthfulness as we strive vainly to hold onto that life which, from our perspective, passes all too quickly. Can you imagine life that does not pass away? We live in a world of poverty in terms of direct knowledge of God. Can you imagine living in the very presence of God? That is where eternal life is. We live in a world of fear, loss, and confusion. Can you imagine the joy and surety of possessing that which is our very own, so that no one could take it away? That is at least part of what eternal means. Are you interested in these true riches? Do you want that which is your very own? Then the gospel of Jesus Christ is for you.

Jesus assures us of the gift of eternal life because he is the one who wins it for us and he is the one who gives it to us. Eternal life is not the whole of the gospel, but it is a part of the gospel, and the gospel would not be complete without it. When Jesus taught this lesson about eternal life to his disciples, he was on his way to Jerusalem to die. That would seem to be a strange coincidence, except that it was by dying on the cross that Jesus defeated the power of death. By suffering the worst that death could do, Jesus allowed death to spend itself and so undo itself. In the death of Christ, death itself has died. In the death of death, Christ has won eternal life. In recognition of this great victory, God rewarded Jesus with resurrection. Now the risen Christ lives and reigns forever. And since he is the one who has won eternal life for us, he is also the one who gives eternal life to us.

Now, given this good news of the true riches that are our very own, (2) why are the affirmations made in the form of a negative question? "If then you have not been faithful in the unrighteous wealth, who will entrust to you the true riches? And if you have not been faithful in that which is another's, who will give you that which is your own?" The good news is presented here in a question because the question includes a warning about the danger of our forfeiting the true riches of eternal life. The good news is presented here in a question because we are at great risk of turning our back to the very good that Jesus extends to us. There is another terrible and negative option available to us. There is another attraction for our interest. There is another suitor for our hearts. There is something glittering there, and, yes, it is gold. The gods that the fathers had served beyond the river and in Egypt had long ago fallen out of fashion, but everyone loves money, and that is the problem. Here is Christ's explanation of our predicament: "No servant can serve two masters, for either he will hate the one and love the other, or he will be devoted to the one and despise the other. You cannot serve God and money."

We live in spiritual danger. We were designed to worship God and created to serve our master. The problem is that we are tempted to worship the wrong god and we are tempted to serve the wrong master. And if we do that, our lives run in the wrong direction, with the wrong results, and all is lost, lost forever. "No servant can serve two masters, for either he will hate the one and love the other, or he will be devoted to the one and despise the other. You cannot serve God and money." That is a simple, exclusive truth. We cannot serve two masters. That is true on an everyday human level, and that is true on a spiritual level. The greatest competition God has in the world is money. Jesus knew that very well. That is why he taught so much about money. So, of these two, which shall we serve? Whom shall we serve? To whom shall we be faithful? God or money?

Lord, help us! Christ lived and died and lives again so that we may serve God and not money. Christ taught us this gospel and asked us this question so that we may serve God and not money. Why is it so hard for us? Money is not evil in and of itself. Money is, in fact, very useful. The problem is, of course, that in addition to using it we begin to love it. But money is not supposed to be loved. God is to be loved. God is to be loved because God made us. Money cannot do that. God is to be loved because God sustains us. Money cannot do that. God is to be loved because God saves us. Money cannot do that. God is to be loved because God loves us. Money certainly cannot do that. So, the choices are clear. Whom shall we serve? To whom shall we be faithful? Jesus urges us to love, serve, and be faithful to God.

What, then, of money? If we are not to love it, we are certainly to use it! That is what money is for. In the parable of the dishonest manager, Jesus makes the point of how it is possible to use money to secure one's life, up to a point, in this world. "And the manager said to himself, ' . . . I have decided what to do, so that when I am removed from management, people may receive me into their houses.'" As Jesus observed, "The sons of this world are more shrewd in dealing with their own generation than the sons of light." Then Jesus builds on that to teach us that there is a use of money in this world that is appropriate to our life in the world yet to come. "I tell you, make friends for yourselves by means of unrighteous wealth, so that when it fails they may receive you into the eternal dwellings." This cannot possibly mean that we can buy our way into heaven. We cannot do that, and besides, Jesus has already done that for us.

So what does this mean? Jesus was teaching this to people who were already his disciples. This is not so much about salvation as it is about Christian life. If the way of the world is to use money for one's own good, the way of the world to come is to use money for others' good. Just as shrewd people know how to get ahead here, let us learn how to do here what is commendable there. "One who is faithful in a very little is also faithful in much, and one who is dishonest in a very little is also dishonest in much." All the money in the world is so very little in comparison to the riches that await us.

It would be foolish to be deceived and captured by what we see here. If we are greedy with what little we have here, it is unlikely that we will ever be entrusted with more there. But if we are generous with whatever we do have here, the good master will give us more in the world to come. Do you see? We are not encouraged to irresponsibility with our money. But we are urged toward a higher, holy responsibility. We are to use our resources to the glory of God and to the benefit of those in need. And if we cannot honor, serve, and be faithful to God with our money and with how we use it here, how could he possibly ever entrust us with something important there, such as eternal life?

As our Lord and Savior has said, "If then you have not been faithful in the unrighteous wealth, who will entrust to you the true riches? And if you have not been faithful in that which is another's, who will give you that which is your own?"

To God be the glory forever and ever! Amen.

44

Do They Not Hear?

LUKE 16:19–31; AMOS 6:1–7

"FATHER ABRAHAM, HAVE MERCY on me, and send Lazarus to dip the end of his finger in water and cool my tongue, for I am in anguish in this flame." No. "Then I beg you, father, to send him to my father's house—for I have five brothers—so that he may warn them, lest they also come into this place of torment." No. "Father Abraham . . . if someone goes to them from the dead, they will repent." No. These three desperate requests from hell, too little too late, and the three unequivocally negative answers from heaven certainly serve to gain our attention. If we have failed to be listening up until this point in Luke I hope and trust that we are listening now. In an indulgent age in which people would like to believe that heaven always says yes to every human request, this is sobering and startling to say the least. No, no, and no. What can this possibly mean? Where is the good news?

As is so often the case, the gospel, the good news of Jesus Christ, forms the un-spoken presupposition, the necessary foundation, of what is said. Let us look for that here. First (1), Abraham said, "Child, remember that you in your lifetime received your good things, and Lazarus in like manner bad things; but now he is comforted here, and you are in anguish. And besides all this, between us and you a great chasm has been fixed, in order that those who would pass from here to you may not be able, and none may cross from there to us." That is to say, (a) there is a reversal of circum-stances from this life to the next, and (b) that reversal is itself irreversible. There is (a) a reversal of circumstances from this life to the next, a reversal of apparent blessing and curse here and now with real curse and blessing then and there, and (b) once that final reversal has occurred it can never be undone again. Well, he certainly has my atten-tion now! I live a life of significant ease and comfort, in a nation of great wealth. I live in a warm home, I enjoy good food, and I have wonderful medical care. He certainly has my attention now. The idea of a reversal is more than a little frightening.

And yet, the foundation of what is being said here about the final reversal is that the God and Father of Jesus Christ, Creator and Redeemer of the world, will not put up with evil forever. There will be a day of reckoning. There will be a day of justice. There will be an end to all that opposes God. And that is good. As it is written in the hymn we learned so long ago, "This is my Father's world: Oh, let me ne'er forget / That though the wrong seems oft so strong, God is the Ruler yet."[1] The wrong in our world seems incomparably strong. The wrong in our churches is more than we can admit. The wrong in our lives is more than we can bear. One day, the wrong will be undone. One day, the wrong will be defeated. One day, the wrong will be put away forever and ever.

The difference between us and the rich man in the teaching to whom this was told is that it was too late for him. He had missed his opportunity. After poor Lazarus died and went to heaven, "The rich man also died and was buried, and in Hades, being in torment, he lifted up his eyes and saw Abraham far off and Lazarus at his side." Suddenly he realized that something was wrong. For perhaps the first time ever, he asked for help. But it was too late. "Abraham said, 'Child, remember that you in your lifetime received your good things, and Lazarus in like manner bad things; but now he is comforted here, and you are in anguish.'" I doubt that remembering did him much good. In fact, I am certain that it did him no good at all. He had his heaven here on earth, so he did not have it afterwards. However, we are allowed to overhear his exchange with Abraham precisely so that we can come to this realization now, in this life, while there is still time for us to change, while there is still time for us to help those in need, and so that we can avoid hell later.

Note carefully that there is nothing in this teaching to suggest that there is anything wrong with being rich. Father Abraham himself was wealthy, and there he was in heaven. However, such privilege does bring great opportunity and therefore great responsibility. And privilege today, compared to what is going on in much of the world, means having food, water, medicine, clothing, shelter, and electricity. The rich man's problem was not that he was rich. Wealth is a blessing. The rich man's problem was that he was stupid, heartless, faithless, and uncaring. Fortunately, there is a cure for all of that. There is a cure for such stupidity, heartlessness, faithlessness, and lack of caring. And that cure is found in the word of God.

Thus, second (2), Abraham said, "They have Moses and the Prophets; let them hear them." This was after the second time that the dead rich man, in hell, thought that maybe Father Abraham could get Lazarus to run a couple of errands for him. Such arrogance, in and of itself, is absolutely astounding. "Could you have Lazarus run down here and bring me a little water?" No. "Then, could you have Lazarus run back home and warn my brothers?" No. The answer here is very interesting: "They

---

1. Babcock, "This Is My Father's World."

have Moses and the Prophets; let them hear them." By "Moses" Abraham indicated the first five books of the Old Testament, and by "the Prophets" he meant all the rest. They have the Bible. Let them read, study, absorb, and inwardly digest that. Let them hear, believe, and obey that. That is all they need. Can you imagine? In the midst of a final conversation about life and death, about eternal reward and punishment, Abraham pointed the unbelieving brothers toward the foundation that we in the church call the ordinary means of grace: the reading and preaching of the word of God. That was all they needed. They did not need Lazarus to tell them. They needed to listen to the reading and preaching of the word of God that they already had.

So, what was the problem? The problem was that they, like their deceased brother, scorned the word of God. They rejected the word of God. They ridiculed the word of God. They belittled the word of God. They absented themselves from worship and therefore from the reading, preaching, and hearing of the word of God. It was too late for the dead man. But Jesus told this story for the living, so that they might hear it before the great reversal. And Luke has recorded it for us so that we might hear it before the great and irreversible reversal, so that we might hear it in time, so that we might hear it in this life, so that we might learn from and avoid their problem, so that we today might hear the word of God. Do we? We have it. It has been given to us. Do we hear it?

Third (3), and finally, Abraham said, "If they do not hear Moses and the Prophets, neither will they be convinced if someone should rise from the dead." The dead, formerly rich man wanted something more for his unbelieving brothers, more than the Bible, something spectacular, a miracle, such as a resurrection from the dead, if only Abraham would send back Lazarus to them. Surely that should get their attention! No. If they do not believe the word of God, neither will they believe any miracles. We have all that we need in the word of God. What a wonderful gift! Let us not neglect it.

Note what is accomplished by this last, double teaching. For starters (a), Abraham affirms the sufficiency of the ordinary means of grace, the reading and preaching of the word of God. Those are what we need to get right with God. Those are what we need to turn our lives around. Those are what we need to love and care for one another. The word of God is good and important. Moreover (b), a note of irony is introduced. We realize, of course, that not very long after this teaching Jesus Christ himself did come back from the dead and, true to his word, many did not believe. Those who had already rejected the word of God continued to reject him. But what these teachings, taken together, mean for us as a foundation is that we do not have to see the resurrection, we do not have to witness the risen Lord Jesus Christ, in order to believe in him as the risen Lord Jesus Christ precisely as testimony is made to him in the reading and preaching of the word of God. The word of God alone is sufficient for our salvation, sufficient to keep us out of hell, sufficient to win us for heaven.

That is to say, we are, of course, the living brothers still today. We are the ones for whom this teaching was given and for whom it has been preserved. We are the ones who still have time to hear, to believe, to repent, and to obey the word of God. What is this word of God? The God and Father of Jesus Christ created us, and we are not our own. This life is good because God made it, and yet this life is not all there is. There is also a life beyond this one, and it is largely shaped by our decisions here. If here we want to have things all to ourselves, we will eventually, there, be all by ourselves. If here we are willing to care for others, we will eventually, there, be cared for ourselves. This is not to say that we do not all need forgiveness. Forgiveness is why Jesus came, died, rose, and will come again. And this is not to say that we can earn our salvation. There is nothing in this teaching that says that Lazarus was good or righteous or deserving. I suppose that is suggested. But there is no indication that he was charitable toward others, since, of course, he had absolutely nothing with which to be charitable. The one thing he did give, if we can understand it this way—the one thing he did give the rich man was an opportunity to help. That is valuable indeed. But this teaching is not really about Lazarus. This teaching is, instead, about the rich man who squandered his opportunity to help Lazarus and so left him to fulfill his name, which means "Helped by God." Lord, help us not to make the same mistake! Avoiding that squandering is the one thing that this teaching is all about.

At least part of what this teaching does mean yet today is that those of us who have the means to help those in need are being given an opportunity to show that we love God more than money, to show that we love neighbor more than money, to show that we care, to show that we have heard the word of God read and preached, and to show that we do believe in the resurrection to new and different life. That is to say, we have an opportunity to help Lazarus today. A poor man has been laid at our doorstep. We dare not neglect him. We should note that while Christianity is a religion of forgiveness and therefore of many chances, it is not a religion of infinite chances. The chances are limited to this life. Now is the time to respond. Now is the time to believe. Now is the time to obey. Now is the time to give. When this life is over, there are no more opportunities.

When Albert Schweitzer was a young Christian medical student, he was confronted with this very teaching of Jesus Christ. He came to the conclusion at that time that the entire continent of Africa was Lazarus for him, lying at the doorstep of Europe. So, instead of practicing medicine in Europe, he went to Africa, built a hospital, and spent his life there. That is to say, the word of God in this teaching turned his life around. And now it is our turn to hear, believe, and obey. In the providence and wisdom of God, this reading from the word of God, this reading about hearing the word of God and learning from it to help those in need, this reading has been brought into our hearing and into our worship today to encourage us to help those in need. We who have ample resources have an opportunity today to help those who have none.

"Father Abraham, have mercy on me, and send Lazarus to dip the end of his finger in water and cool my tongue, for I am in anguish in this flame." No. "Then I beg you, father, to send him to my father's house—for I have five brothers—so that he may warn them, lest they also come into this place of torment." No. "Father Abraham . . . if someone goes to them from the dead, they will repent." No. These three desperate requests from hell, too little too late, and the three unequivocally negative answers from heaven certainly serve to gain our attention. If we have failed to be listening up until this point in Luke I hope and trust that we are listening now. In an indulgent age in which people would like to believe that heaven always says yes to every human request, this is sobering and startling to say the least. No, no, and no. But the foundation undergirding this threefold no from Abraham is the yes, yes, and yes of God. Yes (1), God's justice shall be served, and be served eternally and irrevocably. Yes (2), God's word is sufficient for us and for our salvation. And Yes (3), Jesus Christ has been raised from the dead, and his resurrection is the promise of our own. Are we willing to hear this word, to believe this word, and to obey this word?

To God be the glory forever and ever! Amen.

45

Increase Our Faith!

LUKE 17:1–19; 2 KINGS 5:9–17

"INCREASE OUR FAITH!" THAT is what the apostles asked of the Lord: "Increase our faith!" The first twelve, the chosen recipients of power and authority over all demons and to cure diseases, sent out to proclaim the kingdom of God and to heal, who were soon enough to sit at table with him and to receive the new covenant—these apostles asked of the Lord, "Increase our faith!" The first thing this makes me think is that if they needed more faith, how much more do I need more faith! And I want to come back to that at the end, but it is not the best place to begin. Let us begin instead with the simple, straightforward request of the apostles, "Increase our faith!"

We need to look at both the content and the context. Part of the content is the assumption and therefore the affirmation that the apostles already have some faith. It may not be much, but they already have some faith. It may not be what they want it to be, and it may not be what God wants it to be, but they already have some faith. That is clear. Apart from this reality, the request would make no sense at all. The only time before this in the Gospel according to Luke that the word "faith" has been applied to the apostles was when Jesus asked the disciples, after he calmed a storm at sea, "Where is your faith?" Nevertheless, this very request to increase their faith made by the apostles in today's reading both assumes and therefore affirms that they already have some faith in God and also in his Christ.

In fact, if we consider to whom their request is addressed, that strengthens this conclusion even more. The apostles addressed their request for increased faith to Jesus. They were talking to him. But faith, of course, is a gift from God. It is not a human accomplishment. It is not a human gift. To ask Jesus for faith or even for an increase in faith is to acknowledge that Jesus acts on behalf of God and, indeed, that he is God.

The simple request "Increase our faith!" is nothing less than a prayer, and not a bad one to make our own. Prayers are addressed to God. That this one is addressed to Jesus already indicates faith not only in God but also and especially in Jesus, the Son of God, God himself with us and for us. They may not have understood this entirely. They were, after all, asking for an increase in faith. But at this point, on the way to Jerusalem, between the manger and the cross, at least they had enough faith to ask Jesus to increase their faith. And maybe that is enough. If we have enough faith to ask for more faith, maybe that in and of itself is saving faith. Lord help us! The day we are content with our faith is the day we are in a lot of trouble.

It is no accident that as Luke records the story for us he does not use the name of Jesus in this sentence but uses a title for him: "The apostles said to the Lord, 'Increase our faith!'" This is not a part of their request, but it is certainly a part of their faith and understanding, and Luke has recorded it for it to become part of our faith and understanding. At one level, the word "Lord" could be used when speaking to someone, not unlike the way we use the word "Sir" today. And at another level, the word "Lord" could indicate a man of high rank and power. But throughout both the Old and New Testaments, the word "Lord" is used as a title for God Almighty, and its application to Jesus here and throughout the New Testament indicates nothing less than that Jesus is God Almighty with us and for us. Thanks be to God!

Beyond the content and the addressee of this request, the immediate context is also of great importance. It was immediately after the teachings on temptation and forgiveness that the apostles asked for an increase in faith. Jesus said to his disciples, "If your brother sins, rebuke him, and if he repents, forgive him, and if he sins against you seven times in the day, and turns to you seven times, saying, 'I repent,' you must forgive him." It was then that the apostles said to the Lord, "Increase our faith!" It was then that they knew they needed some help. Forgiveness seven times a day? Every day? Day after day? For the rest of our lives? Can this be for real? "Increase our faith!" Worshiping God is one thing. Forgiving your brother is quite another. At least, we would like for it to be quite another. Somehow, Jesus ties these together in a knot so tight that we cannot undo it. Loving and serving God not only leads to loving and forgiving brother; loving and serving God also requires, and indeed cannot exist without, loving and forgiving brother. The two go together. No wonder the apostles prayed, "Increase our faith!"

Of course, the two belong together in the other direction also. True love of neighbor requires, and cannot exist without, love of God. Apart from the knowledge and love of God, there may be some modicum of care for neighbor, some common humanity, some shared sympathy, but not the true love to which we are called. In fact, apart from the knowledge and love of God, there may be no love for neighbor, but only fear, contempt, disrespect, and disregard. But only with the knowledge and love of God are we even remotely capable of knowing others as creatures of God, as children of God, as loved ones of God, as forgiven sinners, and as ones for whom

Christ died. Apart from the knowledge and love of God, such true knowledge and love of neighbor is simply impossible. So, just as we cannot love God without loving neighbor, we cannot love neighbor without loving God. The two go together. Again, no wonder the apostles prayed, "Increase our faith!" They needed more faith in order to be able to forgive. They also needed to forgive in order to be able to have more faith.

The answer Jesus gives to their prayer request seems a strange one. The Lord said, "If you had faith like a grain of mustard seed, you could say to this mulberry tree, 'Be uprooted and planted in the sea,' and it would obey you." Whatever else that means, it at least means that even the tiniest amount of faith is capable of great and wonderful things. It occurs to me that it might take a lot more faith to forgive one's brother seven times a day than to move a tree into the ocean, but even the tiniest amount of faith is headed in the right direction. And with an increase, we might even acknowledge the risen and living Jesus Christ as Lord and Savior.

Immediately after this teaching about faith, Jesus goes into a discourse about the nature of Christian duty. Again, the two go together.

> Will any one of you who has a servant plowing or keeping sheep say to him when he has come in from the field, "Come at once and sit down at table"? Will he not rather say to him, "Prepare supper for me, and dress properly, and serve me while I eat and drink, and afterward you will eat and drink"? Does he thank the servant because he did what was commanded? So you also, when you have done all that you were commanded, say, "We are unworthy servants; we have only done what was our duty."

That is to say, God does not owe us anything. We might think that God owes us everything, but God does not owe us anything. We belong to God. If we do anything for God, that is what we are supposed to do, and we earn no special favor by doing it.

This conjunction of faith and duty suggests, among other things, that faith leads to duty, that faith is at least part of our duty, and that duty cannot be fulfilled without faith, just as faith is not faith if it does not lead to obedience. The Christian faith, faith in the God and Father of Jesus Christ, calls us to a life of glorifying and serving God, a life of worship and of work, a life of praise and of good works. This is who we are. This is why we were created. This is why we are here. This is what we are all about.

At the same time, the Christian life is not merely one of duty, or even one of only faith and duty. We are also recipients of grace, and therefore our lives are intended for gratitude. This is what we see in the healing of the lepers. Jesus had set his face like a flint to go to Jerusalem, the city that did not know the things that make for peace, the city that did not know the time of its visitation by the Son of God, the city known for killing the prophets who spoke the word of God, the city which would, in fact, kill Jesus. It was on his journey to the cross that Jesus was met by ten lepers who cried out to him for mercy. Jesus extended his mercy to the ten and sent them on their way to be healed. Then one came back to praise God and to give thanks to Jesus Christ.

What is going on here? Not only was leprosy physically horrible, but also the people who had this disease were, by law and custom, regarded as ritually unclean, religiously cursed, and therefore socially outcast. In their hour of greatest need, they could not enter the temple, could not attend or participate in worship, could not live inside the city limits, and could not be touched by another person, because of the ritual uncleanness. The lepers were no longer a part of the human family. They were as good as dead. This is why they stood at a distance and cried out, "Jesus, Master, have mercy on us." Heal us, make us whole, restore us to life, and reunite us with the great human family!

Jesus sent them to the priests. Why? The priests were entrusted with determining who had leprosy and who did not, who was clean and who was unclean. The priests held the key to the door of reentry into the human community, into the exercise of faith and worship. "Go and show yourselves to the priests," Jesus said. And away they went. But here is something very peculiar. Jesus did not heal them before he sent them away. He sent them away first, and then they were healed on the way. All ten obeyed Jesus and went to see the priests. With sores still on their arms, they went on their way to the priests to ask to be declared clean! What a wonderful confidence in the word of God!

Then one—just one!—returned praising God and thanking Jesus. The one was no more obedient than the nine, that one was no more clean than the nine, but the one was more grateful than the other nine put together! And this gratitude is the main goal of God's grace. The one former leper who returned was also a foreigner, a Samaritan, a people hated and despised ethnically, nationally, and religiously by the people of Israel. This one was a double outsider, a leper and a foreigner, and he outshone the nine sons of Israel who also had been healed.

Of all the ten who were healed, the one who returned to give thanks was the only one who put his healing to good use. He returned, praising God with a loud voice, fell on his face at Jesus' feet (that posture is an act of worship in and of itself), and gave Jesus thanks. To the one who returned it was given to know that the wonderful power of God Almighty, which we know as grace, was at work in a unique way in the person, ministry, and teaching of Jesus Christ, both to heal the individual and so to make the community whole again, and this healing grace elicited from him a profound, joyous, and overflowing gratitude.

This story has been preserved for two thousand years now for your sake and mine, in order that we may know the grace of God Almighty in our own lives and in order that we may respond with the appropriate gratitude. It is the goal of grace to elicit gratitude from us. What good did it do, in the grand scheme of things, for the other nine lepers to be healed, if they missed a chance to worship God, neglected their opportunity to thank Jesus Christ, and returned to their normal pre-leprous lives—perhaps good, useful, productive, and happy lives, in and of themselves—but missed a chance to converse and commune with their Lord and Master, to praise their

Maker and Redeemer? And what good would it do for us, if we were to fail to realize that this story is for, and even about, us here today? We have all been created in the image of God; we have been given life and breath; we have been forgiven of our sin; we have been redeemed by the mighty work of Christ on the cross; we have been pursued by the relentless love of God, which always seeks us out and always finds us, no matter how far we might have run, how hard we might have struggled, or how deeply we might have hidden. God has healed us of our disease, so that we may return here this morning for the high and holy privilege of praising God and giving God our thanks.

The grace of God is at work in Jesus Christ to regather us into a community of gratitude toward God. God, whose majesty is beyond our comprehension, whose holiness and power are such that to glimpse them would be fatal, the Lord of heaven and earth, has drawn near to us in Jesus Christ. God, for the sake of his own glory, has reclaimed us from all the false claims that the powers of the world make on us, reversed our stubborn march into oblivion, and recalled us as God's own people. This is why God has gathered us here. We do not come by virtue of our own decision or by the strength of our own effort alone. We are called by the word of God, carried by the hand of God, brought by the grace of God, here, today, to be God's people in this time and in this place.

The next move is ours. Do we live thankless lives, or do we come back here to worship and to give thanks? When our lives have been lived and all is said and done, will Jesus Christ look around and have to say of us, "Were not ten cleansed? Where are the nine?" Or will he be able to say even to us, "Rise and go your way; your faith has made you well"? So it is that Luke has recorded the apostles' prayer in order that we might make it our own: "Increase our faith!"

To God be the glory forever and ever! Amen.

46

Must I Lose My Life to Keep It?

LUKE 17:20–37; GENESIS 6:5–22

"WHOEVER SEEKS TO PRESERVE his life will lose it, but whoever loses his life will keep it." Yes, that is a strange and backwards saying, paradoxical at best if not downright contradictory. But it comes to us from Jesus Christ himself, which suggests at the very least that it is worthy of our attention. This is more than a riddle. This is more than a clever saying. This is actually an invitation to life itself. "Whoever seeks to preserve his life will lose it, but whoever loses his life will keep it." Of course, if you do not care about life, you are free to set this aside. If losing or keeping life does not matter to you one way or the other, you can quit listening right now. But if you are at all interested in life, not only life in general but your very own life in particular, this teaching is for you. And if you are at all interested in eternal life, which is what the word "keep" means here, as in keep your life forever, then this teaching is especially for you, here, now, at this very moment.

"Whoever seeks to preserve his life will lose it, but whoever loses his life will keep it." What in the world is Jesus telling us here? At the end of a whole series of warnings about what not to do on the day of the Son of Man—do not go out, do not follow them, do not go down into the house, do not turn back, all things not to do in order not to lose one's life—Jesus tells us that any efforts to save our own life will forfeit it and that in fact losing our own life will be the only way to save it. Come with me into the strange and backwards world of the gospel.

First of all (1), there is an underlying affirmation here of the reality of eternal life. This is the truth, this is the hope, this is the promise, and this is the foundation. Beyond all the ongoing teachings of the already-but-not-yet qualities of the kingdom of God, beyond all the mystery and even terror of the suddenly coming day of the Son of Man, and in the midst of this strange and paradoxical warning, there is an affirmation of the reality of eternal life. What good news this is! Life here is often short, hard, and brutish, red in tooth and claw. This life is transient. This life comes to an end all too soon. But life here is not all there is. There is a life beyond this life, a life beyond death, a life beyond pain, disease, decline, and decay, an eternal life. That is the first thing Jesus is teaching us here. And that eternal life does not devalue this life. That life does not mean this life is unimportant. Far from it. Instead, that eternal life provides perspective, that life provides direction, that life provides meaning and purpose, and that life alone gives this life its true importance. Without that eternal life, nothing here would matter. People could do whatever they wanted without concern for consequence. But with that eternal life, things here and now take on eternal significance. What we think, say, and do has eternal implications.

Now, we know that our life here is a gift from God. It is he who made us, and we are his. We did not and cannot create ourselves. What Jesus is telling us in today's reading is that there is also another life, a life beyond this life, an eternal life, not a simple extension of this life, but not unrelated to this life. And that eternal life is also a gift from God. We cannot create it ourselves. We cannot earn it or achieve it. We can only receive it as a gift from God. Life here ends with words unspoken, kindnesses not returned, and good intentions not fulfilled. What Jesus is telling us is that there is a life beyond here where our now limited understanding can be made whole, where unfinished deeds can be finished, and where what is wrong can be made right.[1] As the Apostle Paul put it, "For now we see in a mirror dimly, but then face to face. Now I know in part; then I shall know fully, even as I have been fully known" (1 Corinthians 13:12).

The prospect of eternal life changes everything. It simultaneously raises the value of this life and relativizes the value of this life. That is to say, because this life is not all there is, this life is not absolute. It is good, important, and wonderful, but it is not of absolute value. It is not all there is. At the same time, precisely because there is a life beyond this life, an eternal life, what we think, say, and do here is of eternal significance. So, this life is more important than we could imagine it to be without eternal life, and yet at the same time the this-worldly tendency to absolutize this life is undercut and swept away. The prospect of eternal life provides both of these two correctives: it takes away the danger of absolutizing and therefore overvaluing this life, and it takes away the mistake of undervaluing this life. So the prospect of eternal life beyond here both lifts this life to its true importance and also prevents us from thinking too highly of it. The underlying affirmation in today's reading of the reality of this eternal life is good news, and it is the first thing Jesus teaches us here.

"Whoever seeks to preserve his life will lose it, but whoever loses his life will keep it." Second (2), and before we even get to eternal life, there is also a direct teaching here

1. Compare Niebuhr, *Nature and Destiny of Man*, 2.81–90, where he writes that the sacrificial love of Christ completes, clarifies, and corrects what is incomplete, unclear, and incorrect in this life.

that there will be a day of judgment on all self-centeredness. "Whoever seeks to preserve his life will lose it." That is as clear as can be. It may sound backwards to us, but it is as clear as can be. "Whoever seeks to preserve his life will lose it." Self-centeredness, self-servingness, self-protection, self-promotion, and self-preservation here all forfeit the life beyond here! It is that simple. There will be a terrible day of judgment. We were all created to be centered upon God. What sin means is that we have become centered upon ourselves. And that is wrong. It cannot last. It cannot sustain itself. It will not be allowed to continue. There will be a day of judgment that will bring an end to all self-centeredness forever.

We need to realize that this judgment is not arbitrary. God is not capricious. There is a reason for all of this. And part of the reason for this judgment—beyond what I already said, that we were created to be centered upon God—is that one time in human history one person refused to be self-centered, refused to try to preserve his own life, insisted instead upon being God-centered, persevered in that even to the point of losing his own life, and so revealed the poverty of self-centeredness. As Jesus taught the disciples about the Son of Man, which was a title for himself, "He must suffer many things and be rejected by this generation." Suffering many things included betrayal, false arrest, wrongful conviction, and crucifixion. Being rejected by this generation included being mocked, scoffed at, railed at, and killed. And through it all Jesus refused to consider himself, refused to seek to preserve his own life, refused to abandon his faith in God, refused to hate, and refused to sin. Our judgment on him in this world, yours and mine—yes, we were there when they crucified our Lord— our rejection of who he was and what he stood for, became his judgment on us. His God-centeredness was never broken. Our self-centeredness therefore stands exposed, condemned, and forever rejected. But there is more to this than judgment. There is also invitation, promise, and good hope.

"Whoever seeks to preserve his life will lose it, but whoever loses his life will keep it." That self-centered life here forfeits eternal life we understand, "but whoever loses his life will keep it." This is something new. This is something different. This is the third and final point of this teaching (3): "Whoever loses his life will keep it." This changes everything. Not only is there an affirmation of eternal life, and not only will there be a day of judgment, but also there is now an invitation into eternal life. What we have here is the gospel invitation to lose our life in and to Jesus Christ, which loss in turn alone carries us safe through the aforementioned day of judgment and which loss of self-centered life alone leads to the ultimate gift of eternal life, God-centered life, life as it was meant to be, forever and ever. Are you interested? Would you like to receive this?

Jesus is inviting us to lose our lives in him so that we may find our lives in him. This runs against everything else we think we know in this world. This runs against every instinct for self-preservation. This runs against every encouragement of the world for us to seek self-fulfillment, self-promotion, and self-satisfaction. But what

Jesus is telling us is that every instinct for self-protection leads to death, while true life is found and saved only by following him to the cross, only by dying to self, only by living not for ourselves but for him alone. Life is not and cannot be fulfilled in selfish self-fulfillment; life is fulfilled only in selfless self-emptying and self-denial all in the name and for the sake of Jesus Christ. That may sound backward to us, but that is the way it is. Nobody asked whether we liked it, but this is reality. This is the truth. This is the gospel. And if we profess Jesus as Lord, we have to abandon all claims to being our own lords. We cannot have it both ways. You see, the Christian faith is not about human potential. It is about the grace of God doing for us what we cannot do for ourselves. Thanks be to God, his way is the way to life!

I have been told—and I must say that I offer this only as an illustration, not as advice on white-water rafting, so do not try this on a river unless you confirm it with someone else, though it does make sense to me—that there are certain structures on the rivers, such as waterfalls, that create a kind of turbulence from which it can be very difficult to escape. If you were to fall out of a raft and to be swept into this kind of turbulence, the downward force of the water would be exactly matched by the upward buoyancy of the life jacket, so that you would go neither up nor down but would be held in that position, underwater, and so would drown there. The very life jacket that was meant to save life would in those circumstances contribute to the ending of life. In this situation, the only way out of the turbulence would be to slip out of the life jacket, or as we sometimes call it, the life preserver, so to fall out the bottom of the turbulence, and then to come up somewhere down stream. That is to say, keeping the life preserver on would end one's life, while losing the life preserver would lead to keeping one's life.

Just so, Jesus is calling us to a total redirection of our lives, an abandoning of self-centeredness, a turning around, a following of him, and a taking up of God-centeredness. We cannot possess our own life. Indeed, our own life is not our own to possess. The tighter we grasp it, the less we live. The harder we hold on, the more likely we are to drown. So, the Christian life points away from self and toward Jesus Christ. Again, what we have here is the gospel invitation to lose our life in and to Jesus Christ, which loss alone in turn carries us safe through the aforementioned day of judgment and which loss of self-centered life alone leads to the ultimate gift of eternal life, God-centered life, life as it was meant to be, forever and ever. Of course, if you do not care about life, you are free to set this aside. If losing or keeping life does not matter to you one way or the other, you can quit listening right now. But if you are at all interested in life, not only life in general but your own life in particular, this teaching is for you. And if you are at all interested in eternal life, which is what the word "keep" means here, as in keep your life forever, then this teaching is especially for you, here, now, at this very moment. "Whoever seeks to preserve his life will lose it, but whoever loses his life will keep it."

To God be the glory forever and ever! Amen.

47

Will He Find Faith?

LUKE 18:1–14; PSALM 34:1–22

"WILL NOT GOD GIVE justice to his elect, who cry to him day and night? Will he delay long over them?" Again and again we have found that the Gospel according to Luke reads like a catechism, with key questions pointing to the main affirmation of the passage. This is no exception. "Will not God give justice to his elect, who cry to him day and night? Will he delay long over them?" And as we have seen again and again, the repetition and variation of the question serve to emphasize it and therefore to elevate its importance. This is no exception. "Will not God give justice to his elect, who cry to him day and night? Will he delay long over them?" Jesus answers his own two questions, quickly and directly: "I tell you, he will give justice to them speedily." Yes, God will give justice to his elect, who cry to him day and night. No, he will not delay long over them. "I tell you, he will give justice to them speedily." This is good news. This is the major affirmation of the text: God will give justice to his elect, and he will do so speedily.

And then, as soon as that point is made, Jesus rushes on to another question: "Nevertheless, when the Son of Man comes, will he find faith on earth?" And this question is not simply a catechism question. This question is not so much about teaching the faith as it is about inquiring into our faith. This question is direct, personal, and aimed right at you and me. "When the Son of Man comes"—and we remember that "Son of Man" is a title by which Jesus refers to himself—"When the Son of Man comes, will he find faith on earth?" Will you have faith? Will I have faith? That is the real question. It is aimed right at us. And no one else can answer it for us.

It is, I am convinced, to help us answer this third question that Jesus tells us the second parable, ostensibly about appropriate prayer and yet therefore at the same time also about the nature of true faith. That is to say, what Jesus is looking for in us with his question about faith he also sets before us in the second man in this second parable. So, there is still an element of the teaching catechism here, though we will find soon enough that we come back to direct, personal inquiry. "When the Son of Man comes, will he find faith on earth?"

> Two men went up into the temple to pray, one a Pharisee and the other a tax collector. The Pharisee, standing by himself, prayed thus: "God, I thank you that I am not like other men, extortioners, unjust, adulterers, or even like this tax collector. I fast twice a week; I give tithes of all that I get." But the tax collector, standing far off, would not even lift up his eyes to heaven, but beat his breast, saying, "God, be merciful to me, a sinner!" I tell you, this man went down to his house justified, rather than the other.

It is no accident that Jesus "told this parable to some who trusted in themselves that they were righteous, and treated others with contempt." And it is no accident that Luke recorded this introduction for us so that we might know exactly what the parable intends to address. That is to say, trusting in oneself that one is righteous is not faithful, is not Christian, and will not be tolerated. Moreover, treating others with contempt is not faithful, is not Christian, and will not be tolerated. These two negative qualities are not only named but are also illustrated in the parable. The Pharisee in the parable both trusted in himself that he was righteous and also therefore treated others with contempt. This, then, in introduction and parable, is both the naming and also the illustrating of that which is not Christian faith, of that which the Son of Man does *not* want to find when he returns, but with which we are all too familiar.

"The Pharisee, standing by himself, prayed thus: 'God, I thank you that I am not like other men, extortioners, unjust, adulterers, or even like this tax collector.'" This parable works better than any other parable I know. It gets me every time. You know what I mean. I have no sooner read about this despicable character than I break into a prayer of thanksgiving, "God, I thank you that I am not like that miserable Pharisee!" Then before I can say "Amen," it hits me: by my praying that prayer, I *am* that Pharisee, trusting in myself that I am righteous and treating him with contempt! And then Jesus has me right where he wants me. Now I am ready to listen. Now I know I need some help. If my self-righteousness and contempt constitute the opposite of Christian faith, what is true faith?

"The tax collector, standing far off, would not even lift up his eyes to heaven, but beat his breast, saying, 'God, be merciful to me, a sinner!'" Now, that is Christian faith. The tax collector, working against his own people, widely assumed to be crooked, well despised and perhaps deservedly so, made no pretense of self-righteousness. He did not look down upon anyone else. He simply begged for mercy. Why did he do that? Not only because he needed it, but also and even more so because he believed and knew that God is merciful. That is the only possible basis for such a painful and exquisite prayer. He prayed that prayer because he believed and knew that God is merciful. There is no other explanation. And such knowledge of God's mercy is Christian faith. "I tell you, this man went down to his house justified, rather than the other." More of that in a moment.

Fifteen hundred years after Jesus told this parable, John Calvin, a theologian and reformer of the church, wrote, "Now we shall possess a right definition of faith if we call it a firm and certain knowledge of God's benevolence toward us, founded upon the truth of the freely given promise in Christ, both revealed to our minds and sealed upon our hearts through the Holy Spirit."[1] Faith, then, is not believing in something that we cannot know. It is, instead, "a firm and certain knowledge of God's benevolence toward us." It has to do with something we do know. That is to say, faith is knowing, in and through Jesus Christ, by the Holy Spirit, that God is merciful. And it is on the basis of this faith knowledge alone that we are made brave to pray, "God, be merciful to me, a sinner!" It is on the basis of this faith knowledge alone that we are healed of our sickness of trusting in ourselves that we are righteous. It is on the basis of this faith knowledge alone that we are relieved of that nastiness of treating others with contempt. It is through such knowing faith alone that we are, by the grace of God in Jesus Christ, justified. So let us join the tax collector in praying, "God, be merciful to me, a sinner!" This is the gospel invitation to us in today's reading.

Now, do you remember the first two questions and their answer? "Will not God give justice to his elect, who cry to him day and night? Will he delay long over them? I tell you, he will give justice to them speedily." It is these first two questions and their answer at the end of the first parable that provide the basis for the affirmative answer to the tax collector's prayer. It is these first two questions and their answer that provide the basis for the conclusion of the second parable, "I tell you, this man went down to his house justified, rather than the other." At the same time, it is the tax collector's prayer in the second parable that not only demonstrates for us the nature of Christian faith but that also tells us what the elect are to cry out for and that tells us what we ought always to pray for without losing heart. Let us examine this content a little more closely. You see, the poor widow in the first parable was up against an "unrighteous judge," "who neither feared God nor respected man." He did not care about her. He did not care about justice. He did not care about what was right. He had no inclination whatsoever to help her. And yet, because she kept coming to him and wore him down, he finally gave in, relented, and gave her the justice against her adversary for which she had asked so many times.

What a strange parable! Does it mean that God is like the unrighteous judge, so that we must weary him with our prayers? *No*, not at all! Of course not! What it means, instead, is quite the opposite: that God is not like him at all, that God is quick to answer prayer, that God does not delay, that God speedily gives justice. Thanks be to God! The point of this parable, that we "ought always to pray and not lose heart," is

1. Calvin, *Institutes*, III.2.7, 1:551.

not that we should pray out of despair and certainly not that we should pray desperately, but that we should pray and not lose heart, that we should pray confidently, that we should pray joyfully, that we should pray boldly, so that we ought always to pray believing and knowing that God is merciful, just as the tax collector prayed. Is this how we pray today?

There is a great divide in humanity between those who believe in the God and Father of Jesus Christ and those who do not. There is a great divide in humanity between those who trust in themselves that they are righteous and so treat others with contempt, and those who stand far off, do not even lift up their eyes to heaven, but beat their breast, saying, "God, be merciful to me, a sinner!" There is a great divide in humanity between those who pray boldly and gladly and those who try to make it through life on their own. And this great divide has immense and eternal implications, "For everyone who exalts himself will be humbled, but the one who humbles himself will be exalted." This great divide will lead to a great reversal of everything we see in the world here, "For everyone who exalts himself will be humbled, but the one who humbles himself will be exalted." We dare not ignore this.

So while the first parable tells us that the God and Father of Jesus Christ is eager to give justice speedily, the second parable tells us that the justice he gives is our justification. The justice that God gives to us is the forgiveness of our sin, the restoration to right relationship with God. That is what we ought always to pray for. That is the mercy for which we cry. The adversaries against which we seek justice are not of flesh and blood. The adversaries against which we seek justice are sin, death, and evil. And while they attack us from without, they also well up from within us. So the only justice we can have against them is the justification that God alone gladly gives to us: the forgiveness of a sinner, the mercy given to, and received by, those who believe and know that God is merciful. So let us always pray, "God, be merciful to me, a sinner!" Let this be our prayer, so that when the Son of Man comes, he will find such faith on earth, and he will find it in us.

To God be the glory forever and ever! Amen.

48

Who Can Be Saved?

"WHO CAN BE SAVED?" This is the final and most anguished of three questions in today's reading. There is a fearfulness about it, a yearning for assistance and for assurance. Perhaps you are familiar with that anxiety yourself. "Who can be saved?" The question appreciates the difficulty, indeed the impossibility so far as human effort is concerned, of being saved. Thus this question points to the most important affirmation made in today's reading: "What is impossible with men is possible with God." "Who can be saved?" We want to be clear, of course, that salvation is not the only concern of the gospel or the Christian faith. It is the starting point of the Christian life, not the end point. And it is much less important than, for instance, the glory of God. But it is the concern of today's reading. So we would do well to pursue this question today. We would do well to make this concern our own concern if it is not already such.

"Who can be saved?" This final (3) and climactic question arises in response to a previous exchange initiated by the prior (2) question, "What must I do to inherit eternal life?" This question has its own problems, which we will explore in just a moment. But for now we need to realize that both of these questions, along with their answers, expand upon the first (1) teaching of Jesus in today's reading: his teaching about the kingdom of God and about its being entered only by those who receive it like a child. That connection is not immediately obvious. These two adult questions do not seem to be about children. But they are about receiving the kingdom of God, which is the one theme that runs throughout all three sections of this reading. In fact, these two very different questions and their two very different answers explore and explain two opposite approaches to the kingdom of God and therefore two opposite understandings of the gospel of Jesus Christ. One is wrong. The other is right. One seems to be very grown up. The other is childlike. We need to know which is which. We need to know which one to take up as our very own.

"Who can be saved?" Let us (1) begin at the beginning. You remember what happened. Jesus was teaching away, one parable after another, when people started bringing in their children, even babies, right up to him so that he could bless them. What a mess! After all, children are noisy, squirmy, and distracting, and they can hardly be expected to listen, let alone to get something out of his teachings. Some sharp-eyed and sharper-tongued disciples thought they would make a quick end to the intrusion and get those children out of there. But Jesus put a quick end to their blockade, calling the children to himself, and welcoming them with this remarkable teaching: "Let the children come to me, and do not hinder them, for to such belongs the kingdom of God. Truly, I say to you, whoever does not receive the kingdom of God like a child shall not enter it." That stands everything on its head. In the middle of a crowd of adults, Jesus said, "Whoever does not receive the kingdom of God like a child shall not enter it." No wonder this teaching calls for some explanation. "Whoever does not receive the kingdom of God like a child shall not enter it."

Then next (2), as if those words had never been spoken, "a ruler asked him, 'Good Teacher, what must I do to inherit eternal life?'" As if the teaching of the necessity of a childlike reception of the kingdom had never been uttered, "a ruler asked him, 'Good Teacher, what must I do to inherit eternal life?'" The juxtaposition is startling. In the sharpest possible contrast with the way a child receives a blessing simply for being a child, not for any good work he or she has ever done, this ruler wanted to know what *he* had to *do* to inherit eternal life, to earn a blessing, to receive salvation, and so to enter the kingdom. We must suppose that it is good to want all those things, and surely we should want them ourselves, but how did this man get so far off the mark? Why did he think he could accomplish this himself? Was he some strange superhuman? Or did he perhaps, instead, articulate something that is deep within us all, that we want to make our own way in the world, to earn our keep, to avoid making others go out of their way for us, and so to be beholden to no one? Maybe it is not that unusual after all. We have a deep-set drive toward self-justification.

"What must I do to inherit eternal life?" One possibility, theoretically, would be to obey perfectly and completely the Old Testament law, summarized in the Ten Commandments. Surely if one could do that, he or she would deserve to earn eternal life. So Jesus quizzes the ruler in this regard with a quick summary of the second table of the commandments, having to do with duty to neighbor: "You know the commandments: 'Do not commit adultery, Do not murder, Do not steal, Do not bear false witness, Honor your father and mother.'" It is not insignificant that the tenth commandment, "You shall not covet," is omitted here. We shall return to that in a moment. As for now, the ruler says, with a straight face, "All these I have kept from my youth." Jesus does not contest his answer. So far, so good.

However, the importance of the matter at hand calls for greater scrutiny. The desire for self-justification often works hand in hand with the power of self-deception. Jesus knew all along where the sticking point was. He allowed the ruler to articulate what he had done, in order to show him all the more clearly what he had not done and what, indeed, he could not do. So Jesus said to the ruler, "One thing you still lack. Sell all that you have and distribute to the poor, and you will have treasure in heaven; and come, follow me." That was a conversation stopper. Not another word was exchanged between them. "Sell all that you have and distribute to the poor." Notice what has happened here. In violation of the tenth commandment, "You shall not covet," the ruler coveted the wealth that admittedly was his own but that Jesus asked him to distribute to the poor. He came asking for eternal life, but Jesus made him face the reality that he was more attached to the things of this life. It appears that he had never seen that so clearly as at this precise moment.

In fact, the ruler's attachment to his wealth may have gone beyond covetousness. His attachment to his wealth seems also to have constituted a violation of the very first commandment, "You shall have no other gods before me."[1] That is to say, it was not only the case that he coveted his own wealth. It was also the case that he depended upon it for life, meaning, purpose, security, identity, value, and happiness. It was who he was. As Martin Luther said, "Whatever your heart clings to and confides in, that is really your God."[2] It was not simply the case that the ruler had great wealth. It was, instead, the much more intractable problem that his wealth had him. Instead of it belonging to him, he belonged to it. And so he became very sad. He could not sell it. He could not give it away. He could not let it go. He could not earn eternal life.

The ruler's sadness became the occasion for sadness on the part of Jesus. "How difficult it is for those who have wealth to enter the kingdom of God! For it is easier for a camel to go through the eye of a needle than for a rich person to enter the kingdom of God." What an exaggeration to make a point! Or so we would like to believe. I think Jesus was *not* exaggerating but instead was speaking entirely literally and seriously. "How difficult it is for those who have wealth to enter the kingdom of God! For it is easier for a camel to go through the eye of a needle than for a rich person to enter the kingdom of God." You see, money is a good and useful thing. But it is also a very dangerous thing. The danger is that instead of using it we begin to love it, and then we begin to love it absolutely. Such absolute love is to be reserved for God alone. And therein lies the problem.

It is important for us individually not to be trapped by money, and one way to exercise our freedom over it is to give it away. The history of philosophy tells of a man in ancient Greece who freed himself from the grip of wealth by throwing all of his money into the sea. But that was stupid. It accomplished what he wanted, but the value was lost to humanity. Jesus, by way of contrast, did not urge simple sacrifice, but

1. Compare Colossians 3:5, where Paul equates covetousness with idolatry.
2. Luther, "Large Catechism," Ten Commandments, First Commandment.

sacrifice with a point, a purpose, a reason, and a mission. "Sell all that you have and distribute to the poor." There were people in desperate need of the very thing holding that man back from God. Giving substantial and sacrificial offerings to and through the church can help us to moderate our immoderate love for money today, can help us to declare our independence from that hard master, can help us to pledge our allegiance to God, and can help us to help those in need. Of course, it is also important for us as the church not to be trapped by money. The church is not in the business of getting rich. We receive many offerings, and we give away much of that, also. And I hope and believe that by the end of this year Mattoax and Pine Grove Presbyterian Churches will have given away more money for the mission of the church here and nationally and internationally than we have ever done before.

We should note that while others can and have given away their wealth, so that it is not impossible, nevertheless it was the sticking point for this man. And presumably even those who give away their wealth have other sticking points at other places in their lives. Perhaps other people do not covet wealth but also do not keep the Sabbath, or do not honor their parents, or do not refrain from murdering, or do not refrain from adultery, or do not refrain from stealing, and on and on. Perhaps other people do not covet wealth, but all people have at least one area of shortcoming, at least one sticking point, at least one place at which they do not obey the law, and I suspect most of us have many such places. Perhaps, we think, we are among those other people for whom covetousness might not be a problem, so we might as well hang onto our wealth while we try to figure out our other problems. But the other people who first heard this teaching, even as poor as they may have been, at least seemed to realize from this exchange the seriousness of their own situation and therefore of the whole human predicament.

"How difficult it is for those who have wealth to enter the kingdom of God! For it is easier for a camel to go through the eye of a needle than for a rich person to enter the kingdom of God." It was (3) those who heard these words who said, "Then who can be saved?" If entering the kingdom of God is that difficult, how can anyone be saved? If entering the kingdom of God is that difficult, how can I be saved? The despair in this question is appropriate. If obeying the whole law perfectly is impossible, so that there is nothing any one of us can do to save himself or herself, the question is right on target. But note also that the verb has changed from the active voice to the passive voice. The attention has shifted from what we can do or cannot do to what can be done for us by another. And that clue points directly to the answer. "What is impossible with men is possible with God." Here is the good news. "What is impossible with men is possible with God." Here is the gospel. "What is impossible with men is possible with God." Thanks be to God! Even though there is nothing we can do to inherit eternal life, it is still possible for God to save us. It is still possible for God, acting in and through Jesus Christ, to save us, to turn us around, to reclaim us for himself, to justify us, to bring us into the kingdom, and so to give us eternal life. Yes, it is still possible for God to save us, and it is the gospel that he does in fact save us.

Today's Bible reading tells us again that the greatest, the deepest, the most important, and the most profound human need that we have is to be in right relationship with God. There are many other important things about human life, good and useful in and of themselves, but none of them is as important as this one. And we get into trouble when we give those other things priority over this one. Part of what we are told again and again is that our deepest needs are not physical, not food or clothing or shelter, as important as they are. Our deepest needs are not emotional, not friends and family, as important as they are. Our deepest needs are not psychological, or social or political, or economic, or financial, or national, or military, or anything else. Our deepest need is to be in right relationship with God. We were made for that. That is what human life is all about. And without that, nothing else counts for anything.

So how do we meet this need? (a) Actively earning eternal life is not a possibility. There is not one of us who can keep the law perfectly. And yet (b), receiving salvation is a possibility. Receiving the kingdom of God like a child is the only way to enter it. It is sheer gift. Now, we have to know, we have to realize that these two ways—on the one hand earning it on our own and by ourselves, and on the other hand receiving it as a sheer gift from Jesus Christ—these two ways are in direct opposition to each other. They are entirely contradictory; they are mutually exclusive; they cannot touch each other; they cannot be merged; they cannot come together at all. There is no way to mix the two or to use part of one and part of the other. We cannot possibly (a) say, "I am basically a good person; I deserve to go to Heaven," *and* also (b) receive the forgiveness of our sin at the same time. It is one way or the other. "Who can be saved?" (a) *Not* the one who trusts in his or her own actions or supposed goodness! "Who can be saved?" (b) *Only* those who trust in the goodness and saving action of God! "Who can be saved?" "Let the children come to me, and do not hinder them, for to such belongs the kingdom of God. Truly, I say to you, whoever does not receive the kingdom of God like a child shall not enter it."

To God be the glory forever and ever! Amen.

49

What Do You Want Me to Do?

LUKE 18:31–43; ISAIAH 50:4–9

"WHAT DO YOU WANT me to do for you?" This is the question in today's reading. This is our clue as to what is most important in this passage. This is what points us to the good news for our lives. "What do you want me to do for you?" It was Jesus, of course, who asked this question. It was not one of his disciples trying to be helpful. It was not a bystander looking for a job. It was the Lord of the universe, going up to Jerusalem, who stopped at the outskirts of Jericho to help a blind beggar. "What do you want me to do for you?" The question is as fresh today as it was nearly two thousand years ago. For just as Jesus of Nazareth asked this to the blind beggar, so does the risen Lord Jesus Christ continue to ask it to us yet today, "What do you want me to do for you?" "What do you want me to do?" "What do you want?"

The blind man said, "Lord, let me recover my sight." No sooner had he requested it than the Lord did it. We do not know *how* the Lord did it, other than the sheer power of his will and word. There is no description of any surgery. There is no mention of any salve or medicine. We simply know that he did it. Jesus said to him, "Recover your sight," and immediately the man recovered his sight. For with his very next breath, Jesus continued, "Your faith has made you well," referring to the healing as already done, accomplished, and finished. In the twinkling of an eye, the blind man saw. Immediately he recovered his sight and, what is more, followed Jesus, glorifying God. And yet as wonderful as that was for him then, we may be left still wondering what it has to do with us today.

"What do you want me to do for you?" This is the question in today's reading. This is our clue as to what is most important in this passage. This points us to the good news for our lives. A number of affirmations are made here. One (1) is that Jesus

Christ wants to *help*. That may seem a small thing, but it is really quite remarkable. Jesus was on his way to Jerusalem. He had important business there. As long ago as Luke 9, Jesus had "set his face to go to Jerusalem." He had walked from Galilee, through Samaria, and into Judea. And now in Luke 18, Jesus was at Jericho, the last city before Jerusalem, so he was almost at his destination. And he was surrounded by a crowd, pressing into the city, and the crowd was determined to silence any distractions. But Jesus stopped in the middle of the road because he wanted to help.

"What do you want me to do for you?" A second (2) affirmation made here is that Jesus *can* help. It is not only the case that Jesus wants to help. That is nice. It is also the case that Jesus can help. There is a tremendous difference between the two. The basis for this second affirmation may be found in the shift of titles used here for Jesus. When the blind man heard the commotion and asked what it all meant, the crowd told him, "Jesus of Nazareth is passing by." Humanly speaking, that was a perfectly good way to refer to him. Jesus was his name, Nazareth was his hometown, so "Jesus of Nazareth" said who he was and where he was from. But the blind man knew better. "Jesus, Son of David, have mercy on me!" And the more they tried to silence him, he cried out all the more, "Son of David, have mercy on me!"

"Son of David" is not a place name. "Son of David" has to do with royalty. In fact, "Son of David" has to do with eternity. And so, "Son of David" has to do with divinity. A thousand years earlier, the prophet Nathan had spoken the word of the Lord to King David:

> I will raise up your offspring after you, who shall come from your body, and I will establish his kingdom. . . . I will establish the throne of his kingdom forever. . . . And your house and your kingdom shall be made sure forever before me. Your throne shall be established forever. (2 Samuel 7:12, 13, 16)

And the angel Gabriel had built upon this earlier word of the Lord to tell the virgin Mary:

> And behold, you will conceive in your womb and bear a son, and you shall call his name Jesus. He will be great and will be called the Son of the Most High. And the Lord God will give to him the throne of his father David, and he will reign over the house of Jacob forever, and of his kingdom there will be no end. (Luke 1:31–33)

So while the seeing crowd thought Jesus was from Nazareth, the blind beggar knew that Jesus was from God and knew that he was God. How the blind man knew this we do not know, other than to say that he saw this by the eyes of faith. So, it is not only the case that Jesus wants to help. It is also the case that, as the Son of God, he can help. There is a tremendous difference.

"What do you want me to do for you?" A third (3) affirmation being made here is that Jesus Christ *does* help. It is not only the case that Jesus wants to help. It is not only the case that Jesus can help. It is also the case that Jesus does help. In this case, he gives sight. The man whom he helped was blind, unemployed, impoverished, reduced to begging, apparently pushed outside the city, publicly rebuked, and, most likely, spurned and despised. For Jesus to give him sight was for Jesus to give him life itself. The man would have an opportunity to work, to contribute, to mean something, and to be somebody. And even more important that all that put together, the man whom Jesus healed also followed Jesus and glorified God. He followed Jesus and glorified God. Such discipleship and worship are what we were made for. These are what we are saved for. These are the purpose of our lives and the meaning of our existence.

You remember the first question and answer of the Westminster Shorter Catechism: "Q. 1. What is the chief end of man? A. Man's chief end is to glorify God, and to enjoy him forever." We might say today in today's language that the ultimate purpose of human existence is to glorify God and to enjoy him forever. The authors of the catechism probably learned this great truth from today's gospel reading, among others. So it was that the formerly blind man followed Jesus and glorified God. It does not get any better than this. The man's life was complete. And somehow, with the one blind man's healing, even the rebuking crowd and all the seeing but unseeing people finally saw what was going on and gave praise to God. There was a multiplying effect. That is to say, they were healed too.

"What do you want me to do for you?" The already tremendous significance of this healing of the blind man and effectively blind crowd is only heightened when it is set in the larger context of the rest of the reading and of the situation of the disciples:

> And taking the twelve, he [Jesus] said to them, "See, we are going up to Jerusalem, and everything that is written about the Son of Man by the prophets will be accomplished. For he will be delivered over to the Gentiles and will be mocked and shamefully treated and spit upon. And after flogging him, they will kill him, and on the third day he will rise." But they understood none of these things. This saying was hidden from them, and they did not grasp what was said.

They were in worse shape than the blind man! Jesus told them explicitly about his betrayal, condemnation, suffering, death, and resurrection. "But they understood none of these things. This saying was hidden from them, and they did not grasp what was said." The seeing disciples did not understand who Jesus was. But the blind beggar knew who Jesus was. The contrast is startling. And the good news here is that Jesus Christ (1) wants to, (2) can, and (3) does heal the sick, even including giving sight to the blind. That is to say, there is hope yet even for the disciples. There is hope yet even for us.

"What do you want me to do for you?" The gospel point of these juxtaposed stories is for the disciples to take up the blind man's answer, "Lord, let me recover my sight," and make it their own answer. Indeed, the gospel point of these juxtaposed stories is for all of us who are and who would be disciples to take up the blind man's answer, "Lord, let me recover my sight," and make it our very own answer, here and today. This is an open invitation to us, to you and to me. The good news here is that the Lord Jesus (1) wants to, (2) can, and (3) does give sight. Do you want to see? Do you want to know? Do you want to understand? Do you want what is hidden to be revealed? Do you want to grasp the sayings of Jesus? Do you want to follow Jesus? Do you want to glorify God? Do you? "What do you want me to do for you?" "Lord, let me recover my sight." Jesus (1) wants to do that. Jesus (2) can do that. And Jesus (3) does do that even for you and me. Thanks be to God!

Jesus said, "Your faith has made you well." This does not mean that faith is magic. It does not mean that faith can somehow work apart from the saving grace of God in Jesus Christ. What it does mean is that faith is precisely a knowing confidence in the goodness, power, and willingness of God to help us in and through Jesus Christ. The blind man had faith that Jesus could and would help him. As John Calvin wrote centuries later, "Now we shall possess a right definition of faith if we call it a firm and certain knowledge of God's benevolence toward us, founded upon the truth of the freely given promise in Christ, both revealed to our minds and sealed upon our hearts through the Holy Spirit."[1] So faith is not believing in something that you do not know. Faith is knowing, in Jesus Christ, that God is good. And today's reading is an invitation to us all to have that faith that God is good.

Today's reading is an invitation to us all to be confident that God in Jesus Christ can and will help us. And today's reading is an invitation to us all to use our faith, to exercise our faith, and to act upon the basis of our faith to ask Jesus to give us sight and understanding. There are many other things we could ask for. But they might not be the right things to ask for. This is what today's reading is urging us to ask for today. This is what is important here and now.

> See, we are going up to Jerusalem, and everything that is written about the Son of Man by the prophets will be accomplished. For he will be delivered over to the Gentiles and will be mocked and shamefully treated and spit upon. And after flogging him, they will kill him, and on the third day he will rise.

As the Apostles' Creed summarizes this, he "suffered under Pontius Pilate, was crucified, dead, and buried; he descended into hell; the third day he rose again from the dead." The saving work of Jesus Christ for us was concentrated into his death and resurrection. We delight in his parables. We exult in his healings. But the important part is this hard part, this horrible part, this part we do not want to see or to contemplate: he suffered for us, he bled for us, he died for us, on our account and for our sake. This is what we need to see, as hard as it may be to look at. This is what we need to understand and to grasp. And while such knowledge may not be simply humanly

---

1. Calvin, *Institutes*, III.2.7, 1:551.

possible, we have good confidence that our Lord can give us that sight and grant us that understanding. He paid the price to win the privilege to be able to heal us.

Even the poor disciples eventually received this healing. Do you remember what it says in Luke 24? After the crucifixion and after the resurrection, two of the disciples were going to Emmaus, and Jesus himself drew near and went with them. "But their eyes were kept from recognizing him." They were still blind. But he talked to them along the way, and they invited him to stay with them. And then, "when he was at table with them, he took bread and blessed and broke it and gave it to them. And their eyes were opened, and they recognized him." Finally! By the end of this gospel we are reading, the disciples' eyes were opened, and they knew who Jesus was. Their blindness was healed, and they understood that the crucified one had been resurrected. Finally it all made sense. Thanks be to God! And since their blind eyes were opened, there is hope even for us yet today.

"What do you want me to do for you?" "What do you want me to do?" "What do you want?" Do you want Jesus to restore your sight? Do you want Jesus to give you understanding? Do you want Jesus to call you his very own? Then tell him so! Ask him to do for you what you cannot do for yourself. Ask him to do for you what you want him to do for you. Ask him to do for you what he came to do and died to do and now lives again to do for you and for me. "Lord, let me recover my sight." Take away my blindness. Let me see that in your crucifixion you willingly poured out your life for me so that my sin might be forgiven. Let me see that in your resurrection God vindicated your sacrifice so that I might have eternal life. Grant me grace that I may both follow you and glorify God. And may all the people, when they see it, give praise to God!

To God be the glory forever and ever! Amen.

50

Why Did the Son of Man Come?

LUKE 19:1–27; EXODUS 34:1–9

"HE HAS GONE IN to be the guest of a man who is a sinner." This grumbling on the part of the unnamed crowd implies that they had a question about Jesus: "Why has he gone in to be the guest of a sinner?" Perhaps Luke recorded their grumbling so that Theophilus, to whom Luke dedicated this gospel, and all his other early readers could recognize in it a concern of their own: "Why did Jesus associate with sinners?" And perhaps their question anticipates our own question: "Why in the world would the Son of God go in to be with such a notorious sinner?" Why, indeed? It is also the case that this implied question points us directly toward the main affirmation of the text, the most important teaching in today's reading. They all grumbled, "He has gone in to be the guest of a man who is a sinner." But Jesus said, "The Son of Man came to seek and to save the lost."

"The Son of Man came to seek and to save the lost." This is good news, indeed! This is why he came—not only to seek the lost but also even to save the lost. Jesus did not come to entertain us. He did not come to teach philosophy. He did not come to spark a revolution. He did not come to rectify inequalities. Jesus came to seek and to save the lost. There is nothing greater than this to be done. And it would behoove us to realize that we are among those for whom he came. The only people whom Jesus never helped were the ones who did not want help. But to those who wanted help, to those who knew they were lost, to those who could not find their way, Jesus gave life itself. And he continues to do so for us today. In strange and wonderful ways, with far reaching consequences, he continues to give life even today.

The conversion of Zacchaeus in today's reading may be the single most remarkable event in the ministry of Jesus recorded up to this point. We have learned that he healed the blind, cleansed lepers, released the paralyzed, raised the dead, and preached good news to the poor. He calmed the sea, cast out demons, fed the five thousand, challenged the Pharisees, and predicted the future. And more than all of that, in today's reading, the last event recorded before his triumphant entry into Jerusalem, Jesus set a man free from the love of money. This may be his greatest miracle. Jesus knew that the love of money was his greatest enemy. He had called disciples to follow him. He had led people to faith. But Jesus set Zacchaeus free from the love of money, and this may have been his greatest work prior to the cross.

"Why has he gone in to be the guest of a sinner?" "The Son of Man came to seek and to save the lost." And the proof of that is the salvation that Jesus brought to Zacchaeus when he set him free from the love of money. Let us consider the circumstances of his conversion, and let us so realize that this record of his conversion is an invitation to us for our own conversion. Jesus "entered Jericho and was passing through." He had already healed a blind man on his way into the city. "There was a man named Zacchaeus. He was a chief tax collector and was rich." That is to say, Zacchaeus was a sinner extraordinaire. As a tax collector, he was working for the occupying Romans and against his own people. As a chief tax collector, he oversaw others who betrayed their own people. And as a rich chief tax collector, he undoubtedly cheated and defrauded his people, given that the Roman Empire did not overpay him. Zacchaeus was a sinner extraordinaire.

And yet, Zacchaeus "was seeking to see who Jesus was." Somehow, he had heard of Jesus before, as have we. He knew something of his teachings and his mighty works. Something deep within Zacchaeus was stirred. So, this was more than idle curiosity. This was an act of hope. He wanted to see who Jesus was, to know who Jesus was, indeed, to know Jesus. Zacchaeus "was seeking to see who Jesus was, but on account of the crowd he could not, because he was small of stature." How odd that of all the important things in this reading, we remember this incidental thing, that Zacchaeus was a little man. Of course, it provided the occasion for the invitation that Jesus extended to him. And it may have been symbolic of his moral stature. "So he ran on ahead and climbed up into a sycamore tree to see him, for he was about to pass that way." Yes, Zacchaeus was up a tree, in more ways than one. And yet, he is to be commended for his perseverance in his desire to see Jesus. We should try so hard.

"And when Jesus came to the place, he looked up and said to him, 'Zacchaeus, hurry and come down, for I must stay at your house today.'" "Zacchaeus, hurry and come down, for I must stay at your house today." What grace filled words are these! Jesus knew him by name, even as he knows you and me by name. Jesus called him by name, urged him to hurry down from the tree, and invited himself into his home, into his life, into his heart, and into his soul. "Zacchaeus, hurry and come down, for I must stay at your house today." "So he hurried and came down and received him joyfully." What a wonderful response! What a gracious response to the grace-filled self-invitation! Zacchaeus did not protest that his house was not clean. He did not worry about not having enough food. "He hurried and came down and received him joyfully."

And that is what really got the crowd going. Zacchaeus received Jesus gladly. "And when they saw it, they all grumbled, 'He has gone in to be the guest of a man who is a sinner.'" Not that any of them had invited Jesus in for dinner! But they grumbled and groused and complained anyway. After all, Jesus was on his way to Jerusalem to conduct important business, to inaugurate the kingdom of God. Now he had been turned aside into the home of this miserable sinner. How could this be anything other than an unfortunate interruption? "He has gone in to be the guest of a man who is a sinner." This grumbling on the part of the unnamed crowd implies that they had a question about Jesus: "Why has he gone in to be the guest of a sinner?" And perhaps their question anticipates our own question: "Why in the world would the Son of God go in to be with such a notorious sinner?" It is also the case that this implied question points us directly toward the main affirmation of the text. And Jesus said, "The Son of Man came to seek and to save the lost."

But we are getting ahead of ourselves. We are almost at the heart of the story. Not only did Zacchaeus hurry and come down and receive Jesus gladly, and not only did Zacchaeus extend to him the appropriate hospitality, but also, and ever so much more, "Zacchaeus stood and said to the Lord, 'Behold, Lord, the half of my goods I give to the poor. And if I have defrauded anyone of anything, I restore it fourfold.'" There is the proof of his conversion! Nothing else could account for such a change in such a man. "Zacchaeus stood," as well he should have. This was a sign of respect. We stand today when we affirm our faith and when we sing our hymns of praise. "Zacchaeus stood and said to the Lord, 'Behold, Lord,'" not what a tax collector would say to a teacher, but a profession of faith in Jesus as Lord and Savior, a profession confirmed by what followed.

"Zacchaeus stood and said to the Lord, 'Behold, Lord, the half of my goods I give to the poor.'" And again I say, this conversion of Zacchaeus may have been the greatest work Jesus did prior to the cross. What a miracle! Zacchaeus "was a chief tax collector and was rich." And Jesus set him free from the love of money. The love of money is a harsh and cruel master. But Jesus saved this man, set him free, and turned his life around. He set him free, not simply for the sake of freedom, but so that he would be free to do good works, and so he was. "Behold, Lord, the half of my goods I give to the poor." When else has the world seen such gratitude, such graciousness, such generosity, such an outpouring of heart and substance? No one told Zacchaeus he had to do this. This was not a prerequisite of his salvation. This was the joyful over pouring of his heart in response to the love that Jesus had already given him.

And there is more. Zacchaeus continued, "And if I have defrauded anyone of anything, I restore it fourfold." To understand this, it is important for us to realize that there are two ways to say "if" in Greek, the language in which Luke is written, and they have different implications. One word for "if" indicates an assumption contrary to fact. "If I were the President of the United States of America (and we all know that I am not), then I would do thus and so." This same word for "if" could also be used to express an unsure possibility. "If I go to town tomorrow (and right now I do not know whether I can or not), then I will pick up something for you at the store." But the other word for "if" actually indicates a simple assumption of fact. "If I am the temporary supply pastor (and we all know that I am), then I am preaching this morning." We do not normally speak this way in English. We would say, "Since I am the temporary supply pastor, I am preaching this morning." But it is this second way that Zacchaeus uses in today's reading. "If I have defrauded anyone of anything (and we all know that I have), I restore it fourfold." That is to say, this is not a question of something that might have happened. This is a confession of sin that did happen. And it leads directly to an extraordinary promise of restitution.

It is significant that this confession of sin does not precede but actually follows his conversion. The Christian faith is often misconstrued to suggest that it is necessary for one to repent before one can be saved. But if we were good enough to repent before we were saved, we would not need to be saved. Repentance, then, is not a prerequisite for the grace of God. Repentance is, instead, a necessary consequence of the grace of God. Repentance does not lead to grace. Repentance flows out of grace. And therefore repentance is not a once-in-a-lifetime event, to be completed prior to coming to faith. Repentance is a daily, ongoing event for the rest of our lives, as we evermore completely turn away from the life that was our past and as we evermore fully turn toward God and his Christ. In technical language, while conversion and justification can occur in a moment, sanctification is a lifetime of increasing obedience.

"And Zacchaeus stood and said to the Lord, 'Behold, Lord, the half of my goods I give to the poor. And if I have defrauded anyone of anything [or as we would say, since we all know that I have defrauded many of much], I restore it fourfold.' And Jesus said to him, 'Today salvation has come to this house, since he also is a son of Abraham. For the Son of Man came to seek and to save the lost.'" When Jesus heard this profession of faith, this pledge of gratitude, this confession of sin, and this promise of restitution, he named it "salvation." This is not at all to say that Zacchaeus was saved because he did these things. Quite the opposite. Zacchaeus did all these things because he was already saved. These were the evidences. These were the proof. These were the incontrovertible demonstration after the fact that already he had been converted, that already he had been saved, and that already Jesus had set him free from the love of money.

Just in case we still do not realize the magnitude of this conversion, remember that as recently as the immediately prior chapter Jesus himself said, "How difficult it is for those who have wealth to enter the kingdom of God! For it is easier for a camel to go through the eye of a needle than for a rich person to enter the kingdom of God." And now it has happened! No wonder Jesus named it salvation. It was not something Zacchaeus accomplished on his own. It was not something he accomplished at all. It was something done to him and for him. It was the grace of God poured out upon him. It was the grace of God in Jesus Christ, who invited himself into his home, into his life, into his heart, and into his soul, that turned him around, set him free from the love of money, and gave him life.

Are you interested? Would you like to see who Jesus is? He is eager yet today to come into your home, to come into your life, to come into your heart, and to come into your soul. And when he does, you will never be the same again. I promise you that. Your life will never be the same again. Whatever it is that you love more than God will be knocked out of first place, as Zacchaeus demonstrated in gracious and marvelous ways. The grace of God in Jesus Christ is a strange and wonderful and powerful thing. You may find yourself standing to pledge your faith in God and in his Christ. You may find yourself sharing with those who have not: food for the hungry, housing for the homeless, comfort for the distraught, the gospel for the lost. You may find yourself making amends for what you have done wrong. You may find yourself rejoicing.

And what if all of this is old hat to you? What if you have been a believer for lo these many years, or even decades, or most of your life? What if you cannot even remember not being Christian? Is there anything in this grace of conversion for you? Well, yes, of course there is. You remember that the grace of conversion leads to the grace of repentance and that repentance involves a lifetime of turning away from sin and turning toward God, of actions of graciousness and obedience. And Jesus makes that very point explicitly in today's reading. "As they heard these things"—which is to say, as they heard what Zacchaeus said and what Jesus said about salvation—"he proceeded to tell a parable, because he was near to Jerusalem, and because they supposed that the kingdom of God was to appear immediately." They thought heaven would come as soon as he got to Jerusalem.

But that is not the way it was. That is not at all the way it is. The whole point of the parable is that the Lord may be away in a far country for a long time. And in the meantime, we are to be involved in the business of the Lord. We who belong to him, we who are his, we who were converted years ago, are to live our Christian lives day in and day out, year after year, in the unrelenting pursuit of the business of our Lord. He has entrusted us with resources to use during this interim. He is coming back. There will be an accounting. Have we used the resources he gave us? Have we generated a return? Are we ready to report what the increase has been? Or are we like the sorry servant who took what was given and wrapped it up for safekeeping?

These are serious questions. They are asked here for our benefit, so that we can consider them now, before he returns. How can we, as individual Christians, be faithful? How can we, as a church, be faithful? How can we live appropriately to the grace God has already given us? How can we live appropriately to the kingdom that is to come? How can we stand and profess our faith in a world that belittles and ridicules faith? How can we out think the best minds of the secular world? How can we show that we love the Lord more than we love our money? How can we pour ourselves out in the effort to make right all that we have done wrong? How can we take the wonderful heritage that we have received, the faith of the centuries, the mission of the church, the learning of the world, our culture, our society, our government, and turn them all to the service of the Lord and to the business of his kingdom?

No wonder that "when they saw it, they all grumbled, 'He has gone in to be the guest of a man who is a sinner.'" Maybe they knew that when Jesus started associating with sinners the world would never be same. Would that we quit looking down on the sinners and realize that we are the sinners for whom he came! And then the miracles would start flowing. In what may have been the greatest miracle he ever performed, Jesus set Zacchaeus free from the love of money. It was amazing! "Zacchaeus stood and said to the Lord, 'Behold, Lord, the half of my goods I give to the poor. And if I have defrauded anyone of anything, I restore it fourfold.'" From what do you need to be set free? The love of money? The love of something else? Whatever it is, help has arrived. Thanks be to God! Jesus said, "Today salvation has come to this house. . . . For the Son of Man came to seek and to save the lost."

To God be the glory forever and ever! Amen.

51

In Whose Name?

LUKE 19:28–48; ISAIAH 59:14–20

"BLESSED IS THE KING who comes in the name of the Lord!" These are not the un-knowing words of an enthusiastic but fickle crowd, as we often characterize those around Jesus at his entrance into Jerusalem. These constitute, instead, a profession of faith and a hymn of praise on the part of "the whole multitude of his disciples," who "began to rejoice and praise God with a loud voice for all the mighty works that they had seen." "Blessed is the King who comes in the name of the Lord!" They had seen what Jesus had done. They had heard what he had taught. They had followed him to Jerusalem. They knew who he was. They may not have understood his entire ministry then as well as they would after his crucifixion and resurrection, but they knew who he was, and we would do well to hear their witness to us.

"Blessed is the King who comes in the name of the Lord!" They were singing Psalm 118, which says, "Blessed is he who comes in the name of the LORD!" (v. 26a). This is high praise, indeed. Psalm 118 is a tremendous hymn of praise and thanksgiv-ing specifically for deliverance and salvation. "Oh give thanks to the LORD, for he is good; for his steadfast love endures forever!" (v. 1). "The LORD is my strength and my song; he has become my salvation" (v. 14). And, as we say every Sunday morn-ing, "This is the day that the LORD has made; let us rejoice and be glad in it" (v. 24). Moreover, it is clear in this psalm that it is the Lord God himself who is the agent of this salvation and therefore the object of this praise. "This is the LORD's doing; it is marvelous in our eyes" (v. 23). "Save us, we pray, O LORD! O LORD, we pray, give us success!" (v. 25). "You are my God, and I will give thanks to you; you are my God; I will extol you" (v. 28).

That is to say, when the disciples praise Jesus as the one "who comes in the name of the LORD," they are acknowledging him not only as one who comes from God but particularly as God himself among them. He is not only a messenger but is actually God himself. The multitude of disciples are singing to Jesus a hymn written to be sung to God. And they are doing this not to dishonor God but to worship Jesus as God. No wonder the Pharisees said to him, "Teacher, rebuke your disciples." They were not worried about the crowd, as such, but they knew blasphemy when they heard it. And this was blasphemy, unless it was true. There could be nothing in between. That it might have been true was an option they did not consider. Luke has recorded this incident for our benefit so that we might hear the witness of those first disciples and so that we might join them in professing our own faith and in worshiping Jesus as God.

"Blessed is the King who comes in the name of the LORD!" Again, Psalm 118, which they were quoting, says, "Blessed is he who comes in the name of the LORD!" For the multitude of disciples to have changed the pronoun "he" to the title "King" does not mean that they could not remember the psalm accurately. But it does indicate that they fully expected Jesus to initiate and to inaugurate the kingdom of God about which he taught them so much. The kingdom of God would surely come, and Jesus was none other than the king of the kingdom of God, none other than God himself with them. It was in Luke 9 that Jesus "set his face to go to Jerusalem." It is now in chapter 19 that Jesus is entering Jerusalem, the holy city, the capital city, surely to be the seat of government of the kingdom of God. Maybe they did not yet understand the nature of that kingdom or the price that Jesus would pay for it, but they knew and understood who he was, and we would do well to hear their witness to us. Jesus is God, and Jesus is King of the kingdom of God.

There is more. Jesus "entered the temple and began to drive out those who sold, saying to them, 'It is written, "My house shall be a house of prayer," but you have made it a den of robbers.'" The temple is the place of priests. There the priests lead worship. There the priests offer sacrifices to the Lord. That is the reason for the temple. That Jesus cleansed the temple of its abuses and then also occupied it himself means clearly both that he was purifying and preparing it for true worship and also that he is our one true priest. He is the one who leads our true worship of God. He is the one who offers true sacrifice. In fact, he is the one who not only offered the true sacrifice but also actually offered himself as the one true, perfect, complete, and efficacious sacrifice on the cross outside Jerusalem. We have no other priest. We need no other priest. Jesus is our great high priest.

Moreover, Jesus "was teaching daily in the temple. The chief priests and the scribes and the principal men of the people were seeking to destroy him, but they did not find anything they could do, for all the people were hanging on his words." Jesus, who came "in the name of the Lord," was also speaking the word of the Lord. The prophets of old had spoken the word of the Lord on behalf of the Lord. Jesus spoke the word of the Lord as the Lord. Jesus is the prophet par excellence, the prophet without peer, the true and final prophet, the prophet who speaks the word of God with authority. He is the one to whom we should listen. He is the one whom we should believe. He is the one whom we should obey. As it is written in the Theological Declaration of Barmen, a document in our church's book of confessions of faith, "Jesus Christ, as he is attested for us in Holy Scripture, is the one Word of God which we have to hear and which we have to trust and obey in life and in death."

All of this is to say that in these few verses, Luke sets Jesus before us as Prophet, Priest, and King, indeed as God himself with us and for us. Is that of interest to you? Is that of concern to you? Should that be of interest to the world? It may be of interest to us simply because it is the truth. It may also be of interest to us because of the human predicament and the fallen condition of the world. Are you are perfectly satisfied with what Hollywood teaches the world about what is good and true and beautiful and honorable? Then maybe you would not be interested in the Prophet who speaks the true word of God. Are you perfectly satisfied with our society's glorification of violence, sex, lust, power, and abuse in our world? Then maybe you would not be interested in the Priest who offers himself for our salvation, redemption, and renewal. Are you perfectly satisfied with how the rulers of this world rule this world with terrorism, with war, with exploitation? Then maybe you would not be interested in the King who establishes the peaceful, just, and righteous kingdom of God.

But if you share with me, even in the midst of profound gratitude for life, a profound dissatisfaction with the gone-wrongness of life, a profound dissatisfaction with the emptiness of what the world offers, and a profound dissatisfaction with the fear of what seems likely to come, then maybe you are interested in what Luke has to say. Maybe you are interested in the gospel of Jesus Christ. Maybe you are interested in who he is and what he does as Prophet, Priest, and King. Maybe you are interested in acknowledging him as God himself with us and for us. Maybe you are interested in serving him as Lord and Savior. Maybe you are interested in singing his praises. Maybe you are interested in sharing his gospel around the world.

What we have read together this morning is not simply ancient history. Yes, what we have read together is an ancient account of the triumphant entry of Jesus into the city of Jerusalem. But what we have read is also the word of the living God spoken to us today, to you and to me, about who Jesus is, about what he has done and is doing, and about how he does it. We know, of course, that his victory was hard won. He did not simply ride into the city and take it over. He died a horrible death outside the city later that week. But that apparent defeat was his real victory. That cross is the altar where he gave himself. There he broke the power of sin, death, and evil, once and for all. There he became true Prophet, Priest, and King in ways his disciples could not have anticipated. There he showed us the awesome reality of God with us and for us. From there he calls us to be his very own. And for the sacrifice that he made, God rewarded him with resurrection.

"Blessed is the King who comes in the name of the Lord!" These are not the unknowing words of an enthusiastic but fickle crowd, as we often characterize those around Jesus at his entrance into Jerusalem. These constitute, instead, a profession of faith and a hymn of praise on the part of "the whole multitude of his disciples," who "began to rejoice and praise God with a loud voice for all the mighty works that they had seen." "Blessed is the King who comes in the name of the Lord!" They had seen what Jesus had done. They had heard what he had taught. They had followed him to Jerusalem. They knew who he was. They may not have understood his ministry then as well as they would after his crucifixion and resurrection, but they knew who he was, and we would do well to hear their witness to us, to receive their witness to us, and so to join them in their hymn of praise. Let us praise and worship God. Let us believe in God and in his Christ. Let us give thanks to God, not only in our prayers but also and especially in our offerings and in our lives. Let us obey God and his Christ. Let us serve him well with all that we are and all that we have. "Blessed is the King who comes in the name of the Lord!"

To God be the glory forever and ever! Amen.

52

By What Authority?

LUKE 20:1–26; EXODUS 3:1–15

"TELL US BY WHAT authority you do these things, or who it is that gave you this authority." Thus the religious leaders of the day questioned Jesus. By what authority do you do these things? Who gave you this authority? That is, who do you think you are? Why do you think you can get away with this? These questions asked of Jesus then are not unlike the questions asked today to those who would follow Jesus. Who do you think you are? Why do you think Jesus is so special? What gives you the right to tell me about him? Why should I be interested? Are not all religions the same, anyway? Or, are they not all contradictory? And, do they not all lead to war and hatred? Why should anyone pay any attention? I can be moral without them. Keep Jesus and your beliefs about him to yourself!

Thus, by what authority do you do these things? And, who gave you this authority? We have heard them all before, these hostile and faithless questions. We shall hear them all again. Even at Thanksgiving, some people will not realize that it is the God and Father of Jesus Christ to whom we give thanks. Even at Christmas, some people will be embarrassed to name the name of Jesus Christ and will say instead, "Happy Holidays!" Even at Easter, some people will think that Easter has to do with pagan celebrations of the return of life at spring rather than with the life, death, and resurrection of Jesus Christ. Even in America, today, a nation founded by people seeking freedom of religion, freedom of worship, and freedom of expression, there is tremendous pressure to think of the Christian faith as personal, private, and therefore insignificant, if not juvenile and downright false.

So, by what authority do you do these things? Who gave you this authority? Thus the chief priests and the scribes with the elders questioned Jesus. These are not bad questions, really. Admittedly, they were hostile questions. And if you have to ask these questions to Jesus you may never grasp the answers. Nevertheless, Luke has preserved these questions for us in his gospel, which in many ways seems to function as a catechism, a question-and-answer teaching device, and I believe that Luke has preserved these questions for us in order to set before us the answers of the true nature of the authority of Jesus Christ and of the true source of that authority. And with that, Luke himself is following Jesus in "teaching the people in the temple and preaching the gospel."

By what authority do you do these things? Who gave you this authority? There is, of course, a short answer, and then there is a long answer. There is a short answer that Jesus gave when he responded to their question by asking them another question. "Was the baptism of John from heaven or from man?" That was a tough one. It could have been received as an invitation to faith, an invitation to discipleship, an invitation to follow Jesus. But since it was not so received, this question became a conversation stopper. "Was the baptism of John from heaven or from man?" They realized that if they said, "From heaven," he would say, "Why did you not believe him?" But if they said, "From man," all the people would stone them to death, for the people were convinced that John was a prophet. So the questioners answered that they did not know where John's baptism came from. And Jesus said to them, "Neither will I tell you by what authority I do these things." Jesus did not answer his questioners directly, which was a very powerful way of saying that he did not answer to them. Jesus was not there to be a conversation partner. He was not there to dialogue. Jesus was there to teach. He was there to preach. The point is not for us to give a witty reply. The point is for us to listen, to learn, to believe, and to obey. The fact that they failed to do so then stands as a warning for us not to fail to do so now.

And yet, the question remains: By what authority do you do these things? Who gave you this authority? We have heard the short answer. There is also a longer answer, a fuller answer, one Jesus articulates here in a parable and its application, which the questioners did not miss, an answer also embodied in his life and in his subsequent death and resurrection.[1] After his refusal to give a direct answer, Jesus does go on immediately to establish before the same hearers: (1) that he is the Son of God; (2) that his rejection will become the occasion of their judgment; (3) that precisely as the rejected stone he will become the cornerstone, which is to say of a new building, a new temple, a new people of God; and (4) that he did not mind mixing it up with the rabid worshipers of Caesar. That is not bad for an indirect answer. Let us take up these each of these four one at a time.

---

1. Tillich (*New Being*, 79–91) asserts that Jesus refuses to answer the question and even that an answer is impossible. I disagree. Yes, Jesus refuses to answer the question directly. But Luke 20:9–26 includes several answers, albeit indirect, and the text also indicates that the religious authorities realized exactly what Jesus was saying.

By what authority do you do these things? Who gave you this authority? First of all (1), Jesus does these things by his authority as the Son of God. And, by definition, it was God who gave him this authority. He made this point by telling them an old story with a new twist. The parable of the vineyard came right out of Isaiah 5, written hundreds of years earlier. His hearers knew it well. Their own rabbis preached on it from time to time. A man had a vineyard. He cared for it. But it did not yield to him the harvest he was due. And there were consequences to this failure. As Isaiah tells the story, the vineyard is the people of Israel, and it is the vineyard itself that is at fault. As Jesus retells the story, he introduces a new level of detail. The vineyard had been entrusted to the care of tenants, and that was where the problem was. The vineyard itself was productive, but the persons who were responsible for it failed to yield the harvest to the owner of the vineyard. In that the vineyard was still Israel, these tenants, there caretakers, were the leaders of the people, that is to say, the chief priests and the scribes and the elders, the very people questioning Jesus. And there would be consequences to their failures.

Jesus also introduces another level of detail to this old story. The owner was not an unreasonable man. He sent a series of servants to the tenants, seeking the harvest that was due to him. That is to say, he gave them every opportunity to do what was right, to do what was honorable, to do what was good, to give to him what was his own. Clearly, the servants were the prophets sent from God to the people of Israel: Moses, Elijah, Elisha, Isaiah, Jeremiah, Ezekiel, and so forth. Their messages had not been heeded. The official leadership of the nation was in constant tension with the prophets. So were the servants rejected and beaten.

There is more. "Then the owner of the vineyard said, 'What shall I do? I will send my beloved son; perhaps they will respect him.'" Does this language sound familiar? It appears once earlier, in Luke 3:22, at the baptism of Jesus, where a voice said from heaven, "You are my beloved Son; with you I am well pleased." That is to say, God is the owner of the vineyard. The vineyard is the people of Israel, the people of God. The tenants are the rulers and leaders of the people. The servants were the prophets. And now the owner sends his beloved son to the vineyard, which is to say that God sends his beloved Son to Israel, and God has already identified his beloved Son as none other than Jesus Christ. That is at least part of what this parable means. That is the first part of the longer answer. Those who say simply that Jesus did not answer the question asked of him must have failed to read this longer answer. This says that (1) Jesus does these things by his authority as the Son of God. And, by definition, it was God who gave him this authority. And there is more to this answer.

By what authority do you do these things? Who gave you this authority? Second (2), the parable of the vineyard prophesies that the leaders of the people of Israel will reject and kill the beloved Son of God, and of course we all know that this prophecy came true. Moreover, Jesus concludes the parable of the vineyard with the prophecy that his rejection will become the occasion of their judgment. That is to say, Jesus, as the Son of God, is the one who has such authority that the leaders of the people of God will be judged on the basis of how they treat or mistreat him. If the leaders of the people of God do not honor, believe, respect, worship, and serve Jesus Christ, God will destroy them and raise up other leaders in their place. The people were horrified at this. But we all know that it came true.

Of course, it is a word of warning that continues to speak to us today. If the leaders of the Christian church do not honor, believe, respect, worship, and serve Jesus Christ, God will destroy them and raise up other leaders in their place. If the leaders of the Presbyterian Church (U.S.A.) do not honor, believe, respect, worship, and serve Jesus Christ, God will destroy them and raise up other leaders in their place. If we, the leaders of Mattoax and Pine Grove Presbyterian Churches, do not honor, believe, respect, worship, and serve Jesus Christ, God will destroy us and raise up other leaders in our place. That is the way it is. This ancient question and answer continue to speak to us today. Jesus, as the Son of God, is (1) the one who has such authority that (2) the leaders of the people of God will be judged on the basis of how they treat or mistreat him.

By what authority do you do these things? Who gave you this authority? Turning directly to those who objected to his parable of the vineyard, Jesus added the third (3) point to his longer answer by saying that precisely as the rejected stone he will become the cornerstone, which is to say the cornerstone of a new building, a new temple, indeed a new people of God. This quotation comes from Psalm 118:22, another portion of Scripture with which they were familiar, indeed the very hymn that the people had sung to Jesus during his entry into Jerusalem in the chapter immediately prior to this one. They had to know that verse. Again, by applying this to himself, Jesus prophesied his own rejection. He also prophesied his resurrection and glorification. And again he emphasized that people would be judged by their relationship to him. "Everyone who falls on that stone will be broken to pieces, and when it falls on anyone, it will crush him." Jesus carries the authority (1) not only of the Son of God, and (2) not only of the Crucified One, but also (3) as the risen, living, and final Judge of the universe.

By what authority do you do these things? Who gave you this authority? Fourth and finally (4), as the scribes and chief priests perceived that he had told his parable against them, and as they sent spies to catch him in something he might say, Jesus also showed that he had the freedom, the courage, and therefore the authority of one who did not mind mixing it up with the rabid worshipers of Caesar. This was no inconsiderable courage in and of itself. Caesar himself was hailed as a son of god, but Jesus taught that his own authority as the Son of God was greater. The governor did indeed have authority and jurisdiction, and Jesus would come into contact with that soon enough, with his arrest, trial, conviction, and execution later that week, but still his own authority was greater. So he was free, and he was brave. Jesus did not mind a bit mixing it up even with the rabid worshipers of Caesar.

"Teacher, we know that you speak and teach rightly, and show no partiality, but truly teach the way of God." They did not really believe that. If they had, they would have followed him! But they thought it sounded nice, as if it might have drawn them into his favor before they asked their hard question. "Is it lawful for us to give tribute to Caesar, or not?" This is not a question seeking information for an answer. This is a trap. Given the volatility of the day, this could have been a death sentence. Speaking in favor of taxes is never a popular thing. Speaking against Caesar is seldom a wise thing. "But he perceived their craftiness, and said to them, "Show me a denarius. Whose likeness and inscription does it have?" They said, "Caesar's." That is, once again he responded to their question with a question of his own and put them in the position of answering him. Then he said to them, "Then render to Caesar the things that are Caesar's, and to God the things that are God's." This, again, was a conversation stopper. They could not reply at all. Apparently, the state can legitimately demand some things from us, including taxes and obedience. At the same time, there are some things the state cannot demand from us, such as worship and absolute obedience. His answer places on us the responsibility of sorting these things out. There is a higher power than the state. There is One to whom all things, including ourselves and the state itself, belong. There is One who demands and deserves our all. And this One is present with us and for us in the person of Jesus Christ. He is not afraid of Caesar. He is not afraid of those who are afraid of Caesar. This too is part of the longer answer that Jesus gives to the question of his authority. Jesus carries the authority (1) not only of the Son of God, (2) not only of the Crucified One, and (3) not only as the risen, living, and final Judge of the universe, but also (4) as one who is free and brave. And his entire answer to the question of his identity and authority continues to stand until this day. Enough said?

By what authority do you do these things? Who gave you this authority? That is, who do you think you are? Why do you think you can get away with this? These questions asked of Jesus then are not unlike the questions asked today to those who would follow Jesus. Who do you think you are? Why do you think Jesus is so special? What gives you the right to tell me about him? Why should I be interested? Jesus looked directly at them and said, "What then is this that is written: 'The stone that the builders rejected has become the cornerstone'? Everyone who falls on that stone will be broken to pieces, and when it falls on anyone, it will crush him."

To God be the glory forever and ever! Amen.

53

Are the Dead Raised?

LUKE 20:27–47; 1 CHRONICLES 29:10–18

"HE IS NOT GOD of the dead, but of the living, for all live to him." Listen to the whole sentence: "He is not God of the dead, but of the living, for all live to him." Thus said Jesus Christ, and he said it to those who did not believe in the resurrection. Luke has preserved it for us who are still in the land of the living in order that we may believe in the resurrection. The whole meaning is contained in the first part of the sentence, "He is not God of the dead, but of the living," but Jesus clarifies and strengthens it in the end of the sentence, "for all live to him." All live to God. That is to say, God makes alive to himself not only those who are alive here and now but also those who used to live here and have since died to us here. But they are not dead to God. For all live to God. And for that reason, he is not God of the dead, but of the living.

I stress the clarification because without that it is possible to hear the sentence as if it meant exactly the opposite of what it means. For instance, I once told a lady, "He is not God of the dead, but of the living," only to discover that I had horrified her. "I hope he is God of the dead!" she said. Then I realized that she had taken what I had said to mean that God had abandoned the dead. That, of course, is not the case. So, "He is not God of the dead" does not mean simply "He is not God of the dead." It means, instead, that the dead are not dead to him. It means that God somehow makes even the dead alive to him. It means that the Creator of heaven and earth and all that is in them is more powerful than death and does not yield to the power of death. It means that the one who made us for himself is faithful to us and keeps us for his very own forever. It means that the God and Father of Jesus Christ gives us good hope and that we need not despair. And that, of course, was the point that Jesus was making.

"He is not God of the dead, but of the living, for all live to him." With this, Jesus reached the pinnacle of his public teaching. Even "some of the scribes answered, 'Teacher, you have spoken well.' For they no longer dared to ask him any question." That said it all. The God and Father of Jesus Christ is Lord of the universe, he holds the power of life and death, and he chooses to use that power so that even the dead live to him. The power of death, which eventually claims us every one, is a second-rate power at best and has been undone. The power of evil, which deals in the fear of death, is hereby deprived of its greatest weapon. The power of sin, which permeates our lives and causes us to deserve death, is shown to be a broken power that shall not accomplish its ultimate goal. The God and Father of Jesus Christ is the living God. God is the God of life. God is the God of the living. For all—even the dead—live to him. Thanks be to God!

Jesus built to this pinnacle of his teaching by an argument from Scripture, in Exodus 3: "That the dead are raised, even Moses showed, in the passage about the bush, where he calls the Lord the God of Abraham and the God of Isaac and the God of Jacob." More than thirteen hundred years earlier than Jesus, and about five hundred years after Abraham, Isaac, and Jacob, when God revealed himself to Moses at the burning bush, he had identified himself as the God of Abraham, the God of Isaac, and the God of Jacob. Jesus makes much of the fact that God did not identify himself to Moses as the God who *used to be* the God of Abraham, the God who *used to be* the God of Isaac, and the God who *used to be* the God of Jacob, five hundred earlier when they had been alive. God did not identify himself to Moses as the God merely of the formerly living. God did not identify himself to Moses as the God of the dead. Instead, God refused to acknowledge to Moses even that the formerly living were dead. In a startling way, God identified himself to Moses as the God of the formerly living who were also the yet living and alive Abraham, Isaac, and Jacob. Thus Moses learned the name of God before he returned to Egypt to face Pharaoh. But he may or may not have realized all the implications of that revelation. So King David addressed God, several hundred years later, the same way in his prayer that we read this morning, but he may or may not have realized what this meant in terms of the resurrection. But Jesus realized all of the implications. Jesus understood entirely what this revelation meant. And at least part of what it meant was that Jesus did not invent the idea of resurrection. Its truth and reality went all the way back at least to the initial self-revelation of God to Moses. The resurrection was right there in the Scriptures. It was in the word of God. It was not a novelty. His questioners should have known that. So should have we.

Jesus brought forward from Exodus this scriptural argument for the truth and reality of the resurrection to support the answer he had already given about the nature of the resurrection: "The sons of this age marry and are given in marriage, but those who are considered worthy to attain to that age and to the resurrection from the dead neither marry nor are given in marriage, for they cannot die anymore, because they are equal to angels and are sons of God, being sons of the resurrection." That is to say, the question asked of him by the Sadducees, who did not even believe in the resurrection, was shown to rest on a false premise. They intended, by their carefully constructed question having to do with a series of legally required marriages, not to receive an answer or information from Jesus but to demonstrate and to prove that the whole notion of resurrection was absurd and ridiculous. "In the resurrection, therefore, whose wife will the woman be? Husband number one? Three? Seven?" They thought that the conclusion would have to be that there was no resurrection. But instead, their premise—that people marry in the resurrection—was wrong. So their implied conclusion was wrong. And the possibility that they were wrong was a possibility they had not considered.

"The sons of this age marry and are given in marriage." Marriage, procreation, and family are a part of this age, a part of this life, a part of God's good creation, a part of the order of creation. Thanks be to God! These are good. They are God's good gifts to us. They are part of God's intention for our lives here. We are grateful for them. We honor them. In fact, we would do well not to try to invent new and different ways to order human life here, ways contradictory of marriage, procreation, and family. To do so would be to reject, and to rebel against, God's good order for this life. There is a divine givenness to this order of creation that includes husband, wife, and children.

"But those who are considered worthy to attain to that age and to the resurrection from the dead neither marry nor are given in marriage." This is now and that is then. While marriage is a God-given part of the order of creation here, it is not a part at all of the kingdom yet to come. That is a different order of existence. It is a different way of life. It is a different age. Apparently, the communion of the saints in the kingdom yet to come will far exceed the earthly relationships of marriage and family, as well as those of race, ethnicity, language, friendship, fellowship, community, state, and nation which we share here. Given the joy and privilege of marriage, we have to think that some people will be upset to learn that there is no marriage in that age. Given the difficulty and distress of some marriages, there may be some who will be grateful to learn that there is no marriage in that age. But that is neither here not there, for Jesus does not expound upon that here. What he emphasizes instead is the reality and nature of the resurrection. The premise of the absurd question is rejected. The conclusion of the Sadducees is rejected. The resurrection is affirmed.

"Those who are considered worthy to attain to that age and to the resurrection from the dead neither marry nor are given in marriage, for they cannot die anymore, because they are equal to angels and are sons of God, being sons of the resurrection." "They cannot die anymore." Once, they had died. We know that all too well. Once, they had died. But in that age, "They cannot die anymore." Thanks be to God! They have been made alive again, and "they cannot die anymore." It is not possible. It is not permitted. It does not happen. It cannot happen. God does not allow it. "They cannot die anymore." Can you imagine that? What a glorious age that is!

"They are equal to angels and are sons of God, being sons of the resurrection." This does not say that they *are* angels. This does not say that they receive wings. But it does say that God has raised them from the dead and so adopted them as his very own. What more could there be? What joy theirs must be! It would be hard for us to do better than to join our voices to King David's in his ancient prayer:

> Blessed are you, O LORD, the God of Israel our father, forever and ever. Yours, O LORD, is the greatness and the power and the glory and the victory and the majesty, for all that is in the heavens and in the earth is yours. Yours is the kingdom, O LORD, and you are exalted as head above all. Both riches and honor come from you, and you rule over all. In your hand are power and might, and in your hand it is to make great and to give strength to all. And now we thank you, our God, and praise your glorious name. (1 Chronicles 29:10b–13)

All of this emphasis on the truth, reality, and nature of the resurrection in the age to come, in the kingdom of the God of life, does not belittle, detract from, lessen, or denigrate this life in any way. In fact, quite the opposite is true. The truth, reality, and nature of the resurrection in the age to come enlarge, add to, enhance, and ennoble this life in every way. Apart from the resurrection, this life would be cold, dark, and brutal. Apart from the resurrection, there would be no perspective. Apart from the resurrection, there would be no hope. Apart from the resurrection, life would have little or no value. Apart from the resurrection, every action here would be final. But with the resurrection, we know that God raises the dead to life so the power of death to disrupt and to destroy is undone. With the resurrection, God adopts the resurrected as his own children, so none are left as orphans. With the resurrection, all the kingdoms of this world must yield to that kingdom yet to come, so none who rule here are absolute. With the resurrection, all the evil of this world must come to an end. With the resurrection, life is elevated to its true value, for what life we have here is only the beginning of that resurrection life which is to come.

So it is that "He is not God of the dead, but of the living, for all live to him." That is to say, God makes alive to himself not only those who are alive here and now but also those who used to live here and have since died to us here. But they are not dead to God. For all live to God. And for that reason, he is not God of the dead, but of the living. Once his opponents had been reduced to silence on that point, Jesus continued to speak to them, to frame questions they dared not ask, to give answers they could not imagine. Early in the Gospel according to Luke, Jesus had been introduced as the son of King David, the rightful heir to his throne, which he had vacated a thousand years earlier. But now, as his enemies sought to destroy and to kill him, Jesus showed that even such title of royalty was not enough to say who he was. Turning once again to the Scriptures, this time Psalm 110, Jesus showed that King David referred to the Messiah as his Lord. That is to say, Jesus is not only the son of David but is also even far more important than David. And again, this was already recorded in ancient Scripture. Jesus Christ is greater than King David, and more to the point, Jesus Christ is the very Son of God. That is to say, Jesus himself is God with us and for us. Jesus not only teaches us about God, the God of life and of resurrection. More than that, Jesus himself is the very one to whom the dead are not dead. He is the one who somehow makes even the dead alive to him. He is the creator of heaven and earth and all that is in them who is more powerful than death and who does not yield to the power of death. He is one who made us for himself, is faithful to us, and keeps us for his very own forever. He is the one who gives us good hope so that we need not despair. Indeed, Jesus Christ himself is none other than the God of life and of resurrection, the one of whom it is said, "He is not God of the dead, but of the living, for all live to him."

To God be the glory forever and ever! Amen.

54

When Will These Things Be?

LUKE 21:1–19; MALACHI 3:16—4:3

AS TIME MARCHES ON and our very lives hurry to their end, certain very somber questions arise. Who are we? Whose are we? Where are we headed? What does it all mean? Where does it all end? What is there beyond? Who is in control? Why do we die? Shall we meet again? What is real? What is true? What is eternal? What is worthwhile? To what shall we cling? It is clear that this world cannot last forever. The kingdoms of this world totter and fall. Our individual lives likely will endure even much more briefly. We cannot ignore forever these realities that press down upon us.

So it was that the hearers of Jesus Christ, when he was in the temple teaching them about, among other things, the unimaginable destruction of the temple—so it was that his hearers cried out to him, "Teacher, when will these things be, and what will be the sign when these things are about to take place?" Again, "When will these things be?" When will the temple be torn down, stone from stone? When will this center of all proper worship be destroyed? When will the symbol and the reality of the presence of God with us be removed? When will the meaning of our lives thus be disrupted if not destroyed? And will it be the Romans who do this? Will it be another as yet unnamed and unknown enemy? Or will it be, perhaps, the very judgment of God Almighty upon us? "When will these things be?"

Their question then is not unlike our own questions now. So it is that their question becomes our question. When, indeed, will these things be? Sooner or later? How will we know? What shall we do? There is an old saw about the man who said he never worried about those people carrying signs saying "The End Is Near" until he saw two of them synchronizing their watches. That would tend to get your attention. But even apart from those who claim to know too much about the precise timing of the end of time—and the Scriptures are clear that it is not up to us to know the precise time—it is necessarily the case that the more time passes, the closer we are to the end. And even if we deceive ourselves into a false complacency with the assumption that the end continues to lie in the far distant future, having little or nothing to do with us, it becomes increasingly difficult to avoid facing the distinct but not unrelated reality of our own demise. The calendar may run out on that personal reality before it does on the larger reality. We can try to deny our own mortality, but we shall not succeed in that for very long. And, of course, the urgency and the poignancy of the matter are heightened by the hard reality that death has already come for so many of those whom we love. Thus it would seem to be not only necessary and pertinent but also a good and useful thing to take up as our very own question now the ancient question of the hearers of Jesus then with, all of its related concerns: "When will these things be?"

And even more important than their question is, of course, the answer that Jesus gave them which Luke has recorded for us. The answer Jesus gave includes (1) a major affirmation, (2) a related warning, and then (3) an invitation, in that order. First (1), the major affirmation is subtle but significant. Within a few days and perhaps even hours of the end of his own earthly life, Jesus addressed the concerns of his hearers by saying, "See that you are not led astray. For many will come in my name, saying, 'I am he!' and, 'The time is at hand!' Do not go after them." Again, "See that you are not led astray." If it is possible to be led astray, then it is possible *not* to be led astray. That is to say, there is an order to the world. There is truth. There is discernible reality. There is a way and a path that we are to follow. And one way to express this major affirmation would be by saying that God is in control. The God and Father of Jesus Christ is in control of the universe.

It is possible to put an even finer point on this. "Many will come in my name, saying, 'I am he!' and, 'The time is at hand!' Do not go after them." That is to say, do not follow the false Christs. Do not follow the would-be Christs. Do not fall for the gospel of prosperity. Do not fall for the gospel of political correctness. Do not fall for the gospel of so-called progressive theology. Do not fall for any gospel derived from a selective reading of Scripture. Do not fall for the honey of forgiveness apart from the rigor of repentance and renewal. Do not follow the false saviors. Do not follow the ideologues. Do not follow the liars. Follow, instead, the one true Christ. Follow the crucified and risen Christ. Follow Jesus Christ, and you will not go astray. This is part of the gospel of Jesus Christ. This embodies the major affirmation of the teaching of Jesus Christ about the end of time. God is in control. Therefore, stay the course with Jesus Christ. Do not be led astray. This is a tremendous comfort in times of distress and confusion. "When will these things be?" Whenever they are to come, follow Jesus Christ, and so "See that you are not led astray."

Second (2), following this affirmation there is also a related warning. Jesus continued, "And when you hear of wars and tumults, do not be terrified, for these things must first take place, but the end will not be at once." Again, "Do not be terrified, for these things must take place." In these in-between times in which we live, these ongoing times of expectation between the first and second comings of Christ, between his earthly life and his return, between the propagation of the gospel and the end of time, it is necessary that great and terrible things will happen. There will be wars and rumors of war. There will be tumults and upheavals. These things will be frightening. They will be confusing. And they have to happen. But do not, Jesus says, be confused or taken in by them, for they do not mean that the end has come. They do not mean that the end is near. They are a part of the ongoing reality of human existence, year after year, millennium after millennium.

Near the beginning of the movie *The Gladiator*, the emperor of the Roman Empire says to his general that he has been emperor for twenty-seven years and that the empire has been at war for twenty-five of those years. War consumed his entire reign. The movie is fiction, but the point is well made. Our own history consists of one war after another. They are terrible and terrifying things. We can justify them or we can bemoan them, but they go on. Whatever else they mean, they do not mean that the end of the world has come. It would seem, then, that part of the role of the Christian church would be not to overestimate the wars, not to overinflate them, not to treat them as if they were something more important than they are. Such modesty about the importance of war would be a part of not taking ourselves too seriously. We are not in control of the universe. There is Another who has that responsibility. We are not the ones who will determine when the end of the world will come. There is Another who will make that determination. This warning is part of the gospel of Jesus Christ. We are to live in these in-between times without being terrified by the events of these in-between times. In an age of terror, that is a whole lot of gospel.

Third (3), on the basis of his major affirmation that God is in control and of his related warning for us not to be confused, Jesus also extends to us a strange and wonderful invitation to faithfulness:

> Nation will rise against nation, and kingdom against kingdom. There will be great earthquakes, and in various places famines and pestilences. And there will be terrors and great signs from heaven. But before all this they will lay their hands on you and persecute you, delivering you up to the synagogues and prisons, and you will be brought before kings and governors for my name's sake. This will be your opportunity to bear witness.

Again, "This will be your opportunity to bear witness." Wars we know about. Earthquakes we know about. Famines we know about. Pestilences worse than the world has ever before known we now know about. Tsunamis and hurricanes and tornados we know about. Surely the question has been raised: Can this be the end? Are we living in the end times? "But before all this they will lay their hands on you and persecute you, delivering you up to the synagogues and prisons, and you will be brought before kings and governors for my name's sake." This brings it close to home. This is different from distant disasters. What in the world is this all about? Who will be laying hands on us? Who will haul us before the authorities? And yet, "This will be your opportunity to bear witness." In the providence of God and during the upheavals of the world, this is an invitation to, and therefore an opportunity for, us to be faithful.

This invitation suggests that the most significant sign of the end of time will not be war, earthquake, famine, or pestilence. This invitation suggests instead that the most significant sign of the end of time will be massive persecution of the Christian church. "They will lay their hands on you and persecute you, delivering you up to the synagogues and prisons, and you will be brought before kings and governors for my name's sake." This persecution is not something with which we are immediately or personally familiar. And for that I am grateful. And yet, "This will be your opportunity to bear witness." What appears to be, and what actually will be, persecution of the Christian church will also be, at the same time and by the same token, an unprecedented opportunity for us to bear witness to the persecuted Christ. It is because of his persecution that we will be persecuted. It is because of his persecution that we will have opportunity to bear witness. It is because of his persecution that we have good hope for the world to come.

So, "When will these things be?" The ancient question seems to have a greater urgency now than when it was first asked. They spoke of the fall of the temple in Jerusalem. But the fallen temple has been replaced by the risen Lord Jesus Christ. So now we ask of the persecution of the church of this same Jesus Christ. And that could have to do with us. "When will these things be?" And yet, "This will be your opportunity to bear witness." It would seem important to be well prepared for this, but Jesus warns us against being overly prepared. "Settle it therefore in your minds not to meditate beforehand how to answer, for I will give you a mouth and wisdom, which none of your adversaries will be able to withstand or contradict." Note carefully that such avoidance of preparation for this witness before kings and governors has nothing to do with avoidance of preparation for the ongoing preaching the gospel before the church! There are some who wrongly believe that this passage means that preachers should not prepare before they enter the pulpit. But this passage has nothing to do with that, with the regular preaching of the gospel such as we are involved in at this very moment. This passage has to do with testimony at trial. This has to do with defending the faith before a hostile court. Indeed, this very well may have to do with dying at the hands of unbelievers, as did Jesus himself. The Greek word for witness is "martyr." "Martyr" literally means "witness." But so many early witnesses to the Christian faith were killed for their faith that the word "martyr" has come to mean someone who dies for and by witnessing to his or her faith. We should be prepared to stand up for our faith and even to die for our faith.

"This will be your opportunity to bear witness. Settle it therefore in your minds not to meditate beforehand how to answer, for I will give you a mouth and wisdom, which none of your adversaries will be able to withstand or contradict." This invitation is not unlike what the Lord spoke through the prophet Malachi concerning the day of the Lord:

> For you who fear my name, the sun of righteousness shall rise with healing in its wings. You shall go out leaping like calves from the stall. And you shall tread down the wicked, for they will be ashes under the soles of your feet, on the day when I act, says the LORD of hosts.

The reason we are not to prepare what we are to say is that it is the Lord who takes action. It is the Lord who gives "mouth and wisdom" to his witnesses. It is the Lord who does battle with the powers that be. Sometimes the witnesses were given beautiful and powerful words with which to tell kings and governors of the providence of God and the sacrifice of Jesus Christ. And sometimes the martyrs were given the wisdom and the courage to speak by their suffering and so to tell again and unmistakably of Jesus Christ who died for the world. God help us! "You will be delivered up even by parents and brothers and relatives and friends, and some of you they will put to death. You will be hated by all for my name's sake. But not a hair of your head will perish. By your endurance you will gain your lives." Again, "Some of you they will put to death. . . . By your endurance you will gain your lives." It does not say that we will "save" our lives. It says that we will "gain" our lives. That is to say, Jesus is not talking here about this life. He is talking about the life to come. God, grant us the grace to endure! "This will be your opportunity to bear witness." This is part of the gospel of Jesus Christ, that he would deign to use even us, unworthy servants though we are, as his very witnesses. God, grant us the grace to accept and so to fulfill your invitation.

So it is that as time marches on and our very lives hurry to their end, certain very somber questions arise. Who are we? Whose are we? Where are we headed? What does it all mean? Where does it all end? What is there beyond? Who is in control? Why do we die? Shall we meet again? What is real? What is true? What is eternal? What is worthwhile? To what shall we cling? It is clear that this world cannot last forever. The kingdoms of this world totter and fall. Our individual lives likely will endure even much more briefly. As we are driven to face the end of time, we ask with the hearers of Christ from of old, "When will these things be?" The answer comes in three parts. First (1), Jesus gives us a major affirmation: "See that you are not led astray," for God is in control. Second (2), Jesus gives us a related warning: "Do not be terrified for these things must take place." And third (3), Jesus gives us a strange, wonderful, and gracious invitation: "This will be your opportunity to bear witness."

To God be the glory forever and ever! Amen.

55

Give Us Strength!

LUKE 21:20–38; ISAIAH 63:16—64:4

"STAY AWAKE AT ALL times, praying that you may have strength to escape all these things that are going to take place, and to stand before the Son of Man." After everything else that Jesus Christ had to say about the end of time, Jerusalem surrounded by armies, terrors and signs, fear and foreboding, he concluded with this: "Stay awake at all times, praying that you may have strength to escape all these things that are going to take place, and to stand before the Son of Man." We know something today—more than we want to know—about terrors and signs, fear and foreboding. Perhaps that has always been the human condition. But today it is our condition. Today it is our turn to live in the face of uncertainty. So even as we look back with great joy to the birth and life of our Lord and Savior, Jesus Christ, and as we look forward to his return with him as our only confidence, we would do well for the present to remember his teaching, "Stay awake at all times, praying that you may have strength to escape all these things that are going to take place, and to stand before the Son of Man."

The good news here in today's reading is not only that time will have an end but also, and even more so, that at the end of time we shall meet the Son of Man, none other than Jesus Christ, our Lord and Savior. Thanks be to God! This is our great hope. This is our great joy. It is not only the case that Jesus was born among us as one of us. It is not only the case that he lived among us as one of us and that he died for us as one of us. It is not only the case that God raised him from the dead and that he ascended into heaven. But it is also the case that this very same Jesus Christ who lived and died and lives again for us is also the Lord of the universe, whom we shall meet at the end of time. Thanks be to God! This is why his life, death, and resurrection are so important. The story of Jesus Christ would be a sad story if it had to do only with the past. The great joy of Christianity is that the goodness of God to us back then also gives us good hope and confidence that God will yet again be good to us in the future. He already gave us his only Son! What more could we ask? That gift is not insignificant! Moreover, that gift is not temporary. That gift is not passing or fleeting or inconsequential. God gave us his only Son! And in that gift, in that birth, life, death, and resurrection, the goal of all creation was revealed, and the end of time was made known.

So again, the good news here in today's reading is that at the end of time we shall meet the Son of Man, none other than Jesus Christ, our Lord and Savior, crucified and risen, returning in strength and glory. We shall not at the end of time come face to face with Moses, as wonderful as that might be. We shall not at the end of time encounter Mohammed as our judge. Thank God! It is not the Buddha whom we shall find seated at the right hand of the Father. Neither shall it be Darwin, Freud, or Marx with whom we have to deal. Nor shall sin, death, or evil have the last word. Instead, the only one with whom we have to do, both now and then—or we might say especially then and therefore now also—is none other than God himself, and God has come to us and made himself known to us in Jesus Christ. What joy! What relief! What goodness! This is our redemption. The great uncertainty about the end of time—the Day of the Lord, Judgment Day—has been removed. There is still much that is unknown. But this we do know: that then we shall meet Jesus face to face. We shall know as we have been known. And in this we rejoice. As Jesus himself put it, "Then they will see the Son of Man coming in a cloud with power and great glory." Not, that is to say, in the manifest weakness of a preacher in the temple, not in the shame and humiliation of a criminal hanging on a cross, and not, we should say, coming merely in the heart or even the imagination of the believer, but coming instead in truth and reality. "Then they will see the Son of Man coming in a cloud with power and great glory. Now when these things begin to take place, straighten up and raise your heads, because your redemption is drawing near." That is good news! We long for the day of our final redemption.

In the meantime, back in the here and now, in the midst of all of our own struggles and heartaches and pain and sin and hurtfulness of each other, "Stay awake at all times, praying that you may have strength to escape all these things that are going to take place, and to stand before the Son of Man." There is more for us here. Not only will the Son of Man come at the end of time, but also there is good hope that we shall be there at the end of time to meet him. That is the goal of this prayer. That is what we are being told to pray for. That does not mean that it is automatic, but it does mean that it is at least possible. Otherwise, we would not be told to pray for it. God does not trifle with us. In that we are being told to pray for this, for strength to stand before the Son of Man, then we have good reason to be of great joy and to turn to God with earnest gratitude, for it is the will of God for us to meet his Son at the end of time. And "If God is for us, who can be against us?" (Romans 8:31).

What then shall we do? "Stay awake at all times, praying that you may have strength to escape all these things that are going to take place, and to stand before the

Son of Man." I do not take this to mean literally that we must "stay awake at all times." That is not possible. I have already said that God does not trifle with us. Besides, it says in the Psalms that the Lord gives sleep to his beloved (Psalm 127:2). So, "Stay awake at all times" means always to be alert and to be ready at any time for the end of time. But I do take this teaching to mean literally that we are to pray, and pray and pray and pray, that we "may have strength to escape all these things that are going to take place, and to stand before the Son of Man." We are commanded throughout the Scriptures to pray. And for us to be commanded to pray means that we are graciously given permission to pray, permission to stand before the throne of God Almighty, permission to pour out our hearts, permission to sing God's praises, to give thanks for his blessings, and to ask him—yes, to ask him—for all that he wills to give us.

It is a miracle, really. We can ask for faith. We can ask for grace. We can ask for mercy and forgiveness. We can ask for wisdom. We can ask for renewal. We can ask for healing. We can ask for guidance. We can ask that our hearts not "be weighed down with dissipation and drunkenness and cares of this life," and that the day not "come upon [you] suddenly like a trap." And we can ask for strength for the living of our lives. We can ask for strength to be faithful followers of Jesus Christ. We can ask for strength to love one another, to care for one another, to forgive one another. We can ask for strength to escape the terror that is to come. We can ask for strength to stand before the Son of Man. There is nothing greater that we need to do. So let us pray and pray and pray.

How are we to do this? We can pray when we awake and pray before we go to sleep. We can pray before we eat and pray before our work for the day. And we can pray together here on Sunday mornings as we gather to glorify God, to hear the word of God, and to give thanks to God. We can pray together here, Sunday after Sunday, in our services for the worship of God. We can pray together here on special occasions as when, for instance, parents stand before God and before us, profess their faith in Jesus Christ as Lord and Savior, and present their infant son or daughter for the sacrament of baptism. They stake their lives and their future on the goodness and grace of God made known to us in Jesus Christ, and we reaffirm our faith right along with them. "Straighten up and raise your heads, because your redemption is drawing near." We can pray together here from time to time as we gather around the Communion table, where we remember that Jesus gave himself for us. We can pray together here, every Sunday, among the gathered people of God at Mattoax and Pine Grove Presbyterian Churches. This is who we are. This is what we do. "From of old no one has heard or perceived by the ear, no eye has seen a God besides you, who acts for those who wait for him."

Time hurries on. The end necessarily draws nearer and nearer, for each of us individually as well as for the world as a whole. And we know something today—more than we want to know—about terrors and signs, fear and foreboding. Perhaps that has always been the human condition. But today it is our condition. Today it is our turn to live in the face of uncertainty. So at this time, on this day in our lives, as we look back with great joy to the birth, life, death, and resurrection of our Lord and Savior, and as we look forward to his return with him as our only confidence, we would do well for the present to remember that after everything else Jesus Christ had to say about the end of time—terrors and signs, fear and foreboding—he concluded with this gospel teaching: "Stay awake at all times, praying that you may have strength to escape all these things that are going to take place, and to stand before the Son of Man."

To God be the glory forever and ever! Amen.

56

Who Is the Greatest?

LUKE 22:1–38; ISAIAH 43:16–21

"A DISPUTE ALSO AROSE among them, as to which of them was to be regarded as the greatest." Can you believe it? The first twelve disciples, hand-picked by Jesus himself, sent out as his apostles, had not even left the table from the Last Supper before they were arguing among themselves about which one of them was the greatest. Jesus said, "This is my body, which is given for you. Do this in remembrance of me." In a fit of amnesia, "A dispute also arose among them, as to which of them was to be regarded as the greatest." Jesus said, "This cup that is poured out for you is the new covenant in my blood." In apparent, utter disinterest, "A dispute also arose among them, as to which of them was to be regarded as the greatest." Jesus warned, "Behold, the hand of him who betrays me is with me on the table." As if that did not matter to them, "A dispute also arose among them, as to which of them was to be regarded as the greatest."

Apart from what we know only too well about the depth and tenacity of sin, this would be incomprehensible. It is a wonder the early church ever survived the first disciples. Not that reason for disappointment about leaders has been unusual in the history of the church. I believe it was Balmer Kelly, a professor of New Testament at Union Theological Seminary, who used to say that the church's survival of two thousand years of ministers was proof enough that it is an institution of divine origin. And we could easily imagine an argument about supposed greatness taking place at a presbytery meeting or maybe even at a session meeting. But it is disconcerting to see such a dispute arise among the very first ministers at the beginning of the church, in the presence of Jesus Christ himself. It is absolutely astounding.

Jesus took this dispute very seriously. He not only offered a new and corrective teaching, a redefinition of the nature and practice of greatness especially within the

Christian church, but also, and even more so, he proclaimed the gospel about himself, the gospel of his birth, life, death, and resurrection, his ministry of servanthood. "The kings of the Gentiles exercise lordship over them, and those in authority over them are called benefactors. But not so with you. Rather, let the greatest among you become as the youngest, and the leader as one who serves. For who is the greater, one who reclines at table or one who serves? Is it not the one who reclines at table? But I am among you as the one who serves." "Who is the greater?" "I am among you as the one who serves." "Who is the greater?" "I am among you as the one who serves." This is very strange.

The world in which we live measures greatness in terms of power. Thus it has always been. "The kings of the Gentiles exercise lordship over them, and those in authority over them are called benefactors." Just because they are called benefactors does not mean that they are benefactors. And just because they lord it over others does not mean that they are lords. But the ones who have power over others are regarded as great, so that the ones who do not have power lust after it. People want power to go where they want to go when they want to go, power to buy what they want to buy when they want to buy it, and especially power to have other people wait on them and serve them and do what they want them to do all the time. That is power, and that is the measure of greatness in the world in which we live. Thus it was with the Romans, and thus it is with the Americans.

By way of contrast, the true Lord of the world in which we live measures greatness in terms of service. "For who is the greater, one who reclines at table or one who serves? Is it not the one who reclines at table? But I am among you as the one who serves." "Who is the greater?" Jesus understands that in the eyes of the world the one receiving the service of others is greater than the one providing the service. He understands that very well. But he rejects it. He rejects it out of hand. He rejects it, and he forges a new and opposite course in the world. "I am among you as the one who serves." I am among you as one who rejects the world's measure of greatness by power. I am among you as one who refuses to lord it over others. I am among you as one who refuses to seek false titles. I am among you as one who serves, as one who is lowly, as one who is humble, as one who lays down his life for you. Thus the Lord of the world in which we live rejects the world's measure of greatness in terms of power and replaces it with its opposite, measuring greatness in terms of service. He is truly great precisely because he serves.

There are at least three particular ways in relation to today's reading in which Jesus especially serves us. Those are Communion, the cross, and, strangely enough, Christmas. Of course, we could add more ways about his parables and healings. But for now, let us look at these three. The first (1) and most obvious in today's reading has to do with his self-offering in the Last Supper, which became the basis for our celebration of the Lord's Supper, otherwise known as Communion. "He took bread, and when he had given thanks, he broke it and gave it to them, saying, 'This is my body, which is given for you. Do this in remembrance of me.' And likewise the cup after they had eaten, saying, 'This cup that is poured out for you is the new covenant in my blood.'" Jesus redefined the ancient Passover meal, which for centuries had been a remembrance of the long-ago deliverance in the exodus from Egypt, as a remembrance of himself and of his offering of himself for you and for me, and thus as an occasion for hope for the even greater deliverance in Christ. It is not only that he hosted the meal or even that he served the meal to his disciples. It is even more that he became the meal, identifying his body as bread for our nourishment and his blood as drink for our sustenance. As John Calvin wrote of this passage, Christ is our food and drink, that is to say, he alone is sufficient for all that belongs to our salvation. That is service beyond mere serving. That is self-giving far beyond charity. That is gospel self-offering such as the world had never known. "I am among you as the one who serves."

The service that Jesus extends to us in Communion points ahead, of course, to the greater service (2) he extends to us on the cross. What he talked about with the bread and the wine, the offering of his own body and blood, he made real in his willing self-sacrifice on the cross. The new covenant that he named at the dinner table he sealed with his blood on the cross. On the one hand he is our great high priest, presiding over the offering of the final sacrifice at the high altar of the cross. On the other hand, and at the same time, he is himself the content of the offering, the sacrificial lamb that is given up at the altar of the cross. As both priest and lamb, he gave his own body and blood, giving to conquer sin and evil, dying in order that we might live. "I am among you as the one who serves."

The service of Communion and the service of the cross are both based on an earlier service that forms the basis of them both, an earlier self-humbling that sets the pattern for them both, an earlier self-giving that we especially remember and acknowledge at Christmas. Without that, he could not have performed the others. Consider the message of Christmas as enshrined in the Nicene Creed:

> The only-begotten Son of God, begotten of the Father before all worlds, God of God, Light of Light, Very God of Very God, begotten, not made, being of one substance with the Father, by whom all things were made . . . for us men, and for our salvation, came down from heaven, and was incarnate by the Holy Spirit of the Virgin Mary, and was made man.

As Jesus said, "I am among you as the one who serves." This is gospel. This is good news. This is the redefinition of the nature and practice of greatness away from the possession and exercise of power. This is the redefinition of the nature and practice of greatness in terms of the birth, life, and death of a servant. This is the establishment of a new covenant. This is our salvation. Thanks be to God!

It is on the basis of Christ's service at the first Christmas and so still now, at Communion every time we receive it, and on the cross once and for all, that Jesus Christ also commands us to live lives of Christian service. Having redefined the nature of greatness, he redefines the practice of greatness, especially within the Christian church, especially for us yet today. "The kings of the Gentiles exercise lordship over them, and those in authority over them are called benefactors. But not so with you. Rather, let the greatest among you become as the youngest, and the leader as one who serves." "Not so with you." Do not be deceived. Do not be drawn into the false ways of the world, defining greatness in terms of power. Instead, follow me, defining greatness in terms of service. "Let the greatest among you become as the youngest, and the leader as one who serves." Let the very greatest in the Christian church be as a youth or a little child, expecting no special privilege or prominence. Let your leader be a servant. There is no higher greatness in the church.

In that Jesus Christ came to be a servant, how much more are all of us who would follow him to be servants. We gather here to worship God, and then we go forth to serve—at home, at school, at work, at play, serving as we have been served, giving because God has given to us. This is the basis of all evangelism, of all mission, of all stewardship, and of all benevolence. The life of discipleship is not an easy trip to heaven. To follow Jesus Christ is to swim against the stream of the world in which we live. Let us prepare ourselves for faithfulness. When young parents stand before us to reaffirm their faith, taking their stand with Jesus Christ, the Suffering Servant, they do so with eyes wide open, knowing that the world about us has little respect for such commitment. We give thanks for their witness to the faith. When we baptize their infant daughter or son in the name of the Father, and of the Son, and of the Holy Spirit, knowing that such baptism is an eternal sign that the child belongs not to the world and not to the enemies of God but instead to the God and Father of our Lord Jesus Christ, there is a part of us that holds our breath, knowing that the Christian life will not be easy for that little girl or boy, anymore than it is for any of us. But at the same time, we also rejoice at the overflowing goodness of God, who names us as his very own children. Thanks be to God!

Despite the undeniably disconcerting aspect of the disciples' dinner table argument—"A dispute also arose among them, as to which of them was to be regarded as the greatest"—nevertheless it is good for us that the disciples were so out of touch with what Jesus had done at the first Christmas, what Jesus was doing at the Last Supper, and what Jesus was about to do on the cross. For that gave Jesus Christ the opportunity to ask, to answer, and to redefine the answer to the question about the nature and practice of greatness. "For who is the greater, one who reclines at table or one who serves? Is it not the one who reclines at table? But I am among you as the one who serves."

To God be the glory forever and ever! Amen.

57

What Is the Father's Will?

Luke 22:39–53; Isaiah 51:17–23

"Father, if you are willing, remove this cup from me. Nevertheless, not my will, but yours, be done." What an agonizing prayer! What a profound act of faith! "Father, if you are willing, remove this cup from me. Nevertheless, not my will, but yours, be done." Jesus begins by crying out to his Father! And thus the message and the hope of Christmas long ago are fulfilled. Remember, the angel Gabriel had told Mary years earlier that Jesus would be the Son of God. And now the purpose of that sonship is coming to its fulfillment. So the point of Christmas is not simply that the Son of God came to be born among us as the baby Jesus, as wonderful as that is. Instead, the very point of Christmas is that the Son of God came to be born among us as the baby Jesus precisely in order to die for us as the man Jesus. And so Jesus ended his brave prayer to his Father, "Not my will, but yours, be done."

The two parts of this prayer on the Mount of Olives the night before his crucifixion reflect the two-sided miracle of Christmas. One the one hand, Jesus knelt down and prayed, "Father, if you are willing, remove this cup from me." Here we see the humanity of Jesus Christ. "Father, if you are willing, remove this cup from me." Jesus did not want to die! Jesus did not look forward to the cross! He was seeking an alternative. If there were any other way possible, he would have preferred it. In his struggle, we see our humanity. In his agony, we see ourselves. "Father, if you are willing, remove this cup from me." Remove this betrayal, trial, and crucifixion from me. Take away this horrible death. And so we do not have here a Savior who is immune to human feeling, loss, suffering, and pain. We do not have here a Savior who floats above the messiness of our human life, unaffected by it. We do not have here a Savior who is naive about the cruelties of religion and of government or about the cost of defeating sin, death, and evil. Instead, we do have here the one person in all of human history who does know the cost of sin, the cost of our sin, and that is precisely why he wanted to know whether there was any alternative to the cross.

And yet, at the very same time, kneeling down in the depths of prayer, Jesus also found the grace, courage, and obedience to do what had to be done. "Father, if you are willing, remove this cup from me. Nevertheless, not my will, but yours, be done." Surely here we see the divinity of Jesus Christ, and in this joining of his humanity and his divinity we see the truth and reality and reason of Christmas. Jesus here offered to God his perfect obedience to God's will, the obedience that alone could defeat the powers of sin, death, and evil, even when that obedience cost him his life. In this willing sacrifice, in this submission, we see his divinity: "Nevertheless, not my will, but yours, be done." Surely this is not a simple human possibility.

"There appeared to him an angel from heaven, strengthening him. And being in an agony he prayed more earnestly; and his sweat became like great drops of blood falling down to the ground. And when he rose from prayer . . ." "[W]hen he rose from prayer," never again did he ask to escape from the cross! The possibility of a release was raised only in the midst of his growing resolve: "Not my will, but yours, be done." Did you catch the echo of the Lord's Prayer? "Father . . . your will be done." How better for Jesus to teach us to pray than for him to pray the same prayer under the worst possible circumstances! "And when he rose from prayer," he was ready to meet his betrayer, to go to trial, and to hang on the cross, for you and for me.

So it is that Jesus Christ—staring into the face of betrayal by one of his own disciples and of desertion by all the rest, staring into the face of death, staring into the face of divine judgment, not because of anything he had done but for your sins and for mine—so it is that Jesus Christ struggled, prayed, and won the victory for you and for me. He came to peace with doing the will of God even when it was God's will that he go to the cross and die for you and for me. Thanks be to God that Jesus met the challenge! Thanks be to God that the adult Jesus fulfilled the ancient hope of Christmas! Thanks be to God not only that Jesus was born but also that he was willing to suffer and to die on our account!

Now, the obedience of Jesus Christ to the will of God, even when that obedience cost him his life, shows us that the will of God was more important to Jesus than his own life. He started out asking to be saved from the cross. He ended up submitting to the cross. How could this be? The glory of God, the majesty of God, and the will of God are more important to Jesus than his own life. This raises the question: Should the glory of God, the majesty of God, and the will of God be more important to us than our lives or our salvation? Salvation is important, or God would not have sent Christ to bring it to us. And yet, our ultimate purpose is to glorify God. Salvation itself is not the goal, but the way we get to the greater goal.

Jesus shows us something on the Mount of Olives. Others think the universe is self-contained, that this world is all there is, that what you see is what you get. And yet, such a view cannot make sense of our lives. If this world were all there is, it would make no sense whatsoever to sacrifice one's life. But if there is another world, a larger reality, a greater truth, then it would make sense to suffer loss here—even to die—in order to align oneself with larger purposes, patterns, truth, reality, and the divine will. Life here is so good that we want to live forever. But with pain and disease and suffering and death we do not live forever here. Love here is so good that we yearn for perfect love. But love here is marred. Why do we want more than the world can give? Where do we get the ideas that such things exist? If the world were self-contained, all there is of reality, how would we even be able to aspire to something more, something beyond the world? Yet, here we are in a broken world yearning for eternal life and perfect love.

Something within human life points beyond this life. Something within this old world points beyond this world. Jesus knew that life cannot be satisfied here in this world. The world that we see around us is not all there is to the world. The world we touch and hear and smell is not all there is to reality. There is another world beyond this world, a greater reality, a larger context without which this world makes no sense and within which alone it does make sense. The angel of the Lord had revealed this years earlier, saying to the shepherds and so to us, "Fear not, for behold, I bring you good news of a great joy that will be for all the people. For unto you is born this day in the city of David a Savior, who is Christ the Lord" (Luke 2:10). So Jesus came to peace with doing the larger will of God, even though it meant his death on a cross in this world. He had faith that the will of God for his life was good, even though God willed the end of his life as we know it here.

In today's reading we see, on the one hand, the humanity of Jesus Christ in that he did not want to die, and he did not want to face judgment on our account. On the other hand, we see his divinity in that Jesus knew what would happen and still submitted himself to the will of God. And this is the meaning and outcome of his birth at Christmas. Jesus came to peace with obeying and doing the will of God even when it did not lead to his own immediate good and led instead to a horrible death. It was God's will that his only Son would bear an unspeakable burden on our behalf. It is our burden, but we cannot carry it; God in Christ has carried it for us. So, we are the beneficiaries of Christ's struggle in prayer on the Mount of Olives. We are the recipients of God's grace. Our sin is forgiven because he paid the price. Our guilt is removed because he took it on himself. The burdens that crush our lives have been lifted off of us and placed upon him so that we can live anew. God has done for us what we cannot do for ourselves. Jesus Christ has obeyed the will of God when we have not. His obedience has been counted for us.

So where does this leave us now? Having been forgiven, having been graced, we are now able—at least some of the time, on a good day, in partial and broken ways—to obey the will of God ourselves. This is a new possibility for us. Yes, we, like the disciples, are still weak. But after his resurrection, Christ regathered them as his very own. Thus they and we learn again not to rely on human strength but instead to trust in God alone. And if Jesus Christ had to pray so hard that night—Jesus, fully human but also fully divine, Jesus, the very Son of God—to seek, to discern, and to obey the will of God, think of what we need to do in terms of prayer! Consider also that the disciples, who failed to pray, but who slept through the night, were utterly unprepared for the onslaught that came upon them. We need to pray!

There are at least three aspects to our doing the will of God today. The first (1) is to seek the will of God. The second (2) is to discern the will of God. And the third (3) is to obey the will of God. First (1), then, we are to seek the will of God. We have to listen for it, and that is hard to do in a noisy world, where we hear many voices. The world says, "Grab all you can!" Jesus says, "Whoever would save his life will lose it, but whoever loses his life for my sake will save it" (Luke 9:24). That means for us to give all we can, which is the opposite of what the world says. The best place we can seek the will of God is in the word of God, the Bible. And the best way for us to seek the will of God in the Scriptures is through prayer, study, and worship.

Second (2), we are to discern the will of God. It takes wisdom to discern will of God, and it takes modesty in what we claim. At a conference on preaching a few years ago, a speaker told of seeing children at a school for the blind come in from the playground and have to sandpaper their fingertips to make them sensitive enough to be able to read Braille! How can we make ourselves sensitive enough to discern the will of God in the word of God? One principle that we can learn from today's reading about God's will for Jesus is that any conclusion we reach that is to our benefit is suspect! There is nothing here about the Christian life being easy. If the cross was good enough for Jesus, it may be good enough for us too. Sometimes God works not so much through our victories as through our suffering. In the example of Jesus Christ, we can discern the will of God.

Third (3), we are to obey the will of God. That is not easy. The philosopher Plato taught that to know the truth is to do it. In his estimation, the entire human problem is simply one of ignorance. There is no such thing as evil or ill will, just lack of information. That problem is solved by education. If people knew what was right, they would do it. But the Apostle Paul wrote to the contrary, "I do not do what I want, but I do the very thing I hate. . . . I do not do the good I want, but the evil I do not want is what I keep on doing" (Romans 7:15b, 19). Here is a more profound and accurate description and analysis of the human predicament. Even when we discern the good, we cannot necessarily do it! We need God's help! We need God's help to seek, to discern, and especially to obey God's will.

What, then, is the will of God for us? We find the will of God for us in the Ten Commandments about duty to God and duty to neighbor, which is why we read those almost every Sunday. We find the will of God for us in the Great Commandment to love God and to love neighbor, which is why we read that on every Sunday we do not read the other. We find the will of God for us at Christmas in the birth of the Christ child. We find the will of God for us at Good Friday in the crucifixion of the Christ. We find the will of God for us at Easter in the resurrection of the Christ. And we find the will of God for us at Pentecost in the sending of the apostles into all the world. The will of God for us is that the gospel of Jesus Christ is to be proclaimed to all the nations of the world and to the ends of the earth, until everyone has heard it and has opportunity to believe.

So Jesus knelt down and prayed, "Father, if you are willing, remove this cup from me. Nevertheless, not my will, but yours, be done." Thanks be to God that Jesus Christ won the victory for which he had been born at Christmas, all those years later in the struggle of prayer that night at the Mount of Olives! Thanks be to God that Jesus Christ came to terms with doing the will of God and never looked back! He stood and went forth from prayer strengthened, determined, and obedient, all to our benefit. Now it is our turn. Now we are called upon (1) to seek, (2) to discern, and (3) to obey the will of God for our lives and for the church. To do this, we may have to pray all night long. Are we ready to pray with Jesus, "Father . . . not my will, but yours, be done"?

To God be the glory forever and ever! Amen.

58

Are You the Son of God?

LUKE 22:54–71; DANIEL 7:9–14

"ARE YOU THE SON of God?" Therein lies the question of Jesus Christ. Everything depends upon this. Who is he? "Are you the Son of God?" This question of his identity is asked in today's reading from his trial before the council. In effect this question of his identity is asked throughout the gospel of his entire life, death, and resurrection. Indeed, this question of his identity is precisely the question of Christmas, the question of Jesus Christ to which the gospel of crucifixion and resurrection provides the answer. And, of course, this question of his identity is our question yet today, the question that we have to ask, the question that we have to answer about him, and therefore the question and the answer with which we have to live and to die. We may find that it is not Jesus who is on trial here. So what good news can today's reading bring to bear upon this pressing question?

"Are you the Son of God?" Thus the council queried Jesus, in order to condemn him. Let us review what Luke has already taught us about this. The angel Gabriel had already announced to Mary, years earlier, who Jesus is, in words we read every Christmas:

> Do not be afraid, Mary, for you have found favor with God. And behold, you
> will conceive in your womb and bear a son, and you shall call his name Jesus.
> He will be great and will be called the Son of the Most High. And the Lord
> God will give to him the throne of his father David, and he will reign over the
> house of Jacob forever, and of his kingdom there will be no end. . . . The Holy
> Spirit will come upon you, and the power of the Most High will overshadow

> you; therefore the child to be born will be called holy—the Son of God. (Luke
> 1:30–33, 35)

This is the good news of Christmas.

"Are you the Son of God?" Elizabeth, kinswoman of Mary and mother of John the Baptist, speaking under the authority of the Holy Spirit, had already said so to Mary: "Blessed are you among women, and blessed is the fruit of your womb! And why is this granted to me that the mother of my Lord should come to me?" (1:49–43). "Are you the Son of God?" Zechariah, father of John the Baptist, also speaking under the authority of the Holy Spirit, had already said so: "Blessed be the Lord God of Israel, for he has visited and redeemed his people and has raised up a horn of salvation for us in the house of his servant David" (1:68–69). "Are you the Son of God?" The angel of the Lord who spoke to the "shepherds out in the field, keeping watch over their flock by night," had already said so: "Fear not, for behold, I bring you good news of a great joy that will be for all the people. For unto you is born this day in the city of David a Savior, who is Christ the Lord" (2:8–11). This is the good news of Christmas.

"Are you the Son of God?" Righteous and devout Simeon, to whom it had been revealed "by the Holy Spirit that he would not see death before he had seen the Lord's Christ," had already said so in the temple even as he took the baby Jesus up in his arms: "Lord, now you are letting your servant depart in peace, according to your word; for my eyes have seen your salvation that you have prepared in the presence of all peoples, a light for revelation to the Gentiles, and for glory to your people Israel" (2:25–32). The prophetess Anna, also at the temple at that very hour, gave thanks to God for the redemption she recognized in Jesus Christ (2:36–38). "Are you the Son of God?" Jesus himself had answered the question as a child when his parents found him in the temple at Jerusalem: "Why were you looking for me? Did you not know that I must be in my Father's house?" (2:49). Can we not hear all these witnesses and so realize who Jesus is?

"Are you the Son of God?" John the Baptist had already said as much, fulfilling in his own ministry the ancient prophecy of Isaiah: "The voice of one crying in the wilderness: Prepare the way of the Lord" (3:4). The voice of God himself had already said so, speaking from heaven when Jesus was baptized: "You are my beloved Son; with you I am well pleased" (3:22, cf. 9:35). Luke had already said so in his genealogy of Jesus: ". . . Son of David . . . son of Abraham . . . son of Adam, son of God" (3:23, 31, 34, 38). And all of this is from only the first three chapters of Luke. He has told us over and over and over again that Jesus Christ is the Son of God so that we would be ready and able to answer this question near the end of the gospel. How stubborn could the council be? How hard-hearted is the world? More to the point, where do we stand in the great scheme of things, the trial of Jesus, the trial of the world, even our own trial?

It gets worse. Even the devil knows full well who Jesus is. That is the basis of his temptations in the wilderness. The devil said to Jesus, "If you are the Son of

God"—and the question is written in such a way as to indicate that he is—"command this stone to become bread" (4:3). And again, the devil said to him "If you are the Son of God"—and again, the question is written in such a way as to indicate that he is—"throw yourself down from here" (4:9). Even the devil's underling demons and unclean spirits knew who Jesus is and said as much as he threw them out of the people they possessed: "What have you to do with us, Jesus of Nazareth? Have you come to destroy us? I know who you are—the Holy One of God" (4:34). And, "You are the Son of God!" (4:41, cf. 8:28). This carries us up through chapter four of Luke. Then come more miracles and healings, teachings and professions of faith. But this is enough for now. This is enough for us to realize that the good news of Christmas at the beginning of the gospel, that Jesus is the Son of God, is the answer to the questions raised by his life, death, and resurrection, and especially to the question asked of him at his trial.

On the morning of the last day of his earthly life, Christ, born the Son of God so many years earlier, stood before the full assembly of the ministers and the elders of the people of God to answer precisely that question. The irony is overwhelming. They represented the entire people of God gathered in council, yet they all conspired together to extinguish the one hope of salvation.[1] They pretended to ask if Jesus is the Christ, but he knew that they were not interested, and he told them so.[2] They presumed to judge him, though he was without fault, without knowing that he was the prophesied Son of Man who will sit in judgment on them and on all the universe. As it is written in Daniel 7:14, "And to him was given dominion and glory and a kingdom, that all peoples, nations, and languages should serve him; his dominion is an everlasting dominion, which shall not pass away, and his kingdom one that shall not be destroyed."

So the elders and priests seized upon his words and twisted them to ask, "Are you the Son of God?" Sadly enough, the council thus spoke the truth it did not even realize and asked a question it did not want an answer. They were not seeking information. They were not seeking truth. They were not seeking knowledge. They certainly were not seeking faith. They were determined to convict and so to execute Jesus, and any excuse would do. This one served admirably. Claiming to be the Son of God would be a terrible act of blasphemy, unless, of course, it happened to be true, which was a possibility they never considered. Jesus knew, of course, what was going on. His response to them, "You say that I am," indicates that they said the right words but did not believe them, that they said the right words but did not act upon them, that they said the right words but did not live by them. Here is an important warning for us. Anyone can *say* that Jesus is the Son of God. Even the devil and his demons say that. And they actually know that. But somehow they do not believe that. They do not believe in him. They do not trust in him. They do not live for him. So the point of the question now turns against us. Given the Christmas truth that Jesus is the Son of God, the question becomes: Do we believe in him? Do we trust him? Do we live for him?

1. Calvin, *Harmony of the Gospels*, 3:164.
2. Craddock, *Luke*, 266.

The council was not alone in their disdain for Christ, their contempt for the Son of God. "The men who were holding Jesus in custody were mocking him as they beat him. They also blindfolded him and kept asking him, 'Prophesy! Who is it that struck you?' And they said many other things against him, blaspheming him." To the one who had never done wrong, they did wrong. The one who never hated, they despised. The one who did not hurt others, they hurt. The one who was the light of the world, who saw and knew all things, they blindfolded and ridiculed, while their own eyes remained uncovered but they still could not see who he was or what was going on. In short, they refused to acknowledge that he was the Son of God. And their failure stands to warn us against our own.

The problem strikes even closer to home than the council or the guard. It ran to the inner circle of the disciples. "And immediately, while he [Peter] was still speaking, the rooster crowed. And the Lord turned and looked at Peter. And Peter remembered the saying of the Lord, how he had said to him, 'Before the rooster crows today, you will deny me three times.' And he went out and wept bitterly." The outward details of the denial are well known. The inner reality was that Peter failed to recognize that Jesus was the Son of God. To acknowledge him as the Son of God would call for honor, worship, and obedience. To refuse honor, worship, and obedience would indicate a lack of acknowledgment of Jesus as the Son of God. Again, there is no advantage in our criticizing Peter. His failure is remembered as a warning against our own.

"Are you the Son of God?" There is no more important question before us. If Jesus is not the Son of God, all is lost. Sin will run its course. Death will be forever. Evil will reign unopposed. We will be left to faithlessness, self-servingness, and anarchy. But if Jesus *is* the Son of God, that changes everything. Sin, death, and evil are conquered. Our self-centeredness is undone. We are called to faith, worship, and obedience. Surely we can see the importance of the great truth that Jesus is the Son of God.

So now, given the gospel truth that Jesus is the Son of God, there is still the question of whether we acknowledge him as the Son of God. The council did not know that he was the Son of God and so could not acknowledge him as such. Of course, they did not want to know, and that was a great deal of the problem, but it was still the case that they could not acknowledge him. The demons did know that he was the Son of God but they refused to yield him faith. They acknowledged him in their own way, and they obeyed him, though admittedly unwillingly. But they did not believe in him. But here is the question for us: Since we have now been told the truth about who Jesus is, and since we now know who Jesus is, do we believe in him as the Son of God? Do we believe in the ancient truth and reality of Christmas? Do we acknowledge Jesus as Son of God, as Savior, and as Lord? Do we entrust our lives to him, giving ourselves to him without reservation, or do we foolishly acknowledge "still other events and powers, figures and truths, as God's revelation"?[3]

---

3. Presbyterian Church, *Book of Confessions*, 249.

From time to time, people stand and profess their faith before God and these congregations. With worship, nurture, and Bible study, they come to a saving faith in Jesus as the Son of God. They know what the gospel is all about. They know today what the ancient council was trying to deny then. And so they share with us the privilege not only of remembering the birth of Christ but also of witnessing the rebirth of new Christians. Thanks be to God! As these people stake their lives on the gospel, their profession of the Christian faith is an invitation to all of us to reaffirm our own faith and to put our lives on the line for the Lord again.

"Are you the Son of God?" Therein lies the question of Jesus Christ. This question of his identity is asked in today's reading at his trial before the council. And this is our question yet today, the question that we have to ask about him, the question that we have to answer about him and us, and therefore the question and the answer with which we have to live and to die. It is not Jesus who is on trial here.

To God be the glory forever and ever! Amen.

59

What Evil Has He Done?

LUKE 23:1–25; DEUTERONOMY 21:22–23

"WHAT EVIL HAS HE done?" Thus asked Pilate about Jesus Christ with a question that points unfailingly to the good news for us in today's reading, the good news that Pilate announced in his own answer to his question, his gospel answer given no less that three times: "I have found in him no guilt deserving death." Even Pilate could see that. "What evil has he done?" None! Pilate's three negative answers to his own question constituted an official declaration on the part of the Roman Empire that Jesus was not guilty. More of that in just a moment. "What evil has he done?" None! Luke, by reporting Pilate's "not guilty" declaration, announced to the world that one time in human history there lived a man who did no evil—none at all, not ever, not even a hint of it—and that this one life accomplished something so good, so powerful, and so far reaching that it can be nothing less than an act of God that continues to affect us even today.

"What evil has he done?" Pilate, speaking officially on behalf of the Roman Empire, the nation to that date most fully governed by law, three times declared that Jesus was not guilty, and this ruling is the first (1) part of the good news for us today. Pilate said once, "I find no guilt in this man." Twice, "I did not find this man guilty of any of your charges against him. . . . Nothing deserving death has been done by him." And three times, "I have found in him no guilt deserving death." And yet, the voices of Christ's accusers prevailed, as they urgently demanded with loud cries that he should be crucified. So the passage ends with Pilate handing over Jesus to be crucified, and this is his terrible legacy, as recorded in the Apostles' Creed, that Jesus "suffered under Pontius Pilate."

How is it that Jesus was not guilty but was crucified anyway? What does it mean for you and me today that the one who did not deserve to die was both rejected by the ministers and elders of the people of God and also executed by the government and military power of the state? Where is the good news? What is the gospel here? How is it that life for the world flows out of this death by crucifixion?

You and I know, as we look back over the years past and look forward in hope of better years to come—when we are honest with ourselves—that we are not innocent. We may or may not be guilty of flagrant outer crimes, but we know that we are not innocent of the countless wrongs of thought, word, and deed that we have committed against God, against neighbor, and against loved ones. Some of these we cannot even name, let alone admit. Some we cannot bear. Some we cannot live with. We do not mention this in church to be hurtful or accusatory and especially not to wallow in undue fascination with our wrongdoing. Far from it! We acknowledge here our lack of innocence only to seek and to receive the healing, forgiveness, cleansing, freedom, and release we so desperately desire and need.

If Jesus had deserved to die, his death would have been like every other death. It would not and could not have helped us at all. But the point here is that Jesus did not deserve to die. "What evil has he done?" He was not guilty. How odd that we had to have a Roman governor declare that to us! The people of God did not see it. The disciples were no longer on the scene. The mocking soldiers had no concern or interest. So it was left to a politician who did not worship God to declare that God's Christ was not guilty. The significance of this declaration is that it is an official pronouncement of a court of law. Christ's purity is not simply a matter of Christian piety. It is not an invention of wishful disciples. It is not the opinion of the author of the gospel. Instead, it was an official, legal declaration bearing all the authority of the Roman Empire: Jesus was not guilty of any of the charges brought against him. Jesus did not deserve to die! But he was crucified anyway.

The second (2) part of the good news in today's reading is that Jesus refused to defend himself. The religious leaders despised him on the presumption of blasphemy, and they accused him before the court of criminal activity against the throne and against the state. Jesus never denied it, never tried to defend himself, never tried to sidestep or to evade the crushing weight of the lies being amassed against him. Jesus could have defended himself against such charges, but he refused to do so. Instead, he offered no defense, he sought no escape, and he did not plead for mercy. He stood and took what was coming to him. More to the point, he stood and took what was coming to us! Thanks be to God!

Jesus had nothing coming to him, in terms of conviction or punishment. We are the ones who are guilty. We are the ones who try every strategy we can to escape justice. We are the ones who deserve conviction and punishment. So, the third (3) part of the good news for us today is that the only one among us who deserved no punishment at all has taken all our punishment away from us and placed it upon himself, without complaint, being crucified, dead, and buried. All our guilt was placed on his head. At the same time, Pilate's finding of "not guilty" for Jesus has been applied to us. So in his trial and in his crucifixion, Jesus fulfilled the ancient prophecy from Isaiah about the Servant of the Lord:

> He was oppressed, and he was afflicted,
>   yet he opened not his mouth;
> like a lamb that is led to the slaughter,
>   and like a sheep that before its shearers is silent,
>   so he opened not his mouth.
> By oppression and judgment he was taken away;
>   and as for his generation, who considered
> that he was cut off out of the land of the living,
>   stricken for the transgression of my people?
> And they made his grave with the wicked
>   and with a rich man in his death,
> although he had done no violence,
>   and there was no deceit in his mouth. (Isaiah 53:7–9)

This exchange of life and death—his for ours—is made explicit at the end of today's reading. The people shouted for the release of Barabbas, who was guilty of the charge of insurrection brought against Jesus and who was also a murderer. Then they shouted for the crucifixion of Jesus. Pilate gave in to their demands, releasing the insurrectionist and murderer and handing over the "not guilty" Jesus to be crucified. Do you remember that at the beginning of his ministry Jesus said he was sent to proclaim liberty to the captives (Luke 4:18)? This proclamation was fulfilled—not easily, not cheaply, but at the awful price of his actually exchanging places with the captives, with convicted criminals. Jesus was condemned while captive Barabbas—of all people!—was given his liberty. Jesus was crucified, not for all the apparently good people of the world, but literally for, and in the place of, a murderer. The life of Jesus was given for the life of Barabbas.

And the same thing is being done for us. Christ offered no defense of his innocence and so gave his life for us, in order that we who are as guilty as sin might be forgiven, and set free, and live. The Apostle Paul wrote of it to the Romans in this way: "For while we were still weak, at the right time Christ died for the ungodly. For one will scarcely die for a righteous person—though perhaps for a good person one would dare even to die—but God shows his love for us in that while we were still sinners, Christ died for us" (Romans 5:6–8).

As it is written in the Old Testament, anyone who is hanged on a tree is under God's curse. To be under the curse of God is a terrible, deathly, damning situation. It was so horrible that the law said to take the body down and bury it before sundown, so that the curse did not spread and defile the Promised Land! The significance of Christ being killed by hanging him on a tree, or impaling him on a wooden cross, was that by Old Testament law he was under the curse of God Almighty, creator of heaven and earth, his very Father. That is, Jesus took on himself the divine curse that we deserve, in order that we might live under the divine blessing that rightly belonged to him. Again, the Apostle Paul wrote of this to the Galatians, "Christ redeemed us from the curse of the law by becoming a curse for us—for it is written, 'Cursed is everyone who is hanged on a tree'—so that in Christ Jesus the blessing of Abraham might come to the Gentiles, so that we might receive the promised Spirit through faith" (Galatians 3:13–14).

Here, then, is the good news for us. First (1), not only is Jesus not guilty, but also his lack of guilt was officially declared three times by the full authority of the Roman Empire. Second (2), though faced with charges of capital offenses, Jesus refused to defend himself and chose instead to suffer punishment on our behalf. So third (3), Jesus wrongly received and yet graciously accepted a sentence of death in order that we might live. He was willing to undergo a curse from God in order that we might be blessed by God.

These three parts of the good news of Jesus Christ for us lead to three parts of the Christian life within us. First (1), then, Christianity is not about our being innocent, or our trying to be innocent, or our pretending to be innocent. Jesus is the only one who is not guilty. If the Christian faith required that people be innocent, we would not and could not be included. We know that. We do not always want to admit it, but deep down we know it. Therefore, we rejoice in and give thanks for the saving innocence of Jesus Christ. We regret, despise, and weep for the loss of our innocence, but there is nothing we can do about that now. We cannot recover it. But we can be, and have been, forgiven. We can be, and have been, given a fresh new start. We can, and are called, to seek, to discern, and to obey the will of God for our lives. That is why we gather here, in prayer and fellowship, to hear the reading and preaching of the word of God.

Second (2), Christianity is not about defending ourselves. We are bound to come under attack from time to time. But look at the example given to us. They said terrible things about Christ, and he did not find himself under the compulsion to have to refute all the accusations. There were times when the Apostle Paul defended himself and did so quite vigorously, but if we look at those instances carefully, what we find is that he was not defending himself personally but was instead defending the content and freedom of the gospel against those who were attempting to change it into something else. Some of us today labor under a tremendous need to be right. Christ labored under the commitment to obey God and to serve humanity. His example of suffering wrong and false accusations continues to be an impressive guide to Christian life and piety.

And third (3), Jesus Christ provides the one, strong, sure hope we have for life and for the world. The greatest problem in the world is not death, poverty, or disease, but the loss of hope. If we hope in ourselves, we find that we are weak and failing. If we hope in others, we find that they betray and desert us. If we hope in government or the economy or history, we find that they do not save us. And if we have no hope, we cannot face the dawning day, and we cannot live. But there is One upon whom we can depend and on whom we can rely. There is One who has never failed us or deserted us. There is One who calls us by name as his very own. There is One who is our one sure hope, in life and in death. And his name is Jesus Christ.

Cling to him, as to no other, for he holds us close to himself. Disease may ravage us, but God can resurrect us. Society may collapse upon us, but the kingdom of God does not fail. Family and friends may desert us, but Jesus Christ never abandons us. We too often hate ourselves, but Jesus never stops loving us. In all the changing world, here is the rock upon which we can base our lives. In all the shouting, lying, and mocking confusion of today's reading, Jesus quietly and serenely went about doing what he was called to do, obeying God, fulfilling all righteousness, and effecting the salvation of humanity. Here is our one good hope. Christ gives us life beyond this life, and therefore he gives us hope and life within this life.

"What evil has he done?" "We found this man misleading our nation and forbidding us to give tribute to Caesar, and saying that he himself is Christ, a king." Pilate avoided the implication of the "not guilty" verdict that he had three times announced. Herod, frustrated by the refusal of Jesus to answer his questions, had his men dress up Jesus in an elegant robe like the king he was accused of saying that he was. The people cried out for the death of their Savior, the only one who could save them from their sin. And Barabbas walked free while Jesus took his place on death row. But the great truth that Pilate did not discern and that Herod did not know, that the people never dreamed and that to which Barabbas never gave a second thought, is that "not guilty," defenseless, and suffering Jesus was and is also the King of the universe, the King of all times and places, the King of their lives, the King of your life, and the King of my life! "What evil has he done?" None at all, not ever, not even a hint of it. Thanks be to God! So let us acknowledge, worship, and obey the crucified and resurrected Jesus Christ as our Lord and King!

To God be the glory forever and ever! Amen.

60

Are You Not the Christ?

LUKE 23:26–56; ISAIAH 52:13—53:12

"ARE YOU NOT THE Christ?" Therein lies the question posed by and at the crucifixion of the Christ, here articulated by a criminal himself crucified. "Are you not the Christ?" The question expresses some wonderment. It betrays some confusion. It leads into some difficulties. But it is the right question. Finally someone asks it out loud. And Luke has recorded it for our edification. "Are you not the Christ?" The question is asked in such a way as to expect a positive answer. Yes, he is the Christ! Yes, he is! He is the Christ despite the crucifixion. That is the source of the confusion. Indeed, he is the Christ by virtue of the crucifixion. That is the cause of the wonderment. Thanks be to God!

"Are you not the Christ?" The affirmation lying behind this was called into question by the context in which it was being asked. How could the Christ be crucified? How could the Anointed one of God be killed? How could the Savior not be saved? How could the Victor be defeated? How could the Healer of all diseases be hanging on a cross? How could the Teacher be silenced? How could the One of whom the angels sang, the One whom Mary bore, the One whom the shepherds came to see, how could this one meet such an untimely end? What about the kingdom without end? What about good news of great joy for all the people? What about peace on earth among those with whom he is pleased? What about good news to the poor? What about liberty to the captives and recovery of sight to the blind? What about the new covenant? Did not the crucifixion call all of this into question?

"Are you not the Christ?" It was a cry of desperation, really. The poor criminal who asked the question was probably misled by all the disbelief being voiced around him. "The rulers scoffed at him [Jesus], saying, 'He saved others; let him save himself, if he is the Christ of God, his Chosen One!' The soldiers also mocked him [Jesus], coming up and offering him sour wine and saying, 'If you are the King of the Jews, save yourself!'" It was to their voices that the first criminal added his own, saying, "Are you not the Christ? Save yourself and us!" It is no accident that all their voices at the cross echoed that of the devil years earlier in the wilderness, who had tempted Jesus by saying, "If you are the Son of God, throw yourself down from here" (Luke 4:9). The devil, the rulers, the soldiers, and one of the criminals were united in making sport of Jesus and in insisting that he come down from the cross. This, of course, was the one thing he would not do. "Are you not the Christ?" Right assumption. Right question. Wrong conclusion. Yes, he was the Christ. But no, he would not save himself. No, no, no, no, no! He would not save himself. He could do many things. But the one thing he would not do was save himself. If he had saved himself, he would have ceased to be the Christ. And then he could not have saved us. So it was a terrible choice. He did not come down from the cross and did not save himself. Instead, he stayed on the cross and died so that he could fulfill his office as the Christ and save us.

"Are you not the Christ?" Right assumption. Right question. And the other criminal followed it through to reach the right conclusion. This second criminal rebuked the first one, saying, "Do you not fear God, since you are under the same sentence of condemnation? And we indeed justly, for we are receiving the due reward of our deeds; but this man has done nothing wrong." This, by the way, is both a confession of sin and also a profession of faith. Even the Roman centurion in charge of the crucifying Jesus concurred, praising God and saying, "Certainly this man was innocent!" "Do you not fear God?" Somehow, in the midst of the blood and gore, in the midst of the mockery, in the midst of the pain and confusion, this second criminal realized that the appropriate response to Christ crucified was to fear and to honor God. Something holy was happening there. The long-awaited servant of the Lord was taking on the sin of the world. The one who had done nothing wrong was taking on the gonewrongness of the rest of us. Christ chose not to save himself. Christ chose instead to die so that you and I may live.

"Are you not the Christ?" Yes, he is the Christ. Yes, he is. Right assumption. Right question. And this second criminal even arrived at the right conclusion. And then, on the basis of his new faith, he said, "Jesus, remember me when you come into your kingdom." What a wonderful prayer! "Jesus, remember me when you come into your kingdom." With this, the second criminal acknowledged Jesus as King. He placed his own well-being in the hands of the suffering and dying Christ. He placed his only hope in the resurrection yet to come. He refused to mock Jesus as did the others who stupidly and hatefully asked him to do the one thing he would not do. The second criminal chose instead to honor Christ by trusting him to do the one thing he came to earth to do: to die for us and so to save us. "Jesus, remember me when you come into your kingdom."

"Are you not the Christ?" Jesus said to this second criminal, "Truly, I say to you, today you will be with me in Paradise." You see, Jesus is the Christ not only because he was born at Bethlehem and not only because he was raised on Easter, but also and especially because he refused to save himself, refused to come down from the cross, refused to avoid the suffering, refused to avoid death, and he chose instead to suffer and to die for you and for me, on our account, in order that he might forgive our sin, and in order that we might then live. As Isaiah had written of him centuries earlier:

> Surely he has borne our griefs
>> and carried our sorrows;
> yet we esteemed him stricken,
>> smitten by God, and afflicted.
> But he was wounded for our transgressions;
>> he was crushed for our iniquities;
> upon him was the chastisement that brought us peace,
>> and with his stripes we are healed.
> All we like sheep have gone astray;
>> we have turned every one to his own way;
> and the LORD has laid on him
>> the iniquity of us all. (Isaiah 53:4–6)

What is the significance of the death of Jesus Christ? First (1), while the sinlessness of his life and death show his divinity, his death shows us his humanity. Jesus died as one of us. As each of us die, we can realize that he has gone before us. Moreover, the death of Jesus shows us the seriousness of the human predicament. If the human condition were just a little problem, we would not need this much help. But if the Son of God had to die to get us out, we are obviously in way over our heads, in a situation we cannot make right ourselves. If we could make things right with God by trying a little harder, then that is all it would take. But we cannot, and so we do not. We have, individually and as a whole human race, become self-centered instead of God-centered, and only God can re-center us correctly again.

Second (2), the death of Jesus shows the extent of the love of God. This shows us how far God is willing to go for us. God could have written us off. He could have started a new creation. Instead, God so loved the world that he gave his only son. Jesus so loved us that he was willing to pay the price. He gave his life for us. His executioners thought they took it from him, but they did not take anything that he did not give.

For instance: If someone fell in front of an oncoming truck and were killed, that would be an accident. If someone stepped in front of an oncoming truck on purpose and was killed, that would be suicide. If someone pushed another person in front of an oncoming truck and that person was killed, that would be murder. But if someone jumped in front of an oncoming truck in order to push someone else out of the way, and in the process was killed himself or herself, that would be an act of courage, heroism, life-giving sacrifice, and even salvation. And that is what Jesus did for us on the cross: he leapt in front of the onslaught of sin, death, and evil, and he gave his life that we might live.

Third (3), what Jesus did, he did in obedience to God. What is the great commandment? "You shall love the Lord your God with all your heart, and with all your soul, and with all your strength, and with all your mind, and your neighbor as yourself" (Luke 10:27). Most of us love God with our little finger, maybe. We love ourselves a lot more than we love all our neighbors put together. Jesus Christ obeyed the great commandment, not only on pretty, sunny days, but on that dark day we know as Good Friday, loving God under the worst possible circumstances of conviction and execution, loving neighbor in the person of scoffing leaders and soldiers who executed him. Even for them he prayed, "Father, forgive them; for they know not what they do."

Fourth (4), as John Calvin pointed out of this passage and so of the crucifixion centuries afterward, a wonderful exchange occurs here between Christ and us. Christ willingly suffered insult and mockery to make us stand before God pure and unstained. Christ endured all the ugliness of the crucifixion to restore the image of God to us. Christ was thrown out of the city onto Golgotha so that we might be taken into the kingdom of God. Christ was stripped of his clothes so that we might be clothed with the garments of righteousness. Christ endured being counted among the wicked in order to bring us into the company of holy angels. All that he took upon himself was a relief to us. It was for our sake and for our salvation that the Son of God willed to stay on the cross and so to endure torment, agony, and death. There is a wonderful exchange here, in which Christ takes on the curse in order that we might be forgiven.[1] Let us never neglect or be ungrateful for these benefits.

How does the crucifixion and death of Jesus Christ two thousand years ago affect and apply to our lives today? First (1), surely, today's reading inspires us to yearn for eternal fellowship with Christ. We can do no better than to pray with the second criminal, "Jesus, remember me." Of all the billions of human beings who have lived and died, this one shows us what it is all about. This is where God is present with us. This is the one to whom we want to be attached and related. We yearn for the fellowship with Christ. Eventually the relationship will be completed and perfected in heaven. As for now, it is begun here in limited but real ways, meeting God and his Christ in the fellowship of Christian believers, the communion of love and grace.

Second (2), as we are being drawn into that fellowship, we are being called upon to love God and to love neighbor. Since God in Jesus Christ loves us so much that he is willing to suffer, to be humiliated, and to die on our account, it is clear that we are to love God in return and to love one another in a like manner. How wonderful is the love of God! We have no higher calling than to love God in return. It is the purpose of human life. And our love for God overflows into love for each other. If Christ can die for our sins, surely we can forgive one another. If Christ can share our suffering, surely we can care for one another. If Christ can suffer uncalled for humiliation on

---

1. Calvin, *Harmony of the Gospels*, 3:189–99.

our account, surely we can keep hurtful words and thoughts to ourselves. Christ died alone so that we might live in fellowship. Surely this is a great deal of what we are about as the church that bears his name.

Third (3), even as Jesus fulfilled his office of Christ by being a servant of the Lord, so all of us who would follow him—not only ministers, elders, and deacons but also all the members of his church—are to fulfill our offices and our Christian lives by being servants of the Lord. We are not here to lord it over others. We are not here for our honor. We are not here for the prominence. We are here to glorify God and to serve God. And the pattern of our service, the standard for our lives, has been set by the life, ministry, and service of our Lord and Master, Jesus Christ. We cannot and need not repeat Christ's sacrifice. He was sinless, and we are not. We cannot and need not add anything to Christ's sacrifice. It was perfect and complete. And yet, we are called to follow him in the paths of service and even, if necessary, in the paths of suffering.

"Are you not the Christ?" Therein lies the question posed by and at the crucifixion of the Christ, here articulated by a criminal himself crucified. The question expresses some wonderment. It betrays some confusion. It leads into some difficulties. But it is the right question. Finally someone asks it out loud. "Are you not the Christ?" The good news is that, yes, he is the Christ! Yes, he is!

To God be the glory forever and ever! Amen.

61

Why Seek the Living Among the Dead?

LUKE 24:1–12; EXODUS 15:1–11

"WHY DO YOU SEEK the living among the dead?" This is the question with which the two men at the tomb greeted the women who went there seeking Jesus. It is an odd question, because its assumption that Jesus was alive challenged what the women had seen with their own eyes, that Jesus was crucified, dead, and buried. "Why do you seek the living among the dead?" The women in turn went and asked the same question to the male apostles, except that the men were not yet seeking Jesus anywhere, which was even worse. They too assumed that he was still dead. "Why do you seek the living among the dead?" Luke preserved this question not only for Theophilus, for whom he wrote this gospel, but also even for us yet today, challenging again the age old fear and faith of humanity that death is final, that death has the last word, and that the dead stay dead. "Why do you seek the living among the dead?" Is that not one of the strangest questions ever asked?

The stated assumption of the question, the major affirmation to which it leads us, is none other than the good news of Easter. Jesus Christ, who had been crucified, dead, and buried on Friday, is here and now on the following Sunday morning referred to as "the living." "The living" usually applies to people before they are crucified, dead, and buried. Here, "the living" is applied to Jesus Christ after he was crucified, dead, and buried. It seems out of sequence. It seems out of time. It seems wrong. And yet, the tomb was empty. The stone was rolled away. The women did not find the body. He was not there. He was not among the dead. He was, instead, again among the living.

Indeed, the two men at the tomb affirmed the same, explicitly: "He is not here, but has risen." That was new. That was different. That was unanticipated.

"He is not here, but has risen." This is the good news of Easter, that God has raised Jesus Christ from the dead. This is the very content of the gospel, that God has raised Jesus Christ from the dead. This is the major affirmation of the Christian faith, that God has raised Jesus Christ from the dead. This is the great hope of all humanity, that God has raised Jesus Christ from the dead. Indeed, this is more than we have dared to hope, that God has raised Jesus Christ from the dead. This is what we need more than we need anything else, that God has raised Jesus Christ from the dead. This is what we cannot do for ourselves, that God has raised Jesus Christ from the dead. This is more than we have been bold to imagine, that God has raised Jesus Christ from the dead. This is the courage by which alone we live, that God has raised Jesus Christ from the dead. This is, if not exactly the answer, the rebuttal to the question posed at the tomb: "Why do you seek the living among the dead?" "He is not here, but has risen." Thanks be to God!

It is important for us to realize that the two men at the tomb did not speak on their own authority. They referred the women and so us back to the teachings of Jesus Christ himself: "Remember how he told you, while he was still in Galilee, that the Son of Man must be delivered into the hands of sinful men and be crucified and on the third day rise." "Remember how he told you . . . that the Son of man must . . . rise." The basis of Christian faith is the word of God in the teachings of Jesus Christ. "Remember how he told you . . . that the Son of man must . . . rise." That is to say, faith comes from remembering the word of God. Remembering the word of God comes from hearing it. Hearing the word of God comes it being read and preached. Reading and preaching the word of God comes from the Bible and, in this case, from the very teachings of Jesus Christ himself. That is why we are here, Sunday after Sunday, reading, preaching, hearing, and remembering the word of God.

"Remember how he told you, while he was still in Galilee, that the Son of man must be delivered into the hands of sinful men, and be crucified, and on the third day rise." Yes, that is what he said, and that is how it happened. On Thursday evening, Jesus was betrayed and arrested. During the night he was tried. On Friday he was crucified. Given that all this came true, why, on Sunday morning, do we expect to find him still in the grave? Why, on Sunday, are we perplexed by the empty tomb? Why do we seek the living among the dead? Why? Because we do not remember what he told us. Such faithlessness is a result of not remembering the word. Not remembering the word comes from not hearing it. Not hearing the word comes from a lack of reading and preaching the word. But on that day, the women "remembered his words." So on that day, they believed in the resurrection. And on that day, they first preached the resurrection.

The facts of the situation were simple, in a way: the tomb was open and empty, and the body was nowhere to be found. But such facts alone led to perplexity. The truth of the situation had to come from beyond the bare facts. The truth of the situation had to come from the word of God. When and only when the women "remembered his words" did they know the truth, and only then did they understand the facts. What is the great truth of Easter? "He is not here, but has risen." Jesus Christ, who was crucified, dead, and buried, is now alive! This is the most important truth of the universe: Jesus Christ is alive! The one who was rejected by the people of God and executed by the state has been accepted and made alive again by God. The one who was born in a barn and laid in a feed trough, the one who was executed on a cross and laid in a tomb, has now been raised from the grave. This had never happened before. But now it has happened, and it is the most important thing that has ever happened.

This great truth of Easter, that Jesus has risen from the dead, means that death has been defeated. Our old enemy—the end of all life as we know it, the destroyer of all dreams, the breaker of all hopes, the crushing burden of all life, the end of all breath, the loss of all love, the fear of all hearts, the way of all flesh, the abyss into which all fall—death itself has now been defeated. Its power has been broken. Its might has been undone. Its reign has been taken away. Its terror has been removed. This one time, God has recreated new life on the other side of death, in a way that is forever beyond the reach and power of death. God alone is God! Death is not God. Death is exposed as the second rate power it is. Death continues today only by the permission of God, and the day is coming when it will not continue, when its permission will be withdrawn, when its power will be ended, and when its reign will be taken away. The truth of Easter is a sign and a promise of that final victory yet to come.

That God raised Jesus Christ from the dead is also God's vindication of his entire life, his teachings, preaching, ministry, and healings, and his sufferings, sacrifice, and death—of everything we have read about for the last sixteen months. Though the world rejected Jesus Christ, God accepted him. Though the world cast him aside, God lifted him up. Though the world buried him in the ground, God raised him to heaven. Were his prophecies outlandish? As it turns out, they were exactly right. Were his teachings extreme? Perhaps, but they too were correct. Was his call to discipleship demanding? Yes, absolutely, and with every good reason. Was his self-sacrifice ridiculous? It was extravagant and outlandish, and it was exactly what the situation demanded. Were his faith in God, his hope in God, and his love of God insane? No, they were entirely justified. And by raising him from the dead, God vindicated everything Jesus did, everything Jesus said, everything that Jesus was, and everything that Jesus was about. God refused to lose any of that. God refused to let death hold any of it. So God regathered all of that to himself and made Jesus alive again.

How can we believe in the resurrection of Jesus Christ today, two thousand years after it happened? One of the consequences of the resurrection was the empty tomb. That by itself is not sufficient for faith, but the empty tomb is necessary to the faith. Without it there would be no resurrection, no faith, and no Christianity.

So, Christian faith in God and in his Christ is based not only on the empty tomb but also and more so on the word of God and on the witness of those whom the risen Lord encountered. The two men reminded the women of what Jesus had told them, "and they remembered his words." Later that day, the risen Lord himself explained to his disciples how the Law, Prophets, and Psalms pointed ahead to him and told of his suffering, his rising, and his glory. He reminded them of his own teaching. So faith comes from the word of God, as the Holy Spirit bears testimony to it in our hearts. Moreover, we know and believe that Jesus Christ has risen from the tomb and is alive by the witness of the women who went to the tomb. We know and believe this by the witness of the apostles, who did not know or believe it themselves at first but came to know and to believe it with all their hearts.

Soon after the resurrection, the apostles, who had been cowering behind locked doors in fear for their own lives after seeing what had happened to Jesus, were standing on the street corners declaring that this same Jesus was alive and was Lord of the universe. Tradition has it that eventually all of them were arrested and killed for preaching the resurrection. So, why did they do that? Not for the fun of it. Not because they wanted to preserve the memory of the dead Jesus. Not because they were stupid. Not for hope of fame or fortune. There is no human accounting for the courage of their witness to the resurrection and their preaching of the gospel. The only possible reason that they could have been preaching that Jesus was alive is that Jesus was, in fact, alive.

Consider this also: no one ever produced the body. Despite denials of the resurrection by the religious establishment and by the officials of the state, despite the problems being created by street preaching and the rapidly growing Christian church, no one ever produced the body. The easiest way to silence, to shame, and to ridicule the apostles, and the quickest and most effective way to put an end to their talk about Jesus having risen from the grave, would have been to produce the body—to have dug it up, to have paraded it through the streets, and to have shown it to everyone. But no one did that. Instead, they were faced with the incontrovertible fact that the tomb was empty. The body was not there. The people of God who rejected Jesus were incapable of producing the body. The full military force of the Roman Empire was incapable of producing the body. That would have nipped Christianity in the bud, but they did not, because they could not, produce the body. And the apostles continued to preach, so more and more people believed the good news that the two men at the tomb had announced to the women, that Christ has risen from the dead!

What does this ancient word of God have to do with us yet today? The resurrection of Jesus Christ is the basic and central content of the Christian faith. God has raised him from the dead. Moreover, the resurrection of Jesus Christ is the basis of all the rest of the Christian faith. Without it we would have nothing, but with it we have everything. The resurrection demonstrates the power of God. It establishes the truth of the Scriptures. It confirms the identity of Jesus as the Christ. It shows that the power of God, who created the world, is greater than the power of death, which can only take away life. God, who made us, has saved us for himself and reclaimed us as his very own.

Moreover, the resurrection of Jesus Christ constitutes the defeat of death once and for all and so is the promise of resurrection life for us. God did not raise Jesus merely for his own sake. In his resurrection the power of death is broken, death is robbed of its false appearance of being absolute, and we are given the promise and good hope of life with God beyond life and death on this earth. Because God raised Jesus from the dead and made him alive again, so shall God raise us from the dead and make us alive again. In his resurrection God has defeated death, so his victory is the promise of our own resurrection and that of those whom we love.

Where does that leave us in the meantime? There are implications not only for our deaths, but also for our lives. Since the power of death is broken, the life-robbing fear of death is diminished, so we can go about our lives with confidence, dignity, poise, joy, and good hope. We can worship God our Creator gladly, safe in the knowledge that he is also our Redeemer. We can thank God for the forgiveness of sin, because sin and evil were defeated on the cross. And we can bear witness to the resurrection of Jesus Christ and share the good news of the gospel with all people.

This witnessing started in today's reading: the two men at the tomb bore witness to the women, and the women bore witness to the apostles. The apostles have borne witness to us. Now it is our turn. We are responsible for being faithful. We are responsible for bearing witness. We are called to share the great truth of the universe, that Jesus is alive. There is no one in the world who does not need to hear the word of God, the good news of the resurrection of Jesus Christ.

"Remember how he told you, while he was still in Galilee, that the Son of Man must be delivered into the hands of sinful men and be crucified and on the third day rise." "Why do you seek the living among the dead?" This is the question with which the two men at the tomb greeted the women who went there seeking Jesus. It is an odd question, because its assumption that Jesus was still alive challenged what the women had seen with their own eyes: that Jesus was crucified, dead, and buried. "Why do you seek the living among the dead?" Luke preserved this question not only for Theophilus but also even for us yet today, challenging the age-old fear and faith of humanity that death is final, that death has the last word, and that the dead stay dead. "Why do you seek the living among the dead?" "He is not here, but has risen."

To God be the glory forever and ever! Amen.

62

Was It Not Necessary?

LUKE 24:13–35; ISAIAH 25:6–9

"WAS IT NOT NECESSARY that the Christ should suffer these things and enter into his glory?" "Was it not necessary that the Christ should suffer?" Here is the question, near the end of the Gospel according to Luke, that reaches back over everything that has happened to Jesus up to this point and that gathers it all together into the overarching plan of God. Here is the question, recorded in Luke not only for the sake of history be even more for our continuing benefit, both to help bring even us to an understanding of Christ's death and so also to help bring even us to an abiding faith in Christ's resurrection.

"Was it not necessary that the Christ should suffer?" Necessary! Required! Part of the divine will, the eternal decrees, God's good plan for the salvation of the world! Standing behind, beyond, above, and underneath every human decision that contributed to this suffering was this prior divine plan for our salvation.

This insistence upon divine necessity in the death of Jesus Christ is not at all to say that the evil that men did to Jesus was not evil, for it was evil. But it is to say that God both rules the world and overrules the world. God works in obvious ways, such as the faithfulness and orderliness of the universe; God also works in hidden ways, such as the rise and fall of empires; and God even works in very strange ways, such as through the evil deeds of evil men, and yet even then, God always, always, always accomplishes his own good purposes.

"Was it not necessary that the Christ should suffer?" Yes, of course it was. Consider with me the implications of this question about the necessity of the suffering of Christ. Of all the evil things that were done to Jesus, not one of them was outside the will of God. That is to say, none of them caught God by surprise. None of them undid the good purposes of God. None of them overwhelmed or overcame God. None of them defeated the eternal will of God for the salvation of the world.

Quite the opposite: God used the greatest evil in the history of humanity for the salvation of evil humanity. The suffering of Christ was not pointless. The suffering of Christ was not capricious. The suffering of Christ was not arbitrary. The suffering of Christ was not in vain. The suffering of Christ was not for nothing. The suffering of Christ was not wasted. Instead, the suffering of Christ was designed, willed, and intended by God, and also freely entered into by Christ, in order to absorb, to conquer, and to defeat the very agents of suffering, even sin, death, and evil themselves.

Another way of saying this is that the gospel is not a tragedy in which evil deeds undid a good man. The gospel is a love story in which Jesus Christ gave himself to the forces of evil precisely in order to win us to himself. And that was the only way to accomplish what he did. Sin, death, and evil did their worst to him, and he died. But he did not sin. He did not abandon his faith in God. He did not disobey God. He did not return evil for evil. His love was never broken. And so he won the victory.

The power of evil was spent upon him—exhausted, emptied, defeated, and forever undone. The power of sin was destroyed. And though he was given to death as a part of the test by sin and evil, death was not allowed to hold him, and God raised him back to life. "Was it not necessary?" That was the only way that sin, death, and evil could be defeated. The only way! And so he did it. He did it for you and for me. Thanks be to God!

In order to lead these two former followers and so even us into faith, Jesus walked them through all of what we know as the Old Testament. "Beginning with Moses and all the Prophets, he interpreted to them in all the Scriptures the things concerning himself." How many times have I wished that we had those interpretations! Why did not Luke record them for us? And yet, the Holy Spirit has opened these Scriptures even to us. For instance, Genesis 22 tells of Abraham being ordered to sacrifice his only son, Isaac, and this makes sense only in context of God himself sacrificing his only Son, Jesus. Genesis 45 and 50 tell of Joseph forgiving his brothers who had sold him into slavery with the assurance, "You meant evil against me, but God meant it for good," which Jesus as well could have said to those who crucified him.

It was from Psalm 22 that Jesus quoted the cry of dereliction, "My God, my God, why have you forsaken me?," and from which his detractors received their taunt, whether they realized it or not, "He trusts in the Lord; let him deliver him; let him rescue him, for he delights in him!" Isaiah 42 tells that God put his Spirit upon his chosen servant. We now know who that was. Isaiah 50 tells that the Lord God helped his servant so that he was not disgraced, which is to say that by the resurrection God vindicated Christ's sacrifice on the cross. Isaiah 52 tells that his servant's appearance was marred beyond human semblance. Isaiah 53 tells that he was wounded for our transgressions, that he was crushed for our iniquities, that he bore the chastisement that brought us peace, and that with his stripes we are healed. Those stripes, of course, were the wounds made by a whip prior to crucifixion. Page after page, chapter after chapter, all of Scripture points ahead to Jesus Christ. "Did not our hearts burn within us while he talked to us on the road, while he opened to us the Scriptures?" This is where we come to know him. Thanks be to God!

But this suffering is not the whole story. "Was it not necessary that the Christ should suffer these things and enter into his glory?" "Was it not necessary that the Christ should . . . enter into his glory?" Here is the question, near the end of the Gospel according to Luke, that not only points to the resurrection but also points ahead to the ascension, to the glorification, and to the return of Christ, and that gathers it all together into the overarching plan of God. Here is the question, recorded in Luke for our continuing benefit, both to help bring even us to an understanding of Christ's death and so also and especially to help bring even us to an abiding faith in Christ's resurrection.

"Was it not necessary that the Christ should . . . enter into his glory?" Necessary! Required! Part of the divine will, the eternal decrees, God's good plan for the salvation of the world! "Was it not necessary that the Christ should . . . enter into his glory?" The question that Jesus poses for us has a second half, just as necessary as the first, being in fact the very goal and purpose that the first half serves.

Consider with me the implications of this second half of the question, about the necessity of Christ entering his glory. Death did not have the last word. The crucifixion was not the end of the road. The tomb could not hold Jesus long. God raised Jesus from the dead, not only for his own sake but also as the promise of your resurrection and of mine. God lifted Jesus into heaven, establishing the fellowship into which we shall be drawn. God promises his return, when Jesus shall reign forever and ever, and when God's overruling shall become his explicit ruling. All of this was as much a part of the plan, as important, as necessary, as all the previous suffering. In fact, it was necessary for Christ to be raised from the dead for death to be conquered. It was necessary for Christ to ascend to heaven to be restored to God. It is necessary for Christ to return to fulfill his kingdom and to gather us unto himself. Even as the suffering first half of the plan has been completed, so are we given ever-increasing confidence that God shall complete the glorious second half also.

All of this, too, was foretold by Scripture. "Beginning with Moses and all the Prophets, he interpreted to them in all the Scriptures the things concerning himself." Exodus 14 and 15 tell of Israel's escape from death through the sea, even as Christ escaped from the tomb. Joshua 24 tells of Joshua calling the people of Israel to faith, even as Jesus, his namesake, calls us to faith. Samuel tells of King David ruling the people of God, even as Jesus would rule the kingdom of God. Psalm 46 tells of the victory of the Lord, even as Jesus won the victory.

Isaiah 25 tells of God's victory over death, and he made that come true in Jesus Christ. Isaiah 43 depicts the return from the exile in Babylon as a new exodus and points ahead to the even greater exodus from the grave, which began at Easter. Isaiah

65 tells of God creating a new heaven and a new earth, and it all started in Jerusalem. Amos 5 calls for justice to roll down like waters and righteousness like an ever-flowing stream. That has come true in Jesus Christ. Malachi 4 tells of the great and awesome day of the Lord. That day has dawned in Jesus Christ. Page after page, chapter after chapter, all of Scripture points ahead to Jesus Christ. "Did not our hearts burn within us while he talked to us on the road, while he opened to us the Scriptures?" This is where we come to know him. And knowing him is why we still read and preach the Scriptures today. Thanks be to God!

This interpretation from the Scriptures of the necessity of both the suffering and the glory of the Christ became, along with and in the context of the meal, the means by which he led these two former followers first to faith and then also to witness. "When he was at table with them, he took the bread and blessed and broke it and gave it to them. And their eyes were opened, and they recognized him." That is faith. They knew the risen Lord Jesus Christ. "And they rose that same hour and returned to Jerusalem. And they found the eleven and those who were with them. . . . Then they told what had happened on the road, and how he was known to them in the breaking of the bread." That is witness. They told others about the risen Lord Jesus Christ.

Luke has recorded both of these results not so much for historical interest, as significant as that is, as for your sake and for mine, and not only as encouragements to lead us both to faith and so also to witness, but in fact as the very means that God himself uses yet today to lead even us both to faith and so also to witness. This is the point of this reading. This is the point of this gospel. This is the point of the entire life, ministry, death, and resurrection of Jesus Christ, that we should both believe in him and also bear witness to him. May God himself open our eyes! May God himself cause even us to recognize Jesus as the Christ! And may God himself grant even us the grace to proclaim to all the world today the good news of the resurrection, "The Lord has risen indeed!"

With this good news of the resurrection, the ancient prophecy has been fulfilled. God has given us the word of hope we have needed to go on living. We have needed and longed for the word of forgiveness to cleanse us from our sin and guilt. We have needed the word of acceptance to restore us to right relationship with God and with each other. We have needed the word of challenge to urge us along the way. And most of all we have needed the word of reassurance that this world is not all there is, that this life is not all there is, that death is not the end of it all, and that there is something more, beyond this, where the unclarities of life here are made clear, where the errors of life here are made correct, and where the gaping incompletenesses of life here are made whole.

This is the good word of hope we receive with the resurrection of Jesus Christ, for the good news that Jesus is alive again is also the promise that God will make even us alive, that we shall join Jesus Christ in the resurrection, and that the table fellowship of the kingdom of God is forever. One day there shall be no more Mattoax and

Pine Grove Presbyterian Churches. One day there shall be no more United States of America. One day there shall be no more earth or sun. But even then you and I shall continue to live eternally in the presence of God our Father and of his Son, Jesus Christ our Lord. That is at least part of what the resurrection means.

"Was it not necessary that the Christ should suffer these things and enter into his glory?" Here is the question, near the end of the Gospel according to Luke, that reaches back over everything that had happened to Jesus up to this point and that not only points to the resurrection but also points ahead to the ascension, to the glorification, and to the return of Christ, and gathers it all together into the overarching plan of God. Here is the question, recorded in the Gospel according to Luke for our continuing benefit, both to help bring even us to an understanding of Christ's death and so also and even more so to help bring even us to an abiding faith in Christ's resurrection.

"Was it not necessary that the Christ should suffer these things and enter into his glory?" Yes, yes it was. And we are grateful for all that he has done for us.

To God be the glory forever and ever! Amen.

63

Why Are You Troubled?

LUKE 24:36–53; ISAIAH 52:7–12

"WHY ARE YOU TROUBLED, and why do doubts arise in your hearts?" Here is a question for the disciples. Here is a question for Theophilus. Here is a question for you and for me. "Why are you troubled, and why do doubts arise in your hearts?" Yes, I know it is two questions, but the two are actually parallel ways of asking one and the same question, probably to make sure that we hear it. "Why are you troubled, and why do doubts arise in your hearts?" Well, the first disciples to whom Jesus asked this question were troubled because he was the one asking it! He had been crucified on Friday, dead and buried, and yet, "As they were talking about these things, Jesus himself stood among them, and said to them, 'Peace to you'"! No wonder "they were startled and frightened." In fact, they "thought they saw a spirit." That was the only way they could make sense of the situation, at first. But that understanding was the very opposite of the truth. That was the antithesis of the reality before them. That was an act of doubt. That was a failure of faith. And that was the reason for the question.

"Why are you troubled, and why do doubts arise in your hearts?" You see, Jesus was not looking for information. He was not quizzing them. This was not a test. Instead, this was an invitation to faith. This was an invitation to believe. This was an invitation to life. This was an invitation to joy. This was an invitation to discipleship. And it continues to be so for you and for me, today. Jesus acknowledges that we are troubled in order to give us peace. He acknowledges that doubts arise in our hearts so that he can give us faith. With this question at the end of the gospel, we move beyond catechetical instruction about the faith into the very gift of faith itself. Are you interested? Would you like to receive the gift that Christ gives us?

"Why are you troubled, and why do doubts arise in your hearts?" The disciples were troubled because they were confronted with the risen Lord Jesus Christ, and that challenged everything they thought they knew about the world in which they lived. Dead men do not live, but there he was! What could they say? Jesus presented them with the evidence not only of his being alive but also and especially of the physical reality of his resurrected body: "'See my hands and my feet, that it is I myself. Touch me, and see. For a spirit does not have flesh and bones as you see that I have.' And when he had said this, he showed them his hands and his feet." Do you catch the significance of that? For the second time, hands and feet. We would say, "Look at my face!" That is how we recognize people. But his hands and his feet bore the marks of the cross, the holes from the nails, the wounds of his suffering on our behalf. It could be no other than the Christ, alive again. The resurrected one was none other than the crucified one.

"And while they still disbelieved for joy and were marveling, he said to them, 'Have you anything here to eat?' They gave him a piece of broiled fish, and he took it and ate before them." After all, ghosts do not eat broiled fish! In case his hands and feet were not enough, he showed them that he could eat. He was alive!

> The LORD has comforted his people;
>   he has redeemed Jerusalem.
> The LORD has bared his holy arm
>   before the eyes of all the nations,
> and all the ends of the earth
>   shall see the salvation of our God. (Isaiah 52:9b–10)

And so it was that the first disciples were neither to be troubled nor to have doubts arising in their hearts. That is to say, the very question Jesus had asked them contained within itself the implicit promise of help. The very purpose of the question was to ease their trouble and to allay their doubts. And so the very purpose of the question is also to ease our trouble and to allay our doubts. Jesus intends to take those away from us. Thanks be to God!

There is more. Jesus "said to them, 'These are my words that I spoke to you while I was still with you, that everything written about me in the Law of Moses and the Prophets and the Psalms must be fulfilled.'" The whole Old Testament! It all pointed ahead to him. Do you see now why we try to read each book so carefully? Then Jesus "opened their minds to understand the Scriptures." He did not invite them to be open minded, he did not encourage them to be open minded, he did not plead with them to be open minded, he did not try to convince them with clever arguments to be open minded, but instead he opened their minds himself, and he gave them what they needed. Jesus "opened their minds to understand the Scriptures, and said to them, 'Thus it is written, that the Christ should suffer and on the third day rise from the dead.'" Yes, he was to suffer, die, and be raised. It was all there! They had not understood it before, but it was all there. His resurrection was new, but it was not sheer novelty. It was the fulfillment of the ancient word of God.

Then Jesus "opened their minds to understand the Scriptures, and said to them, 'Thus it is written, that the Christ should suffer and on the third day rise from the dead, and that repentance and forgiveness of sins should be proclaimed in his name to all nations, beginning from Jerusalem. You are witnesses of these things.'" This is the purpose of it all, that repentance and forgiveness of sins should be proclaimed in his name to all nations. And that is what they went and did. We can read about that in volume two of Luke's gospel, otherwise known as the Acts of the Apostles. That is what they went and did, proclaiming the resurrection of Jesus Christ, proclaiming repentance and the forgiveness of sins. Thus has the gospel been preached even to us. Thus are we yet to preach the gospel to others. "How beautiful upon the mountains are the feet of him who brings good news" (Isaiah 52:7).

"Why are you troubled, and why do doubts arise in your hearts?" The disciples were troubled because they were confronted with the risen Lord Jesus Christ, and that challenged everything they thought they knew about the world in which they lived. We, on the other hand, are troubled in part because we are confronted with the physical absence of Jesus Christ, and that allows the world in which we live to challenge everything we believe. Our circumstances may be the opposite of those of the disciples, but our troubling is not so unlike theirs that it cannot be addressed by the same gospel. They saw the risen Lord whom they did not expect, while we do not see the risen Lord whom we very much need. Someday he shall return. But what are we to do in the meantime? How are we not to be troubled?

Jesus prepared even the first disciples for his immediate departure and physical absence. "Behold, I am sending the promise of my Father upon you. But stay in the city until you are clothed with power from on high." The promise and the power are none other than the Holy Spirit. The promise and the power are the very presence of God with us during the bodily absence of Jesus Christ. The promise and the power are the gifts of God to the Christian church. The promise and the power are here for us today. The promise and the power sustain us in these continuing, in between times.

"Then he led them out as far as Bethany, and lifting up his hands he blessed them. While he blessed them, he parted from them and was carried up into heaven. And they worshiped him and returned to Jerusalem with great joy, and were continually in the temple blessing God." They worshiped him and were continually in the temple blessing God. They worshiped him and were continually blessing God. We do the same.

> Bless the Lord, O my soul,
> and all that is within me,
> bless his holy name!
> Bless the Lord, O my soul,
> and forget not all his benefits. (Psalm 103:1–2)

Christ made himself known to them in his risen body. Christ opened their minds to all the Scriptures said about him, so that we seek him in the Scriptures still today, week in and week out. And Christ led them into ongoing worship, so that we realize yet today that the ultimate purpose of our existence is to glorify God and to enjoy him forever. So do we continue to worship God gladly yet today.

"Why are you troubled, and why do doubts arise in your hearts?" We are troubled not only by the physical absence of Jesus Christ but also in part because we live in troubled times. We live in a time when evil men are eager to commit evil deeds. We live in a time of terror and of horror. We live in an age when doubt is worn as a badge of honor. We live in a time when the Christian faith is under attack from both inside and outside the church. We live in a time when some would abandon the faith and others would destroy it. We live in a time when we realize that even more difficult times may lie ahead for the Christian church. What are we to do? How can we face such troubles and doubts?

The faith that we have received from Jesus Christ is both nourished by, and also expressed in, the worship of God into which we have been led by Jesus Christ. First of all (1), we are nourished here by the word of God. Jesus "opened their minds to understand the Scriptures." We are enlivened by the word of God. We are sustained by the word of God. Come what may, we shall continue to gather here to hear the word of God, by which alone we live. No one can take that away from us.

Second (2), we are nourished here by the sacrament of the Lord's Supper. They "were continually in the temple blessing God." We are made alive by the work of Jesus Christ here. We are drawn into communion here with God, with his Christ, and with all the communion of saints. Come what may, we shall continue to gather here around this table to be nourished at this feast by the body and blood of Christ, by his life and by his death, by his sacrifice and by his victory, and so by his resurrection. No one can take that away from us. Here we have pulpit and table, word and sacrament, one gospel, "one Lord, one faith, one baptism, one God and Father of all, who is over all and through all and in all" (Ephesians 4:5–6).

"Why are you troubled, and why do doubts arise in your hearts?" Jesus Christ is not looking for information. He is not quizzing us. This is not a test. Instead, this is an invitation to faith. This is an invitation to believe. This is an invitation to life. This is an invitation to joy. This is an invitation to discipleship. The risen Lord Jesus Christ acknowledges that we are troubled in order to give us peace. He acknowledges that doubts arise in our hearts in order that he can give us faith. With this question at the end of the gospel, we move beyond catechetical instruction about the faith into the very gift of faith itself. Are you interested? Would you like to receive the gift that Christ gives us?

To God be the glory forever and ever! Amen.

Appendix A

Questions in Luke

As I preached through the Gospel according to Luke, I divided it into sixty-three passages. I did so largely on the basis of the questions I found in the text, questions which usually point to the most important affirmation of each passage. It was this pattern of question and answer that suggested to me that Luke was presenting the gospel in the form of a catechism. For a brief discussion of how this works, see the Preface. Some of these passages could be divided further, but the ones left undivided here hold things together, such as faith and action, or faith and gratitude.

It occurred to me that it might be helpful to move beyond my initial impressions about the importance of these questions by looking at some actual numbers. Here is what I found: of all sixty-three passages, forty-six of them include direct questions (referenced below by verse, in parentheses, alongside the number and title of the sermon in which they appear; one question, in 11:13, is punctuated in the text as an exclamation). These make up fully 73 percent of the whole, or nearly three quarters of the passages.

Direct Questions in Luke

1	How Shall I Know?	(1:18)
2	How Will This Be?	(1:34)
3	Why Me?	(1:43)
4	What Then?	(1:66)
7	Did You Not Know?	(2:49)
8	What Shall We Do?	(3:10, 12, 14)
11	Is Not This . . . ?	(4:22)
12	What Is This Word?	(4:36)
14	Who Can Forgive?	(5:21)
15	Why with Sinners?	(5:30)
16	Good or Harm?	(6:9)

18	What Benefit?	(6:32, 33, 34)
19	Why Do You Call Me "Lord"?	(6:46)
21	Who Is to Come?	(7:18, 20)
22	Who Forgives Sins?	(7:49)
24	Who Commands Winds and Water?	(8:25)
26	Who Is This?	(9:9)
27	Who Do You Say That I Am?	(9:20)
28	Who Is the Greatest?	(9:46)
31	What Shall I Do?	(10:25)
32	How Much More!	(11:13)
33	How Will His Kingdom Stand?	(11:18)
34	Did Not He Make You?	(11:40)
36	Why Are You Anxious?	(12:26)
37	Who Is Faithful?	(12:42)
38	Worse Than All the Others?	(13:2, 4)
39	What Is the Kingdom of God?	(13:18)
40	Is It Lawful to Heal?	(14:3)
41	Do You Not Count the Cost?	(14:28)
42	Do You Not Go After the Lost?	(15:3, 8)
43	Who Will Entrust to You the True Riches?	(16:3)
46	Must I Lose My Life to Keep It?	(17:37)
47	Will He Find Faith?	(18:8)
48	Who Can Be Saved?	(18:26)
49	What Do You Want Me to Do?	(18:41)
50	Why Did the Son of Man Come?	(19:23)
51	In Whose Name?	(19:31, 33)
53	Are the Dead Raised?	(20:41)
54	When Will These Things Be?	(21:7)
56	Who Is the Greatest?	(22:27)
58	Are You the Son of God?	(22:70)
59	What Evil Has He Done?	(23:22)
60	Are You Not the Christ?	(23:39)
61	Why Seek the Living Among the Dead?	(24:5)
62	Was It Not Necessary?	(24:26)
63	Why Are You Troubled?	(24:38)

Seven more passages include imperatives (referenced below in braces, in the same manner as above). While these are not exactly catechetical questions, they are nevertheless commandments or at least requests for action, and as such they call for and require a response, an answer. Again, the request points to the major affirmation of the passage. In some of these titles, I have cast the imperative as a question. These seven make up an additional 11 percent of the passages. Taken together, the passages with direct questions and those with imperatives account for 84 percent of the whole, or more than five sixths of the passages.

Imperatives in Luke

13	Let Down Your Nets!	{5:4}
25	Only Believe!	{8:50}
35	Fear Not!	{12:4}
44	Do They Not Hear?	{16:29}
45	Increase Our Faith!	{17:5}
52	By What Authority?	{20:2}
57	What Is the Father's Will?	{22:42}

All ten of the remaining passages are written in such a way as to include an implied question (referenced below in brackets). The question does not appear in the grammatical form of a question, but it is there in the background, undergirding and informing the passage, constituting the foundation apart from which the passage cannot be understood. In some of these titles, I have articulated the question. These ten make up the remaining 16 percent of the passages.

Implied Questions in Luke

5	What Good News?	[2:10]
6	How Long?	[2:25]
9	Whose Son?	[3:23]
10	Whom Shall You Serve?	[4:8]
17	Blessing or Woe?	[6:20–26]
20	Say the Word!	[7:7]
23	Take Care How You Hear!	[8:10]
29	How Shall We Follow?	[9:57, 59, 61]
30	Who Hears You?	[10:16]
55	Give Us Strength!	[21:36]

It is especially striking that among the forty-six passages with direct questions, the question is repeated in four of the passages. In two of these, the question appears three times. The same thing happens with one of the implied questions. All of this repetition is clearly for emphasis. In these passages Luke makes a special effort to be sure that we get the point.

REPEATED QUESTIONS IN LUKE

8	What Shall We Do?	(3:10, 12, 14)
18	What Benefit?	(6:32, 33, 34)
21	Who Is to Come?	(7:18, 20)
29	How Shall We Follow?	[9:57, 59, 61]
38	Worse than All the Others?	(13:2, 4)

Finally, it is also the case that thirty-seven passages of all three types above include additional questions (referenced below with a plus sign and numeral alongside the verse) that seem to be incidental and thus do not serve the larger purpose of presenting the gospel in the form of a catechism. Perhaps it would be more accurate to say that I did not deal with these questions in this series of sermons. If the Gospel according to Luke were divided into shorter and therefore more passages, perhaps these questions, too, would gain more prominence.

INCIDENTAL QUESTIONS IN LUKE

7	Did You Not Know?	(2:49) + 2
8	What Shall We Do?	(3:10, 12, 14) + 1
12	What Is This Word?	(4:36) + 2
14	Who Can Forgive?	(5:21) + 3
15	Why with Sinners?	(5:30) + 1
16	Good or Harm?	(6:9) + 2
19	Why Do You Call Me "Lord"?	(6:46) + 4
21	Who Is to Come?	(7:18, 20) + 8
22	Who Forgives Sins?	(7:49) + 2
24	Who Commands Winds and Water?	(8:25) + 3
27	Who Do You Say That I Am?	(9:20) + 2
28	Who Is the Greatest?	(9:46) + 1
29	How Shall We Follow?	[9:57, 59, 61] + 1
31	What Shall I Do?	(10:25) + 5
32	How Much More!	(11:13) + 2
33	How Will His Kingdom Stand?	(11:18) + 1
36	Why Are You Anxious?	(12:26) + 3
37	Who Is Faithful?	(12:42) + 4
38	Worse Than All the Others?	(13:2, 4) + 3
39	What Is the Kingdom of God?	(13:18) + 3
40	Is It Lawful to Heal?	(14:3) + 1
41	Do You Not Count the Cost?	(14:28) + 2
43	Who Will Entrust to You the True Riches?	(16:3) + 5
45	Increase Our Faith!	{17:5} + 5

Appendix B

Texts, Psalms, and Hymns

The sermons in this book are based on the readings from Luke. At the same time, each reading was paired with a reading from the Old Testament and sometimes with a psalm also. And each Sunday, of course, hymns were sung as a part of the service. In case any of this information might also be helpful (even as a starting point) to others who are called to preach and to lead worship in this way, it is provided below.

1. How Shall I Know? (Luke 1:1–25)
   Daniel 9:1–15, 20–23
   "O Come, O Come, Emmanuel"
   "Let All Mortal Flesh Keep Silence"
   "Lift Up Your Heads, Ye Mighty Gates"

2. How Will This Be? (Luke 1:26–38)
   Job 38:1–11
   "Come, Thou Long-Expected Jesus"
   "What Child Is This"
   "Angels, from the Realms of Glory"

3. Why Me? (Luke 1:39–56)
   Jeremiah 31:7–14
   "Gentle Mary Laid Her Child"
   "Lo, How a Rose E'er Blooming"
   "O Little Town of Bethlehem"

4. What Then? (Luke 1:57–80)
   Jeremiah 1:1–10
   "Song of Zechariah"
   "Angels We Have Heard on High"
   "O Come, All Ye Faithful"

5.   What Good News? (Luke 2:1–21)
   Micah 5:1–5a
   "Angels, from the Realms of Glory"
   "Hark, the Herald Angels Sing"
   "Joy to the World!"
   "What Child Is This"
   "Silent Night! Holy Night!"

6.   How Long? (Luke 2:22–40)
   Isaiah 49:1–6
   "Joy to the World!"
   "Once in Royal David's City"
   "O Sing a Song of Bethlehem"

7.   Did You Not Know? (Luke 2:41–52)
   Isaiah 45:18–25
   "All Beautiful the March of Days"
   "Immortal, Invisible, God Only Wise"
   "God of Our Life"

8.   What Shall We Do? (Luke 3:1–20)
   Isaiah 40:1–11
   "Lift Up Your Heads, Ye Mighty Gates"
   "Prepare the Way"
   "Guide Me, O Thou Great Jehovah"

9.   Whose Son? (Luke 3:21–38)
   Isaiah 42:1–9
   "Come, Thou Almighty King"
   "God Himself Is with Us"
   "All Hail the Power of Jesus' Name!"

10.   Whom Shall You Serve? (Luke 4:1–13)
    Deuteronomy 6:1–15
    "It Is Good to Sing Thy Praises"
    "I Sing the Mighty Power of God"
    "Call Jehovah Thy Salvation"

11.   Is Not This . . . ? (Luke 4:14–30)
    Isaiah 61:1–11
    "O for a Thousand Tongues to Sing"
    "Be Thou My Vision"
    "Jesus, Thou Joy of Loving Hearts"

12.   What Is This Word? (Luke 4:31–44)
Deuteronomy 18:9–18
"All Creatures of Our God and King"
"I to the Hills Will Lift My Eyes"
"God of Grace and God of Glory"

13.   Let Down Your Nets! (Luke 5:1–11)
Isaiah 9:1–7
"Joyful, Joyful, We Adore Thee"
"Christ Is Made the Sure Foundation"
"Lord, Dismiss Us with Thy Blessing"

14.   Who Can Forgive? (Luke 5:12–26)
Isaiah 11:1–9
"I Greet Thee, Who My Sure Redeemer Art"
"Love Divine, All Loves Excelling"
"Amazing Grace—How Sweet the Sound"

15.   Why with Sinners? (Luke 5:27–39)
Zechariah 7:4–10
"O Worship the King, All Glorious Above!"
"God of Compassion, In Mercy Befriend Us"
"Ye Servants of God, Your Master Proclaim"

16.   Good or Harm? (Luke 6:1–11)
1 Samuel 21:1–6
"Praise, My Soul, the King of Heaven"
"O Master, Let Me Walk with Thee"
"Jesus, Thy Boundless Love to Me"

17.   Blessing or Woe? (Luke 6:12–26)
Jeremiah 17:5–8, Psalm 1
"Blessing and Honor and Power and Glory"
"God of Our Life"
"Lead On, O King Eternal"

18.   What Benefit? (Luke 6:27–36)
1 Samuel 26:6–12
"When Morning Gilds the Skies"
"O God of Love, O King of Peace"
"God the Omnipotent!"

19.   Why Do You Call Me "Lord"? (Luke 6:37–49)
      Isaiah 55:1–3, 6–13
      "It Is Good to Sing Thy Praises"
      "My Hope Is Built on Nothing Less"
      "How Firm a Foundation"

20.   Say the Word! (Luke 7:1–17)
      1 Kings 17:17–24
      "Rejoice, the Lord Is King"
      "I Greet Thee, Who My Sure Redeemer Art"
      "Now Thank We All Our God"

21.   Who Is to Come? (Luke 7:18–35)
      Deuteronomy 18:15–22
      "All Hail the Power of Jesus' Name"
      "Of the Father's Love Begotten"
      "I to the Hills Will Lift My Eyes"

22.   Who Forgives Sins? (Luke 7:36–50)
      2 Samuel 12:1–7a, Psalm 32
      "All People That on Earth Do Dwell"
      "When I Survey the Wondrous Cross"
      "My Faith Looks Up to Thee"

23.   Take Care How You Hear! (Luke 8:1–21)
      Isaiah 6:1–13
      "Holy, Holy, Holy! Lord God Almighty!"
      "God the Omnipotent!"
      "Holy God, We Praise Your Name"

24.   Who Commands Winds and Water? (Luke 8:22–39)
      Psalm 107:1–3, 23–32
      "I Sing the Mighty Power of God"
      "God Is Our Refuge and Our Strength"
      "Now Thank We All Our God"

25.   Only Believe! (Luke 8:40–56)
      Ezekiel 34:1–16
      "Lift High the Cross"
      "All Glory, Laud, and Honor"
      "Ride On! Ride On in Majesty!"

33.   How Will His Kingdom Stand? (Luke 11:14–36)
    2 Kings 1:2–16
    "Holy, Holy, Holy! Lord God Almighty!"
    "Jesus Shall Reign Where'er the Sun"
    "All Hail the Power of Jesus' Name!"

34.   Did Not He Make You? (Luke 11:37–54)
    Job 40:1–14
    "All People That on Earth Do Dwell"
    "Before Jehovah's Awful Throne"
    "Joyful, Joyful, We Adore Thee"

35.   Fear Not! (Luke 12:1–12)
    Jeremiah 20:7–12
    "We Gather Together"
    "Be Still, My Soul"
    "I to the Hills Will Lift My Eyes"

36.   Why Are You Anxious? (Luke 12:13–34)
    Ecclesiastes 1:1–2; 2:18–26
    "O God, Our Help in Ages Past"
    "Baptized in Water"
    "My Faith Looks Up to Thee"

37.   Who Is Faithful? (Luke 12:35–59)
    2 Kings 17:33–41
    "Praise Ye the Lord, the Almighty"
    "Child of Blessing, Child of Promise"
    "O Beautiful for Spacious Skies"

38.   Worse than All the Others? (Luke 13:1–17)
    Exodus 3:1–15
    "The God of Abraham Praise"
    "Bless, O My Soul! the Living God"
    "Praise, My Soul, the King of Heaven"

39.   What Is the Kingdom of God? (Luke 13:18–35)
    Isaiah 66:18–24
    "Christ Is Made the Sure Foundation"
    "Lord of Light, Your Name Outshining"
    "Glorious Things of Thee Are Spoken"

40. Is It Lawful to Heal? (Luke 14:1–24)
Exodus 20:8–11
"It Is Good to Sing Thy Praises"
"O Savior, in This Quiet Place"
"O God, What You Ordain Is Right"

41. Do You Not Count the Cost? (Luke 14:25–35)
Proverbs 24:3–6
"O God, Our Help in Ages Past"
"When I Survey the Wondrous Cross"
"'Take Up Thy Cross,' the Saviour Said"

42. Do You Not Go After the Lost? (Luke 15:1–32)
Exodus 32:7–14
"O Worship the King All Glorious Above"
"Amazing Grace—How Sweet the Sound"
"Jesus Shall Reign Where'er the Sun"

43. Who Will Entrust to You the True Riches? (Luke 16:1–18)
Joshua 24:1–27
"We Praise Thee, O God, Our Redeemer"
"How Firm a Foundation"
"My Faith Looks Up to Thee"

44. Do They Not Hear? (Luke 16:19–31)
Amos 6:1–7
"A Mighty Fortress Is Our God"
"The Word of God Incarnate"
"Lead On, O King Eternal"

45. Increase Our Faith! (Luke 17:1–19)
2 Kings 5:9–17
"Now Thank We All Our God"
"O Splendor of God's Glory Bright"
"Christ, of All My Hopes the Ground"

46. Must I Lose My Life to Keep It? (Luke 17:20–37)
Genesis 6:5–22
"Hail to the Lord's Anointed"
"Jesus Shall Reign Where'er the Sun"
"God the Omnipotent!"

47. Will He Find Faith? (Luke 18:1–14)
    Psalm 34:1–22
    "Immortal, Invisible, God Only Wise"
    "I to the Hills Will Lift My Eyes"
    "Guide Me, O Thou Great Jehovah"

48. Who Can Be Saved? (Luke 18:15–30)
    Exodus 20:1–17
    "All Beautiful the March of Days"
    "As with Gladness Men of Old"
    "God of Our Life"

49. What Do You Want Me to Do? (Luke 18:31–43)
    Isaiah 50:4–9
    "O for a Thousand Tongues to Sing"
    "Open My Eyes That I May See"
    "When I Survey the Wondrous Cross"

50. Why Did the Son of Man Come? (Luke 19:1–27)
    Exodus 34:1–9
    "Joyful, Joyful, We Adore Thee"
    "We Give Thee but Thine Own"
    "O Master, Let Me Walk with Thee"

51. In Whose Name? (Luke 19:28–48)
    Isaiah 59:14–20
    "All Glory, Laud and Honor"
    "Hosanna, Loud Hosanna"
    "Be Thou My Vision"

52. By What Authority? (Luke 20:1–26)
    Exodus 3:1–15
    "Christ Is Made the Sure Foundation"
    "Now Thank We All Our God"
    "All Hail the Power of Jesus' Name!"

53. Are the Dead Raised? (Luke 20:27–47)
    1 Chronicles 29:10–18
    "Sing Praise to God Who Reigns Above"
    "The Strife Is O'er, the Battle Done"
    "Thine Is the Glory"

54. When Will These Things Be? (Luke 21:1–19)
Malachi 3:16—4:3
"Come, Ye Thankful People, Come"
"We Gather Together"
"We Plow the Fields"

55. Give Us Strength! (Luke 21:20–38)
Isaiah 63:16–64:4
"Come, Thou Long-Expected Jesus"
"Rejoice! Rejoice, Believers"
"Let All Mortal Flesh Keep Silence"

56. Who Is the Greatest? (Luke 22:1–38)
Isaiah 43:16–21
"The First Noel"
"Hark, the Herald Angels Sing"
"Angels We Have Heard on High"

57. What Is the Father's Will? (Luke 22:39–53)
Isaiah 51:17–23
"Praise to the Lord, the Almighty"
"On This Day Earth Shall Ring"
"O God, Beyond All Praising"

58. Are You the Son of God? (Luke 22:54–71)
Daniel 7:9–14
"O Come, All Ye Faithful"
"Gentle Mary Laid Her Child"
"Joy to the World!"

59. What Evil Has He Done? (Luke 23:1–25)
Deuteronomy 21:22–23
"All Beautiful the March of Days"
"In the Bleak Midwinter"
"Alleluia! Sing to Jesus"

60. Are You Not the Christ? (Luke 23:26–56)
Isaiah 52:13—53:12
"All Glory, Laud and Honor"
"O Sacred Head, Now Wounded"
"Lift High the Cross"

61.   Why Seek the Living Among the Dead? (Luke 24:1–12)
      Exodus 15:1–11
      "Jesus Christ Is Risen Today"
      "The Day of Resurrection!"
      "Thine Is the Glory"

62.   Was It Not Necessary? (Luke 24:13–35)
      Isaiah 25:6–9
      "The Strife Is O'er, the Battle Won"
      "What Wondrous Love Is This"
      "Crown Him with Many Crowns"

63.   Why Are You Troubled? (Luke 24:36–53)
      Isaiah 52:7–12
      "Praise the Lord, His Glories Show"
      "Be Still, My Soul"
      "How Firm a Foundation"

Bibliography

Babcock, Maltbie D. "This Is My Father's World." 1901.

Calvin, John. *A Harmony of the Gospels: Matthew, Mark and Luke.* Translated by A. W. Morrison, T. H. L. Parker, and A. W. Morrison, edited by David W. Torrance and Thomas F. Torrance. 3 vols. Calvin's New Testament Commentaries. Grand Rapids: Eerdmans, 1972.

———. *Calvin: Institutes of the Christian Religion.* Translated from the 1559 Latin edition by Ford Lewis Battles, edited by John T. McNeill. 2 vols. Library of Christian Classics. Philadelphia, PA: Westminster, 1960.

Craddock, Fred B. *Luke.* Interpretation. Louisville: John Knox, 1990.

Jackson, Thomas. "Stonewall Jackson at the Battle of Bull Run." Online: http://www .sonofthesouth.net/leefoundation/jackson/stonewall-battle-bull-run.html.

Johnson, Ben Campbell. *Rethinking Evangelism: A Theological Approach.* Philadelphia: Westminster, 1987.

Leith, John H. *Basic Christian Doctrine.* Louisville: Westminster John Knox, 1993.

Luther, Martin. "Large Catechism." In *The Book of Concord: The Confessions of the Evangelical Lutheran Church,* edited by Robert Kolb and Timothy J. Wengert, translated by Charles Arand et al. Minneapolis: Fortress, 2000.

McPherson, James M. *For Cause and Comrades: Why Men Fought in the Civil War.* New York: Oxford University Press, 1997.

Niebuhr, Reinhold. *The Nature and Destiny of Man.* 2 vols. New York: Scribner's, 1964.

Oden, Thomas C. *The Rebirth of Orthodoxy: Signs of New Life in Christianity.* San Francisco: HarperSanFrancisco, 2002.

Old, Hughes Oliphant. "The Ministry of the Word." In *Worship That Is Reformed According to Scripture,* edited by John H. Leith and John W. Kuykendall, 57–85. Guides to the Reformed Tradition. Atlanta: John Knox, 1984.

———. *The Reading and Preaching of the Scriptures in the Worship of the Christian Church.* 7 vols. Grand Rapids: Eerdmans, 1998–2010.

———. *Worship Reformed According to Scripture.* Rev. ed. Louisville: Westminster John Knox, 2002.

Presbyterian Church U.S.A. *Book of Common Worship.* Louisville: Westminster John Knox, 1993.

———. *Book of Confessions.* Part I of *The Constitution of the Presbyterian Church (U.S.A.).* Louisville: Office of the General Assembly, 2004.

———. *Book of Order* (2011–2013). Part II of *The Constitution of the Presbyterian Church (U.S.A.).* Louisville: Office of the General Assembly, 2011.

Redhead, John A. *Learning to Have Faith.* New York: Abingdon, 1955.

Bibliography

Temple, William. *Nature, Man and God: Being the Gifford Lectures Delivered in the University of Glasgow in the Academical Years 1932–1933 and 1933–1934.* New York: Macmillan Company, 1949.

Tillich, Paul. *The New Being.* New York: Scribner's, 1965.